Conversations

Roy Newquist

RAND McNALLY & COMPANY

To my MOTHER
who started it all

Contents

Introduction

I am sure no one in CONVERSATIONS needs an introduction. As writer, editor, critic, or publisher, each of the company is well-known—often on several levels.

Perhaps "levels" is the key word in describing the composition of this book. There is a tendency, particularly in critical and academic circles, to become cliquish in assessing the literary output. When A and B come into favor, C and D are cast out; E and F, because they write for mass appeal, are never "in" to begin with. Such selectivity must determine the outlook of critic and academician, of course, because what they strive for is the identity of literature as it is produced within their time. But the clique and claque do occasionally swerve from objective appraisal.

Such selectivity is *not* the province of this book. There is a large and varied audience that reads; there are a number of small audiences that are significant because their support gives our literary output the spectrum deserved. The cast in CONVERSATIONS speaks, at one time or another, to all these audiences. A critic's favorite and a litterateur's anathema are often side by side. I think this is as it should be, since they speak not only of their art or craft, but of their citizenship in the world about them. Levels of observation and feeling are intensely varied—and often intense. Surprisingly often, there is an absolute sharing of outlook and belief, however varied the product written or presented.

Perhaps it is all very representative of democracy itself, wherein everyone is given voice.

The rewarding and stimulating thing about all of these voices is the manner in which they are raised. It is not just a matter of speaking well (which almost all of them do; their dialogue, only slightly reorganized and smoothed, is not too far from the cadence of their writing), but it is the way they speak up, and speak sharply, on vital issues.

Virtually all, for example, touch heavily upon the problems of the Negro and the imperatives of integration. Not that there is a solidarity of viewpoint—Lerone Bennett, Jr. and William Melvin Kelley, even as

Negroes, cannot agree—but there is virtual unanimity in the depth of concern which I believe exposes the conscience of the communicator.

Nor is the racial issue the only bone of contention presented.

Robert Penn Warren and Eleanor Clark express disdain for the "free money and free advice" so many young writers now regard as their due.

Irving Wallace traces his exacting process of research, his insistence upon accuracy, before staging an assault upon certain organs of criticism.

As a conscientious Catholic, *Ramparts* editor Edward M. Keating launches an attack upon the Catholic press.

What is the torment of a writer's block? Laura Z. Hobson explains its misery. What is the price of early success? Evan Hunter is paying it —because he hasn't written another *Blackboard Jungle*.

How do philosophers view America's role in our nuclear world? Will and Ariel Durant regard it rather calmly; Dr. Arnold Toynbee politely rages. The specter of censorship? French publisher Maurice Girodias is explicit in his contempt.

Is it immoral to write a best seller, as many critics seem to think? Helen Gurley Brown, Rona Jaffe, and Jacqueline Susann don't think so.

But there are many other issues, and many other voices, and I think the cast is in good voice. Thus I believe that anyone who writes, anyone who reads, will be gratified by the occasional twinges of shock embedded in the dialogues CONVERSATIONS contains.

—R. N.

Conversations

"... I think that the Negro artist has an obligation ... to the Negro people ... to understand the revolution, to project it, and even to participate in it. ..."

Lerone Bennett, Jr.

Lerone Bennett, Jr.

N: *Lerone Bennett, Jr., is senior editor of* Ebony *magazine. His writing stands at the helm of that considerable body of distinguished work concerned with the activities and welfare of the American Negro. However, Mr. Bennett has also authored a series of penetrating books dealing with the Negro past and present and with Negro leadership in all fields of endeavor. These include* What Manner of Man, *a biography of Martin Luther King, Jr.;* The Negro Mood, *an assessment of the forces at work in the Negro's struggle for equality;* Before the Mayflower, *a study of the Negro in America dating from the first enforced arrivals; and* Confrontations Black and White, *a frank assessment of the present "condition" of the racial problem and what must be done to resolve it successfully.*

The first time I met Lerone Bennett, he had just finished Confrontations Black and White. *I asked him why he wrote it.*

BENNETT: I wanted to give the so-called Negro revolution a larger context. It seems to me, from the work I have done in Negro history, that the present upheaval is the result of a long series of developments, and that it had its tangible beginning with the Negro migration to the North after World War I.

I don't think it is something that happened in the 1960's. The roots lie deep; what we have now is the manifestation of generations of movement and struggle and change.

I wanted to show why this movement won't die down, but will become stronger by the end of the decade. You see, the Negro in the urban North gained a new impression of himself before World War II. The war accented racial consciousness, and after the war he became aware of his own power, numerically and geographically.

Now, I don't mean "power" in the sense that the Negro wants to rule those cities in which he is becoming numerically equal to the white population or even outnumbering the whites. He simply wants an equal chance when it comes to education, jobs, professional opportunities, voting. In many respects the "Negro problem" has now become a "white problem" as the whites have fled to the suburbs and let the Negro population move toward a majority.

14

What I hoped to show, in essence, is the inevitability of change, whether the social structure changes peaceably or through abrasive action.

N: *Does the present struggle relate to the struggle for identity waves of immigrants have encountered?*

BENNETT: I can't see any association simply because, in the first place, we have a racial aspect which America didn't have with the Italians, or the Irish, or the Jews. In the second place, the Negro is not an immigrant.

The Negro does not present a language problem, for example, and the majority of Negroes are Christians, not at odds with the majority of American whites as far as faith is concerned. But he is a Negro, and the separation on the racial basis has been so strong he has never been regarded as an equal by a majority of whites.

Decade after decade goes by, generation after generation, and he is still not accepted in the way the Italian, Irish, and Jewish immigrants were. He finds that just waiting for acceptance gets him nowhere.

This is why the Negro revolution, in all its phases, is so strong now, and why it's not going to weaken until the Negro has obtained identity.

N: *Born in Clarksdale, Mississippi, graduated from Morehouse College in Atlanta, Bennett lives and writes in Chicago. This interview continues as he describes his work at* Ebony.

BENNETT: I guess I've always written — at least after I was ten years old. In high school I edited the school paper, then went to college in Atlanta and edited the paper and the yearbook.

There were a few digressions in the earlier years. At one time I wanted to become a lawyer, and there was a period when I played in a jazz band. But I guess I'm pretty much like anyone who writes: it's inevitable.

I worked as a reporter for a daily newspaper in Atlanta, and came to Chicago in 1953 to work on *Jet*. I was transferred to *Ebony* in 1954, and I've been with the magazine ever since.

As senior editor I'm primarily concerned with long-term projects. This is delightful in many ways because I can go into a project of almost book-size and develop it over a year and a half. For example, the project I'm working on now is titled *Black Power U. S. A.* It will eventually be a book; I've been working on it for a year and I'll be with it at least eight or nine months longer. Basically, it's a research job. It's the story of the period between 1867 and 1877, when Negroes had a great deal of political power in America. It's very similar to what's going on now. As you know, we're getting voting rights in the South: a great number of Negroes are voting in Alabama. The marvelous thing is the fact that

this happened before, and in almost the same way. The Negroes voted in
Alabama and sent three Negroes to Congress. Selma was the center of
black political power in the state. There were Negro judges in Selma,
Negro members of the city council, and the police force was predomi-
nantly Negro. An astonishing period. As I mentioned, it's a research
job. I've been working at the Library of Congress in Washington and
the Newberry Library here in Chicago. We have old newspapers on
microfilm—for example, the New Orleans *Tribune*, a Negro newspaper
which was published from 1865 to 1872. So I've been working with
these papers and with the basic scholarly books in the field, and writing
condensed chapters for the magazine. I will then take four or five
months more and expand the chapters for the book.

From time to time I do a special story for the magazine, but for the
last six or seven years I've been assigned to special projects, to material
that takes from two to four months to work out. This is not at all
different from research work for a book.

The reason for study at the Library of Congress and the Howard
University Library, and for going to the old Reconstruction capitals in
New Orleans, Jackson, and Charleston, is to get on-the-spot fill-in.
What I'm trying to do in this series and the subsequent book is to give
the actual feel of that time, what it actually meant for Negroes to be a
majority in a state. For example, South Carolina had a majority of
Negroes in the legislature. The overwhelming black voting majority in
the state lasted for ten years, from 1867 to 1877, until it was destroyed
by Ku Klux Klan terror. And there was what is called the "Bargain of
1877," when Rutherford B. Hayes said in so many words that he would
withdraw federal troops from the South and give Southerners "home
rule" in return for the several needed votes which elected him President. With the withdrawal of troops Negro power dwindled until
Negroes were pushed out of power entirely.

Although Negroes had voting majorities in South Carolina and
Mississippi, and perhaps in Louisiana and Florida, they did not try to
seize all political power for themselves. They said to the whites, "We
want to cooperate with you; we don't want to create a black state, we
want an integrated state." As a result, in almost all of the Southern
states the whites held a disproportionately large number of offices. I
don't think that Negroes demonstrated enough independent political
action or independence; this was one of the major reasons for the
downfall of Reconstruction, and the Ku Klux Klan terror. You find, in
going back that far, some distressing parallels in the kind of political
servitude we see in certain big city machines. Certainly Chicago is a
good example, where Negroes have great voting power potential but

dissipate that potential by following unworthy Negro leaders and unworthy white leaders. Certainly this seems to indicate a need for greater political education and an equal need for political independence on the parts of voters and leaders.

N: *Was there not a great difference between then and now in the educational level of the Southern Negro? I've read about that period in at least some breadth, and I've come across frequent statements that the Southern Negro was not ready for political power.*

BENNETT: I don't agree with that. The whole rise of Afro-Asia indicates that there is no direct correlation between literacy and political astuteness. Even what happens in Chicago indicates that. Most people do not vote for a candidate on the basis of what they read; they vote instinctively, emotionally, their whole lives.

It is true that at least 80 percent of the Negroes in the South were illiterate then, about the same proportion of illiterates as you will find in India today. But as in India today, the voters understood the issues and voted for the issues. A larger proportion of Negro voters registered and voted then than register and vote in Chicago today. From my research it seems to me that the level of political consciousness in South Carolina is the same as it is in Chicago almost a century later. I don't think people need degrees to vote. I'm all in favor of the one-man, one-vote idea. But from an analytical standpoint one must admit that there was a lack of trained leadership and there was not enough time to develop this leadership; this was one of the major reasons for the overthrow of the Reconstruction government.

Today the problem is not a lack of educated leadership; I do not think that the average, educated, middle-class Negro today is a good leader, an effective leader, simply because he has a degree. I think that more than that is needed; he needs a political consciousness, an understanding of the whole political landscape. He needs, above all, some distance from the values he is trying to change, and certainly a close connection with the masses of people. We've not gotten this, generally, from educated, middle-class Negroes today.

N: *I'd like to turn to the Negro writer — to what you think is the obligation (that may be too sweeping a word) of the Negro writer.*

BENNETT: I don't think I disagree with the word "obligation" particularly. I think that the Negro artist has an obligation. I think that any artist has, first of all, an obligation to people, and I think the Negro artist has an obligation to the Negro people. Certainly at this crucial juncture, where we find the Negro involved in a sort of quasi-revolution, it is the obligation of the Negro artist to understand that revolution, to project it, and even to participate in it. When people are going through a tremendous social upheaval, I don't see how the artist who embodies their consciousness can remain relevant unless he keeps pace with the people.

I'm afraid that some Negro writers have not kept pace with the changing consciousness and the developing consciousness of the Negro people; therefore they may be reflecting a reality that existed, if it existed at all, ten or fifteen years ago. Reality is changing fast. If the consciousness that artist is supposed to embody is migrating, and if he fails to keep pace with that migration, then his work won't reflect the reality of what is happening in the world of his time. I think the Negro artist has an obligation to take a leading role in this struggle.

It seems to me that the Negro artist has a duty to try to guide and sharpen the sensibilities of his people; this too would apply to an artist of any race anywhere. It seems to me that it is also the duty of a white writer, at this time, to take part in the struggle of life that is going on about him so that he can reflect what America *is* at this particular time. I must confess that I read American white novelists and (with the exception of Mailer) wonder what country they're writing about.

I simply don't get any sense of the white artist being involved with this time, the artist reflecting and writing about what is happening now. If this is true of white writers, I think it would be well for Negro writers to avoid the pitfall and involve themselves in the struggle so that they can produce a great art which will celebrate the people and lift them to higher stages of aesthetic and social development. Last summer, on my vacation, I went down to Buckingham Fountain and marched every day in the anti-Daley and anti-Willis demonstrations. I got arrested one day on State Street and was put in jail; I stayed in jail eight or nine hours. I didn't go to jail to get material (I've not written anything about this), but after going to Mississippi and speaking in Selma I felt that, as a man, I had an obligation to become involved in the struggle and go to jail here.

It was one of the most fantastic days I've ever spent. In the lockup some fellows came up and said, "You're a writer," and I said, "I don't want to talk about art, I'm here as a man." It was a great feeling to be there as a man. It may sound ridiculous at first hearing, but wasn't it Tolstoy who said that nobody knows what kind of country he lives in who's never been in jail?

Certainly part of my education as a man in society is not only to learn about Negroes, but what happens to people when they go to jail in this society. How poor white drunks are treated in jail, how poor whites are treated in jail, how all poor people are treated in jail. Coming in that kind of contact with policemen in our society, I think I learned something I could not learn in seven hundred books about what I think is a deep sickness in our society which has nothing to do, specifically, with policemen or race—a deep sickness that relates to the whole environment in which we operate.

I don't think going to jail was an artistic experience; I think it was an experience having to do with my life at this time, the life of people at this time. I think it was helpful. I don't intend to write anything about this especially, but I do have a greater understanding of what happens to people who go to jail in America, especially people who are not powerful and not rich.

What I'm trying to say is that the artist, any artist, must get in touch with reality. One might get a sort of reality in middle-class integrated cocktail parties, and I guess a novel can be written about that kind of reality, but it isn't the only reality for the Negro people in America. In fact, it's only a very tiny part of their reality. The greater reality is somewhere else, and if one confines oneself to middle-class integrated cocktail parties, or to the podium lecturing to white English students, it seems to me that one loses contact with the larger part of reality that should be at the command of the artist who wants to reflect what happened at the time when he lived.

N: *As far as you yourself are concerned—as editor, writer—what are your ambitions?*

BENNETT: There are a number of things I would like to do. Almost by accident, you see, I got involved in doing this series of nonfiction projects. It's been gratifying, and I can get lost in the 1860's and 1870's. It's like a detective story, trying to put facts together from old musty books. Because of what seems to be a journalistic default in this area, I've had the good fortune to be of some small help to a great many kids, Negro and white, who've not been exposed to a lot of material regarding our common past. About both the Negro and white pasts in America. I still have a few projects in the area. I've completed *Pioneers and Protest* and I'm completing *Black Power U.S.A.*

If I could get some time, I would like to write more poetry. I have completed a book of poetry—some of the poems have been published, but not the book—and there are things I would like to say in that form. Also, I started a novel before getting involved in the nonfiction projects, and I would like to complete that. I don't know whether I can do it in the way I started, but there is so much material that should be explored. I don't know how interested publishers are in that type of material, but for the Negro artist there is so much to explore and to say. For example, a good novel could be written about people involved in a protest movement in any city; what happens to them while they're involved. Young white kids, young black kids. A struggle of that sort in a

Southern or Northern city could provide a great landscape for a novel. A lot of material like this is contained in the Reconstruction period. A man like Pinchback, a fantastic man who served briefly as governor of Louisiana—a Negro, a daring, bold, extraordinary man, would be great to work with. And there's so much more material waiting to be utilized in the form of a novel, perhaps in a play. I'd like to see if I could work some of this material into a novel.

I'd even like to do a play utilizing this matter. It would make, I think, splendid theater. Above all, I'd like to express, in fictional form, some of the things I feel and see. I haven't the vaguest idea of where the novel is going; it may be that the novel is an inadequate form for conveying certain experiences that are available to Negro writers. Many Negro writers, especially Baldwin, are more compelling in essays than they are in the novel form. The Victorian form of the novel may not be suited for what we want to say. John Killens, the Negro novelist, has just come out with a book of beautiful essays. LeRoi Jones has done several things in essay form. But before I'm used up I would like to take a stab at developing this rich lode of material in poetry, in fiction, perhaps for the theater. The form will have to be worked out.

N: *What advice would you have for the young writer? You can work in the general area of the oncoming writer, or concentrate on the talented young Negro, whichever you prefer.*

BENNETT: I tend to think that a young person moving in the direction of any form of creative work will find his own way, some way, without the benefit of advice. In spite of the fact that I don't think one can give advice to the artist, I would say that the artist—Negro or white—if he wants to be an artist, must simply make up his mind that he is going to be one and hold fast to that ambition despite anything that might happen.

I think it's a great deal more difficult for a Negro to be an artist in our society than it is for a white person. The Negro has a great many more obstacles. It might also be true that he has many more advantages. He inherits a cause, something bigger than himself, and to a great degree he inherits (I'm not talking about genetics) from his environment a greater drive toward aesthetic things.

In the Negro community, as distinguished from the white community, I believe you find, just in everyday life, a greater appreciation of rhythm, a greater delight in words used simply for the pleasure of using words. There is a great tradition in the Negro community, starting with the Negro preacher who builds a great crescendo of sound: people go to church to hear artistic preaching. Not many young Negroes are religiously inclined, but the artistic-religious tradition is still a force in the black community.

The delight in colors, the delight in rhythm, a less obsessive orientation to machines—I think these things are pluses for the potential artist, and these things are found in abundance in the Negro community. I'm afraid the Negro artist faces an essentially more difficult start; but once he's on his way he has certain advantages.

At this point in history I also believe that any artist, particularly the Negro artist, must find a completely new language—if necessary, completely new forms in which to articulate his experience. We have assumed, in the Western world, that the experiences and forms of Anglo-Saxon articulation are the goal and the standard. Now the world is in the process of reabsorbing 60 to 80 percent of the people of the world: the Asians, Africans, Latin Americans. The young Negro artist should look forward to making the same sort of leaps in literature and on the stage as were made in modern art, where the reabsorption already shows. It seems to me that he comes to this task with a slight advantage, because he views America from two standpoints: from the standpoint of being a Negro and from the standpoint of being an American. It may be, having these standpoints forced on him, that he can bring more objectivity to the task of creating new forms of literature, new languages, the all-embracing literature and art we've not had before.

This may sound utopian, but I don't think we've yet had the great cultural leaps and explosions we will and must have. I don't think that Negro artists, generally, have brought to literature the same freedom and inventiveness great Negro jazz musicians have brought to music. If we could get Negro novelists and playwrights to stand in front of their experience with the same freedom and lack of preconceived notions that distinguish the greatest jazz musicians, we would have a fantastic renaissance, not only in Negro literature but in all American literature. We haven't seen anything like this yet, but I believe we're going to get it. We know about Baldwin, Wright, Killens, and the other great Negro writers, but the kids who are involved, say, in the struggle in Chicago and in the South (and many of them are writing poetry and novels while they're marching) are capable of enormous contributions.

To a great extent Negro artists have come out of the middle class. The Negro middle class has been a sounding board or an echo of the white middle class. One goes to college, is given values, and these values are essentially "white" values. Some of these values are important and should be preserved, but it is not necessarily true that because a value is European in origin it is preeminent.

What happens is that Negro kids in college begin to see the world through white eyes, through Hemingway's eyes or Faulkner's eyes, which is absurd. Faulkner is a great artist, but it is ridiculous for a potential Negro artist in the South to see what Faulkner saw. A Negro kid in Oxford, Mississippi, isn't seeing or living Faulkner's Oxford. But what happens is that he begins to see through Faulkner's eyes, begins to make a world which, in essence, was Faulkner's world, not his world. I meet any number of kids who are starting to see all over again, which is the most difficult thing in the world to do. The kind of education we get today in America doesn't encourage us to see what's there.

What I'm trying to say is that if we eventually get enough Negro artists in America who are trying to find a new language and define new forms, to say as honestly and passionately as they can, "This is what I see," "This is my vision," and if we get enough honest white writers at the same time trying to see what's there and trying to project what's there, and if there's enough honesty on both sides of the racial lines, then we can have a blending of the two, and what great art it would be. Heretofore, I'm afraid, Faulkner's vision or Hemingway's vision has been defined as *the* vision. Nobody has *the* vision.

I think the result of clear vision and honesty and passion on the part of both Negro and white writers will result in a great human experience.

I don't think one gets to the human or to the man by holding onto these two abstract notions—"the human" and "man." I think one gets to the universal by starting with the particular, and I think the particular is the universal, the singular is the universal. People say that Negroes should write about human beings and not about Negroes. Well, Negroes *are* human beings. A writer writes about a particular man in history, a man in a particular place in a particular time. If he happens to be white he writes about one sort of world, and if he does it well enough he touches the human, he touches "man." The same thing applies when a Negro writes about a black man in a particular city in a particular place in a particular time. If he does it well enough he touches the human, he touches "man."

I don't think it's possible, in art, to start with the abstract, say, the human, and reach the particular, say man. I think one starts with the particular and by working with passion and honesty and compassion one creates the human, one creates man, and someone reading it will say, "Although it's a white man or a Negro man who has transcended certain problems, he stands here for man—for all men."

To return to this business of trying to find a new language. When Picasso and the modernists first saw African masks they were led to certain discoveries. Perhaps they looked on them as exotic things; I don't know. Perhaps they looked on them with surprise, but the fact that the masks struck them, touched them, and moved them deeply enough to create something new meant that human was talking to human. This is essentially what I mean by the fact that the concrete, done well enough in any medium, touches and becomes the universal or the total human.

"...A writer should come to grips with life around him; I think he should interpret.... After all, great fiction mirrors the times. I think a great writer must be involved with society."

Van Allen Bradley

Van Allen Bradley

BRADLEY: I was born in Albertville, Alabama, on Sand Mountain, and grew up in northern Alabama. I went to college in Arkansas for two years — a small one, Harding College, then transferred to the School of Journalism at the University of Missouri. I received my bachelor's degree in 1933, then spent a year free-lancing (for want of a better term). Actually, I lived in the hills of Alabama waiting for something to show up. Nothing showed up, so I went out to look for a job in 1934 and found one on the *Nashville Tennessean*. I wrote my first book reviews for Jennings Perry, who edited their Sunday magazine, and I wrote poetry and took it rather seriously. The "fugitives" were in Nashville — Allen Tate, Robert Penn Warren, that distinguished group of Southern writers — and I fancied myself to be at least on the periphery of their group, so I wrote a few poems that Perry published, then went on to book reviews.

I realized that I wasn't going to get rich down there. I made $15.00 a week as a reporter and I thought I could make more money elsewhere and I almost doubled my salary by going to the *Omaha Bee-News*. After that Hearst paper was suspended in 1937 I came on to Chicago, working for the *Tribune* until 1942, when I resigned because of disagreement with certain *Tribune* policies. I didn't have another job but I said, "I quit," and was lucky to get a job right away on the *Chicago Sun*.

I became chief of the copy desk — I'd headed the copy desk on the Hearst paper in Omaha. I was primarily a copy reader, but I did some book reviewing for them — I guess this has always been in my blood. I think I was one of the first Faulkner fans in northern Alabama; I lived one hundred miles or so from Faulkner country and his work always struck home to me and I remained a Faulkner fan through high school and college. *Sanctuary* and *Light in August*, and *As I Lay Dying* were *the* great books of the period to me, and I wrote an essay on Faulkner's work for one of my English courses at Missouri which won a high honor in one of the campus literary competitions.

At any rate, I continued as head of the copy desk on the *Sun* until the merger of the *Chicago Sun* and the *Chicago Times*; then, because of adjustments in the makeup of the newspaper, I was displaced as chief and made second-in-command. I didn't care to be displaced; I felt I'd earned the job, and the fact that the publisher had made the mistake of buying another paper didn't seem any reason why I should be sacrificed, so I again said, "I quit."

I went to the *Chicago Daily News* as Literary Editor (this was in 1948) and I've been with them ever since. I must say the job has been the great joy of my life because it has allowed me to live with books, build my own library, and come and go as I please. My hours are my own. It's a great newspaper. I don't have to punch a clock; I have the time I want to read, see people, speak, lecture, do the things I want. As long as I produce a readable book page, everyone is satisfied.

N: *You've also written a number of books?*

BRADLEY: I still haven't written the books I really want to write. I'd like to do something truly creative and I may do it yet, someday, but the books I've written are primarily hack work, designed to help make a living.

My first book, *Music for the Millions*, was actually a subsidized business history, but I make no apologies for it. I think it is a very good piece of business Americana; as a matter of fact it was so reviewed by the organs of the trade. It was the history of the W. W. Kimball Company, a piano and organ manufacturer, turned out for their one hundredth birthday, but good enough to be published by a legitimate book publishing company, the Henry Regnery Company of Chicago. The Piano Trade Magazine devoted an eleven-page review to it, and called it "the best history of the music business ever written in America," so I felt rather pleased with it.

I've ghostwritten a book for someone — I won't mention it — and I've done two in the field of rare books that came out of my interest in rare books. I've been a book collector all my life; since I was a kid I've collected the works of my favorite authors, so I have a fairly large library, over 15,000 books in my home. I'm not a specialist collector, but I do have several good collections. I've even sold some of the collections when I've needed money.

I've built the collections in various fields. For example, I've one on the raising of pheasants because I like them and raise them at my place out in the country. I have a collection of works of my favorite authors, a virtually complete collection of Nelson Algren's works inscribed to me by him. I did this with Faulkner's works and with Hemingway's. I had some of the rarest Hemingway material in existence, but I sold that collection when I was putting my son through college. It's expensive putting a couple of kids through school and building a house in the country at the same time.

About ten years ago I got the idea for a column, later syndicated, titled "Gold in Your Attic," which dealt with those things that make a book rare, what its value is, etc. The rare book business is a great mystery to most people. They don't understand it and often wonder what their books are worth, so I thought, "Why not inform the public about rare book values?" Out of this syndicated column have grown two books, *Gold in Your Attic* and *More Gold in Your Attic.* I've finished a third book in the field, *The Gold in Your Attic Guide to Rare English Books.* The first two dealt primarily with rare American books. And I'm almost ready to publish a revision of the first one because the rare-book business has moved ahead, considerably, since it first came out. I've also in the works, a more sophisticated book about rare books for Putnam, and an anthology on Chicago. A collection of writings about Chicago written by Chicagoans and by famous people who've visited here. That's for Doubleday. So it's a matter of four books going at one time, and trying to get them done is quite a problem.

N: *Recently, we seem to have become involved in a literary storm in a teacup relating to the duties of the literary critic and the book reviewer. How do you distinguish between the two?*

BRADLEY: It has always seemed to me that the newspaper reviewer's function is somewhat different from that of the highbrow critic who writes for quarterly reviews and the literary journals.

First of all, the newspaper book reviewer's space is limited. How much can be done as a literary appraisal of a book, in detail and depth, in 350 to 500 words? Most book reviews in most newspapers have to be limited to that kind of space. *The New York Times* has a full book section, and there's *Book Week,* but most of the newspapers in the country have a limited amount of space to devote to book reviews. For that reason the majority of the reviews are short. There are exceptions; I will some-times do a very long review, or one of my reviewers will go to 1,000 or 1,250 words, but these occasions are infrequent. As a consequence, the newspaper's function is to tell the reader what the book is all about, what the author is trying to do, and whether or not he succeeded in doing it. Is the book worth the expenditure of $5.95? It's a simple function, but by the same token it can be a valuable function. It can retain the essence of critical analysis, but it is a different breed of cat from the long magazine piece or the very erudite piece that would be of little interest to the general audience.

N: *Considering the limitations of space in the* Chicago Daily News *for book reviews, how do you handle the allocation of books for review?*

BRADLEY: Since I have a limited amount of space on my book pages I prefer to devote my space to favorable reviews, to books that are good. I try to make some sort of analysis or prejudgment of a book before I assign it for review. I have to do a preliminary sorting of the wheat from the chaff. I receive a tremendous number of books every week and we can only review a small number of them, so I try to select those books that seem, for one reason or another, to require attention. Now, if a well-known or highly talented writer turns out a bad book, I think we should review it; we should say it's a bad book, even at length. On the other hand, if a book is bad and it's just an ordinary book by an ordinary writer, there's no point in bothering with it.

But I do think we have a duty as a review medium to let people know what is going on, what should be read.

What I try to do is to cover the books that seem significant and that are newsworthy and books people will be talking about and books that have some local interest. My coverage is about the same you would find in a weekly news magazine; I think we cover approximately the same books. However, we do have additional supplemental features on our book pages. We have a column on paperbacks, a column of reviews of children's books, and I write the rare book column plus a weekly column covering some local books, some local literary topics and sometimes national topics, depending upon what I think should be covered. Out of the 28,000-30,000 books published each year we review six to eight books per week. This means that only first-rate books, newsworthy books, bad books by famous people, or books of exceptional local interest make it.

N: *Over the span of time when you have more or less "lived" with books are there any trends you've observed, or movements in contemporary literature, that invite comment?*

BRADLEY: I think we've been in a state of trying to find ourselves ever since the war. I don't think any really great novelists have emerged since the prewar days. Who do we have to take the place of Faulkner? Who do we have to take the place of Hemingway? I've been looking for the replacements since 1948, and I've been book reviewing on a full-time basis. I don't know what has happened, but it seems that the postwar crop of writers has been preoccupied with personal problems. A contemplation of the navel, as it were. We don't have many writers today who are able to get out of themselves. I'm ruling out such things as the historical novel which is adventure, storytelling, not literature.

The great novels are those that come to grips with life itself. The great novelists come to grips with life; they don't shabbily proclaim, "I'm the great person to be concerned with; my twisted personality is the thing everybody is interested in." I frankly think everybody is rather sick of twisted personalities. I think they're sick of this type of novel. I, and many other reviewers, have been looking for the great novelist who would deal with the great problems of today in broad terms, not in a personal, narrow sense.

Faulkner dealt in broad terms; so did Hemingway. But in the last twenty years I don't think anyone has come along who deserves to be called great. I think we have a few writers who show definite promise. There are people like Styron, a good novelist who shows the influence of Faulkner; *Lie Down in Darkness* was an exceptional first novel, and his most recent one, *Set This House on Fire*, is good. People like John Updike are fine, very fine writers, but what have they to say?

Salinger is rather a dead issue. *The Catcher in the Rye* caught the voice of his generation. For a time it was popular with college kids, but I don't think it is a great novel. It's still popular, still read and discussed, but Salinger hasn't come through with anything since that matches it.

Reynolds Price has come along with a few good novels—*A Long and Happy Life* and *A Generous Man*. There are a lot of good novelists, but no first-rate ones that I can see. Maybe I've grown cynical or expect too much, but I still wonder who's going to replace Faulkner and Hemingway. I do think it's a disaster, in most cases, for a writer to turn out a very successful first novel. He's always trying to live up to that first novel, and so often he fails. I think it's better to start, as Nelson Algren did, with *Somebody in Boots* and *Never Come Morning*. They weren't really noted at the time, so he didn't suffer too much when *The Man with the Golden Arm* made a big splash.

Actually, Algren is one of the really good talents we have in this country. In his old age he could be the next Faulkner. He and Styron and James Jones are probably our best bets. Mailer is kind of kooky, but basically he has a lot on the ball, a lot of fire. He's more or less like Algren, spending too much time showing off, but he may settle down and live up to *The Naked and the Dead*, just as Algren may yet settle down and live up to *The Man with the Golden Arm*.

One other writer I'd like to dwell on a bit—Jones. I think *The Thin Red Line* will probably be rated, a hundred years from now, as one of the great novels of the century despite the popularity of *From Here to Eternity* that sort of eclipses it now. *The Thin Red Line* has some of the same crudities, but it really catches the essence of war. It's a great novel despite the fact that its style isn't all it could be, at times; much better than *Eternity*.

N: *What preparation do you think is valuable in the education or grooming of the young writer?*

BRADLEY: I don't think anyone can be taught to write a great novel; tremendous talent and ambition and a close concern with life goes into that. But as far as the nonfiction fields are concerned, where the mechanical aspects of writing are important, I think a great deal can be taught.

I honestly think that if a person can write a sentence in English, I can teach him how to write salable material. In fact I've done this. I taught writing courses at Northwestern University for some years — feature writing, reporting, copywriting, etc. By the end of each term or semester we produced selling writers.

I think you can teach the mechanical processes of writing poetry, how to research a subject, how to arrange an article a newspaper or magazine will print.

But that great novel depends more upon the writer's vision of existence, his awareness, his talent, his willingness to work. Writing is a very hard job, a very lonely job. The writer who wants to write creatively generally writes, whether he takes a course in college or not.

N: *What advice would you give the oncoming writer?*

BRADLEY: I think, first of all, that a writer should come to grips with life around him; I think he should interpret. After all, great fiction mirrors the times. It is a reflection of the times in which a writer lives. I think a great writer must be involved with society. Mailer certainly is involved; he takes a stand. If he doesn't like something he says so. The same is true of Algren, who fights conformity. He's a rebel, a social critic, in the same sense that James T. Farrell was a social critic in his day and Dreiser in his. To an extent Jones has the overall view of things Mailer and Algren have.

Now, an awareness of society, an awareness of things around us, is the basis upon which a writer can create. And there are so many other valid issues — issues of morality with which the writer can come to grips, issues relating to sex and marriage.

Someday an American writer could write a great book about marriage — about what is happening to marriage in this country and in the world.

Everything that involves life and living is material for the writer. An aware person will come to grips with the life around him and his reactions will reveal themselves in his novels. I would hope that we develop writers who look at things objectively, as Dostoevsky and Dickens did. I once referred to Nelson Algren as "the Dostoevsky of Division Street." I think he was; I think he is. I think he has reflected upon the conditions of Chicago in the era he has written about.

One of the problems with contemporary writing is that there are so many diversions for the writer. A man comes along and writes a good short story and it's published in some little magazine and he's recognized as a writing talent and what happens? He is grabbed off by an advertising agency, the television industry, or—if he can interject a little bit of *Playboy*-type sex into a novel—Hollywood. If he writes a best seller he gets diverted from his central purpose, which is to write books —books that will live.

Commercialism is a real problem. One of the things I've always admired about James Farrell—regardless of how he's been criticized by all these people who harp on his crudeness, etc.—is that he has kept on his course. He has been a noncommercial writer.

I think that to be noncommercial is essential. The writer must disdain the lures if he really wants to create. He's got to write because he wants to write, wants to reflect the life around him. Not because he wants to sell something to *Cosmopolitan* magazine or to Hollywood or to television.

N: *Does the obligation to produce better books extend beyond the writer?*

BRADLEY: I've never quite bought the idea that the public buys or takes what it deserves. I think that publishers have a responsibility, that publishers to a measurable extent dictate public tastes. They're really more powerful than we want to admit.

Right now we have a situation, because of the loosening of the censorship laws and court decisions, where the hardback and paperback publishers are publishing material that couldn't have appeared ten years ago in this country. Some of it is good material, but the overwhelming majority of books of this nature now being published are sheer junk. They're pure pornography. They're published because the publishers figure they will sell. They seem to be outdoing each other in publishing dirty books.

I'm not against calling a spade a spade; certainly the writers I've admired have done it and continue to do it. And I've never been in favor of censorship. What I am against is the outright catering to the moron trade the publishing industry is involved with. Some of the most prominent publishers are in the act, publishing dirty books because they think dirty books will sell. And I personally think that the public is getting fed up with this and that sooner or later we'll get books that don't clinically overemphasize sex. What the hell—sex is a normal part of everyone's life, but there are many other issues in life, many other problems, that deserve equal attention.

I hope that the swing of the pendulum in the other direction isn't a Puritan revolution. I hope we don't get deeply involved in censorship.

But just because Henry Miller did it thirty years ago, why keep doing it? In certain respects, *Tropic of Cancer* and *Tropic of Capricorn* are great books, but the imitations are largely junk, even though they get praised in some very strange places. Miller had the virtue of being a great writer, but most of the present writers of pornography are hacks, and I don't think that publishers honor letters when they publish badly-written dirty books just for quick profit.

N: *How would you define the obligation of the book publisher?*

BRADLEY: I think the American publisher has shirked his obligation, which is to publish good books, in all too many cases. I think a lot of junk is published just because the publishers think junk will sell.

Ironically, this is a myth. I can go back over the best-seller lists and the records of book sales and show you that pornographic novels are not *the* best sellers.

Now, I don't hold any great regard for Hervey Allen, though he was a fine historical novelist with a fantastic attention to detail. He wrote *Anthony Adverse*, which was a runaway best seller. It sold a million copies in hard-cover. By the same token, another novelist who was not a great writer but who had a marvelous sense of narrative — Margaret Mitchell — produced an even bigger best seller in *Gone with the Wind*.

Twenty and thirty years ago we had *real* best sellers. Books that sold a million copies in hardback. I can take you back over the best-seller lists of the last fifteen and twenty years and show you that a book is considered a tremendous best seller today if it sells 250,000 copies. This is absurd. Obviously, the public is ready and willing to absorb books in great quantity if we produce books of quality; they showed this thirty years ago. Now we have thirty or forty million more people than we had when *Anthony Adverse* was published, which means that the potential book market is much greater now than it was then. What have we had in the past twenty years? Mediocre talents, mediocre novels, and publishers with very short vision.

The book publishers are turning out junk, perfectly satisfied to get $750,000 from Hollywood, not caring that it's junk. They're not even particularly looking for good books. Most are content with a short profit. They think a book that will sell 175,000 is great and it goes into paperback and sells a million copies. The paperback sale means nothing because the permanence of the book is measured by its hard-cover sales. The fact that *Peyton Place* sold in huge quantities — still falling well short of the *Anthony Adverse* and *Gone with the Wind* huge quantities — doesn't mean it's a great book or that the public took it to heart. I'm sure they knew it was a piece of junk. Its huge paperback sale didn't change its status as a piece of junk because the hard-cover copies won't be around long, there will be no hard-cover reprint, and the paperbacks will disappear.

The worst thing is the shortsightedness involved in not even looking for good books. They're content with big profits over the short haul rather than books with permanent worth and durability.

There are exceptions, of course. I think there are many good editors in the business, many reputable publishers whose motives are pure. I hope that the potentially good writers who come along connect with those houses.

It means nothing to me that Harold Robbins sells 250,000 copies of *The Carpetbaggers* or that it sells a million copies in paperback; this means nothing. It's still garbage. But it seems to be the thing publishers are willing to settle for. Robbins has done well as a commercial writer but he's not going to go down in American literature with Hawthorne, Melville, Faulkner, and Hemingway.

Best-selling trash isn't a brand-new invention, however. Perhaps the top American novelist from the point of sales was Mrs. E. D. E. N. Southworth who wrote *Ishmael*. She was popular before the turn of the century; every book she wrote sold in huge quantities. She turned out somewhere between fifty and one hundred novels, and not one of them has endured. So there's been quite a period of our literary life when we have not been able to measure the worth of a book by its sales.

On the other hand, some of the really great books of our time have not sold in large quantities. Farrell's *Studs Lonigan* has sold in very small quantities actually, yet it has a permanent place in American literature.

What I mentioned before—the commercial temptation—aids and abets the publisher who wants to get the most money he can for the least in quality. This is a very profitable period for a popular writer. He can sell a book to the hard-cover publisher, sell the reprint rights, sell to TV, get all sorts of second-serial and serialization rights. But is he creating literature?

"My primary obligation . . . is to my poetry, to myself. The poetry is myself. When I sit down to write . . . it's because I've had an impression, an idea, an emotion."

Gwendolyn Brooks

Gwendolyn Brooks

BROOKS: I was born in Topeka, Kansas, on June 7, 1917. I've always resented that fact because my parents were living in Chicago, but my mother wanted me to be born in her home town, with her mother, so when I was due to arrive she went to Topeka. When I was about a month old we came back to Chicago, so I feel that I'm really a native Chicagoan. After all, I grew up here and attended Chicago public schools.

I started writing poetry — according to my mother — when I was about seven years old. At least, I tried to put rhymes together. I don't have any poems on hand that go back quite that far, but I do have some that date to the age of eleven. In fact, I have many old notebooks filled with poems that I'll show to nobody, except to family members, occasionally, when they want to have a good laugh.

We had many books in the house, always, and I was blessed with a very encouraging mother and father. My father used to tell stories to my brother and myself, and sing us old songs and read us old poems.

My parents did nothing professional as far as the arts were concerned. My father brought home books and music because he worked at the McKinley Music Publishing Company. They were very fond of him (he was a shipping clerk), and they would give him music and old books. He died in 1959. My mother always wanted to be a pianist; she plays very nicely, to entertain herself, and about twenty years ago she began to compose music. She took a course in harmony at one of the evening schools, then started to compose, though she never attempted anything on a professional basis.

When I was eleven I started to get *Writer's Digest*. I don't know how I saw it; I wasn't in the habit of going to the downtown bookstores. I read all the articles in the magazine and had dreams of selling, selling, selling, the thing that periodicals place so much stress on. I read a lot; we had the *Harvard Classics* at home, and there was a good library at the Forrestville Public School two blocks away. And I wrote, but I didn't sell anything. I believe I did place some poems in those anthologies that require you to buy a number of copies in exchange for the honor of being published.

I saw my first published poem in ~~American Childhood~~ magazine; the pay was six copies of that issue. During my sixteenth and seventeenth years I had seventy-five poems printed in the ~~Chicago Defender~~, in the "Lights and Shadows" column which they no longer have. Aside from these pleasantries I didn't publish a poem in a well-known magazine until I was twenty-eight, even though I had sent poems to poetry magazines for fourteen years. Finally *Poetry* magazine published a group of four. This should encourage youngsters who feel discouraged at not getting anything published. All you have to do is stick it out for fourteen years. I thank the editors, now, for not publishing the first things I sent in. I would have been thoroughly ashamed of them. That, too, should be a lesson to the young.

My last two years of high school were spent at Englewood. There I met a history teacher, Miss Hern, a very strict teacher who paid no attention to me until I did a history report. The report was on a historical novel titled *Janice West*. I hated the book, and in order to make things a little more bearable for myself I wrote the report in rhyme. Miss Hern was fascinated at the idea of someone trying to do such a thing. She became interested in me, and told me that someday I might become a poet.

Also at Englewood I had a journalism teacher named Margaret Anderson. I've been trying to find her for lo, these many years, because she was very encouraging to me. She took time to talk to me, to ask me about my family, whether there were writers in the family, where I got my ideas. And a Horace Williston encouraged me in writing; aside from these three teachers I can't remember anyone outside of my family giving me any encouragement at all. Things were not then as they are now; today so much stress is given to creative writing, to school newspapers and magazines.

I did have some negative experiences. When I was going to Forrestville Elementary School I used to write compositions, and my English teachers were rather skeptical of them. Finally one of them sent a note to my mother, telling her that I was plagiarizing, stealing the works of published writers and using them as compositions. My mother flew to the school and insulted the teacher. She said that my English was better than hers, that I certainly had not plagiarized anything, that everything I turned in was my own work, and that I would sit right there and write something comparable if the teacher wanted me to. The teacher had me do something on that order, then admitted that she guessed I hadn't plagiarized.

From the beginning my mother told me and everybody else that I would be a second Paul Laurence Dunbar. She was positive that my future depended only upon time; time would take care of everything, and I would be published. She had more faith in me than I did. I was convinced I would never be published, and from time to time I would bury the poems I wrote in the back yard to be dug up in the future, the way they do time capsules now. I must have written at least a thousand lousy poems and buried them.

I did show a little enterprise. When I was thirteen I founded a newspaper titled *The Champlain Weekly News*. My mother helped me make copies of the paper, and I sold it to the neighbors for a nickel apiece. It got so that the neighbors were very eager for the weekly news to arrive. Some people rather took me to task because I would listen very eagerly to the neighborhood gossip. My mother wasn't much of a gossip, but she has a good receiver, and the women in the neighborhood loved to tell her their troubles and their tragedies, and I would "accidentally" overhear them. We rented out an apartment upstairs, and I would stand in the vestibule listening to all the life that went on up there. I think everyone was greatly relieved when I gave up my career as newspaperwoman.

I really haven't had an exciting life. I went to Wilson Junior College, and when I graduated I went to Illinois State Employment Service and applied for a job. They gave me a most peculiar one. (So peculiar and memorable that the book I'm writing now, a full-length poem, is based upon it.) They sent me to the Mecca Building—the address was 3838 South State Street—and I was to be a secretary to a Dr. E. N. French, who turned out to be a spiritual advisor. He had a storefront and four secretaries, all of whom were kept busy answering letters, taking the money out of the envelopes, and giving it to him. He would mail the people who sent in money anything they asked for—holy thunderbolts, charms, dusts of different kinds, love potions, heaven knows what all. The secretaries were also expected to help make up some of these charms. He had a regular little bottling operation. Some of his clientele lived or worked in the Mecca Building, and I delivered potions and charms and got to know some of these people. Oh, it was a bleak condition of life.

This was in October of 1936, and I stayed with Dr. French for the most horrible four months of my existence. I still recall vividly how I suffered. But it was my first job, and I hated to go home a failure. Besides, it was depression time, and my father was always poorly paid, so the small amount of money I got ($8.00 a week) was quite a bit for a job of that sort in those lean days. The money helped at home—I can remember my mother being able to buy draperies for the house—so I hated to quit. I stayed until Dr. French informed me that, because he thought I could speak well, he would employ me as his assistant pastor in the church he operated next door. A storefront church, naturally.

Dr. French was the most awesome West Indian; he wore a little black cap, and he was extremely fierce and stern. But I did have enough sense to tell him that I certainly was not going to become an assistant pastor. He said, "You will, or you'll leave. Don't come back to work Monday if you fail to show up Sunday at the church." I didn't show up Sunday, but I did go back to work Monday because I didn't think he meant his threat. Besides, he owed me money. But he told me I was fired, and I didn't get my last money earned, but at least I got out of there and went home from that horrible place for the last time.

After that I joined the NAACP Youth Council. A couple of girl friends asked me to join it because there was so much liveliness going on, dances and things. And it was there that I met my husband. He had been sent by a mutual girl friend of ours, who said that since he was writing poetry, he should join this council to meet a girl who was writing poetry, too. So I was sitting with her, and this glorious man appeared in the doorway and posed for a moment, looking the situation over, and I said, "There is the man I'm going to marry." It seems remarkably bold of me, perhaps farsighted in a blind sort of way. I was always impressed by dignity in a man, and he certainly had that. So my girl friend, having spunk and fire, said, "Hey, boy, this girl wants to meet you." And I met him.

I became publicity director for the NAACP Youth Council, and I was deeply impressed with some of the things these young people were doing. It also turned out to be the first time I was really accepted by people of my own age. You see, the children I went to school with and the people in my neighborhood were not interested in the things I was concerned with. I liked to read, and everyone else considered reading a chore. And I liked to draw, as my brother did. I played the piano a bit, and all these things combined to make me seem a rather strange individual. In the Youth Council, however, I met people who were artists, good pianists, writers. Many of them have become very success-ful. Johnny Johnson (now head of the Johnson Publishing Company) was there when I was, and John Karl, a very famous artist in San Francisco. So for the first time I found myself accepted by the young of my own approximate age, and it was very exciting, and I stayed with it for awhile after I was married.

I got married in September of 1939, and my son was born in October, 1940; after that I was too busy to run around to meetings. But in 1941 Inez Cunningham Stark—a reader for *Poetry* magazine and an eccentric society matron (it doesn't seem right, somehow, to call her that, but none of us who knew her could forget her fantastic John

Fredericks hats) decided that she would like to come to the South Side
Community Arts Center, which was still at 38th and Michigan, and
start a poetry group for the southsiders. This must have been the most
exciting thing that had happened to me because she introduced me to
modern poetry.

I had already been introduced to modern poetry, in a sense, when I
was sixteen. I had written to James Weldon Johnson, who wrote *God's
Trombones*, asking him to look at some of the poems I was enclosing and
tell me what he thought of them. He wrote back and told me that he
saw some hope, but that what I needed to do was to read a great deal of
modern poetry. Not to imitate it, but to absorb it, to know what people
of the present day were doing. He suspected that I was a subscriber to
Wordsworth, Coleridge, and Keats, all of whom were excellent poets
and still have much to give, but that I knew nothing about Eliot or [John
Crowe] Ransom or Frost, or the other contemporary poets I should
have been reading. I regret to this day that I didn't read modern poetry
and fiction and philosophy when I was extremely young. It wasn't my
parents' fault; they had the books at hand, standing firmly in the bookcase in the dining room. I would go and open up the glass doors of that
bookcase and take out fairy tales and simpler things. Foolishly I let the
books that contained the moderns just stand there.

We read modern poetry in this group, and Mrs. Stark had very little
to say. She would start the ball rolling and we would do the rest,
lighting into each other's poems with great spirit. It is the only poetry
group I ever encountered where people really told each other what they
thought; they didn't care how feelings got hurt. Many a young woman
went home crying; many a young man went home mad. It was very
helpful. Oddly enough, Margaret Danner was the worst writer in the
group. Everyone used to laugh at her. No one thought she would ever
do anything. She really started from the bottom, but she grew to be, for
a while, an assistant editor of *Poetry* magazine when Karl Shapiro was
there. She went to Detroit and opened a salon, but I understand she's
back in Chicago, and she's one of our really good poets. There were so
many good poets in that group, most of whom have stopped writing.
Margaret Walker came a few times; she's just published a novel titled
Jubilee.

Many of the poems contained in my first book were written when I
was in that group. This was 1941, 1942. Then many of the men were
sent away to war, and a few of them were killed. I suppose, in a way, an
age had ended.

The next thing that happened of significance—speaking in the
literary sense—was when I spotted a notice in one of the Chicago

newspapers which announced that the Midwestern Writers' Conference was sponsoring a poetry contest, and that manuscripts should be
sent to the Cordin Club at 410 South Michigan. So I sent some of my
poems in. Then, out of the blue, Alice Manning Dickie, who used to be
an editor for *Woman's Home Companion*, came over to see me one
Saturday morning. She had to climb a long flight of stairs to one of the
kitchenette apartments I had not only lived in, but had written so much
about, and she said that she was shocked to discover that I was a Negro.
She must have begun to suspect it when she entered the neighborhood.
(We were living at 623 East Sixty-third Street then.) She wanted to
know how in the world I had heard of the Midwestern Writers' Contest,
and I told her I had seen it in the paper.

The poem had won first prize. The next year I entered and won first
prize again. The third year the Midwestern Writers' Conference was
combined with what was called the Annual Writers' Conference, and
held on the Northwestern University campus. Paul Engle was teaching
a summer course out there, and he became very interested in the work I
was doing. Perhaps this was because he was so unimpressed with the
work others were doing. At any rate, he said it was a relief to find
something worthwhile.

In the contest they had that year I won first prize, and that, Pulitzer
Prize notwithstanding, is the prize that has meant the most to me,
personally. So much was attendant upon it.

The awards ceremony was held at Cahn Auditorium, and the hall
was flooded with people. No one expected a little Negro girl to win a
prize, and when Paul Engle called my name I just sat there. I didn't
expect to win, either. I had thought of how nice it would be to win the
poetry prize again, but I didn't think I would. So I sat there, finding it
hard to believe that he was really calling my name, wanting me to come
up to the stage to get the first prize. When it seemed that I wasn't going
to get up at all, Paul Engle said, "You'd better come up here, Gwendolyn, or I'll give the prize to someone else."

Finally I walked up there. I'll never forget the gasps that went
through the audience. Remember, things were different then, and
Negroes just didn't win prizes of that sort. But poetry doesn't exactly
earn a living, you know — it didn't then, it doesn't now — and at that time
I was primarily a housewife, which is the last thing I'm really interested
in being. I was at home all the time. I enjoyed my son, even though I
was a nervous wreck when I was a mother for the first time; I didn't
understand anything about children, and he was an experiment. I think
he rather senses that. I enjoyed bringing up my daughter more because
I knew a bit more of what to do, what to expect.

In 1944 I sent a collection of poems, nineteen in all, to Harper, because I decided it was time to try to get a book published. I had met Emily Morrison at the first Midwestern Writers' Conference, and she told me that when I had enough poems to make a book, she would like to see them. So I sent all these verses that had no connection, really, but she was canny enough to see a connection in several of the poems, those that dealt with Negroes. She said *that* was my forte, not to write disconnectedly about such things as love, death, and the mysteries of life, but to center my ideas in the background I really knew something about. She thought the best of those poems dealt with Negroes, so I took her at her word and gathered them together and called the collection *A Street in Bronzeville.* My idea was to take my own street and write about a person or incident associated with each of the houses on the block.

Elizabeth Lawrence at Harper replied that indeed they were interested in bringing out a book of my poems, and to take my time. But I couldn't take my time, so I sat down immediately and wrote a long poem and a series of war sonnets. With her letter, incidentally, she sent a copy of a letter from Richard Wright, to whom they had shown the manuscript. He was enthusiastic, but he didn't care for my title. He said no one would understand what "Bronzeville" meant, and it turned out that he was right. Negroes and whites alike are forever asking me what it means. It refers to what used to be, and really is still, the largest Negro area in Chicago. In those days it was very well defined; I know. There was not one Negro east of Cottage Grove Avenue. I used to take my little boy over there on walks, and we counted ourselves lucky when we weren't thrown at.

I wrote those extra poems and they said I'd done enough and that they would bring out the book. It took nine months. It was published on VJ-Day in August, 1945, and attracted a great deal of attention. It wasn't too hard to attract attention with a book in those days; soldiers were reading madly, and books sold well, even poetry. My book had a rather folksy narrative nature, and I guess that is one way to get poetry in front of people: to tell stories. Everyone loves stories, and a surprising number of people can be trapped into a book of verse if there's a promise of a story. The legend on the cover of the book, "Ballads and blues..." promised excitement.

I suppose the next truly big thing that happened to me was being awarded the Pulitzer Prize for Poetry in 1950. It still seems like a thing that couldn't have happened to me. And it came, you might say, out of the blue.

One day a reporter from the *Chicago Sun-Times* called me and said,

"Do you know that you have won the Pulitzer Prize?" I screamed and said something about not believing it. I was stunned. I grabbed my little boy (he was nine at the time); we had been getting ready to go to the movies. Anything was better than sitting home in the dark. We'd had our lights turned off because we hadn't paid the bill; we were very poor. So we went to the movies, but I don't think I saw or heard a thing; I kept believing and not believing I'd won the Pulitzer Prize.

The next day was exciting and a little appalling at the same time. Newspaper reporters and photographers came out, most of them in the daytime, which wasn't too bad. But the *Chicago Tribune* came out at twilight, and they were going to take pictures and would need electricity. I sat there frozen. (I wonder if other people who think of themselves as being sensible do such foolish things.) I sat, waiting in a sort of quiet terror for him to put the plug into the socket. Then came that horrible moment when he put it in, and strangely enough, the lights came on. I still don't know how this happened. My husband said he had done something about the light situation, but that they couldn't have turned them on that quickly. So that's the story of the Pulitzer Prize. Light in darkness.

I mentioned before that one does not make a living from poetry, and that is so sadly true. This is one reason why I've taught for many years — perhaps the better way of putting it would be to say that I've led classes. I don't consider myself a teacher. I don't have teacher's training or certificates, and I'm sure that I've been accepted in schools because my Pulitzer Prize represents a diploma of some sort.

The first person who showed an interest in having me do this sort of work — helping? lightly leading? surely not teaching! — was Mike [Norman] Alexandrof, the president of Columbia College here in Chicago, a communication arts school. He told me he wanted me to conduct a poetry workshop to encourage young people to write. The first classes were in the evening, so I had people of all ages, not just young people. I had one sprightly little woman in her sixties who wanted to write poetry so badly; I saw her a few months ago, and she has been publishing poetry in various magazines and seemed very happy about it.

In these classes I play records — *The Waste Land*, *Spoon River Anthology*, Robert Frost, many other modern poets — Dylan Thomas, Marianne Moore. Then we have panel discussions and debates, and I stress that they must read and read and read and write and write and write. They always seem to be very interested.

I think that the beat poets have had something to do with the interest young people have in poetry. What the beats had to say, while certainly not in the kind of verse I would want to write, related to them, to our world. When I have them write beat poetry as an exercise I tell them, "You will probably never want to write another beat poem, but it's a wonderful muscle-loosening exercise." The beat poets seem to have invested modern poetry with some fresh air and blood it really needed.

The people in the workshops have told me, over and over again, that they had hated poetry because they were forced to memorize it in elementary school and high school, and it was presented to them as something heavy, to be gotten through for the sake of grades. The thing I am interested in doing is in presenting poetry as a living thing, an instrument of pleasure, of release, and they enjoy it when it's given to them that way. I make them write a lot, and once in a while they'll groan about that. Each student must write a book of twenty or twenty-five poems, depending upon the time we have. The few sessions when I've taught a fiction workshop I have them write groups of stories or short novels. My motto could be: "It's all in the doing."

The gratifying thing is that I find a great deal of talent, real talent. I've found people I envy, turning out very good poetry and very good fiction. Most of them are willing to work very hard. There are a few, always, who come there just for the grades, and I try to impress upon them that grades are of little interest to me. I regret the fact that I have to give them. But I have been amazed at the willingness of students, young and old, to put real energy and time and thought into their projects. I know how much *is* put in because I have to read their works and comment on them. And I must comment on every page submitted, because if I leave one unscrawled-upon it's brought to me and I'm asked, "What did you think about this? You didn't write anything, so I'm wondering if you thought it was so bad there was nothing to say."

Teaching, readings, being a mother to a teen-age daughter, and a wife to a fine and talented husband—these things take up time, and the time is well-spent. But I'm still primarily a poet, a necessary and perhaps compulsive thing. And I think that my poetry is related to life in the broad sense of the word, even though the subject matter relates closest to the Negro. Although I called my first book *A Street in Bronzeville*, I hoped that people would recognize instantly that Negroes are just like other people; they have the same hates and loves and fears, the same tragedies and triumphs and deaths, as people of any race or religion or nationality. I did not start writing to be a propagandist. I began writing because I love to write, and wrote about whatever I thought I knew. As I grew older, of course, I realized that it was Negroes that I saw, so I wrote about Negroes.

But take a poem from *Bronzeville*, "The Preacher." It could be about any preacher ruminating behind the sermons, wondering how God is, what He thinks up there, alone. He wouldn't have to be black or brown or yellow or white to wonder about that. A poem like "Kitchenette Building" applies more to Negroes, perhaps, because more Negroes live in kitchenette apartments than the members of other races because they are so cheap and, consequently, so bleak. I've lived in many of them, and wrote from my own experience. But I hope that people can come out of my books feeling, "Well, Negroes are people after all, despite how strange they look with that peculiar color." People still indulge in this feeling; they find what they don't know to be mysterious, and distrust it.

I feel the civil rights movement to be most important, naturally; I belong to the NAACP, contribute what I can afford to give them, and I've given to SNCC. They are young people who are fighting the battle for some of us older ones. I intend to continue to contribute as much as my income will allow. But I'm not active in a speaking or marching sense. I guess I'm too withdrawn.

My primary obligation as a person and a writer is to my poetry, to myself. The poetry is myself. When I sit down to write a poem it's because I've had an impression, an idea, an emotion. I feel something, and I want to put that something on paper. You might say, "Well, because you put it on paper you are obviously trying to interest other people." That is certainly true, but my first commitment is to getting myself onto the paper. Then I hope, naturally, that many, many people will want to read it.

Many writers do feel an urge to save the world, of course, and perhaps some of them have succeeded to some degree. When I was a little girl I felt that I might write something that would have great influence upon the world, but since I came to my senses I have not felt obliged to revolutionize the world in any way. Some things that I have written might sound otherwise, but my first idea is always to put what I thought and felt on paper. I wrote about the Emmett Till murder because it got to me. I was appalled like every civilized being was appalled. I was especially touched because my son was fourteen at the time, and I couldn't help but think that it could have been him down there if I'd sent him to Mississippi. That was a very personal expression. I tried to imagine how the young woman, the one who was whistled at, felt after the murder and after the trial, after her sight of the boy's mother. What it was like to live with a man who had spilled blood. I imagined that she would have certain cringing feelings when he touched her—at least I know I would.

Now I'm working on the long poem, the book-length poem titled, *In the Mecca*, based on my first job experience I mentioned before. So I guess that virtually everything I write comes from life, and must come from life, to have validity.

This is an exciting age to be writing in. I think that the present great interest in form and language was bound to happen, if only as a reaction to the dull sleepiness of the preceding years. I don't think that the present intense concentration on very close, very textured language will last. I think that poets and readers will soon become interested again in presenting life in all its rich and diverse aspects. But I also think the good writing will continue without being as specialized and finicky as it is today. I guess I'm part of the persuasion; I too love to fight with a line or with a phrase. But I think most of the writers, the good writers, will become less self-conscious as time goes on. After all, the important emotions and subjects and ideas are made more exciting through clarity, and the way to that admirable combination of reality and power stand out in Dylan Thomas and T. S. Eliot and Yevtushenko, and are now most enthusiastically found in Voznesensky. Voznesensky seems to be so much a part of today in both language and subject; I think he's a good forerunner of what we may expect from the future.

"...you want to write a book for so many reasons.... The main reason...is because it will make you well-known and beloved and popular and sucessful and famous and respected. You also write...to make money, but that motivation is not first on the list."

Helen Gurley Brown

Helen Gurley Brown

BROWN: I was born in Green Forest, Arkansas, up in the Ozarks in 1922. We moved to Little Rock when I was quite small because my father was elected to the state legislature. When I was ten he was killed in an elevator accident in the state capitol building. They had appropriated funds for a new elevator, but the money got sidetracked somehow, and my father was killed in the line of duty, so to speak.

After that we moved to California, my mother and sister and I, and I went to high school and started as a working girl at the tender age of eighteen. I did have a year at business college; I worked at the same time at a radio station answering mail. No formal education aside from this.

N: *This does not lead to* Sex and the Single Girl *or* Sex and the Office.

BROWN: I really don't know how ladies raised in Little Rock and in most provincial cities can wind up with any interest in sex. People do their very best to disinterest you. They say, "It's all right to make love after you get married. Then the fireworks start and the heavens light up." But before that time you're supposed to feel nothing whatever, so how a girl reared in a Midwestern town maintains her interest in sex is beyond me. But somehow I survived my early training. However, I think you have to live for a while before you know whether you want to write about sex or anything else. There are very few Francoise Sagans.

N: *How did you come to write the books?*

BROWN: I think you want to write a book for so many reasons. I think the main reason you want to write a book is because it will make you well-known and beloved and popular and successful and famous and respected. All of those things enter into it. You also write a book to make money, but that motivation is not first on the list.

Some people write a book because they have to. They're like the great artists; they have to speak up. In my own case I wrote a book because it turned out that after all those many years I could write one. I would have written books a long time ago, if I'd been able to, for all the reasons just mentioned.

As to how they came along: let me quickly say that my husband read some old carbon copies of letters I'd written, and he decided I had a writing style. A year or two later I was very unhappy at one of my jobs. I was out of favor at the office and I said, "Maybe I could write that book you mentioned I should write some day," and he thought about it and decided that what I could write a book about was the single woman, since I'd been single so long myself before I was married.

When I sat down to do it I was better than anyone supposed I might be. In other words, it turned out better than we thought it would. So you couldn't say I was driven to writing a book through a burning, driving ambition. Things simply fell into place.

Before this, I had written a few little things; an article I sent off to *Glamour* which was promptly returned, an article for *Playboy* which was returned, *Esquire* same thing. But that was over a period of perhaps ten years. I'd no other writing experience, really.

With my first book, *Sex and the Single Girl*, the writing period was fairly brief. It took a year, and I wrote it while I had an advertising job, working on weekends and in the evenings and sometimes at the office when nobody would give me any work to do. (At the ad agency I was in, they played favorites and I was out of favor.) With this sort of moonlight writing I finished the book in a year, and what happened afterward was really astonishing. *Sex* has been published in twenty-eight countries now, and in sixteen languages. Nobody's ever been able to figure out why it has done so well, but I think it's this: it was simply the right idea at the right time handled in the right way. Whoever said —was it Voltaire?—that nothing is more powerful than an idea whose time has come, knew what he was talking about.

At the time I wrote about single girls, nobody was championing them. Volumes had been written about this creature, but they all treated the single girl like a scarlet-fever victim, a misfit, and since there happen to be twenty-six million of them in the United States you can't really categorize one-third of the female population as misfits. I didn't know the statistics when I started writing, but it happened that I picked up a torch, I guess you'd say, and became the standard-bearer for this particular group. And in addition to tackling a worthwile subject I tried to write so that I wouldn't put anybody to sleep. The combination, being helpful and constructive, plus the inherent sexiness of the subject and fairly easy-to-take writing, seemed to work out.

You know, when authors talk about themselves and how they happened to write what they wrote it gets to be a bore. It's like a recording artist being interviewed on disc jockey shows. They say, "Then I recorded 'All God's Chillun' Got Molasses Feet' for Columbia and then I moved over to Capitol and then I switched to MGM and I'm opening tomorrow night at . . ." you know. So I'm going to shut up.

N: *In both of your books you advise the single woman to live a little bit more, and explore promise and fulfillment more thoroughly, but you don't actually invite them to be promiscuous.*

BROWN: I have to tread a very fine line. I watch every paragraph in this regard. I can't take a stand for promiscuity. In the first place, I'm not for it. I don't believe in "sleeping around." I don't think it's fun to have too many lovers; it gets very confusing. Therefore, I would never lead a girl toward that kind of activity, nor even encourage her to have one affair (although it certainly can work out well). All I can say is that in many cases an affair does not work out badly.

In personal conversation, if I were talking with a girl and she told me all the circumstances, I could give a direct personal answer or opinion. But when I'm writing a book that's going to hundreds and thousands of young women I really can't take a positive stand and say, "By all means go and have an affair."

In *Sex and the Single Girl* one of my interviewees said she had never known a happy virgin over the age of twenty-two. That's going rather far. And in *Sex and the Office* when I discuss promise and fulfillment, I have to be a lady or nobody is going to pay any attention to me. If I'm a brazen hussie and say, "Have an affair with the chairman of the board; great benefits can be yours," I'd be doing any girl a disservice. She has to choose and pick her partners. The office is where the men are; she can use her feminine wiles. Work hard, but also be a charmer. It seems to me that's going as far as I can go.

It would seem to me that if a girl's religious training absolutely precludes having anything to do with a man before marriage, she can't listen to anyone like me. She must listen to other voices.

Parental verdicts are something else again.

What I'm trying to say is that girls are different, and some of them I couldn't hope to persuade to my way of thinking. But there are girls over thirty who are not strictly religious who aren't living at home with Mommy and Daddy, and who have had affairs. I can certainly say to them, "Look, it's not the end of the world. It's part of living. You may not get married for years. You may never get married."

I think girls are torn because they need men, they're interested in sex. What do you suppose all this "dressing up" is for? Not for other girls, really. But they pretend they are not interested in men and they are shocked when a man makes a serious pass at them.

If I exhort a girl to do anything at all it's to face reality. Like a man she is a sexual creature.

Now, many a girl who remains virginal until her thirty-fourth year can't stand the pressure any more, and ends up being virtually raped.

She can't make herself give herself to anyone who is gentle and kind and takes a calm approach; she can only go over the brink with someone who practically beats her over the head once she gets herself in a position to be beaten over the head. Certainly something *nicer* should have happened to her before.

A girl who is terrified that a man is going to deflower her before her wedding night has a problem, socially. She sets up icy waves around her, and perhaps she can't help it. Something has made her believe that men are dangerous until you marry them, and then they are okay. But that kind of girl has a rough time getting a man to marry her because she doesn't know how to give and take socially. She is inhibited socially because she is ill at ease with men.

This is a rather incendiary subject, and it sounds as though I'm pushing sex, saying, "Go out there and get your share." I'm not, really. I dare say that there are girls so anesthetized that they are happier not doing anything about sex; they would be desperately unhappy if they tried to change, so they should stay as they are.

I also think there is a different moral code for young girls, even girls in their twenties, and women in their thirties and forties. A girl of thirty-six is not a girl of sixteen, yet in this country some persons believe girls of all ages live by the same rules. I'm all for girls staying chaste as long as they can, really, up to a reasonable age. There's no hurry. I think that being innocent when you're young is desirable and lovely. You can make love to a man until you're seventy, so what's the rush? However, to carry innocence past a certain age may defeat its purpose. So, although an affair can bring heartache and disenchantment, being a thirty-nine-year-old virgin may have brought some girls nothing. Neither joy nor heartache, just a void.

I made a speech at a resort in New York recently, at Grossinger's. They can accommodate about six thousand people in their busy season. Here were about sixteen hundred single people from all over this country and from several foreign countries. I talked, and we had a question and answer session afterward, and a number of the young people had questions like, "Mrs. Brown, don't you know that a girl is marked after she has something to do with a man? What is this doctrine you're preaching that will ruin a girl if she does what you suggest?" These are intelligent, reasonably well-off people. (They have to be to pay the hotel bill, anyway.) I just said, "Isn't that insane. She isn't any more marked than if she had just gotten out of the bathtub."

Not much has been said in this country, it seems to me, about sex being fun. If it was fun at all, it was supposed to be fun only for the man. Now girls are getting into the act, and I think we're terribly interested in anything written about it. Many people say, "Well, Helen Gurley Brown, you are placing too much emphasis on sex; can't you talk about something worthwhile?" I'll admit that there's a lot of emphasis, perhaps overemphasis, on sex, but I think we're simply getting away from our puritanical forebears. Now the pendulum is swinging the other way, and everyone wants to talk about it. I think one of these days more people will get around to having satisfactory sex relations and then some of the talk can die down.

N: *What motivated your second book,* Sex and the Office?

BROWN: I figured I really only knew two subjects. One was "being single," which I was for thirty-seven years, and I polished that off with the first book. The other thing I knew in depth was about working: nineteen offices, twenty-three years of experience working in them.

I have to write from the gut. It has to be what I call visceral research. I talk to a lot of people, and I sift what they tell me through my own consciousness. In other words, I don't do a case history of Mrs. A. Von Greenschmidt of Evanston, Illinois; that's no fun. So I talk to loads of people and gather in their opinions and experiences.

By and large, it's my thinking and personal observation and opinions that went into *Sex and the Office* because it's an area I know something about.

Most working girls don't know what they have. They don't make anything out of their jobs. They look all over the place for men — social clubs, church, picnics — and the men aren't there. The men are in the office, right under their noses. They don't seem to realize that.

When they get a little further along in a job, they might begin to catch on. Fun, you know — having lunch with men, going to meetings, having men listen to you. Sometimes you're sent on a trip, to be the only girl with fifteen men. That doesn't lead to orgies; it just leads to some interesting days and evenings. Working is great if a girl works hard and uses her femaleness to have a good time at the office. She spends so much time at work, maybe eight hours a day including lunch hour, that she is a little idiot if she just sits there and thinks, "Oh, if I could only go and roll bandages in the Congo and do something important instead of this." The rewards and the fun are there, right under her nose, and I want to tell her how to get on with it.

I think she should be most discriminating. It seems to me the prerequisite for making love is to like someone enormously. Now, I'm not talking about the act of sex all the way through *Sex and the Office*. When I refer to sex it's the overall appeal between men and women.

I do hear from people who get so outraged and incensed. They call up and say, "Mrs. Brown, who's going to take care of all the fatherless children if these girls do what you suggest?" Well, they presuppose that every girl who has a conversation with a married man in the office is going to wind up in the sack, pregnant the next morning. The percentage of affairs that develop from office repartee is very minute, although some do develop. But a girl who can't be trusted to talk to a man in the office can't be trusted out of her cage. Besides, degradation, death, and fatherless children don't always result from an affair.

The silliest questions come in. Some people assume that because a girl has had an affair she is finished socially, that no decent person will ever have anything to do with her again. Now, I would defy anyone to look at a woman and tell how many affairs she has had. You can't tell by speaking with her or looking at her, and you can't count the rings on her trunk. She can be respected, dignified, kind, compassionate, interesting, and who knows how many men she's slept with?

On the other hand, a perfect bitch, a dreadful girl whom nobody wants to be around, much less marry, can have had no affairs whatever. One thing does not necessarily relate to the other.

N: *How do you think the American male is doing?*

BROWN: I think he's coming along nicely! The American male is nicer, more wonderful than he was ten or twenty years ago. I think men are now quite inclined to recognize a woman's ability and stamina, and they aren't leaving her out of things the way they used to. They've stopped deprecating women, stopped saying, "Women are funny little creatures, and who can understand them?" Perhaps we have lost certain of our prerogatives; I notice that men sometimes let us push the door open ourselves, and on the bus the other day a mailman with a big sack of mail sat on a vacant seat while I stood. But that's exactly as it should be. We're big girls now.

I think American men are finding out what hellishly good fun it is when a woman is treated as an equal and allowed to have a good time.

N: *What are your future plans as far as books are concerned?*

BROWN: I have a contract for three more books, if I ever get them written. I guess I'll have to live a little bit more and collect some ideas. I don't think I should turn out a book every year just to turn one out. Maybe the soil has to lie fallow for a while.

My husband edits my manuscript quite severely. It's too good to be true to have an editor right in the family. As soon as I get a chapter as polished and as gorgeous as I think it can be, I give it to David and he tears it to pieces. By the time it gets to my publisher, Bernard Geis, it's fairly coherent, and they have a terrific editor there, Don Preston, who pulls the final things into shape. He questions the things he doesn't understand and we fight to the mat, but he doesn't change much. He cuts, sometimes, but the editing has been done at home.

You know, there are so many sexier books than mine. Books with more salacious titles. If you want to pick up a sexy title you can do a lot better than *Sex and the Single Girl* and *Sex and the Office*. Originally people tried to talk me out of those titles, said they sounded too much like a Kinsey Report. A biological survey. But I liked the titles, and they weren't chosen because they were the sexiest I could think of. As for the amount of sex dealt with in my books, they could be so much sexier. I think my books are quite moral. Of the people who criticize I think about 60 percent haven't ever read anything I've written, and the others are jealous; most people would like to write a book that sells.

So when something comes along, simple and girlish, they have to find an excuse for its success. It couldn't possibly be because I wrote well or had something to say. Never. It had to be because I wrote something dirty, or it was all because of "that great title." Perhaps those people wouldn't be so jealous and frustrated if they sat down and wrote. But even mentioning sex to certain groups (the Puritan thing, again) is like mentioning vivisection to animal-lovers. They go berserk. Either they wish they had a better sex life than they do, or they're hopelessly frustrated. Methinks they protest altogether too damned much. You never see them picking on a *failure*.

As for the comments about writing books to make money: why do they suppose authors run around the country being interviewed, talking about their book? You want people to read it. Why do you want people to read it? Most importantly, you want them to know what you've said; to get your message across like you want them to listen to you in conversation, you want them to read your book. It's a lovely, gratifying thing. The other reason you do all that promoting is that you want to be a success. You want the next publisher to offer a bigger advance. You want to sell more copies and make more royalties. You want a book club and a paperback deal.

Of course you want your book to be successful. You didn't spend two years of your life writing something you hoped would die like a yellow-fever victim.

Note: *A relatively brief period of time, less than two years, passed before a second interview with Helen Gurley Brown was scheduled. In the meantime she had added another significant accomplishment to her list of successes: she had become the editor-in-chief of* Cosmopolitan *magazine, and had made that once-desultory periodical one of the most talked-about in America and one of the hottest sales items on newsstands.*

This portion of the interview begins with a query as to how the magazine came into her already-busy life.

BROWN: At the time *Sex and the Single Girl* and *Sex and the Office* were on the market I got a lot of mail. The mail continued to run rather heavily, even after the books were in paperback, and all of the letters asked very personal questions.

I know that Abigail Van Buren and Ann Landers and all the other advice-giving ladies get much more mail than I've ever received, but I found my supply impressive because it had never happened to me before. It seemed to me that there could possibly be a magazine that would answer a lot of these questions for the girls who were writing to me. I felt there was a girl out there who wasn't being reached by all the publications that were already on the market. At least if it *was* there these girls weren't taking advantage of it.

My husband, David, and I, sat down together and put together a format that originally had a title, *Femme*. I don't know what the final name would have been, but we worked out a presentation that was about twenty-five pages long, as far as we could go without spending any money. We thought of about two hundred article ideas, twelve to fifteen departments. There was a long pitch at the beginning explaining why there should be such a magazine. It was for the girls who worked, the girl every magazine publisher seemed to have deserted. *Glamour* used to be a magazine for a girl with a job, but *Glamour, Mademoiselle,* all of those magazines had been recently acting as though working was not as important as grooming—once all the other books said that a home and children and one's life with a man were everything. This left twenty-three million women who work with no magazine that was directly appealing to them. And based on my experiences with my books I knew there were a lot of single women nobody was talking to, the girl who was alone at twenty-five or twenty-six, unmarried but probably still hoping to be. Twenty-three million of them, including divorcees and widows.

I really think that anybody could have come up with this magazine format. To digress: the reason people don't get things into the works is because they don't get them into the works. While it is true that David and I had some entree, and could get people to listen to our ideas, we aren't that influential. We simply sat down and did it. One Saturday night near Easter we talked about this magazine with one of my girl friends, and by the next morning David and I were busy writing it. Admittedly, we're a bit nutty; we don't have little children to dye Easter eggs for, and we have the time to devote to ideas.

We prepared our little presentation (I typed it; I'm a good typist) and it went off to two or three different publishing firms. MacFadden-Bartell was one, Dell another, and though we got through their doors, they really weren't interested. It takes a great deal of money to start a magazine. My publisher, Bernard Geis, knew Dick Deems who's the head of all the Hearst magazines. They had worked together at *Esquire*. He said, "I'll take it over to Dick for you," and it turned out that Hearst was just the place for it. They said, "We don't want to start a new magazine, but we're thinking of making some editorial changes in *Cosmopolitan*. Maybe you could take your format and superimpose it on *Cosmo*." It took several months for us to negotiate but we finally worked out a deal.

I thought, at the beginning, I would be considerably curtailed editorially, that they wouldn't let me do articles that were too controversial, and I would have to pussyfoot along. I decided to make those concessions because probably no one would ever let me start a magazine all my own.

But it's really been quite wonderful. They have really given me free range, and I've been able to talk about frigidity and about women being more sexually responsive than men and wives who are having affairs. Sometimes I'm sure they must have bitten their fingernails, but they've given me a chance.

I meant to go slowly. I meant to change the magazine gradually, so that we didn't lose the old readers before we started getting new ones. But when I got here I found that the art director had to do what I said! It was such a heady experience, coming from the world of advertising where the art directors trample all over the copywriters. I had never been a boss before. I knew I was going to be the editor of the magazine, yet I'd never even had my own secretary before. I gradually realized that I was the boss, and that what Lola Gurley Brown wanted, Lola Gurley Brown could get. The art director could say, "I like this picture better" and I could say, "I don't; I like my picture better" and we ended up using my picture. Of course, I have a nice art director. It was absolutely heady, and since I had these prerogatives and could indeed make it my book, every single page the very first issue I brought out was *my Cosmopolitan*, and it has continued to be so ever since. I never deviated from the format David and I worked up in the first place.

I do keep my blinders on. It doesn't matter how marvelous the baby pictures are that come in. It doesn't matter how fantastically good an article on natural childbirth is. They're not for me because my format says we do not do children and domesticity. It doesn't matter that a lot of *Cosmopolitan* readers are mothers, which they are; it's just an area I'm going to stay away from. I've been true to my format. It was either going to work or not work. It worked, so I'm still at it.

N: *Has the circulation of* Cosmopolitan *increased?*

BROWN: It changes every month because we're a newsstand magazine, 98 percent of the way. This means we have no subscriptions we
can rely upon every month. Many magazines have a base circulation.
Glamour has a base circulation of 743,000 copies; *Mademoiselle*, a base of
243,000 copies. I mention them first because they are my immediate
competitors to some extent. What *McCall's* and the *Ladies' Home Journal*
have, I'm not sure, but their base circulations are in the millions.

Anyone can have base circulation by buying it. You make the
magazine expensive enough. You make the subscriptions so inexpensive
that a reader can get ten copies for $1.25 or whatever. You can buy
circulation, but it's quite expensive from the production standpoint to
mail out these copies. You're offering them for twelve cents a copy, and
postage would be twenty cents, so this means you lose money on every
single issue mailed out.

Cosmopolitan is completely a newsstand sale and, of course, the same
number of people don't walk up to the newsstand every month to buy
the magazine. I just got the August figures; we sold over a million
copies. In September we'll probably sell 900,000. Again, to answer your
question, our base rate at *Cosmopolitan* is a guarantee of 800,000 copies
per month. This means that, averaged over a period of twelve months,
we guarantee advertisers that they will reach that many people. When I
came in they had not been meeting this guarantee for several months.
They were down, some months, to 600,000 or 650,000, which meant
that they were going to have to change the ad rate momentarily, if
things didn't pick up. So let's say that I've brought *Cosmopolitan* from
600,000 to over a million some of the time, to 800,000 or 900,000 the rest
of the time. It fluctuates.

I don't know whether this sounds like copping a plea or not. In other
words, I have not gone from 600,000 to 1,500,000 or 2,000,000. I feel I'm
more like the *New Yorker*. *New Yorker* circulation doesn't increase year
after year; it's just that the magazine gets fatter and fatter from
advertising. The *New Yorker* has a devoted following that wouldn't be
without it. And I'm after the *Cosmopolitan* girl who doesn't want to read
about babies and domesticity and Laundromats and teen-age delinquency and college fashion boards. She wants to read the stuff I give
her, and I want that loyal audience of girls. I want my girl, the
Cosmopolitan girl. I'm not after all the people who read *Ladies' Home
Journal*, though it would be nice to have them. But if you're going to put
out a *Reader's Digest*, which can sell to twelve million people, you have to
have a certain type of article. If you're going to have a magazine that can
show a man and woman in bed together, you can't expect that kind of a
market. I'm not going to equal the *Reader's Digest* as far as circulation is

concerned. I'm going to be a more rarified type of book. With loyal readers.

But to answer your question: yes, circulation is up considerably. An important thing to my bosses is the fact that with the February, 1966, issue, we raised the newsstand price from thirty-five to fifty cents a copy, a 43 percent increase, and there wasn't a drop-off in sales. This means they just glided very smoothly along, and each issue sold brings in 43 percent more than it did previously. *Cosmopolitan* is profitable for management.

And one must keep in mind what one is in business for. I keep it firmly in mind that I'm in business to be successful. I'm spending a company's money and I know they want a good return on their money. They are getting it. Advertising, as of next year, will be up 100 percent. That's where the money is, really—not in how many magazines you sell but in how much advertising you carry.

N: *Could you go into your philosophy of the magazine a little more deeply?*

BROWN: We have a very personally-edited book. It's my magazine and we don't take surveys to find what people want. I put in things that I think will interest women and girls because they interest me. I wouldn't say that my objective is to make this a better world generally, except as it is improved by women being more secure within themselves. My objective is to put out an interesting magazine that people will buy. I have no idealistic goals whereby a community is going to be safer or juvenile delinquency is going to be stamped out. I want a magazine that will make girls say, "Gee, there's my friend, *Cosmopolitan*. It seems to understand me. There's a lot of stuff in it I enjoy reading. I kind of get inspired. They have my number. I get this magazine every month because I like it, because everything personally applies to me."

That's my goal, to put out a magazine that is right for this particular girl.

We deal with all subjects of emotion, because I think emotions come first. They really motivate everything we do. I think most decisions are visceral, really. Therefore, every month, *Cosmopolitan* has an article on jealousy, shyness, the uncontrollable temper, or insecurity—things that stem from emotional states.

Then, every month, we have an article about one famous person. That again follows strict guide-rules on my part. We don't come up with someone obscure, and try to lionize that person ourselves. It must be a Julie Andrews or a Julie Christie or a Jane Fonda; somebody who has already begun to make it big. We do one reasonably important non-girlish article per month. Something like "What Vietnam is All About." You know, there are many women who won't admit that they don't know how it all began, and when they read *Time* or *Newsweek*, those magazines aren't going back to explain all over again how it got started; somehow when all this was coming about in the UN in the fifties, we just weren't paying close attention. So we did a very good article on how it all got started and who is doing what, why we can't get out, why some people are so much for it and some so much against it. We had a piece on labor unions which explained in primer fashion to girls how *they* got started, and whether or not they've gone too far. We have somebody doing U.S. foreign policy, why we won't let Red China into the United Nations, etc. I know I'm a reasonably smart woman, but an absolute dumbbell in areas like foreign policy and it's too big a bore for somebody who really knows the subject to sit down with me and explain to me what's going on. I wouldn't like to admit my ignorance, anyway. So these four-page (usually four-page) features cover those things that help a lady understand the world around her a little better.

Nor do I think I'm being patronizing when I say, "Look, I'm in the same boat, so if I'm not too proud to read an article that helps me understand, I don't think you'll be too proud, either."

We do a lot of stuff about men and women because about 90 percent of the mail I get is about a man's relationship with a woman or the other way around. Women writing about men. I'd say that 70 percent of this mail is from women who are mixed up with the wrong man but they won't admit it; they can't stand to hear it. So we have a great deal to say about divorce, about the man who won't marry, the homosexual man, the lukewarm boy. He is different from the homosexual. He's a neuter, for neither boys nor girls. Usually he's for his mother.

Then we do the things all women's magazines do—fashion and beauty, because most women care about those things. I don't think it's immoral. Supposedly it's OK to be wrapped up in painting, and appreciate beautiful pictures; well, I think that looking at beautiful women in beautiful clothes is just another aspect of it. A woman looking her best is hardly a Botticelli, but she is fulfilling a form of creativity and self-expression. I think fashion is fine, and we do something about it.

Actually, you know about my books. The magazine is an extension of everything I've written before, but I would think it is done much better, since we get the finest writers we can get hold of. We get good books, good fiction. I don't write anything for *Cosmopolitan;* I think an editor should edit, and the writer should write. There are writers who are a great deal better than I am, and they're the ones for me.

N: *How do you feel about the comment that* Cosmopolitan *is the feminine counterpart of* Playboy?

BROWN: I'm not insulted by that, although we really are less racy by far. We never show anything that isn't in good taste. Not that *Play-boy* does either, if you keep your sense of humor; I'm mad about the magazine and have always read it every month. I don't think it hurts anybody, and I don't know why people get so excited about it. They say, "Well, if you had a daughter you'd feel differently." That's not true, of course. We're not a *Playboy* because we're not that nude, we're not that sexy, and we don't talk about the things *Playboy* talks about.

To one extent we are like *Playboy* magazine. In *Playboy* there's never anything about a man's family, and we know that *Playboy* men have children and wives, but *Playboy* takes the attitude that they do not. Nothing gets into *Playboy* that is not presumably for the *Playboy* man. They rarely have a woman writer; I think I was the only one. They rarely write an article about a woman. Everything is for the consumption and enjoyment of the *Playboy* man.

Well, every single thing that goes into *Cosmopolitan* is for the consumption and enjoyment and self-improvement of a *Cosmopolitan* girl. We both seem to understand and appreciate our markets, although our market and our approach are quite, quite different.

"There is a great deal of illiterate reviewing being done, and it's better to just go away from it and say nothing. . . . I don't suppose there's really any critic except posterity."

Hortense Calisher

Hortense Calisher

Note: Most writers, when speaking of life and career, work rather well from the standpoint of chronology. Perhaps more give-and-take and urging take place than show up in the interviews on these pages but, on the whole, a pattern is established and maintained.

Similarly, a definite compartmentalization establishes such subject matter as views on other writers, the critics, advice to young writers, etc. The cohesion which (I trust) results in a fluid manuscript comes with a minimum of editing on my part, a minimum of false starts on theirs.

Hortense Calisher is an abrupt exception. Two taped interviews, three years apart (September 1963, June 1966) produced glittering and sensitive fragments of observation I simply cannot link together via bridges or questions. It isn't that she was being capricious or uncooperative. I simply have a feeling that this superb stylist has her own way of making a statement, and that to distort or interrupt a statement she makes would be as sinful as shooting butterflies.

CALISHER: Someone asked me, just last week, if I would come and talk to students. This is one thing I frequently do, but he said, "Will you talk about your work?" and I said, "No, I can't." He asked me if I'd read, and I said I would but that I thought it would be a passive and dull thing to do to students. I began to think about what I would say — apparently I would have to speak for twenty minutes — and I decided it might be interesting for them to learn why I *can't* talk about my work. It has always seemed to me that if you could talk about your work in fully-formed phrases, you wouldn't write it.

The writing is the statement, you see, and it seems to me that the poem or the story or the novel you write is the kind of metaphor you cast on life. You make a statement, you give it a form, and it's like a metaphor in that you cannot break it up. Once you break up a metaphor you don't have it any more.

*　　*　　*

I kept a notebook when I was seven, but I haven't had one since. I keep hoping that I will. All I remember about the notebook is that I read stories out of it to my aunt, and she disapproved, so I didn't write any more. I had the usual writer's history. I wrote poetry while I was in high school, I wrote poetry and short stories while I was in college. I didn't write again for a long period, except for doing an occasional poem, but I could never stop thinking about it.

I came to writing fairly late. My children were young and ready to go off to school when I decided that I would go out of my mind if I didn't write, and that I would try once more to see if I really had anything to offer. I started writing my short stories, and I was lucky; they were published, and they haven't been able to keep me from writing, since.

*   *   *

I didn't react to the fact that my stories were being published when that break came. I reacted to the fact that I was actually going to be able to do, seriously, the thing I had desperately wanted to do all my life.

A woman has a great many excuses she can give herself as to why she can't write—not male excuses. A woman has household things, children, and for a long time I hid behind one or the other. I finally realized that the excuses weren't valid.

I'm so glad to be writing; it's so nice to be accepted. The important thing is to be able to do it, to feel serious about it. If you remember, in *Textures of Life* I describe the young people (and so very young; this generation starts off so early) as saying, "I'm a sculptor," or "I'm a poet." I've heard young people say, "Jenny's coming over tonight. She's a writer."

I could never have done this. To have said in public, "I'm a writer," is more than I could imagine doing. When I was finally published I was able to say, "I am a working writer." This may be a strange and private reaction, but it was mine.

*   *   *

There does seem to be a tendency, here, to distinguish between men and women writers. I think it's based on the rather strange distinctions that are made in this country in dividing things into the feminine and the masculine; there are things that are right for females to do, and things that are right for males to do.

Actually, the male writer in America suffers from this more than women do. We suffer critically in the sense that we are usually reviewed by women writers, by other women generally, and it's a great accolade to be finally reviewed by a man, but this is incidental in this country. The fact that so many of our male writers must flex their virility muscles in peculiar ways must be hard on them. They have to fight through the generation of writers that grew up with me, and in a way repeat the thing that Hemingway did to show that although he was an artist, he could shoot bears or fish. Many young writers still have this difficulty, and I think it comes from the fact that it's not quite all right in America for a man to be an artist. I think it's much, much easier, now; in fact, many of the young male writers I know aren't out shooting bear and seem quite secure.

*   *   *

Everyone gives advice to the young writer, and all of it happens to be good advice. I think it has to be taken where and as it can be applied.

To me, everything is grist for the mill. Experiences. For myself, I like to stay unverbal outside of writing. I certainly would not want to write other kinds of things to make a living. This may be a matter of temperament, because many great writers have done so. Here, in this country, we teach to provide accessory income. We start early, we have to earn a living, and the thing to do (for young writers) is to teach. I didn't prepare for this. When I was younger I thought I wanted to be an editor. Thank God I dropped this idea. I think it would be the worst thing to do, because when you start looking at books from the outside you cannot stay humble, and every writer worth his salt thinks only occasionally from the outside, and stays humble.

As a young person the things I did were quite varied. To list them all will make me sound like Tennessee Williams. There was quite a fashion in the 1930's and 40's to say that you were everything but a writer or dramatist; you dug ditches or whatever. I didn't dig ditches, but I started life as a dancer, and I was going to become a modern dancer until I decided that dancers weren't verbal enough, and I couldn't stand their company, and I wouldn't work hard enough. I got out of school during the Depression and worked during college. I sold at Macy's. I think everyone of my generation sold something or other at Macy's. I sold maternity dresses, stocking-stretchers, that sort of thing. I was also a hostess in a Happiness Candy Shop. I was head of a stocking and hat department. (I wrote a story about that.)

I was a social worker for awhile, and that was an important thing. I was a middle-class young woman of a protective good family, and the only job I could get after I got out of college was as District Visitor for the Welfare Department of New York. I saw homes I'd never seen before, and was projected into that great part of life you would never have seen from the confines of a proper home and the proper schools. This made some rather deep changes in me; I began to have some small insight into social thinking.

*   *   *

If you are a serious writer, or a serious artist of any kind, you write with your whole life. You may not have command of it, but it's there.

In the book out most recently, *The Railway Police* and *The Last Trolley Ride*, the second novelette has a setting in upstate New York. Now, I lived in upstate New York from 1941 to 1946, five years. I loathed it. I had never been away from New York for any length of time, and we had very little money and a new baby and I had no sense about how to make do. A few years later I drove back through the area and I thought, "How could I have been so neurotic? This is the most beautiful landscape in the world." I was in Rochester, and I don't like cities of that size. Perhaps Rochester is a very "cold" town, but I had been too immersed in myself, and I didn't write about it.

But this last novelette I wrote really comes out of that landscape. Some reviewers said that the characters are all mixed up with the landscape. That is intended, the whole sense of the land I didn't know I was sucking in, is there.

You can never tell when you're storing things up. I used have an old friend, not a writer, who had artificial ideas of how writers live, and every time he heard we were going away he'd say, "That's right, that's right, get local color." That isn't it at all. If you did it consciously you'd probably end up being a bore to yourself.

*   *   *

Peculiar things have happened in reviews of the long new novel, *Journal From Ellipsia*. To be alternately beaten and praised in Europe is a new thing, for me.

The English hate it. Partly, I think, because there are some pages on the English they might not find complimentary. Also, I think, because they hate pretensions on the part of Americans. They don't like it when an American slings the King's English around. They would rather have Americans say "prezackly." They would like us to stay in the image they've created for us.

The Irish, who are splendid masters of the language, and know it, don't mind when someone from across the water dares. The Dublin *Times* called *Ellipsia* a breakthrough of a particular kind in coming to terms with the scientific side of our lives. This is really what I think it is. They said that the novel triumphed in a humanistic way, that it pursues the humanistic tradition, that it is about people and keeps its eye on people throughout. This is precisely what I tried to do. When I saw this review I almost went straight up in the air; it's the only one that said this.

It's a difficult novel to understand, I'm afraid, but I don't think it will be as difficult as time goes on. Susan Sontag told me that she put it on a special list, and asked me if I'd seen it. I said "No," and she said, "Well, I think you ought to know that if you had been a writer tabbed by the avant-garde, such as William Burroughs, this novel would have been talked about all over, but nobody expected such an avant-garde book out of you."

I don't know why not. But I'm not equipped to know how people think of me. Yet this theme, this type of writing, is not new to me. In my very first book, *In the Absence of Angels*, there's a story called "Heartburn," which for years has been included in anthologies of weird stories. It's a long road from that story to *Ellipsia*, but there is a direct connection.

I'm not like Truman Capote. I don't invent a form every time I use it. I invent a book. And the novel must change, because every art must change.

Another thing the Dublin man said was how I had broken out of the framework of the nineteenth-century novel. Every novelist must do this, searches for ways to do it. But I don't think you create a form. You create a form for your book, in a way, but it has tag ends, you know. There certainly are traces in *Ellipsia* of the side of literature from which it comes.

I think what scares people is that novels don't stay the same in the sense that they're always in a particular tradition. *Ellipsia* also had linguistic wordplay in it, but this wasn't mentioned, except by the Irish. Badly trained people think of Joyce every time they think of language play. This is odd, because language play has been going on ever since the human race opened its mouth.

*   *   *

The Last Trolley Ride has puzzled people. It puzzled me. I couldn't understand why I was doing it, when I first started writing it. It's about what most persons call "folksy" people. Well, folksy people cover the earth, the United States, but my work has not been identified with them. Yet I know a great many folksy people. I am related through my family, through the families of both of my husbands, to Upstaters, Midwesterners, all sorts of non-New Yorkers. I've lived with these people, so why should I write them out of my existence?

Actually, the novel is, in a peculiar way, a response to that countryside. I began to think of that countryside and its names. The people had come first, but then I saw why. It was also involved with the cycles of life. In a very direct manner I now (particularly now) think the novel also comes, in a peculiar way, out of the war in Vietnam. This is never mentioned, but we are again living wartime, and I have lived through three of them, and was born in time to feel the tag ends of the First World War, so that makes four. If you live that long you begin to recognize cycles in people and in their reactions and you think, "That damned old wheel is turning again." I put it, in the novel, in terms of transportation. I thought of the last trolley ride; when transportation systems die people usually make the last run a picnic. Trolleys are the latest to give way, but our newer forms of transportation will someday be outmoded, too.

But it's hard to talk about my own work. All the facets are in it, and anything I say is only a part.

*   *   *

The American book reviewer with a daily job cannot—unless he is an extraordinary human being—do a competent job on any book, especially if he is a general reviewer who has to know everything about everything. In these terms it is surprising that so much good work does come off, upon occasion, but I think it's done by a very few people.

For example, there is almost no relation between my books and the reviews they get. Sometimes one reviewer will say one particular aspect is good—by "good" I mean "astute," according to what I know. Oftentimes I'm praised for what I find to be mystifying reasons. I also think critics like to think that they can help the writer do better. This is almost never so, excepting in one narrow sense. We all need encouragement, and if we get it there is no doubt we're inclined to do better work, but this is because we're human beings, not because we're writers.

Writers have great rises and slumps in ego. It's very useful to us if something good is said that coincides with our own intentions; in fact, it's pure heaven. But there is a great deal of illiterate reviewing being done, and it's better to just go away from it and say nothing. You spend your life doing something, and if it's misinterpreted it seems wasteful, but I don't suppose there's really any critic except posterity.

I think that the British have a greater air of literacy in their criticism. I don't think the differences are as great (between theirs and ours) as they once were. They buy our best sellers now, and the British picture has changed, although their standards tend to be more severe.

I think it is still true that they try to give American writers a hard time in specific areas, particularly if we are attempting to produce real literature. And they tend to give their own writers an easier time. For example, Iris Murdoch is far more important to them than she is to us, and we are more likely to criticize her for her lapses than they are. Yet nobody chafes an Englishman harder than another Englishman.

I think it's useful to read on both sides of the Atlantic, now. We don't cover them as well as they cover us, but their comment on the American scene can be very enlightening. I don't read reviews very often, so I'm really not qualified to go into this too deeply. When I'm in England I read all the English reviews I can lay my hands on, and we do subscribe to some, here. But I find reading reviews on a steady basis an impossible thing for me to do. I waste so much time and energy wanting to rebut. I'd never write a manuscript; I'd turn into a reviewer because it could be such lively fun.

The only kind of review I really detest, all things considered, is the one which is showing off the reviewer rather than the book reviewed. Reviewing for their own display. There are a few reviewers and critics I love and respect because they brought me to literature. I think this is, perhaps, their real function. A great deal is said, now, about Edmund Wilson, but I remember that when I was a young person I read things and went back to things because he sent me, and I'll be forever grateful to him. I knew nothing about John J. Chapman until I read one of his reviews—what a discovery! He sent me to Dickens with greater appreciation than I'd gained from all my reading about Dickens. And he came at a time when I was young enough to want that guidance.

*   *   *

Who knows what literary health is? The state of being changes so. We can't go on doing the same thing. I don't mean that we have to be original every time we speak, but there is a slow yet definable way in which literature does change. Most often it is subtle rather than obvious.

For example, the most obvious and possibly the most trying change in the novel is what has come to be known as black humor. I don't object to black humor—I love it. But I object to the books which are merely a free ride on disassociation. They bore me; I can't read them. But any kind of morbid humor that is powerful and formed to a recognizable degree I love.

I don't tend to see literature in terms of trends. I tend to view particular books. I don't read current fiction while I'm working, not because I'm afraid of catching something, but because of time. It's just that when you're concentrating on a piece of work the form grows like an embryo, and any other man's creation tends to get in the way, if only in general terms. I'd rather not be walking around with anyone else's imagination, or have his imagination walking around with me, at that time. So I'm always catching up on things later, and by then the book has attained some degree of perspective.

*　　*　　*

I get up early and start to work in the morning. My best hours are when I go straight from bed to typewriter with a cup of coffee, not talking to anybody. I used to work only in the mornings, but now I find that I work longer into the day. I think this is because I'm in New York. I used to spend much of the time in the country, and I could take a break and go for a long walk in the countryside. Now the walk leads me to Saks Fifth Avenue. So I work until 4:30, when I'm hungry for tea, company, and relaxation.

*　　*　　*

The reactions to the book of two novellas—*The Railway Police* and *The Last Trolley Ride*—went as I predicted. People understood one or the other. I suppose it's only human to prefer one over the other, and I predicted that those who liked one would not like the other. There's no doubting the fact that the two novels are very different from each other. Richard Sullivan, for example, plugged for the last one, said it was a notably distinguished novelette, and that he admired my work so much he didn't want to comment on the first.

If you suck somebody in on one piece of work they expect to be sucked in on the second, and if you change the pace and the content— oh, my. People get so upset when you don't do what you've done before.

Art collectors get extremely upset when a painter changes his so-called image, you know. They think it tends to challenge values. I hope book readers have more sense. After all, owning a book is not so serious an expenditure. It's hard for the writer who does try to change his image, or explore, or grow. Yet if I were a critic reviewing the two novelettes I would go back to my early work and discover that certain tendencies reappear, this novel does relate back, etc. After all, a writer has nothing to work with that is new under the sun. He's always saying things in different guises. Proust, Mann, Hemingway, did this all their lives. We would be demons or angels if this weren't true. Yet we try to expand and explore, though the writer who does give you the same thing, the same comfort, every time, has a much easier time of it in his lifetime, particularly in his early periods. Very often the writer who has done something different is roundly scolded for it.

But I feel good for having stretched.

*   *   *

I suppose every writer has some second thoughts, some regrets, about a book that reaches publication. I wish I had cut a little more than I did from one section of *Journal From Ellipsia*. As a matter of fact I sat up all one night cutting that section, and my husband finally stayed my hand and said, "You're going to ruin the book. It's tough, but it's worthwhile, so let it be. Generations will understand it." But then you do find someone who understands it, and you're so pleased. John Barkham understood that book. I think he's the one on this side of the Atlantic who did the most with it and for it, and I thought, "Well, if he understood it I was right, wasn't I?"

When this happens you feel good.

Robert F. Capon

Bed and Board is everything a good marriage manual should be — and seldom is. Perhaps it's because its author, Robert Farrar Capon, is an Episcopal priest who is not only observant and witty in his own right, but speaks from the depths of daily experience in coping with marital problems within his parish. He also has a wife and six children.

How did he come to write the book?

"Actually," Father Capon said, "it started out to be a cookbook — slanted for the large family on a modest income, naturally. But, perhaps, in the back of my mind, I had gotten so irritated by all the marriage and child-rearing manuals which indulge in either gray truths or rosy lies, that I worked my way from board to bed and then to all the other aspects of marriage. I ended up with two paragraphs on food and no recipes.

"When I found myself doing this I knew I would have to be honest, to stay within my own realm of experience. Six kids have given me a lot of experience, and so have the marital problems within my parish. It wasn't hard to hold a line.

"I realized that I couldn't sit on a theological throne in writing the book — that would be as bad as occupying a psychological throne, or a sociological one. It would go too far over the head of the average guy who simply can't understand his children, perhaps never will, but who should learn to avoid blowing his top and spoiling his day.

"Now, in the average book on child-rearing they tell you that a child will respond in a certain way at a certain age. Then in a little footnote at the bottom of the page they say that the child may not do thus and such then because each child possesses tiny bits of originality and this originality should not be squashed.

"What they don't say is the fact that the child acts like a footnote 99 percent of the time, and up to the general rule 1 percent of the time, with the result that the horrified parent doesn't know what to do and, in a state of total confusion, disciplines the child one day and lets him run wild the next.

"This, in turn, reflects upon the kid. Children do not want parents to be playmates or buddies any more than they want them to be prison warden. They want parents to be there, firm and stationary, holding a line in matters of discipline, perhaps making them unhappy some of the time but giving them a firm background all of the time.

"So much of modern child-rearing invites anarchy. And anarchy in the home is the thing that's apt to make a husband come home from the office a bit tense, drink too many martinis to drown out the noise his kids are making, then blow his top when a glass of milk is dumped in his lap. An evening is ruined — but there's no reason why his children couldn't have been quiet enough when he got home to forestall that extra martini.

"You see, we forget, often through the advice given, that a happy home for children isn't one in which they shed their inhibitions and act like a bunch of Zulu warriors. Firm — not harsh, but firm — discipline is something they need for their own security and well-being.

"Most books that deal with marriage, too, can be misleading. They make sex a matter of acrobatics and stopwatch — which it isn't at all. It's something people work out for themselves, and though they might occasionally need advice they don't need to enter statistical columns.

"To get back to the book — I guess I wrote it in the hopes that the reader can find enough reassurance and identification to be able to say, 'Gosh, I'm not so bad after all, even though I don't understand my kids, and blow up at my wife,' and then do something to make the relationship with the children smoother, and the arguments with the spouse less frequent.

"Man being the imperfect being he is, life cannot be lived in absolute harmony all the time. But life being the gift it is, why not make it as happy and constructive as possible?"

Rachel Carson

At the time of her death Rachel Carson was working on the expansion of the text for *The Sense of Wonder*. It is to be regretted that she did not make it all she wanted it to be. Yet, we need feel no sense of omission for it is a beautiful book, a superb evocation of the joy and awe felt by a child's encounter with the world of nature. Thanks to the photographs (mostly by Charles Pratt), it is both a textual and visual bit of reality and warmth, utterly timeless yet forever significant, and deserves a permanent place in the home library.

How did she come to write it?

"I have always believed," she said, "that though a child will discover things for himself and feel a sense of wonder, he will be all the more fulfilled if he shares that discovery with an understanding adult — preferably an adult who has never totally lost the same delight in discovery, who recognizes the mystery and perfection of oh, say a sunset, the roar of the surf, a fawn, a nestful of baby birds.

"In urban society we forget that such things exist. Our sciences seem to feel that such things are outmoded. Yet all these simple but wonderful things were here before we were, and if we keep on as we're going they may be here long after we're gone. Unless we destroy them, too, which we seem quite willing to do.

"If you've ever taken a child by a hand, and shown him a cocoon, and explained to him what it is, and the moth or butterfly that will emerge, then looked at his shining eyes, you've realized that the joy of this discovery exceeds any accomplishment he may later encounter as a nuclear physicist.

"Better yet — if there are enough discoveries like this he may revere life enough to become a nuclear physicist."

Had she always strong objectives as a writer — commitments as powerful as those that showed in *The Silent Spring*?

She smiled. "I've been such a crusader I'm afraid I've made myself quite objectionable to those who believe that man, or science, is the end-all. No, I shouldn't say 'afraid'—I'm proud of the discomfort I've caused them.

"You see, man isn't the total of life. I don't believe he shares any form of exclusivity as being the most important creature on earth. We are meant to share this planet with all forms of animal and vegetable life. Indeed, if we keep on with our ridiculous overbreeding, and crowd out the other forms of life, we could find the endless and exclusive company of other humans to be quite a bore.

"I think almost anyone who has wandered into a wooded area that has been heavily sprayed with an insecticide feels the first twinge of this loneliness and boredom. No insects or animals move. No birds cry out or fly. It's so eerie you would welcome a mosquito to bite you, or a fly to annoy. But because we have lost respect for all forms of life other than our own—and after Hiroshima I wonder how much respect we have for our own—we don't mind poisoning our forests and meadows and lakes and streams.

"The irony, of course, is the way the poisons we sow are ultimately reaped by ourselves, as the insecticides enter our body through the animal and vegetable life we've tainted."

She paused, and I was thankful to hear the bird song in her yard.

"Back to the book I'm working on—call it the joy of discovery, the sense of wonder, whatever—it's the most beautiful thing that can happen to a child. For that matter, it's a beautiful thing for any adult who leads that child, who sees through the child's eyes, and perceives through his other senses, the recreation of a magic moment in his own life.

"Isn't this renewal, this rejuvenation, the reason for life in the first place?"

"I would hope the aspiring writer had guts and talent.... Young people are often asking for kinds of help they never used to ask for ... the arrogance of so many very young 'would-be' writers.... I find this absolutely deplorable. You don't go groveling around for help ... or for advice. This is sickly behavior."

Eleanor Clark

"Anyone who wants to write is going to pay a price.... The aspiring writer has to put a lot more on the line. The gamble is bigger, and ... the reward can be bigger, too. If he's honest and he works, advice is beside the point."

Robert Penn Warren

Eleanor Clark
and
Robert Penn Warren

CLARK: I keep silent about my birth, except for passport applications. It's not my age I'm coy about, but I was born in Los Angeles and I'm embarrassed about it. I packed up and left when I was a few weeks old, and grew up in a migratory sort of way in Connecticut. I consider myself a native of this state, but my sister, who grew up in exactly the same times and places, always claims she comes from New York. We need sorting out, geographically.

I went to dozens of schools, including a little country school for a few years that required three miles of walking each way through swamps and blizzards and things. I even went to Europe to school for a while.

College — Vassar. Not as one of *The Group,* thank you. Like most writers, I started writing when I was minute. I was a lot more concerned with music for a number of years, and thought I was going that way; I worked hard at it, and had a lot of fun, but when I was eight I wrote a book and gave it to my gym teacher. She didn't say a word about it. Then, when I reached college, I wrote a great deal of poetry. I showed my long prize poem to my grandfather, who had been a poet, along with other things, and whose judgment I mightily respected. He looked at it sternly and didn't say anything for a long time. Finally he handed it back to me and said, "All you can hope is that someday you'll grow up and forget about it."

As you can see, I was encouraged right and left.

But at school one publishes in the usual undergraduate way. When I was a Sophomore in college my sister and a friend and myself somehow got out our own magazine. We all published heavily in it, each of us working under five different names. We put it on the market and, oddly enough, it made a little money; I think we each made about $12.00 after paying the printer. But in the big world, I started writing for money as soon as I got out of college. Not much money. I went in to see the people at *The New Republic* — I shouldn't say "went in" because I walked around the block about fifty times, and finally pushed myself into the office, and told them that I intended to write book reviews for them. I subsisted for a long time on such things. I was writing a novel and stories and things at the same time, but for a year the only things that appeared in print were reviews. A lot of them.

I guess I did all the usual things as a youngster. I starved in a garret for a number of years, and did some ghostwriting for refugee psychoanalysts, and worked for a publishing house. Then I started getting my stories published. *Partisan Review, New Directions, Life and Letters* in England. For awhile I sort of coedited *New Letters in America,* in the late 1930's. I published a story in it, naturally.

I suffered frightfully from a political and social conscience. Oh, and by the way, during those early years I sent a short story, very timidly, to the *Southern Review.* Last year I came across the terribly kind rejection letter — not a slip, but a nice long letter explaining why they didn't feel this story was right for them — from the editor, a fellow named Robert Penn Warren. That was our first communication.

N: *How did you two meet?*

CLARK: He claims we met at Katherine Anne Porter's house. I think we met a week earlier, in a restaurant. Anyway, the season was then.

Back to early years — a rather sad note in my life was my first novel, my first published book. I had written a novel before, but I threw it away; I've come back to it now to make it the root of the one I'm writing at present. I worked a long time on this book, interrupted during the World War II years when I took a job with the OSS in Washington. I tried to work nights on it, but didn't manage very well. I wasn't accustomed to an office job, and I would keep reminding myself every night, as I dragged home at six o'clock, of all the literary martyrs who had always worked and written, working so very hard. But it didn't help.

At any rate, I managed to get it finished. It's called *The Bitter Box.* It came out in 1946, after all the struggle and interruption. I haven't looked at it for a long time, but I wouldn't be surprised to read it now, and find it the best thing I've done. Some people think it so.

Unfortunately, *The Bitter Box* was swamped in the publishing procedure. This is what happens to a lot of books. I don't claim to be grieving over it, but it was rather sad to me, after working on it for such a long time, not to have it noticed. It came out the very same day as a book on the man-eating tigers of someplace-or-other came out. I was amazed to see those tigers all over the place that day, and no mention of my small effort, whatever. I was young and hopeful then and expected to be fussed over. Now I know better. There's always some man-eating tiger around on publication day. But I must say that my book has never recovered from those tigers. Other first novels do recover from similar disasters, but mine hasn't.

Come to think of it, my novels seem to be prone to protracted interruption. Not only World War II, but the long hiatus on the present one when I took time out to do *The Oysters of Locmariaquer*. I feel as though I was only the agent in that procedure; I didn't intend to interrupt the novel, but I seemed to have no choice.

We were in Brittany at the time, and I planned to work only on the novel, but the oysters took over in an imperative way—inch by inch forcing themselves upon me. So the novel was put aside. I should be used to this, in a way, because I've been writing it while having children. The life span of the novel—the endless gestation, I should say —has been studded with the vicissitudes of motherhood. I've had other vicissitudes before, wars and my husband and things, but nothing like motherhood. Unrequited love is nothing compared to requited love involving offspring.

N: *What approach to research do you follow in producing nonfiction works like* Rome and a Villa *and* Oysters of Locmariaquer?

CLARK: I'm continually being asked about research. I let myself in for that by doing the Rome book, which did have a lot of so-called facts strewn about in it. In all humility, I have the greatest respect for people's note-taking systems, when they have them, but I simply haven't got one. All the notes for the Rome book, such as they were, were on flyleafs and old cigarette packages. No method whatever. I finally did buy a notebook in Rome, and used it to a certain extent, but I have to do things as they come.

In both the Rome and oyster books the procedure was the same. I wrote a great deal with very little solid information simply because, when I began, I didn't expect to carry either one as far as I finally did. Simply because I was entranced by the subject and the subject matter, I dealt with it rather as a painter deals with colors, and as more precise information became necessary to the pattern I went out and acquired it. In both cases it meant an awful lot of rewriting.

I had to tear things apart I had already written, mend and stretch and modulate them, as I acquired the necessary information. When a pattern grows on you like this, it's sheer hell, and I went through a lot of it.

Obviously this is not a literary technique you would advocate for anyone because it's horribly painful and wasteful. But I, myself, couldn't function any other way in these matters because I have no interest whatever in learning per se, or in doing a work of journalism to present facts. I couldn't care less. I simply have to do those things that take possession of me, and this possession comes only in the stages I've described. I never know, from one stage to the next, how much more is really going to be required of the pattern, because the pattern goes on stretching, growing, imposing itself.

N: *What was the point or germination or origination, with both* Rome *and* Oysters, *if it can be tracked down?*

CLARK: That is the sort of question that exists on a good many levels, isn't it? One can provide a little surface narrative of the genesis of any book; especially with nonfiction the obvious things could be said, but that would not be a very important level of truth.

You bring to your curiosities about life—therefore, about your specific needs to write, to create—a whole mass of experience. This experience includes lackings, yearnings, losses, regrets, nostalgias—I think we can generalize a bit and say that Americans, in general, are nostalgic people in this generation, perhaps for the last two or three generations. And we have certain delights and rages and furies that are apart from the general sense of life; mine involve a relationship to this country, our country.

I have no interest whatever in writing what is generally called a travel book; but the fact is that I was in foreign places these two times when my imagination was struck in a variety of ways and on many levels, and in a way that brought to a focus all of my more or less unformulated feelings about my country. Now I'm speaking privately, personally. We're bound to hate our country sometimes, or misunderstand our own love of it, and it can be that certain images of a foreign place bring these feelings to a moment of truth, compelling you to give shape and words to them. I had known Rome as a child, had lived there, and had put it out of my conscious mind. When I came back I was not aware of having seen the Forum. I knew I had, but when I saw it again it was as though I was seeing it for the first time. Little by little I became aware that I had known it, and then this spaciousness of time in Rome became very exciting to me.

I was on a Guggenheim Fellowship, trying very hard to do what I was supposed to do, but it was torn apart by this tug of Rome. I had never know anything like this except for a return to the American West, which I went back to for the first time since babyhood, and had been absolutely overcome and delighted by the spaciousness of time out there. Arizona, western Nebraska, parts of Wyoming. The sense of geological time, petrified wood, etc., was marvelously enlarging. I felt that I was moving spaciously. But I saw that too briefly for it to settle into anything I could commit myself to, or use, but when I came to Rome it was the same thing in other terms, and I was forced into that marvelous journey into time that Rome is.

I think you write only out of a great trouble. A trouble of excite-ment, a trouble of enlargement, a trouble of displacement in yourself. *Oysters* was the same, for me, because it sprang from an even bigger world—the sea, the truly ancient and endless world of the sea. But it was the same kind of journey, the same kind of trouble.

I don't know whether or not the novel I'm doing will have any of that spaciousness. I would be pleased if it does. It certainly doesn't have it in an obvious way, because after all these years I'm writing my hometown novel. The one you are supposed to do when you're nine-teen. (I did write it at nineteen and mercifully threw it away.) Any spaciousness it might have would be through the wiles and the wilds of people. I hope it's there.

N: *Both you and your husband are such polished writers; how conscious are you of style?*

CLARK: "Style" is a word I'm very shy of. I'm really not aware of it as an entity or demand. It seems to me that as you write, it is terribly important for a certain kind of music to be heard, a certain kind of precision to come into being. I think one develops—perhaps has, to begin with—a loathing of the imprecise. (At the moment I loathe the very imprecise way I'm talking to you, but it *is* dialogue, and I hope it is read as dialogue, not something I've worked over.) This doesn't mean that you won't have sloppy moments, moments when your mind is on something else in the sentence or the paragraph. Things get by you.

I think you develop a working censor as part of your being; you're not conscious of that censorship all the time, but it's got to be there because without it there is no craft. There is only effort. And after you've been at this business for a number of years, this basis of your craft will be inherent. If it's not I'd say you're sunk, and you'd be better off giving it up.

N: *A corny question: How did you feel when* Oysters *won the National Book Award?*

CLARK: I don't know whether or not the question's corny, but it is puzzling. I don't know, really. It's nice to be liked. It's nice to feel that somebody likes what you've done. But it was strenuous. I'm not used to getting up and showing my face in public. I find that a bit abashing. I'm troubled about that, because I think there's a risk of confusion between a public performance and what is supposed to be the point of the whole affair, that which one has written. There seems to be a good deal of that sort of confusion in the book world today. There are other confusions too, and if we were to be hypersensitive about them we'd go off to live on an island and never publish, so I guess we've got to be a little thick-skinned. Still, it was a bit disconcerting. The song and dance aspect.

N: *I'd like to discuss those things in the literary world that you most admire and most dislike.*

CLARK: There you've really got me. Part of my dilemma is the fact that having children has cut down my reading time by about a thousand hours a year. That is probably a literal estimate, like those police estimates of crowds at funerals. I'm not complaining, but there are such horrible gaps in my reading that any opinion I might express on anything except *Winnie-the-Pooh* would be quite irresponsible. I think that when my children get to boarding school I may graduate.

N: *Is there a problem with working schedules? Two writers in the family, two fairly small children —*

CLARK: You've been around here for the past few hours. You've got a sample. Electric trains roaring around, a succession of small animals, a great deal of squawk and babble. But we manage.

N: *Do you and Mr. Warren bounce your work off each other for criticism or comment?*

CLARK: If I were a properly literary wife I would hover over his prolific daily output every night and never do anything else. As it is, he's awfully nice about anything I write, and I'm nice about anything he writes, when life permits. He's just better than I am, and not a mother.

N: *How do you feel about the state of literary criticism and review in the United States?*

CLARK: I write a little criticism, you know, so I'm not in a position to make any horrid generalizations about it. But I guess it's doing all right, limping along as usual.

Recently I did a piece on Edith Wharton for the *New York Review of Books*. It took an elephantine length of time; I wrote it in a day, but it seems to have taken me months to get ready for the day, between the reading and the children. The one thing I learned from that experience — from reading all the Wharton-James business — was what a wretched state criticism was in at the time of their friendship. Edith and Henry got together on their critical tenets, which I should have thought unnecessary for them, but it was impressed upon me that criticism was in a ghastly state in this country fifty years ago. I suppose there were a few fairly decent critics, but by and large the general level of reviewing was appalling. Wharton and James found it absolutely necessary to sit down with their friends and talk and work out certain principles of aesthetic approach to fiction. I can't bear to do this sort of thing. I think both of them paid a very great price for this, but it was a necessary price, due to the way things were at the time.

Compared to that sad state, I would say we're in clover. I think there are a great many very good people around, and a lot of books get the attention and the criticism they deserve. The ordinary level of critical writing — the general run of the press that reviews for the mass, not the scholarly literary quarterlies — seems to operate at a high level.

I don't normally have much appetite for reading reviews of my books, but when *Oysters* came out I had things sent to me from all around the country, and I was happily surprised and delighted by critical pieces and reviews. On the whole I thought that the small city papers (by "small" I mean papers in cities smaller than New York) were much better than those in New York.

N: *If you were to advise, or hope for, the youngster who wants to become a writer, what would you offer?*

CLARK: I would hope the aspiring writer had guts and talent. What else is there to hope for? Perhaps as I've grown older, I've adopted the classic approach to the younger generation: faultfinding. But it does seem to me that young people are often asking for kinds of help they never used to ask for, and I find this very upsetting. I simply don't understand it at all, the arrogance of so many very young "would-be" writers who send letters to all the well-known authors asking them for advice and interviews and assistance. I would no more have dreamed of doing this, at that age, than I would have thought of jumping off the Brooklyn Bridge. I find this absolutely deplorable.

I think you should stand on your own feet, damn it, and know what the price is. You can see the price clearly at seventeen, eighteen. Everyone my age who is a decent writer knew the price at that age, and if they didn't they fell by the wayside. You don't go groveling around for help from established people. Or for advice. This is sickly behavior. You can make friends with an older writer if you happen to meet or know him; you could go knock on his door out of respect. This can be fine if you're worth something, and the older writer recognizes that. A friendship may develop on the basis of a give-and-take that will be valuable to the young writer and the older one. But this business of just indiscriminately expecting the established writer to be throwing out helpful hints, usually to meet a commercial motive, is despicable. Now you'd better talk to my husband; he may not find youth so damnably opportunistic.

*   *   *

WARREN: Born, April 24, 1905. Guthrie, Kentucky, in Clyde County, fifty miles north of Nashville, Tennessee. Population, 1206 or 1305, I forget which. It's still the same — hasn't changed to this day. Half in Tennessee, half in Kentucky, half black, half white.

I went to public schools through my third year of high school in Guthrie, then went away to prep school for a year, and from there to the university.

As a writer I arrived fairly late. I wrote one or two things as a youngster. I remember an overwhelmingly passionate desire to write a poem when I was twelve years old and had a fever. This proves the pathology of art. I actually wanted to be a naval officer; I had an appointment to Annapolis, but had an accident and couldn't go, so I went to Vanderbilt University instead. For three weeks I intended to become a chemical engineer. Then I fell into bad company. I had a freshman English coach named John Ransome. He was the last man to recruit, to want to recruit, anyone to writing, but he couldn't help it because he made it so interesting.

Lots of young people took his courses and decided it would be nice to be a writer, and I was one of them.

I wrote a great deal during college, and went on to graduate school at Berkeley, California, for two years, then to Yale graduate school, then to Oxford for two years.

I came back to the South in the middle of the Depression. I had to go back. I wasn't programmatic about it; I just felt I had to go there. It wasn't really home, it was simply a part of the world I had a stake in. At Oxford, probably out of homesickness, I began to write fiction — the first time since my sophomore year that I'd tried. I'd written poetry, all the time, and published things in literary reviews and in *The New Republic* and *The Nation*, and developed an obsession about American history, but something happened to me at Oxford that simply took me back to the South. Perhaps it was because of the fact that when I was in college in Tennessee I became so involved with the university world, and to misuse a big word, the philosophical world, that even when the Scopes trial was held a few miles away I didn't go to it. Five years later I thought I was a damned fool not to have gone to it, so I came back from Oxford and became wedded to the South again. I could have gotten a bad job elsewhere.

N: *That was during the period when such a disproportionate number of our writers originated in the South.*

WARREN: It's true, I suppose, that for awhile we did produce more than our share. And you're bound to wonder why, if you have lived in the South a great deal of time. I think it happened this way: The world of the South was frozen from 1865 to 1917, when the First World War came along. Things happened there, but the pattern of thought wasn't disturbed. There were no new ideas, no basic changes in society. The First World War shattered the frozen quality of the South. The key element in the South, the most obvious element, at any rate, is the race business. Once the First World War had been fought the South had to recognize the fact of Negro mobility, labor mobility. The Negroes would move from one place to another in the South where they were needed, and leave the South for opportunities up North.

A comparison (a more drastic thing, but nonetheless a comparison) is what happened in fourteenth-century Europe, when the Black Death struck and the labor ratio was changed. Society couldn't be constructed along the same lines afterward. But all sorts of shocks came to the South, beginning in 1917. I remember the people I knew, the college students and older people of the 1920's; they didn't look to New York or the Middle West, wonder what they were like, admire their writers. I madly admired Dreiser, and still do; he's a great writer, but I didn't look to him for guidance. In a strange way the relationship with the Irish and French writers was more important. Particularly the Irish, because ours is a provincial area, speaking provincial English. Our attention was focused on the European rather than the U.S. Northern. The writers, the Southern writers, of my generation, had a European orientation; Pound, Eliot, Crane, Stevens. Yeats and Joyce and the French novelists were our world. I never heard the word "Marx" used except in Hart, Schaffner and Marx until after I left college. This was a strange contradiction; every Southern freshman, literarily inclined, knew *The Waste Land* by heart in 1922. We sat up all night reading Baudelaire, but Marx and Freud were only ugly rumors.

Then our insular world ended. Strange tensions and ferments were bred, running from the question of a "new conscience" – "new discomfort" was the better description – regarding the Negro situation, and new notions of economics, and a sense of a world existing outside us. Just acquiring a sense of the world outside was challenging.

Hope came, too. The poverty of the South was immense, and the mere fact that the possibility existed of improving one's lot was an exciting thing. Even the black man felt this, as the possibility of change took hold.

Actually, I should think that all literary or artistic revivals, or new states of awareness, are based upon shocks of consciousness or moral shocks. You stir a man to a point where he wonders what he can do about an existing state. This happened in New England in the 1830's and 1840's, and in Elizabethan England of the eighteenth century. The Renaissance was a period of change through shock.

Results are always evidenced at different levels and scales. The society that is frozen, fixed in its values and procedures, begins to think about itself in a new way when it is kicked in the can. In literature the society can objectify the issues it finds most urgent. It's not a parlor trick, not a game; it's both a cause and effect of the society waking up to its own problems, its own inner nature. The South had this experience. It was shocked out of what it was. But you can't shock people too much, as Toynbee has noted. Too much challenge is like shooting a man in the heart. It doesn't make him do anything; he's dead. The Civil War, with its dire poverty and total shock, didn't bring change. It had to be just enough shock, the right shock treatment. The war generation in the South during World War I was the real carrier of the shock. Younger people like me benefited from it. We were picked up in the backwash. But the generation of John Crowe Ransom, Allen Tate, William Faulkner—they made the real crossover.

World War II hasn't affected the South as much. Economically, yes —you can see the new prosperity. But there's been less social change. The big thing has been the civil rights movement of the 1950's, which could be regarded as a delayed backwash of World War II. The new mobility, the new investment of money in the South, has benefited Negroes in a backhand, corner-of-the-table way. Without World War II and the new education for whites and Negroes through the GI bill, you wouldn't have had the civil rights movement as it is known in the South and elsewhere; so I suppose that the second war did have deep and significant effects, after all.

N: *In* Who Speaks for the Negro? *you examined the civil rights movement in an extremely frank and intimate manner. What motivated the book, and how was it done, and what did you hope to accomplish?*

WARREN: In one sense it was a purely personal book. You can't be a Southerner and not have the whole race question on your mind in one way or another. It's bound to be there. I simply had an overriding interest. I have my own feelings, and they were informing me of what was happening, but I guess I just wanted to know more, to really inspect my own feelings. I didn't go at it in a "Which side am I on?" approach; that wasn't the point. I knew where I stood at that time on that question. But I wanted to know the shades of feeling. You can't walk into Martin Luther King's office and say, "Let's go out to lunch and have a conversation." He'd say, "I'm busy; what do you want?" You have to have a reason for the project, a reason for yourself.

The key motive was to find out about that world as deeply as I could, to find out about myself as deeply as I could. The only way of "finding out" is to write a book or a poem; if you're a writer you will only do your thinking because you are writing. I must say that I have never had a more fruitful experience. The mere fact of seeing that number of people who feel such an extraordinary degree of commitment; the intelligence, the gaiety that sometimes entered. When you think of the great number of young Negroes of the highest intelligence, the strongest drive, devoting themselves to civil rights, you can only wish they didn't have to fight spooks. I'm not saying that what they've done and what they're doing isn't crucial and valuable, but what if all this energy was put to another purpose? To cancer research, for example? But they're committed to fighting the spooks of society instead of dealing with the real problems of nature, the real problems of man at another level.

America is a story of release of energy at different levels. One can see where each wave of immigrants has had a perfect release of energy, a sudden full entry into American life. The most recent and best-advertised release, artistically, is the Jewish literary impact. A Negro literary impact is just beginning; we are feeling the first stirrings of some extremely talented people. But think of this release of energy not in terms of just a few talented people, but a bang, a racial release. This is what has happened, stage by stage, to the various groups of immigrants. We don't even think about it any more. It is simply assumed. Now the last great reservoir of human energy, ethnically, is the Negro. Once that vast reservoir of energy is released we should run over with vast strengths and talents.

The Negro in a secret and suppressed way has made great contributions to American life, even when he was supposedly cut off from participation. The effect of the Negro has been enormous. We can't even guess what America would have been like without the Negro. No Civil War, a totally different structure of American life, different language, different music. Yet while the Negro has made an enormous impact racially, he's been cut off individually. This full recognition, the full release of energy, could come anytime in the next fifteen to thirty years. And it will be tremendous.

N: *To turn to* All the King's Men. *Could you explain its genesis?*

WARREN: I was writing novels and living in Louisiana, so there you are. It was just that simple. I was living in a melodrama. But all of my novels have come out of the same sort of thing, out of a world I knew something about.

If something doesn't interest me deeply I don't want to fool with it. It never crosses my mind to find a good story to write a novel about. I have to have enough interest in the subject matter to make me want to, have to, write the novel. Anyone knows a thousand good stories, but when you can get worked up about a thing that has a special rub, a special concern, then it simply has to be written.

N: *As a poet and novelist are you aware of a conscious obligation, to whatever quarter that obligation might be owed?*

WARREN: Yes, and I can say it very quickly. Two obligations. One is not to lie. The other is to write as well as I can. You're trying, imaginatively, to set up a world that feels like truth to you. This is the way it really is. It must be that way. And you have to do it as well as you can. You're not going to whip out something worthwhile without feeling it through.

I think your obligation begins at home, always, where you're trying to tell the truth as you see or feel it. And I'll make a remark on the side: I think that if more obligations began at home there would be fewer public troubles. If home truths were applied we'd have a great deal less trouble in the world.

N: *You've done a considerable amount of teaching at the university level, creative writing and literature courses. Has this been satisfying, on the whole?*

WARREN: Let me go behind your question, if I may, without trying to undermine it. I don't see any difference between teaching classes in Shakespeare or classes in writing. It's all the same process: trying to teach people to apply their wits to the problem at hand. Fortunately, most of my teaching has been straight teaching; I can't imagine a worse fate than teaching just writing.

By and large, over the years, I've had an extraordinary range of talented, intelligent students. When you're teaching seniors or graduate students you expect this, of course. As for really memorable experiences in teaching, I don't recall a more extraordinary group of people any-where than the students I had at Louisiana, seniors and graduate students. What this proves, I don't know. Perhaps I was lucky.

N: *As far as your own body of work is concerned, which works have given you the greatest satisfaction?*

WARREN: I have to take two views, a short view and a longer one. When you're doing something, you're committed to it and the work is it. To think beyond that would be death. As far as the long range is concerned, the novels that seem to have brought the most satisfaction to me are *World Enough and Time, The Flood,* and *All the King's Men.* But when it comes to choosing fiction against poetry, it's more complicated. I have to change my metabolism. Many years ago I talked to Moravia about his first novel, and he told me that he thought of it as a poem. I know what he meant. All the novels I have written have seemed to me like big poems, with the chapters and events as metaphors rather than documents. This is the way I think of fiction, from one perspective.

N: *How do you evaluate current literary criticism and review?*

WARREN: I don't. I don't know how to survey it or analyze. It's possible to pick up the paper on a day when something's right, another day when something's wrong.

On the academic side I think that "high-brow academic criticism" as opposed to straight reviewing has passed through a very strange phase where exegesis of a certain sort has become the order of the day, and this is a necessary phase, but it's about run its course. They're moving to something else.

You see this when the works of a particular writer are dealt with. Take the works of Faulkner, now. They've about done the exegesis of most of his novels, for better or worse.

N: *To turn to the younger writer: what advice could you give him, or what would you hope for him?*

WARREN: I'm not an advice-giver. I'm not even an advice-seeker. But I would above all, make him an honest man. If he's a genius, I suppose he can be a little crooked now and then. But anyone who wants to write is going to pay a price, a damned big price. The gamble is big. Anybody with common sense and a reasonably solid character and reasonably good health can make a comfortable living these days, but the aspiring writer has to put a lot more on the line. The gamble is bigger, and I suppose the reward can be bigger, too. If he's honest and he works, advice is beside the point. He'll merely do what he must do, and that is everything.

N: *In considering American literature as a whole, which writers or books or specific events do you regard as landmarks or turning points?*

WARREN: This is a question I shy away from in my own mind, because I want to prowl around the question rather than plow right into it. The context swamps the question for me. I could pick off things for a textbook immediately, but I wouldn't feel the answer would be quite true. You can say *Huckleberry Finn*, and be true and untrue at the same time. It was *the* novel when it came out, and it was and is important, but to regard its enduring popularity is one thing, and to try to evaluate its influence is another.

When Hawthorne wrote his first few stories, nobody read them. Now we look back at them and say, "Ah, that was a great moment," but nobody read them when they came out. They were published in obscure magazines. His best stories were published that way. So at what point do they become a turning point? We now say that those stories were new and fresh, extraordinary and revolutionary, but when they were first published nobody read them.

Melville's poems, published in 1866, now look like world-shaking events, but nobody read them then.

It isn't as simple as saying, "This particular writer changed things when he wrote such-and-such."

The fact that Hawthorne existed is the important fact, but we can't talk about his particular stories because they weren't read or understood or even thought about for years. They had a slow effect. It wasn't until 1850 that *The Scarlet Letter* had any effect at all, and then it was misunderstood. Melville's *Moby Dick* is great, but 115 years ago, when it came out, it was a failure. Now it's a great influence. Conversely, for many years Longfellow was appraised as some sort of god, but nobody could be of less influence than Longfellow for the past seventy-five years.

This is the tangle I get into when I try to answer this question. Just look at the 1930's. *In Dubious Battle* and *Citizen Tom Paine* were talked about in American literature classrooms in the tone of voice reserved for Shakespeare. Now we have to think hard to recall who wrote them. And at the time, the same time, you couldn't get anyone to speak well of *Light in August* or *The Sound and the Fury*.

Note: Later in the evening Eleanor Clark, Robert Penn Warren, and I returned to the subject of the young writer who seems so inclined to seek help from older ones.

N: *Perhaps it's from isolation that the young writer tries so hard to establish contact. There must be a feeling of working in a vacuum if you live apart from fellow writers.*

WARREN: It's true that Eleanor and I were very lucky in having a lot of friends our age, and many who were somewhat older, who were very bright and literary. We didn't have to go out and knock on doors. Rapport was built-in. I don't think we felt lonely or dependent. I could talk about things, the important things, with people my own age, and Eleanor and her sister and their friend could even start their own magazine. I suppose, if you're isolated in a nonliterary community, it can be a different matter entirely.

CLARK: It's something else we're talking about, really. Who could have been more lonely than Sherwood Anderson as a young man? Or Dreiser? Actually, I don't know all the details of their early lives, but they certainly couldn't have lived in a very stimulating environment. And when you think of France, of the great writers of the nineteenth century, it seems they all studied in loneliness in some provincial town.

WARREN: They didn't stay there long, though.

CLARK: Even so, reaching out for communication is not the same as reaching for a handout. Let's make this distinction.

WARREN: I was speaking of the necessity for communication as a thing that comes first—

CLARK: But these people who write to us don't want you to talk; they're writing for a handout. They're writing for a synopsis of your own novels, or an introduction to someone here or there, or for help in getting a grant. This isn't asking for communication—

N: *Or as your friend Peter De Vries says, "While you're up, get me a Grant."*

WARREN: Boy, that's true. You have to dodge getting grants, these days. They're like atomic bombs, all over the place. Few of us have survived the grants. The world is being blighted by them. It's a war against art.

CLARK: This is another important difference between now and the time when we were making it, and starving in garrets. Nobody starves in garrets anymore; there's too much money around.

WARREN: There's no romance in art anymore. So many ways of getting an easy berth.

N: *What do you think of the mechanics of so many best sellers? The personality-oriented book that is sold to paperback and motion picture before it's even written.*

WARREN: And then turns out to be a bad book.

CLARK: The analogy of this very sort of thing is found in almost any poor section of Italy. People come to you wanting a job, and their idea of a job is this: Since you presumably move in a bigger world and have friends in Rome, your friends will know friends who know people in the ministry of something-or-other and, therefore, they will get a back-door job. This is the normal process of thought. Not to go out and do a job well. Of course, there are economic reasons for it, in these cases. And a certain involvement of historical procedures.

WARREN: Not as a saw, but as a way of life.

CLARK: It is, and it becomes a rather depressing commentary on a society. The business of today's young writer has become strangely analogous to this for very different reasons. There's no dire poverty behind their coming to the older writer to say, "Give me a hand." Something else is involved, but the psychology is the same. You go to somebody to get influence. Instead of sitting down and writing the best poem he can write, which is all that goddam well matters, all that matters. You write it or you don't. You're capable of it or you're not capable of it, and this should be all that matters. But in so many cases, it isn't what matters at all. They think first and foremost of climbing the ladder like some sort of awful worthless vine without roots.

WARREN: This is true. Most of them haven't written anything at all.

They're not the compulsive writers who have to write. They are people who don't write, but who do want a swimming pool in California.

Albert Erskine at Random House is a subtle and witty man, and he would say that most writers he knows want to have been writers or to have written. They want the contract, the swimming pool, but they don't want to work. They don't want to live the process.

CLARK: We were talking to John Hersey the other night about students taking LSD and all that. He remarked that what saddened him as much as anything was the way LSD, in so many cases he's seen, is a surrogate poem. It gives the illusion of being a poet and producing a poem without having written a bit of poetry.

WARREN: I wonder if it could ever lead to an A-plus on a term paper.

N: *As far as the young writers are concerned, wasn't there more emphasis on the literary quarterlies—the* Southern Review, Antioch Review, *etc.,—in the days when you, Mr. Warren, were an editor?*

WARREN: You've got to remember that most of the wonderful things that appeared in the quarterlies and reviews weren't things that could be published in popular magazines. There were exceptions; the *Southern Review* published several stories by Katherine Anne Porter and two of her finest novelettes, *Old Mortality* and *Pale Horse, Pale Rider*. She could have published those elsewhere, but she preferred that they be in the *Southern Review*. We published five stories by Eudora Welty, five of her best. This was her choice, too.

CLARK: But a lot of us couldn't have published our stories anywhere but in those reviews and quarterlies. Someone once sold me on the idea of having an agent. It was a disaster. This poor agent looked at my things and she didn't know what they were all about, much less could she sell them for real money. Those stories were at home only in the *Kenyon Review* and the *Partisan Review* and *Life and Letters Today* and the *Southern Review*.

WARREN: Young writers may have had more patience then, more ambition; we had a natural set of contributors, and they seemed proud to have their stuff appear in our little magazines. In Louisiana we had the cream of fiction flowing into the office. Extraordinary first stories— they don't seem to be written any more. We never had a problem filling each issue with prose and poetry we were proud of. I don't really know if the young writer's approach to writing is that much different today. In the money sense everything seems more acute. The *Southern Review* has been revived, and they are paying. But money—I saw this during the few years I was at the Yale drama school. The shadow of Broadway fell over it. The students weren't aiming at writing the play they really wanted to write, or could write; they were trying to write next year's big hit. But perhaps the situation in the off-Broadway theater will change that prestige symbol.

N: *I wonder if young writers get star-struck any more; fall under the influence of someone and worship—*

CLARK: That could be so exciting. I remember when I was about seventeen, and discovered T. S. Eliot. I'll never get over it; I would say it was the guiding influence of my whole career. Eliot was the introduction to Marx and everything else. He broke up the conventional world I had known and presented a literature from which one could assemble a whole new fluctuating world. When he died last year I read all the obituaries I could find and I was absolutely overcome.

WARREN: Ralph Ellison says his life began with *The Waste Land* when he was at Tuskegee. That it changed his world.

N: *A final question for both of you: If either of you were to chart your careers over again are there things you'd do differently?*

CLARK: I'd have married him earlier.

WARREN: Very much earlier.

CLARK: As far as undoing career mistakes are concerned, wouldn't you make others?

WARREN: I'm sure I'd make worse mistakes. I think a man had best settle for what is done the first time around.

CLARK: I feel very lucky in my life. Woman, writer, and mother. I haven't formulated all this, not even to myself, but I'm sure it's a crucial sort of trinity.

Writing is removal; it's got to be. And being a mother is the opposite; it's an involvement. It's got to be, or you're a monster. A man is better able to remove himself from such involvement than a woman; perhaps it's the nature of the male.

But hardly anyone talks about one aspect of motherhood, and I haven't put it into terms for myself. When you have children you're surrounded by an endless and extraordinary creativity all of the time. It's a fantastic experience, and goes on at a pace adults cannot even remember. No experience as a single person can possibly prepare you for the barrage of creativity. It may be the total difference between being a single woman writer and a mother woman writer. Your time is chopped into: you're chauffeuring, you're worrying about colds and measles, you love them and practice piano with them and hundreds of things. And it's all time-consuming but it's lovely. But it isn't the big question as far as one's own writing life is concerned. You learn to accommodate your own impulses to this barrage, and it's a vital and difficult thing; yet if you are living with children who are pouring out inspiration by the mile every single day, it's as though you are looking in on God creating the universe. You somehow must accommodate the nature and proportion of your own creativity to this immense fact. How it is done, I don't know. One does manage—on some days.

WARREN: I think this matter of isolation and involvement is a constant struggle between poles, so to speak, for the writer. This is why we have to get away by ourselves, just to have a relaxation from conscience. But hasn't this always been true? The Anglo-Saxon artists, poets, painters of the nineteenth century were forever flocking to Italy. Now we're flocking to a village in France just to get away from too much social consciousness, and to have our children in a French school for a year.

But we're not expatriates. We're rather the opposite of that. We just have to live and work for awhile away from here, away from tension.

"We must do our best to tell the story well, very well indeed, to involve people, emotion, place, stress, all the things that will hold an audience. All things that hold an audience are called 'entertainment.'"

Richard Condon

Richard Condon

CONDON: I was born in New York, March 18, 1915. I went to DeWitt Clinton High School for a period, then became a night clerk at a hotel in Bermuda, then a waiter on the *President Garfield*, which went around the world twice with me aboard. When I came ashore from that I got a job as a writer of package inserts, the little wrappers that go around toothpaste tubes and are printed in six-point type which no one ever reads. For a short ten-day period I had the illusion of being a writer, but I quickly discovered that one isn't a writer unless he has a reader, and the more effective the readers are at reading the more effective the writer becomes at writing. I went into advertising copywriting, working mostly on hotels and hearing aids.

Then I became Eastern publicity director for Walt Disney Productions, national publicity director for Walt Disney Productions, Eastern publicity manager for Twentieth Century-Fox and director of special events (in California) for Twentieth Century-Fox. After that I founded Richard Condon, Inc., in New York, handling a wide diversification of accounts, from woolens to the Hayes office to *Look* magazine to the Houghton Mifflin Company; twenty-seven accounts altogether, which covered the spectrum, including a book by Louella Parsons titled *The Gay Illiterate*.

In 1947 I was national publicity director for the Freedom Train, the train that carried important documents around the U.S.—the Magna Carta, Bill of Rights, all the key documents of democracy. The train was armed with a squadron of Marines to bayonet the schoolchildren through rapidly so more schoolchildren could come through.

After that I became director of publicity for Cecil B. DeMille on *Samson and Delilah*, and for Jose Ferrer's *Cyrano de Bergerac*. Jose and I went into business and co-produced *Twentieth Century*, a remake of the Hecht-MacArthur play, and we produced *Stalag 17*. Both of these were big hits, and I got the impression that although the producer's place is a happy one, the last of the gentlemen's professions (meaning he got in at eleven in the morning, got out at twelve, had a three hour lunch, and came back to check the receipts), the *real* place in the theater was that of the playwright, because the playwright didn't have to go into the office at all once he finished writing the play.

I wrote a play, *Men of Distinction*, which opened at the 48th Street Theater in April of 1953; this was while I was a vice-president of RKO, in charge of advertising and publicity. Our family joke goes like this: "If it had opened on a Monday night we would have doubled the run and made it until Saturday night." The show closed. Quickly. Within two months I was on my way to Europe in charge of publicity for United Artists in Britain and on the Continent. We lived in Paris for two and a half years, in Madrid for a year and a half. We returned to New York and I left show business — forever, I hope, and I became a novelist on the strength of the six months' severance pay I got from my contract.

I wrote *The Oldest Confession*. Fortunately, the publisher had a big hole in his spring schedule and accepted it one afternoon; he produced the book in three months instead of taking eight or nine. With the increment from the paperback sale and the film sale I was able, with wife, two children, and an aristocratic dachshund, to go on to the second book. I've been writing novels ever since and moving to a new country every two years.

The reason for moving is that when you live in a country where you cannot speak the language you gain much more thinking-time in your sort of isolation. I'm not hostile to people, but I'm antisocial, and if one cannot speak Spanish or Italian or French, one is invited out that much less. If one is riding on a bus, and the two women behind are talking in a language one cannot understand, and they are saying, "If that butcher gives me a roast like that again I'll shove it . . ." it sounds like music. I have been able to gain much more writing time, more isolation to spend in the business of novel writing, which after all is the extension of schizoid fantasy in which it is essential that the day before be as much like today as possible in order to sustain the fantasy. I write on a seven-hour day, seven-day week, and about every ten weeks we cut from Geneva, which is directly in the center of Europe, to go somewhere else. Paris is only fifty minutes away, London an hour and a half. There are lots of places to go and we break the fantasy without any diversions within the fantasy, and come back to carry on in the same pattern.

N: *Could you trace the evolvement of* An Infinity of Mirrors?

CONDON: That particular book is very easy to trace. I have had the conviction that every ten years, at least, someone should remind the world of what happened to eighty million people. It's frequently asked, "How could the Germans do what they did?" but eighty million people go beyond the Germans. If a man who had no education, no political entrée, no credentials beyond an Iron Cross as a corporal in the

German army—if this man, using propaganda only, could take over a nation of eighty million people with the primitive propaganda force he had at hand (compared to the complex and sophisticated communications system we have, for example), it is possible that those eighty million people could be an example for two hundred million people to continually examine, lest it happen to them.

With this in mind I set out to write a story that would be a virtual parable of *Beauty and the Beast*. Most of the novels I've written have been based on, let's say, oversimplified fairy tales or legends because I think the overcommunications industry is closing in on all sides. The pressures put on people, particularly readers, are so great that we no longer have time to do the things we used to do and want to do. The novel takes us back to the days of the cavemen who told a story to a group of thirty other cavemen who didn't want to go out into the lightning and walk among wild beasts. It told the story of the man who did everything for them; he ate and drank and made love for them, traveled for them, and became an archetype experience, sensation, and emotion. And I set out to write a *Beauty and the Beast* laid in that beautiful architectural congregation called Paris and imposed upon by the SS and the German army.

As I began to work on this it became a thing of dynamics, where each element changes place with the other, then goes back to its own place. I realized that I would have to research the background meticulously because there are still forty-five million witnesses to the event. I didn't know how deeply I'd have to research, or how long it would take me. I think I spent too long a time on the book. Three years is too much time for a professional writer to spend on one book. But there were no Americans in the book, so I had to research my principal characters back to their point of origin, then forward again to show what made them move the way they moved. I had to understand the history of the period, and I had to understand what had happened to the oppressor and the oppressed in Germany and France. It became a novel on many levels because the first country to become occupied by the Nazis was Germany, and from there Naziism spread out over the entire Continent. I had to know quite a little about it all, so that my point of focus would become clearer. The point of focus being from 1932 to 1938 in Berlin, and 1940 to 1944 in Paris.

N: *How did* The Manchurian Candidate *evolve?*

CONDON: This was much more of a stunt novel. I worked backward from the ending, which was, "What would have happened if a sniper with a Soviet rifle had shot the nominee for the Presidency of the United States at the convention of 1960?" From then on it became a work of literary logistics, of working all of the departments of the novel technically backward, to the very beginning of, "Where would such a man have begun if he could have done such a thing?" Then, "How could he have been persuaded to do it?" And finally, "If he could have been persuaded to do it, who could have persuaded him?" So it was a matter of understanding American mores, politics, reaction.

In *An Infinity of Mirrors* I had an associate professor of contemporary history in Frankfort work with the German archives, and a newspaperwoman in Paris work on the French and Spanish archives. A German-speaking woman at the National Archives in Washington worked translating captured German documents, and there was a woman in London at the library which contains the foremost anti-Nazi repository and library in the world. Thus I started with a short, forty-page raw plot and began to ask them questions expanding the plot, so that when the answers came back I could advance the novel slowly in twenty- and forty-page sections. This took a great deal of time because I knew nothing at all about Germany or the German army. I knew France only geographically, perhaps its people to a certain extent, but to no profound extent.

But I am an American, and I understood *The Manchurian Candidate* down to its bones; it wrote itself with a great deal of feeling that came effectively from within me, rather unlike the feeling I had throughout the three years spent on *An Infinity of Mirrors*.

N: *You mentioned your moving about. Where have you lived?*

CONDON: We lived in Paris, and I got *The Oldest Confession* out of that, then New York, of course, where I got *The Manchurian Candidate* and *Some Angry Angel*. (I use "we" but not the editorial "we"; somehow my family is involved in the production of these novels.) Then we went to Mexico, and I wrote *A Talent for Loving*, based in Texas and in Mexico from 1941 to 1944, then to Paris to lay down the research lines for *Mirrors* and to Geneva for three years to execute the research and write the book. We were going to move on to Portugal, but for various reasons no one could have anticipated it became necessary not to go to Portugal, so we've decided to stay in Geneva for the next few years because we like the city very much. I'll be fifty, next month, and I think the urge to move from country to country has dulled a bit.

N: *You look forty.*

CONDON: That's the result of a book, *The Pleasure of Fasting*, the only nonfiction book I think I'll ever write. One May I went to a fast farm in England to lose weight. I was forty pounds overweight, and I had reached the point that when I turned over in bed my stomach followed about two minutes later. They had a system of fasting for three days on hot water, then moving to fruit juices and salads and yoghurt. On the first day there I found a book about fasting, and it fascinated me. Anyway, for fourteen days I had hot water three times a day, which is a great deal easier than anyone might imagine. But on the other hand I must advise everyone not to do it unless it's done under qualified medical supervision because it can be very dangerous. I lost twenty-eight pounds, and that was enough for me. But more important was the fact that my blood pressure dropped from two hundred over one-thirty to one-thirty over ninety-five, which is like picking up a gift of six years.

Thus impressed, I began to read more and more about fasting and wrote to New York about it. The book was set and magazine serialization negotiated for and I hired a researcher in New Delhi, another in the Vatican Library, and another in Rome. Another, in England, has an assistant who abstracts German books on fasting; the Germans have more books on fasting than the Canadians have on hockey. We even have a researcher in New York who has an assistant who does a bibliography out of the Library of Congress. I've made a tour of about eleven fasting sanitoria in Europe, and I've completed a tour of seven medical authorities in the U.S. Now, also, because I spent so many years in the film business, I plan to do a book about an American production company in Hamburg, and another set in England in 1921 when the British upper class found out it was done for. A poignant year in history.

I've no end of things I want to do.

N: *In looking about you at the present, as far as the state of culture (literature, in particular) is concerned, what do you find to admire or deplore?*

CONDON: I'd rather talk first about what I most deplore, because it eliminates the other; the others are affected by it. Our system of overcommunication includes all outlets and has replaced our educational system. We are, in effect, educated formally to the eighth grade even though we go on to take our master's; beginning in the sixth grade we're overtaken by the most massive, complex system that has ever been known in history. This may be part of a pattern set down by a Regis Professor of Sociology at Aberdeen University, a thing called "Animal Dispersion and Social Behavior," in which he demonstrated how, in the insect world and in the animal world, when the food supply is threatened, the insect or animal community, depending upon the species, begins to destroy itself, to reduce its number to a more manageable total in terms of food supply. It's possible and probable that the human race considers itself far beyond the instinctual motivation of insects and animals, but it's also possible that this total education toward violence, the total collapse, as it were, of political, social, and religious systems, is preparing us for a destruction within ourselves; in effect, that we don't have to rely on war any more; that it's possible through water pollution and juvenile delinquency and resistance to civil rights and so on, to control our numbers.

Now, since we are the only thinking organism, we have the choice of going along on this instinctual road to destruction or of absolutely extirpating everything from our system of education and wholly revolutionizing it, so that we can prepare ourselves against this total self-destruction.

In promulgating this, the novel and the theater, comic books and television, radio and newspapers, every form of communication, has been brought into play. Which novels oppose this? You could say that we're sorely lacking in novels of compassion. I know that many people may be able to think of novelists who deal with compassion, with the understanding of others from sympathetic and empathetic points of view, but at the moment I can only think of Carson McCullers and John Steinbeck. (I certainly can't include myself.) There is too much of a tendency on the part of novelists to think that they are mirroring their own times, therefore alibiing their method of dealing with violence.

In terms of the people I admire, I suppose the novel I most admire from the "I wish I had written that" point of view is Nigel Dennis's *Scars of Identity*. I admire Joyce Cary, also a compassionate writer, and the early novels of Evelyn Waugh and Miss Mitford. I admire Robert Graves, and the lucidity of Thornton Wilder, but most of all I would look to the novelists like Carson McCullers and John Steinbeck to save us from ourselves.

N: *In the same area, what advice would you give the young writer?*

CONDON: I would warn him against attending classes on creative writing which purport to teach creative writing. These instructions may have cost us three great novels and certainly dozens of good novels because they have told the young man and woman that he or she must only write from his own experience. In the first place, a student from eighteen to twenty-four hasn't had much experience. The consequence of such instruction is that when they finally finish one book it's almost invariably the same book: it's the book of boyhood or girlhood, or one of those inevitable novels of campus life. The second consequence is that they believe, when they finish the first novel, that they have nothing else to write about, and they go on into other pursuits in life.

It's impossible to believe that we have achieved a literary community wherein, in order to express contempt for a writer, they are able to say that he doesn't approach his work to produce art. These young people are told, after they stack up the white or yellow copypaper to sit before the machine to produce art, that the man who created it has nothing to do with its place in art.

I think that a great deal can be served if we realize that the function of the novelist is to entertain and enlighten. If the storyteller sits down to tell stories about what happened to him when he was sixteen years old and under the influence of his lovable Aunt Emma, or his hatable Aunt Emma, or if he thinks he can, in the interchangeability of human experience and human emotion, relate to a Chinese peasant and a Norwegian sea captain without any loss of the depth of emotion, he's off base. The depth of emotion and the transcendence of emotion are given to six men in a century; the rest of us are not able to make that long reach toward total enlightenment and total transcendence of human experience. We must do our best to tell the story well, very well indeed, to involve people, emotion, place, stress, all the things that will hold an audience. All things that hold an audience are called "entertainment."

Learn to entertain first and hope that you have this God-given blessing called art, or the ability to enlighten, because if you do entertain and hope to enlighten, you will have met the function of the novelist which is to function as a teacher in the best sense of the word.

As far as telling him what to do with his career, I think the publishing houses have far more need for material than writers will ever be able to supply. They should bear in mind that all publishing houses today are so competitive that they have people on their staffs who do nothing but scout, yet they're getting less and less material from the formal factories that pretend to teach creative writing because novels are becoming more and more identical.

In the words of Philip Wylie in one of the most fascinating anecdotes regarding writers I've ever heard, there is a story about the man who decided to kill himself. Before he did, he got a pad of paper and a pencil and felt that just before he died the key to life, the key to understanding, would be given to him. He opened the oven door and turned on the gas and put his head in the oven. Fortunately, a neighbor smelled the gas and called the police department and they put a pulmotor on him. He awoke in the hospital and the first thing he said was, "Where is the pad?" They brought it to him and on it there were four scribbled words: "Think in other categories." So you mustn't think in the way your teacher tells you to think. You mustn't think the way your peer group, as they say in England, thinks. You must certainly not think ever, ever, the way the critics think they think. You must think for yourself, and out of that come all the novels that are worthwhile.

N: *How well do you think literary review and criticism function in the United States?*

CONDON: I don't think criticism functions. I think it's self-pity and a form of indulgence and compensation for not being willing to work for a living. I think these men have a high regard for literature and a low regard for writers because they can't imagine themselves as writers, men who have to work long, hard days and do the same work over and over and over again, when they can fool everyone and pretend to be the peer of these writers by doing two or three hours of work a morning.

I think it's a useless form, not as useless as the birds on the backs of crocodiles perhaps, but I have no room for them whatever. And I adjure all young writers, middle-aged writers, and old writers not to believe or accept any criticism, because if you accept the good remarks you have to take the bad ones to heart, too. Neither will advance you because the period of gestation, the time it takes to publish a novel you've finished, is about nine months. By that time the writer should be off on two or three other things. A novel is reviewed ten months after it's turned in. You certainly can't do anything to change that particular work. It's impossible to think that a man whose reflexes have been so vastly conditioned in opposition to your own could have the presumption to criticize this work to (at the most) fifteen hundred people in the United States, and feel that he is influencing a work already printed. If the work criticized can't be changed, and the man who wrote it is ten months away from it and immersed in two other projects, and the critic doesn't know what those two other projects are (and they won't relate to the one at hand), how can the critic justify his existence?

The critic does not reach the reader. He reaches a small coterie of social outcasts who, like him, like to talk about literature as though they hold a proprietary interest in it. The critic in the United States exists only in tiny teaspoonfuls of readers, and the most of these tiny teaspoonfuls have nothing to do with the promotion of the book. They get them from publishers' lists and they loan them to each other. The writer must cultivate his arrogance and have no regard for these parasites.

The reviewer is slightly different. Let's assume that a reviewer performs as a journalistic duty. If a book is published on a certain day, it is his duty as a journalist to report the news of that day. Now, there are so many books published he cannot report on them all, so he selects the book he believes to be the news of that given day. That has nothing to do with criticism.

Reviewing is essential. You can't get along without it. You have to have a conduit, an electrical current to pass the word of the book out to the greatest number of people, on the theory that there are no writers unless there are readers. There can't be readers unless they know about the book, and the reviewer lets them know about the book.

The opinion of the reviewer is not valid because it's an irritant or a counterirritant. Let's say a book comes out such as *Exodus,* and the reviewer who reviews it is a member of an Israel resistance organization, and he gives it a wildly enthusiastic notice. Now, this review is read by a violent anti-Semite in Arizona who becomes so indignant and resentful about the book that he may even go out and buy it. The reviewer tends to let a large number of people learn about the existence of the book that they, in turn, can tell each other about the review with the implication they have read the book. Eventually they become surrogate reviewers by repeating the reviews. Thus the reviewer does lead the book to readers.

N: *A change of subject: What do you think the value of sex in current literature, current creative writing, should be?*

CONDON: In writing about sex in my own novels I've allowed it the percentile equivalent of 20 percent. I reached that 20 percent by complimenting my readers into believing that they live sex, actively or in contemplative thought, about 20 percent of the time. I think that is an enormous percentage, considering the elements constantly involved in earning a living, clothing oneself, driving, commuting. I also think it's too high because if we were all having a more active sex life, physically and mentally, we would be close enough to a surfeit to not need as much vicarious sex life. So when *Candy* came along and when *Peyton Place* came out, I became convinced that the norm of acting out sex and thinking out sex must be somewhere between 6 and 10 percent since the sex in those books was closer to 80 percent.

Let's do this. Suppose everyone within the reach of your newspaper and the sound of your voice and the readership of your book would send in an anonymous letter saying, "Thinking it over, taking measurement, I think about sex and engage in sex —— percent of the time." A norm would be established.

If you can prove to the novelist that your active participation and thought about sex is very low, they'll give you more vicarious sex in novels. If you can establish that what you're getting is the real McCoy and you don't have to read about it, they'll give you less sex in novels. The less sex, the more story.

N: *What image of Richard Condon as a writer would you like to leave the future reader?*

CONDON: Any future reader is a very nebulous thing. Any future critic is only going to use a writer from the past as a club to beat writers of his present. So both the future reader and the future critic can't cancel each other out. However, if I could project the purity of my ego into the future as a tightrope walker might project that thin wire to the other side of the arena, as I walked across it I'd like to walk toward a confirmation of my ability to move people, as we say today, to grab them and hold them and make them believe a fantasy we were living in. That's what a storyteller is.

"I think it's pretty obvious that the United States at the present time is in the same relationship to Western Europe as Rome was to Greece in the century before and the century after Christ."

Will Durant

Will and Ariel Durant

W. DURANT: I was born in 1885 in a little town in Massachusetts named North Adams. I've often resented the fact that the Lord didn't allow me to be born in nearby Williamstown — then I could have gotten a good education just by sticking around. There was a fine college there, you know. In fact, one of our grandsons has just entered Williams College.

My parents were French Canadians, and I was brought up as a good Catholic. They prepared me for the priesthood, on the theory that if any member of the family became a priest or a nun the entire family would go to heaven, no matter what they did on this earth. I was supposed to manage all that, so they were very kind to me and gave me all the education that was available — first with the French school in North Adams, which was taught by nuns who spoke only French in the morning and only English in the afternoon. In 1892 we moved to New Jersey, where I again went to a parochial school and met one of the finest men I've ever known, Father James Mooney. He was an Irishman from Jersey City, but he had been sent to Italy for his postgraduate education and came back almost entirely Italianate, with splendid manners, an impressive, immaculate cleanliness, and a good heart. He took me under his wing, saying that he had found another Thomas Aquinas. He entered me at St. Peter's College in Jersey City in 1900; I was graduated in 1907.

Father Mooney had, of course, assumed that I would enter the seminary after graduating from college. But fortunately or unfortunately I encountered the public library in Jersey City, where I discovered Charles Darwin and Herbert Spencer and Ernst Haeckel and other terrible fellows, and the lovely faith in which I had been reared began to tremble a bit. Also, I had discovered William Randolph Hearst. This is a rather queer combination, Darwin and Hearst, but Hearst was running for mayor at the time and he made speeches which aroused my interest. I used to go to New York in the evening and root for him until I lost my voice.

A touching thing happened one night when I came back from these very late visits to New York. I found my mother sitting in her chair. It was midnight, and I asked her what she was doing up so late. She said, "Willy, I'm so worried that when you go to New York you go to visit bad women." I'd never dreamt that she had this in her mind, but it's an example of how thoughtless we can be to those we love deeply. Night after night she had those worries, and I hadn't the sense to console her, to tell her I was the very best virgin she would ever know.

Ultimately I got over the Hearst affair, but I went off in another radical direction: I became a Socialist. I stood on the streets of Newark, New Jersey, lecturing to all who would come near on the virtues of socialism as the hope of the world. This went on until I noticed that the working people, whom I was describing as the future rulers of America, didn't take any stock in what I said. They smiled and passed on as if to say, "If we were able to rule this country we wouldn't be shining shoes." Only a few white-collar people stayed to listen. So I gradually got over my socialistic evangelism, and was faced with a truly bewildering problem: Should I chart the course I wanted, or should I follow through with all that was planned and hoped for me? Should I break my mother's heart by not going into the seminary? I entered the seminary in 1909, determined to become a good priest whether I believed or not. After two years I began to realize that I was condemning myself to a life of hypocrisy, so I quit and brought a tremendous grief to all of us, but it had to be done. Despite all the heartbreak and recrimination, my mother, Father Mooney, and I recovered.

Then I met Alden Freeman, the son of a former treasurer of Standard Oil. He had money, a great deal of it, and he said, "You need a real education, so you must come with me to Europe." Thus, in 1912, I toured Europe, all the way from what we now call Volgograd to Edinburgh and Dublin and Killarney. When I came back to the United States I had to earn a living, and became a teacher at the Ferrer Modern School in New York—I think it was East 103rd Street. There my loveliest and most brilliant pupil was the lady who is now my wife, so I'll let Mrs. Durant take up the story at this point.

A. DURANT: I probably won't go very far before Will contradicts me, because we cannot remember the exact particulars of the incident that brought us together. It was fated that this man, coming from the environment he just described, should meet up with a person so different in every aspect from himself.

I am a product of New York City as it was at the beginning of the century. I reflected, in my youth, its chaos, its many-tongued immigrant infiltration. It was the time of child labor, a time when exploitation of every sort was accepted in the industrial field, a time when nothing was questioned — except by the voice of the exploited community, which gradually grew louder.

I was also a product of a disunity at home. The first thing I remember, apart from quarrels and a rather constant unhappiness, was my mother telling me, in a whisper, that a great tragedy had taken place, that Tolstoy had died. I wrote, "Today the great Tolstoy died, but I don't know anything about him, or who he was." I tell you this because I want you to know how completely blank my mind truly was in any direction of learning before I met my teacher.

My parents were immigrants from Russia, and I naturally attended schools in the Harlem area. I could not adjust myself to the public school system. One day when I was playing hooky in Central Park, I noticed a woman teacher with a number of children of different sizes and ages. All the children seemed to be confident of her goodwill and friendship. They touched her, they reached into her pockets to take things out. To me this was an extraordinary experience, and I made up my mind that I would follow them to see where they went, and join them if I was allowed. I wanted to be a part of this little group.

I did follow them, and it turned out that they were from an experimental school in progressive education. It had been founded in honor of a Spaniard, Francisco Ferrer, who had been shot to death by the Spanish government for voicing the need to separate church from education in Spain. I went into the school, and when I sat down at someone else's seat in the classroom the teacher came over to me and asked me who I was. I remember telling her that I did not belong to the school, I had never seen it or heard of it, but since I hated where I was going to school I would like to join them. She said it was very interesting, because they themselves were not acknowledged by the public school system, and here I was, a living example, a child who knew the other but preferred this. So I was admitted.

Several weeks later I came to class to find that my teacher wasn't there. A substitute teacher stood at the front of the room, and my surprise amounted to shock. I whispered to a friend, "Who is this man? Where is our beloved teacher? I don't know what this man is saying, because he talks through his nose." My schoolmate burst out laughing, and the teacher said, "You there, what did you say that was so funny? Say it out loud, so that we all may laugh." And I, fresh and unheeding, stood up and said, "Who are you? Where is our teacher? You talk funny; you talk through your nose." I didn't know that he was French and that many Frenchmen talk this way. I had never met one before.

The class burst into laughter, and he said, "You stay after class. I want to talk to you." I knew I was in for it.

After class he looked me square in the eye and said, "The life of a substitute teacher is very hard. You have ridiculed me, you made the class laugh at me, and it will be almost impossible for me to achieve order and continue with the lessons, particularly since, as you know, this school does not believe in any sort of physical punishment."

As he said this and looked at me I began to feel very sorry for him. So I said, "Don't worry; if anybody interrupts you or makes your job hard, I'll murder him." I made up my mind that I would be on Will's side. Fifty-three years later I'm still on his side.

The substitute teacher stayed. After a little while he began to take an emotional interest in me. Being a conscientious teacher—first and always he *is* a teacher—he felt that it was not morally correct of him to remain where he would even unconsciously direct his teachings to the pupil who was of most interest to him. Therefore he resigned.

We met clandestinely at first, then openly, with my mother's consent but not my father's. Within a year we explained to my mother that Will could take my education better in hand, and protect me, if she would give her consent to our marriage. She did, and we were married in the alderman's chamber in the New York City Hall. I was fifteen; he was two months from being twenty-eight. He taught me his way of study even though he did not then know what his direction in life would be, what his needs as a student and scholar would be, yet almost unconsciously he trained me in the direction of his needs.

I must say that the training I received from my teacher led in the direction of the vast research we would later harness into *The Story of Civilization*. Though this wasn't Will's conscious intent, it turned out that every step of my education was a brick in the edifice that turned out to be this fifty-year occupation. As I said, he was unconscious of the way he was bringing me up, yet we were both moving, imperceptibly, into the very fields of study that would take over our lives.

N: *How did you actually begin your roles as historians?*

W. DURANT: That is another strange story. I think it was in 1921 that I read an account of Buckle's death. Now, Henry Thomas Buckle had written an introduction to the history of civilization. He had planned to write the complete history, but he died of dysentery in Damascus at the age of forty. I have the four-volume Brisbane edition of his work, and it was the first historical work I read that aroused my enthusiasm. For some reason the crazy idea came to me to do what Buckle had tried to do. We couldn't approach it then, because I had to give courses of lectures at a school named Labor Temple in New York in order to butter our bread. So I went from 1914 to 1927 lecturing twice a week, forty weeks a year.

Then another fortunate accident happened. E. Haldeman-Julius, who was publishing the Little Blue Books in Girard, Kansas, happened to enter Labor Temple one afternoon and heard my lecture on Plato. He liked it, and a few days later he wrote me from Girard, asking me to write out my lecture as a booklet. I replied, telling him foolishly that I had no time to write these things out. But he wrote again, this time enclosing a check for $150, saying, "I'm paying you in advance to assure you that your time will not be wasted. Whether it's good or not, you'll be paid."

So I wrote the booklet on Plato. He liked it and he asked for another. I wrote on Aristotle; he asked for another. This kept on until— quite by accident, certainly not by design—I had written the eleven booklets which became *The Story of Philosophy*. He brought it to Max Schuster—I think this was in 1925—and since Max was a lover of philosophy as well as a great publisher, he decided to risk publishing the eleven booklets as one volume. He was reconciled to losing some money. I warned him he'd only sell about eleven hundred copies at best. He said, "I think I'll sell fifteen hundred copies." I thought he was a wild enthusiast.

The Story of Philosophy has by this time, sold some three million copies.

Well, I now had enough money to do what I wanted to do. Since many of my Labor Temple lectures were on the history of civilization I can safely say that we have been working on this enterprise from 1921 on, actually gathering far more material than I could use in the lectures. Thus in 1927 we began to give nearly all of our time to *The Story of Civilization*, and as the result of eight years of work the first volume, *Our Oriental Heritage*, came out in 1935. It was the most difficult of all the volumes for us to write; though we made two trips through Asia, the material was new to us.

These, then, are the chance incidents that led us to our life's work.

N: *What are your working methods? From research to the actual writing?*

W. DURANT: We have the advantage of knowing what our job has to be, day after day. After completing any given volume we have to decide precisely what the next volume is going to cover, and we divide the job into chapters. Then we consider what we must read to create each chapter.

Usually we read about five hundred volumes for each of our books. I don't mean to say that we read these books aloud to each other, but we do read them at approximately the same time, discuss them, and make notes. The hundreds of cards in this file are some of the notes relating to Volume X.

A. DURANT: And that is only a part. We have a thousand notes in typewritten form in galley sheets. Every note we take from our readings includes the name of the book, the author, and the page from which it was taken. The scissored slips are placed exactly where they belong in the detailed outline of our chapter.

W. DURANT: Oddly enough, we have just received a request to explain our method, a request from Dr. Arne Peters in Munich who says that his friend Dr. Heisenberg, the great physicist, is an addict of ours and wanted to know our system. But I don't think anyone else will go through this labor again within the next fifty years.

A. DURANT: If they wanted to do anything like this, they might well have to be subsidized by a government and have anywhere from a hundred to a thousand researchers to help them. There has always been just the two of us; naturally, it has been a complete devotion. Everything else has been secondary, because this must absorb your life.

W. DURANT: It must be a mania. Yet I think that every fifty years a job like this should be done. Research progresses all the time. Already some parts of our first volume, *Our Oriental Heritage*, are antiquated because of the new research. Doubtless, fifty years from now, *The Age of Voltaire* will have to be done again. It isn't that the total outline of history changes, but discoveries are very apt to change perspectives and assumptions regarding social and internal life. Yet I doubt very much, when it *is* done again, that it will be done by one couple. It will be done by a consortium of scholars as in the *Cambridge Modern History*.

A. DURANT: There you have specialists in each field contributing only highly specialized subject matter. That is very different from what we have to do. We cannot become specialists, but we have to be keenly aware of the important findings in every field. It is a very delicate task. Thus far we have been very lucky; we've sailed the stormy seas, and are almost in port. One volume to go, and we will have escaped the clutches of the specialist who might accuse us of oversimplifying or talking down to people. These things we have never wanted to do.

N: *What do you feel the obligation of the historian to be?*

W. DURANT: His first obligation is to have a concept of history. He might have a concept that we would reject. For example, many of the old histories were records of wars and politics and are rather dreary things to read now, unless they were made brilliant by style such as distinguished Gibbon and Macaulay.

Our concept has been what we call "integral history." We believe that the historian should present the whole life of a people at a given period, in all its phases, so that the reader can see how men lived and felt and thought in that age. We feel that in addition to a history of religion, a history of politics, histories of the fifteen decisive battles of the world, histories of philosophies and science and art, there should be a history that attempts to put all these aspects of life together.

Naturally, such a historian must confine himself to a given period of time because it would be impossible to put all this into one volume for all centuries. It would be impossible for the writer of such a history to become a specialist; we must depend upon the specialist. Our task is to put their results together into some sort of unity and perspective, and this is what we have tried to do. So the first thing we must ask of a historian is that he should define his purpose.

A. DURANT: And we hope that his purpose would include total perspective, that the major contributions in each field would be recorded in their interrelation and in proportion to their real influence and significance.

W. DURANT: Working as we do, we make mistakes. Not being specialists we are undoubtedly guilty of errors now and then, the specialist may discover. We do believe that the gap between the specialist and the public has grown so wide that there is a definite need for persons such as ourselves to bridge that gap, to bring the work of the specialist into some sort of unity and correlation, thus making history intelligible to anyone who has even the beginnings of a college education. As to the errors we've made, we hope to correct them in later editions, and they have taught us to watch our step, and that is all to the good.

N: *How conscious are you of literary style, considering that research and the marshaling of facts must be such an exhaustive task?*

A. DURANT: We were conscious of style all the time we worked on that first book, *The Story of Philosophy*. So conscious, in fact, that we read many books aloud together, watching the turn of every phrase and the structure of every sentence. We especially studied the French, who are *the* great stylists. To a certain extent, because Will is a Frenchman, style came to him naturally, and he passed this consciousness on to me. Primarily I should say that the French school of literature, which always aimed at clarity, has been our greatest influence.

W. DURANT: I must add that I owe something to my old friends, the Jesuits. For seven years they were my teachers. They gave me a rather poor education in biology and in history, perhaps because those subjects are rather disagreeable to orthodox Christians. But they were very good on literature. I remember how we went through Addison and Steele and Pope—a great deal of emphasis was put on the early eighteenth century.

We two are utterly out of step with the style of the twentieth century, but somehow we don't mind. I remember how Father Dimnet wrote to us about one of the earlier volumes saying, "Very good, but what old-fashioned style!" Perhaps he thought that he was insulting us, but actually he paid us a compliment.

A. DURANT: As a matter of fact I don't believe that the style in these books is close to the Augustan age of Addison and Steele and Johnson. I believe it is much closer to eighteenth-century French writers like Voltaire and Montesquieu. Maurice Maeterlinck said of Caesar and Christ: "At times one would believe he is listening to Montesquieu." Will forgets that though he started off being steeped in the great English stylists, he also and almost always observed the French. During the last few years we've gone very deeply into the French. I believe that to a great extent his style is a marriage between the masculine Augustan era — Addison, Steele, and even Johnson — and the delicacy and humor and clarity of the French stylists of the eighteenth century. I believe they are quite well wed throughout *The Story of Civilization.*

W. DURANT: We have, perhaps, become infatuated with the eighteenth century. We've given two volumes to it; even so far as music is concerned we have become addicts of Handel and Bach and Mozart. We have more or less passed over Beethoven to the eighteenth, and we wonder why the orchestral programs of today don't give us more of the eighteenth century. There are so many lovely arias in Handel. Naturally, his operas couldn't be sung today because so many of the major roles were intended for castrati, and such "processing" isn't legal. Last year I went so far as to suggest to the program committee of the Hollywood Bowl that they might make a summer's program in which every evening would contain a composition by an eighteenth-century composer and one by a twentieth-century composer. It might disturb the stomach, but it would be a richly educational experience. They turned me down.

N: I love concert music like The Royal Fireworks.

A. DURANT: That's an example of the remarkable influence of Italy. The Germans would have been unbearable in music without the Italians. They need that light, romantic touch to counter the heavy German tread. We are so fortunate that a Latin, a French influence, has come into the English language. English is basically Germanic, but how much more beautiful English style is than the German. The French style, by itself, might be considered too lacy or feminine, abrupt English too heavy or masculine, but the two together become both graceful and strong.

Style is a very important subject; one can write volumes about it, as the French have. "The style is the man. . . ." When Buffon said that, he started a whole new line of thought. Naturally, whatever you do is what you are.

N: *You are now working on the tenth and final volume of* The Story of Civilization. *Looking back over all these years of research and writing, can you find individual men and women, or the color of a particular period that stands out either in terms of influence upon history or in a measure of strong appeal to you as persons and historians?*

W. DURANT: There are two ways of interpreting that question. One would be to name the person in history that has influenced you most, and I would say, first Christ, and after that, Spinoza. But if you ask the question, "What person in history has cast the greatest degree of influence?" it's a much more difficult question. And you can't answer that question from the standpoint of any one civilization. Doubtless, Christ has been the most influential person in our civilization, but to the Asians Buddha would be vastly more important, and to the educated Chinese, Confucius. As a matter of fact, I don't believe that any one individual has been significantly influential among all peoples. Even today we're living in boxes called "nations," and influence seldom rises over the walls of the boxes.

A. DURANT: In this respect our memories are short-lived. In each volume, as we work on a particular era, we will find some outstanding character who enmeshes us emotionally. So for a time—like a mother with many, many children—the last child is the dearest and the most precious. Recently, Voltaire dominated our minds, just as he dominated Europe and his age. But now that we're finished with Voltaire we're being pulled along by Rousseau and his powerful influence, whether we like it or not. The power is there and it's centrifugal and you've got to be in it. Really, it becomes a question of time and place and the necessities of interest.

W. DURANT: Our heroes, our fascinations, do change with each book. It's a little like being unfaithful, perhaps fickle; yet each age does have heroes, and one who stands out above all.

N: *In your latest book you seemed exceptionally struck by Voltaire. In fact, there was an enthusiasm and vitality that ran constant, and made me wonder if you perhaps enjoyed writing this book more than others.*

A. DURANT: You're right.

W. DURANT: Yes, we enjoyed writing about Voltaire, if for one very good reason only: it is exceedingly difficult to be dull when you write about Voltaire. But we also enjoyed writing about Elizabethan England.

A. DURANT: Voltaire was a highly complex character, but the most complex thing about him was his better half—Frederick the Great. The steady relationship between Voltaire and Frederick is unique in history. I think the honors in friendship go to Frederick, who was at all times a little more conscientious, more honest, and more appreciative of Voltaire's genius than can be said of Voltaire's attitudes toward Frederick. I think this relationship, with its contrasts, makes the period more interesting, because every time Frederick comes into the picture there is a high tone of sincerity.

W. DURANT: In the letters between Voltaire and Frederick you'll find that Frederick, though he was about twenty years younger than Voltaire, speaks with more wisdom. For example, he did not share the enthusiasm of the Enlightenment for placing philosophers over states. He warned Voltaire time and time again that he and Diderot and the others were exaggerating the capacity of human beings to reason, and that a civilization led by philosophers would soon go to pieces. Then again, in the years that Voltaire spent with Frederick in Germany, we find that the conduct of Voltaire was not quite as honorable as Frederick's. Voltaire was perhaps the most brilliant writer that ever lived We wish his morals had been as fine as his intellect. However, a combination of fine intellect and questionable morals is always interesting.

A. DURANT: It's a good thing he had a friendly critic in Frederick, because Frederick loved him despite his faults, worshiped his intellect and his genius to a degree that let him forgive other elements in Voltaire. Frederick even predicted that the period would be called "The Age of Voltaire."

N: *To turn finally to the present. Do you find any period or situation in history that parallels our present time? Are there lessons we could learn from study and observation that would help us?*

W. DURANT: I think it's pretty obvious that the United States at the present time is in the same relationship to Western Europe as Rome was to Greece in the century before and the century after Christ. Rome at that time was taking over Greek culture, and toward the end of that period her philosophers, like Marcus Aurelius, were using Greek as the language of literature. Rome, you see, after conquering Greece about 146 B.C., became the protector of Greece and the beneficiary of the Greek heritage.

We are now in the stage of becoming the protector of the European heritage and the protector of Western Europe—even though de Gaulle doesn't realize this. Consequently I think that if we would learn any lessons from history we might study the relationship of Rome to Greece in that age.

At the same time we might ask, "What happened to Rome after

absorbing that heritage?" First she transmitted her culture to France, to Spain, to Portugal, to Italy, to parts of Germany, Austria, Romania, and Yugoslavia. She transmitted even her language to France, Spain, Portugal, and Romania. The language of France was taken from the Roman soldiers who spoke a very debased Latin, and it's amazing how that debased Latin became the beauty of the French language — and the beauty of all the other so-called "Romance" languages, for that matter. They are the most beautiful languages in the world, but they came as corruptions of Latin as spoken by Roman soldiers and immigrants. *Corruptio pessimi optima.*

One of our tasks is to see that we transmit our heritage, and we are doing it better, I believe, than any other nation has ever done before.

The next question would be, "Will we be destroyed as Rome was?" Well, no culture is immortal any more than any individual, except in its transmission of culture. This is the only immortality we can hope for, and it is but a fraction of a moment in geological time. I suppose a time will come when our civilization will end. But all that is in the natural course of things, and we shouldn't worry about it. Death is life's way of renewing itself.

A. DURANT: In one of the volumes, facing that very question, Will said, "Civilization does not die, it migrates. It changes its habitat and its dress, but it lives on."

W. DURANT: May I add that conquest by barbarism can come from within as well as without. Indeed, it was barbarism within the Roman Empire that conquered Rome, rather than the barbarians from beyond her borders. In our own culture we have the terrible problems that come from the fact that we breed faster than we educate, and that we breed from the bottom and die off at the top. Therefore, our energetic President is on the right tack when he urges Congress to vote funds for education.

A. DURANT: Improved education in the use of contraception must be spread also, or every other gain is nullified.

W. DURANT: I believe that some President will one day be brave enough to say that we must make parentage more careful and less reckless. If I had my way I'd make parentage a privilege instead of an accident, but naturally I'm not going to have my way.

A. DURANT: These things lie in the seed of time.

Jesse Hill Ford

Mountains of Gilead established Jesse Hill Ford as one of our finest young writers. However popular and highly praised, it seems due to be eclipsed by his powerful presentation of Southern racial conflict, *The Liberation of Lord Byron Jones*.

What is Ford's background?

"As you can plainly tell from these honeyed tones I'm a Southerner. Born in Alabama, reared in Tennessee, educated at Vanderbilt and the University of Florida.

"It took me a long time to become a bona fide writer. I did some reporting while I was in college, then did some medical reporting in Tennessee before I came to Chicago to write for the American Medical Association.

"It was in Chicago that I really got the bug. I saw writers making a good living at free-lance work so I quit the AMA and went to my wife's hometown, Humboldt, Tennessee, to give it a try. She taught, and her father, who was a doctor, gave me one of the hospital-type rooms just off his office to work in.

"I was not an overnight success. In the first six months I made five dollars. But I'd accumulated all kinds of nice, personal rejection slips from *Atlantic Monthly* and a lot of encouragement from Little, Brown.

"I kept at it, and kept improving, I think, and eventually there were short stories I sold and a novel they published and all of a sudden there was a day when my ever-patient father-in-law and my ever-loving wife heard me say, 'Hot damn, I'm a writer. I can make a living at it.'"

How did *Lord Byron Jones* come about?

"I think there were two rather strong motivations. The first was this whole racial issue as I saw it and felt it in the South. I felt that I could write a valid story, and a powerful one, that could shed a great deal of light on the reality of the situation—not the theories that may or may not hold true.

"In addition, I found myself getting angrier and angrier about much of the fiction that touched on the racial issues. We were fairly inundated with either tracts barely disguised as novels, so unpleasant and one-sided they were unbelievable, and slightly romantic novels in which a nice little kid or two brought a whole town to its senses.

"These were even more unbelievable, and a distortion of truth, because they skipped over the great obstacle to integration in the South. They ignored the fact that for over a century the average Southerner has been taught to believe that the Negro is an inferior person who must be kept in his place—a step below the poorest white.

"Not all Southerners believe this, of course, but a majority either believes it implicitly or finds it convenient to pretend to believe it. And the prejudice is so strong that the resident of a small town who believes in integration is virtually forced to keep his mouth shut or move out. It's a very real and unpleasant situation, and change is going to come slowly, with a lot of give and take, and it will be resisted all the way.

"But eventually a brighter day will have to come. I think it will come in the North, too."

I commented on the fact that *Jones* was a mighty rough, powerful novel, more uncompromising than any other racial novel I'd read. Ford said:

"I think that if you are going to write about an issue or a situation you have to face it squarely if your work is going to be of any honest value. It's a rough, powerful situation, and none of the compromise is going to come easy. But then, change won't come at all if we shy away from the truth.

"And *Lord Byron Jones* may be all fiction—but it's also all truth."

"We are just playing into the hands of the censors when we accept the invitation to argue with them, to plead in favor of freedom, to protest that an artist has certain rights. This is a ridiculous, phony approach. Freedom is whole and cannot be allowed by degrees."

Maurice Girodias

Maurice Girodias

GIRODIAS: I have so far published under the Olympia Press imprint books in English only. My firm was founded in 1953. It is true that my father, Jack Kahane, started the Obelisk Press in the 1930's, which represented the first phase of our family endeavor to publish, in Paris, books which were banned or might have been banned if they had been printed in the English-speaking countries. During the war, in which I remained in France, it was quite out of the question to go on with the normal activities of the Obelisk Press. In 1934, my father had published *Tropic of Cancer* and the famous autobiography of Frank Harris, *My Life and Loves*, a first novel by Cyril Connolly, books by James Hanley, and many other works by writers who were to later achieve a certain degree of fame.

After my father died in 1939 I started a publishing business of my own. I published art books and built a new company called Les Editions du Chene. Throughout the occupation I published books devoted to Matisse, Picasso, and most other important recent French painters. In 1950 I met with rather serious financial difficulties and relinquished my assets to a larger company which absorbed Les Editions du Chene.

It was only in 1953, as I mentioned, that I started the Olympia Press, with a view of making money and also of publishing books by authors I liked. During that year I was fortunate enough to be the first publisher of Samuel Beckett; *Watt* was actually his first full-length novel, the first book he ever wrote directly in English. All his later books were written first in French, then translated into English by the author himself or under his supervision.

N: *How did you happen to come across Beckett? What are your impressions of him and his work?*

GIRODIAS: I have always been fascinated by Beckett's personality. His works were all the more a revelation to me since I had previously been deeply impressed by two other writers of exceptional stature, Joyce and Kafka, and it seemed to me that Beckett had been able to digest the influence of these two and yet retain his own personality. From the start, even when he was unknown, I felt that his work was very strong, very worthwhile. His fame built up very slowly in the United States after *Molloy* was published there a few years ago; it was released by us here in Paris at virtually the same time. As you know, Grove Press has published many of the books we had brought out here, or arranged simultaneous publication.

N: *I'd like to turn to Nabokov. When you published* Lolita *didn't you introduce Nabokov as a vital and growing talent?*

GIRODIAS: I think Nabokov may now have reached his zenith, although *Pale Fire* does reveal his incredible ability to change from one creative mood to another.

When I first read the manuscript of *Lolita* in 1955 I must admit that I was dazzled by its originality and inventiveness. One year after we released *Lolita* it was banned in France by the French government, and I entered a series of legal conflicts with the government. Eventually, much to my surprise, I won my case and the ban was lifted on the English version. But this was shortly before the semirevolution which took place in May of 1958, and it was obvious, after the change of regime, that I would no longer be allowed to win a case against the French police.

N: *What are your impressions of Nabokov as a person, and again, as a talent?*

GIRODIAS: I must keep the two greatly separated in thinking or talking about them. My personal relations with Nabokov have been very difficult, which is not unusual because I think a great writer possesses a certain type of egocentric individuality which publishers are seldom fitted to manage.

But I have always had a great admiration for his work. After I published *Lolita* I discovered his other books; books I had not read before. In fact, I had never heard of Nabokov until I received *Lolita* in manuscript. We published the book with very few changes and no expurgations. During the year following the book's publication, *Lolita* was virtually ignored in France and America. People only started to take an interest in it when it was banned in France and litigation began, which is proof that censorship always helps sell a book.

That same year we published a book that became almost as famous as *Lolita*—*The Ginger Man*, by a young American writer named J. P. Donleavy. This also has a curious story because we released an unexpurgated version in France, and one year later an expurgated version was published in England with a great deal of success. The book never did quite achieve in America the success it deserved, which is unfortunate because I think it is one of the most original humorous novels to have come out since the war. During this same period we have also published books by Henry Miller, one called *Plexus*, another called *Sexus*, which are part of a trilogy entitled *The Rosy Crucifixion*. Another called *Nexus* has been published in part, though the second half of that book has not yet been completed by the author.

N: The Roger Casement Papers *was yours too, wasn't it?*

GIRODIAS: Yes. This involves another complicated story—not literary this time, but political. I first heard about Roger Casement in 1957 when a book by a British writer, Alfred Noyes, was added to the great number of volumes already devoted to his case. I was struck by the extraordinary combination of ill fate, ill luck, and misunderstanding, which is to be found in the story of Roger Casement. I was astounded by the symbolical value of Casement's story, so charged with dramatic power and political significance.

Roger Casement was an Irishman from Ulster who became a British consul at the beginning of the century, and who turned against England after he left the service in 1913. He became one of the leaders of the Irish insurgents.

During his civil service career he had been a British consul in the Congo and later in South America. In both locations, at enormous personal risk, he had denounced the colonial system—that established by the Belgians in the Congo, and by what was know as "the rubber companies" in the Amazon region of Brazil and Peru. This was an unusual attitude for a British consul, but amply justified by the system of inhuman exploitation then prevalent in the Congo and South America, which culminated in veritable genocides; and Casement was no ordinary consul. His investigations were officially presented by the British government in two "white papers" and they caused the world to realize clearly, for the first time, what crimes were being committed in the name of civilization.

Roger Casement became a very important and controversial public figure, but his actions naturally provoked the anger of the special-interest groups in England and Belgium since he had, in effect, put a stop to the colonial evils as then practiced by exposing them.

Casement did no more than follow his natural inclinations when he enlisted in the Irish Nationalist movement in 1913 after having resigned from the civil service. This launched a series of incredible adventures. He was secretly sent by the Irish rebels to New York in 1914 to try to obtain financial help and arms. Then he was sent by the Irish Directory in New York (again secretly) to Germany to plead for German help against England. In Germany he gradually discovered that his good faith had been abused; the Germans despised him, and the Irish conspirators in New York found his personality so irritating that they kept him in Germany under some phony diplomatic pretense. Yet in the spring of 1916, he heard about the preparations to be made for the uprising which was to take place on Easter day. He begged the Germans to send him back to Ireland, and they finally consented to let him go. He traveled secretly as usual, this time in a U-boat. But his intention when he landed on the Irish coast was not to help in the uprising, but to persuade the Irish leaders to call it off. He knew that the Germans, who had promised to bring arms and men into the country just before the rebellion, had no intention of doing so. They were only interested in creating as much confusion in Ireland as possible. Casement knew that the Irish would discover this only at the last minute, and then it would be too late.

He was captured a few hours after his landing and immediately sent to London for trial. But he had just managed to send a message to the leaders of the rebellion in Dublin, informing them of his views, and this only the day before Easter. A gigantic state of confusion followed as a feud developed between the two Irish factions, extremists and moderates. The uprising was called off, and again confirmed, and finally broke out one day later, only to be drowned in a bath of blood by the British army after a week of hopeless struggle.

Casement's personal situation was aggravated by the fact that the British government wanted to obtain a spectacular conviction to focus attention upon this issue rather than upon the defeats the country was enduring in the war. Thus Casement, after a trial that was as unfair as possible, was hanged by the British in 1916. The public prosecutor was F. E. Smith, who had been, only two years before, Casement's bitter, ruthless political adversary in Ireland.

The most involved and colorful aspect of the whole affair was the introduction of Casement's diary into the proceedings. Casement was a homosexual, and quite a delirious one at that. His diaries had fallen into the hands of the British police, and the Conservative government of the day agreed to let the intelligence services use those diaries against Casement to crush his chances of obtaining a reprieve by showing them to influential personalities.

That is why I became so interested in Casement's history. There is something frightening in the fact that a superlatively virtuous society, like the post-Victorian, can destroy a man so easily just because his sexual patterns vary from the average.

N: *In publishing the list the Olympia Press has turned out, do you feel an obligation, on the one hand, to the writers you have brought to market, and on the other, to the public to whom the books are presented?*

GIRODIAS: First I have to consider the two kinds of books I have consistently published since I launched the Olympia Press ten years ago. First come the books I publish simply because I like them. In this category are all the books I've mentioned so far, plus those by Miller, Jean Genet, Durrell, Burroughs, perhaps a half-dozen others. Then there are books which are usually classified as pornography, a word I earnestly despise because it has a purely emotional meaning.

Actually, I have deliberately published those books described as pornography not because I am a bloodthirsty maniac or an irresponsible member of society, but simply because I believe it had to be done.

I will certainly not deny the financial motive. But why not make money by taking advantage of the weaknesses of society if one finds it possible to do so? Actually, every publisher in the world does exactly that, only they are not always quite as frank about it as I am. And when I say that it is a necessary thing to put out books such as *White Thighs* and *Chariot of Flesh* and so forth, I am not trying to find jocular excuses to conceal a feeling of guilt: I really mean it. Reading erotic books is not harmful; sex is not evil. And I believe that the civilization to come will owe much to the cultivation of eroticism, which to me is the only source of art, progress, ambition, and all the other positive impulses in man.

The logical thing, in order to defeat censorship, was to prove that censorship was entirely unnecessary. We undertook to publish books that were so outrageous, so completely frank, that we sometimes astonished ourselves. We have proceeded to do this since 1953 in a methodical manner with the result that we are nearing the point when censorship will be finally abolished in the English-speaking countries. I do not mean that we deserve all the credit for that revolution, but at least we have given it its initial impetus. We have helped prove that censorship is conducted by people who are afraid of their own inner shadows. We have shown that four-letter words in print do not cause physical or moral collapse; that the graphic depiction of an orgasm does not lead to delinquency.

The movement developed in America and shortly afterward in England at an amazing pace. The first significant move came in 1958 with the publication of *Lolita*. Then followed in quick succession those books which had been considered for so very long as the symbols of forbidden literature: *Lady Chatterley's Lover* and *Tropic of Cancer*, both published by Grove Press at great risk and cost, and later, *The Naked Lunch*, by the same firm. The recent publication of *The Memoirs of Fanny Hill* is an even more impressive move because the U.S. courts have plainly admitted that *Fanny Hill* could not be considered a literary masterpiece worth saving from the censors because of its literary quality. Thus the last false excuse was courageously disposed of by the

American judges, and I consider the *Fanny Hill* judgment as even more important than the famous *Ulysses* judgment of thirty years ago. It implies that sex or even deliberate obscenity is not harmful and should not be eliminated as such. A great step forward has thus been taken toward complete freedom.

N: *What books are you planning to publish in the near future?*

GIRODIAS: As far as my firm is concerned, I must admit that this present trend is proving fatal to our activities. We existed because the literary censorship prevailing in the English-speaking countries made it imperative to have, somewhere in the world, a publishing firm able to print the books suppressed in the United States and in England. Now that censorship is receding, our role is nearing its conclusion, unless we start publishing books directly in America, which we shall probably do.

On the other hand, France has followed a very strange evolution in the past few years, going in the opposite direction from the Anglo-Saxon nations. Today in France, censorship reigns supreme, not only over book publishing but over the press, radio, films — all our forms of art and communication. The French have not been totally aware of what has happened because the evolution has been gradual, but at present, publishing is anything but free.

For example, after many litigations and changes of fortune, I have had more than sixty books banned. I was sentenced to one year in jail, and have been assessed enormous fines. I was forbidden to publish books for twenty years. I appealed these sentences, which seem all the more exaggerated since the books I publish are in English and cannot be of great concern to the French public. The magistrates who prosecute me so assiduously are usually quite unable to read the books for which I am being tried. My English-language magazine, *Olympia*, which used to be freely admitted and sold in America and in England, has been banned in France and I've had to discontinue publication. Under yet another jurisdiction I am forbidden to publish any book without submitting three copies to a special censorship board and waiting three months for the decision of this commission. This, of course, makes any publishing activity impossible, but it does not bother me too much since I am under a special personal ban, in any case, as I have just explained. Why I am being so venomously persecuted is hard to understand. The reason may simply be that my attitude generally appears not quite conformist enough to the French judges, and they feel I do not show enough respect for their concept of justice.

N: *And the crowning irony, of course, is the fact that for a century or more France led the way in eliminating the ban on the sensual or erotic and so-called pornographic literature.*

A slight change of subject, but in an overall sense how do you evaluate the quality of fiction being written today?

GIRODIAS: This is a period of transition. People have not adjusted to it yet. Writers are still trying to find a new direction. It is difficult to evaluate what the arts of writing are going to become in the next few years because many attempts at definition are being made, many searchers for a new direction.

In France the *nouveau roman* is the vogue. But it is not really new; it is not even exciting or constructive. It is important, however, insofar as it tends to destroy the old forms, the old rules of the literary game. It does not give us the vivid emotions we should derive from a work of art, as the writings of that school are always more clever than poetic, more technical than revealing of some inner reality.

The trend is the same in America, but I feel that the literary movement in the United States is much stronger and richer than in France and in Europe as a whole. Writers like Kerouac, Burroughs and Ginsberg are essentially iconoclasts, but they have a voice, a power, a style that is still lacking in the works of their European counterparts with a few exceptions, such as Borges, Beckett, and Michaux.

It is Henry Miller who wrote that the modern novel will tend to be more and more autobiographical. I believe this is quite true. But the passage from traditional literature, which was the acme of artificiality even when it achieved greatness, to this new form of autobiographical fiction is far from easy. It is not enough to be brutally frank about the facts of life and cynical about one's own weaknesses, to attain poetic reality. It requires a much deeper effort, a ferocious mental discipline to achieve that sincerity without which the art of the future will never emerge. This is why I consider men like Burroughs or Michaux as prophets, but what they prophesy is yet to come.

This brings us back to the twin problems of freedom of expression and sex in literature, and I would like to make a few remarks before we finish to make my point quite clear.

Actually, this absurd censorship business has obscured all the real issues for too long a time. We are just playing into the hands of the censors when we accept the invitation to argue with them, to plead in favor of freedom, to protest that an artist has certain rights, and all that. This is a ridiculous, phony approach. Freedom is whole and cannot be allowed by degrees. The very fact that we are made to question ourselves about this is degrading; we are no longer in the nineteenth century. We live in a new, vital, inspiring era in which individual freedom will become more and more a basic necessity.

It is not only that the habit of obeying all sorts of mental taboos turns every one of us into a mental cripple, a mental cripple who is usually unaware of the fact that he is one; it is essentially the fact that sex in itself is a creative force which requires cultivation instead of repression.

Eroticism is probably the central, perhaps the only force of evolution in man. What distinguishes the amoeba's way of life from our own, it seems to me, is that the energies of the amoeba are directed towards the survival of the species, whereas our outlook includes desire, ambition, art, conquest; we want to absorb the universe, to make it our own. Sexual eroticism is an elementary expression of that drive; political ambition is just another expression of the same drive, as are science and art, and the purest forms of religious or philosphical mysticism constitute the last consequence of the evolution which starts with sex.

Perhaps you will think that, like all specialists, I have developed a sort of obsessional madness. But even if it is a sign of madness, I think somebody had to say this clearly at last: sex is everything. It is in everything. It is the beat of the universe. And if there is one thing that cannot be detached from sex, both in its simplest and in its most elaborate forms, it is art and, of course, literature.

Donald Hamilton

As far as sales are concerned, James Bond probably holds top honors in the secret agent fiction field. This situation isn't apt to last much longer, however, for an intrepid hard-hitting American named Matt Helm has moved through nine paperback novels to sales of over five million copies.

Matt Helm's creator is a bearded, erudite man who shatters every preconception of what the writer of secret-agent thrillers should look like. His name, Donald Hamilton, sounds Anglo-Saxon.

"Actually, I'm Swedish—born in Sweden, in fact," he said dispelling illusion number one.

"Hamilton is quite a common name in Sweden—some very noble and courageous Hamiltons came there some time ago, and the family flourished. The name remained through generations of Swedes, mostly all of the minor nobility. In fact, if we hadn't come to the United States I'd be a 'Count Hamilton.' Some of my Swedish relatives are a little annoyed that I don't use the title."

Aren't most of the suspense and secret-agent novels being written with more attention to pace and sex than to style?

"I loathe this misconception of writing down to the public just because you're supposed to be working in a popular vein. I have grave doubts about the twelve- to fourteen-year-old mentality the average reader is supposed to have. I think they're a great deal brighter than this, and I don't think they like to be written down to.

"Three-syllable words don't scare them."

Did he base Matt Helm on James Bond?

"No, not at all. I have only read one of Ian Fleming's delightful books, and that was quite some time ago. I've deliberately avoided reading the James Bond novels for fear that I would unintentionally borrow something from him, or bend over too far backward to avoid any similarity.

"The latter is the greatest problem, you know. For example, in my tenth Matt Helm, I had planned to use a midget submarine. Well, a spy story just came out that involved a midget submarine, so my editor suggested that I find something else if I could. It's taken some reworking, but there won't be a baby submarine in my book.

"Fortunately, the variations that can take place within stories of this sort are numerous. But not endless."

Has he had trouble finding new plots, new locales?

"Not at all. Helm has actually been self-generating. I've put the stories in Scandinavia, Canada, Scotland, Maryland, and spent a bit more time in my home area, the Southwest, and there are a great number of situations to use without stretching too far or repeating.

"So far Matt has taken care of himself nicely."

How was the character created?

"He started in what I might call 'just another book.' I've written many types of stories, including westerns like *The Big Country*, which became a rather ambitious motion picture. I've written nonfiction mostly on yachting and photography, two hobbies.

"But when I gave my editor at Gold Medal *Death of a Citizen*, which involved Matt Helm, he immediately saw it as a series. We had problems—like getting rid of the wife and children which might encumber his free-wheeling—but it all started from that."

What were his origins as a writer?

"I didn't start off to be one. My father, who came to Harvard University to join the medical school staff, didn't think that writing was a profitable career, so I intended to become a doctor. I switched to chemistry, got my B.S. from the University of Chicago in 1938, but the urge to write was too much for me, and I went from short stories to a novel to another novel to Matt Helm. Thanks to him, I guess, we live in New Mexico, in Sante Fe, and I think my life is a great deal freer than it would have been had I become a doctor."

"The only thing an artist can really contribute to the world is one truthful and fulfilled person—himself. Anything he writes has to be true…the world as it is…colored by his own sense of beauty, his sense of values, whatever they might be."

James Leo Herlihy

James Leo Herlihy

HERLIHY: Born and reared, Michigan and Ohio. A great many cities in both. My father was a city engineer; my mother a housewife. I had two brothers and two sisters, one older and one younger of each, so I'm right in the middle. I went to a Catholic school until I was in the tenth grade, then switched to a public school and was graduated in 1944.

All through school I worked at various jobs — delivering papers, delivering groceries, writing money orders, working at carnivals, whatever came along. I worked in a war plant until I was seventeen, then joined the Navy. The day the war ended was the day my overseas orders were dated, so I didn't get on any ships. Most of my naval career was spent at Great Lakes.

Then I went to Black Mountain College in North Carolina for a year. A progressive school. It has a strange and interesting history. It was created in 1933 by six educators who had a great passion for education; the only rules they created concerned the fact that you couldn't carry firearms on the campus. There were ninety students and thirty-five teachers when I went there. Some of your classes would be with just one teacher, and many had six or seven students in them, no more. It was a great way to be educated. They really cared about education only in the sense that they led and inspired the student, rather than beating him to death with things that had to do with standards and degrees and getting jobs. It was more concerned with training your mind to learn, to absorb the world, to reach out.

I stayed there for about a year, then hit the road and hitchhiked around. I had various jobs at various places, then went to California.

I had been advised at Black Mountain that I shouldn't be a writer. Isaac Rosenfeld said it wasn't my particular gift, and that I should take one of those tests that tell you what you should do. So I took a test, and it said I should be a writer, but I thought, "Well, those tests can't be any good." The second thing it said I could be was an actor, so I ended up at Pasadena Playhouse, which was where I thought you should go if you wanted to be an actor. In those days it was *the* place to go. I got out there and found that every play I was cast in had me putting my hands in my pockets, standing awkwardly, saying, "Gee, Mr. Smith, I sure do like your daughter." I was so bored that I didn't know what to do, so I started writing plays that I could act in. Soon I found that I was really writing, after all. They did my plays out there, and liked them, and I became a playwright.

Then some friends created a couple of different theaters out there on the Coast—the equivalent of what we have off-Broadway—and we did my plays, and plays by other people. We acted and wrote, painted the scenery, sold the tickets, lived together and fought, and it was marvelous. Eventually, I decided to come East to see what New York was all about, and I proceeded to earn my living here in various ways. I was editor of a house organ for a charity organization, I swept the floor at a sound recording studio, I washed dishes in Woolworth's basement, and I wrapped picnic plates for samples.

Then I wrote a couple of television plays that were done on the old Kraft Theater. And through those first years in New York, Bill Noble and I were working on a play called *Blue Denim*, which was performed on Broadway for about 170 performances and was done as a movie afterward. So I began to make a living as a writer.

No more dishwashing. I'd had about forty-five of those little jobs, altogether. But I had written in all my spare time—even in California I was writing stories that began to be published in *Discovery*, the pocketbook affair they bring out now and then; *Paris Review*, others. After *Blue Denim* I wrote and directed a play titled *Crazy October* which was a mistake. It starred Tallulah Bankhead, Estelle Winwood, and Joan Blondell. We went on the road and tried to make it right, but we couldn't. Stayed out fourteen weeks and finally folded in San Francisco. The next year I published a volume of short stories, and in 1960 the novel, *All Fall Down*, which had a moderately good sale, was on the best-seller list for a few weeks, and was bought by Metro-Goldwyn-Mayer, who almost made a good movie of it despite some very odd casting.

Then I discovered that all the writing I did in 1961, 1962, and 1963 I couldn't stand, and I got scared. I'd finish a novel (I wrote three in this period) and read it over and have the feeling that someone other than myself had written it; they seemed to have been written with an ax to grind, to make a point, not to be novels. So I shoved all three into a drawer and thought, "Well, how am I going to make a living?" I decided to go back to the stage to act, because I needed the money, and I began to get a few jobs. I played the young psycho in *The Zoo Story* (I don't suppose Albee would want me to call him that) in summer stock, and I

played him in Paris, starring in the first Paris production of any of
Albee's plays. We had a pretty good success with it, over there. Then I
did a movie; I played one of Jean Seberg's four lovers in a movie titled
In the French Style, and I was the one that married her in the end. But I
got a good case of the touristas during the making of the picture and lost
forty pounds. Thus I weighed 170 in the first reel and 130 in the last,
and the reels didn't match. You couldn't tell it was the same person. So,
since the first reel wasn't really plot, they cut me out of it, and left me in
as the skeleton who married her in the end.

I came back to New York and gained some weight and acted in
television on the Coast—"Route 66," things like that. And I played *The
Zoo Story* in Boston, and *The Caretaker,* by Pinter, and in 1964 I started
writing *Midnight Cowboy.* I found, just having been away from writing
for a year and a half, that I could make a living some other way. This
had taken the pressure off me, and I was able to write again with a
lighter hand. There wasn't so much at stake; maybe I wasn't so terribly
involved with myself.

You see, *Blue Denim* was a collaboration; it was a big success, and all
that, but it was different in all respects from doing something by myself.
Collaborations are bull sessions. You sit and talk with your collaborator
about what kind of play you want to write together, what sort of
material you have in common to draw from. Somewhere out of days
and days of really talking (both Bill and I love conversation; we
sometimes talked twenty-four hours at a stretch) came *Blue Denim.* I
can't be any more specific about the origins of the play. Conversations,
similar experiences. I think that collaboration worked, because it's a
sound play; it seemed to spring naturally and beautifully from a
situation that seems impossible, at first thought.

Now, those years of not being on the beam were godawful, and I
think they were wrapped up in the frightening aura, not of self-
indulgence, but of terror, of wondering what the hell I was doing,
thinking of myself as a writer. What right had I to write books? I began
by thinking that I had to say something specific, that I had to write in a
way that would end up with an implicit recommendation of how the
world should go. I felt, during those years, that it was a sort of crime to
write out of your own pressures and impulses when so many really big
things were wrong with the world, so many major issues paramount.
How could I dare write out of an individual pressure, an exclusively
personal impetus? I thought I would, must, have a broader view in
mind.

So after limping through three lousy novels with this attitude it
suddenly occurred to me that the only thing an artist can really

contribute to the world is one truthful and fulfilled person: himself. There's a big question concerning whether or not this is possible. But it's what he's got to aim for, and anything he writes, whether it's a novel or a play, has to be true. It can't be bent, it's got to be the world as it is. It will have to be colored by his own senses — his sense of beauty, his sense of values, whatever they might be. They'll come out in his work and be part of his work. But he's not going to try to systematize, which makes for very bad writing. This is just a guess, but I would imagine that sort of writing does more harm than good because it gives a false view. It may be a lovely view; it may be attractive to think that the world can go the way you want it to go, people behave the way you want them to behave, and the ideal can exist — yet I don't think that anything good comes from a snow job. I think that the ultimate good is going to come from people facing the simple home truths about humanity. If a writer is dedicated to truth he's got to be fearless about looking at other people and projecting his findings in his work.

You know who put me onto this? Marlene Dietrich. I met her at a party in Paris when I was playing in *The Zoo Story*. She had come across some of my work, and she said, "What is a writer like you doing here, starring in a play and going to cocktail parties? Why aren't you writing books?" She takes a very dim view of performing. She doesn't think it is of any real importance, and claims that she does it because it's all she can do. But she's a remarkably intelligent woman. I replied, very honestly, that I didn't know what I was doing there; that I was still bound up by the "Is it all right to write from your own personal impulse?" thing. I said it seemed that some of the things I had seen in the world were ugly and unjust and violent and even hideous, and what was new about those elements? What had I to contribute? I really think I had bought a point of view that everything in life is supposed to be the sound of music.

Well, she hit the ceiling. She was marvelous! She said she thought this was the silliest thing she had ever heard, that she had heard other artists sound off the same way, including a sculptor who hadn't worked for four years because he tied himself up in this same knot. She said that if truth can corrupt the world then we'd better be corrupted pretty damned fast and get it over with.

I think that got me to work on *Midnight Cowboy*. Or, out of the sound of music and into the world of roses and horseshit. The main thing about *Midnight Cowboy*, from my own selfish point of view, is that I really dig that character, Joe Buck. I like him. I'd like to take a stick to him, sometimes, and put my arm around him at others, but I really dig him. I think he's got something in him which — if the world is to survive

—is the saving grace: an ability to be committed. Perhaps it's because he's innocent and naïve. But something essential within him gives him the power to be committed. It's an aliveness; he conducts a flirtation with life. He wants to be connected with life, married to it. The quality isn't intelligence—he hasn't got much of that. He hasn't even got a vast imagination. But he has such a commitment to life that he cannot succeed in evil—which, after all, is nonlife. He tried to be a hustler, but he couldn't succeed at that. He tried to con somebody and failed and ended up being conned. This is why I really dig him.

I could have carried the novel to five hundred pages—as a matter of fact, I did, and then cut. I simply hated to put an end to the book because I wanted to stay with him.

On another level *Midnight Cowboy* can be related to the picture we have of the cowboy. I mean the symbol of the cowboy, what he means in our culture.

I have a feeling that the cowboy in American legend is someone who rode into town. This is the way we see him, and the way people all over the world view the cowboy. We think of the cowboy as more the father of our country than George Washington. He's the heroic head, the folklore papa. He rode into town, proud, his jaw squared, ready to defend the beautiful and the just, and he was flawless. He rode at high noon, so there wasn't even a shadow. He was pure, and he would always appear in the blaze of light, and if he left town at the end of the picture it was always into the sunset. He was a glorious, shadowless man.

This concept of the human animal, of the human being, has caused the biggest screw-up in the whole American psyche of any lie we've told ourselves. It's not just the cowboy—it's extended into every aspect of our lives. The whole Jack Armstrong bit.

What I mean is, we create, very diligently, a culture in which it is not possible to be an animal as well as a human being. These two elements are constantly in terrible conflict. The shadow, which is the body, cannot breathe in a culture like this. So the cowboy casts no shadow, the legend casts a big one. If a cat thinks there is something in him that is not true and beautiful, that there are facets of himself that do cast shadows, he has to abandon allegiance to the good things. He has to become bad, to become aligned with the underworld, with the shadowy forces of the world. He can't embrace animal characteristics and be a good person.

Now, it seems to me that it is entirely possible to be a louse and care a great deal about honor and love and virtue and truth. It is perfectly possible to be honorable and loving and virtuous and truthful and steal. In other words, it is perfectly possible to have contradictory elements in one's nature, yet remain a fine example of a human being. We have an inability to embrace the whole man, and this is why I love my character and do not love the antihero or the nonhero.

In fact, the antihero and nonhero put me in a fury with modern fiction. The kind of men I want to cavort with are those who press on, who keep trying. They're going to get everything—the works and the rewards, but they're not going to lie down and let the tractors run over them and the horseshit fall on them. This impatience with non- and antiheroes limits my reading, to say the least.

As you can see, what I like best in art—whether we're immediately concerned with painting, writing, architecture, music—is the feeling that the artist is giving you his aliveness in his work. He's giving you his essential self. Along with it, he's taken a great deal of trouble to learn his craft. When you see the two things together, I'm excited. I feel that Albee does this. Of the new writers I find him the most exciting because he's taken great trouble to learn his craft. How he's gone at it—directly or obliquely—doesn't matter. He does know how to project his view of life onto the stage. *The Zoo Story, The American Dream, Who's Afraid of Virginia Woolf?*, prove it. I'm not referring to how much, or whether or not, I liked these plays; that's beside the point. The plays come painfully and totally alive; they come directly from himself; they're done by a craftsman. Of the new writers, he's the one.

Tennessee Williams—always. He's always alive with a real knowledge of how the theater works, and he always writes with his own sense of life (and I don't mean in a hideous geographical sense). He has enormous craftsmanship. I don't think he has ever bored an audience; he does things to the audience some people think undesirable, but he has never bored them, he has never taken them away from life.

One thing that upsets me is to see people sleeping in a theater. I think it is one of the saddest sights in the world. Men and women here and there nodding off—what the hell are they doing there? Who conned them there in the first place? Who made them come clear onto this lousy island to sit and be bored for two and one-half hours? And it happens all the time. I think it is a crime to bore an audience, and I think that the Theater of the Absurd is a generic term created to defend writers who have not learned how to hold an audience. Writers who have not learned to use form. I'm sure there are playwrights who have been lumped in that generic category who don't belong to it, who are good artists. But I feel that the term itself is a hiding place for playwrights to whom the audience is the last consideration, and I don't think this should be.

Telling a story is as old in the theater as the theater itself, which

makes it as old in the history of art as anything. Go back to mythology
—stories. What this god does to that goddess; damned interesting
stories. Pick up Bulfinch—he's twice as interesting as many modern,
aimless short stories. You're involved. I think that the Theater of the
Absurd is trying to get away without telling stories, though I won't
deny a certain usefulness and popularity. Usefulness in that it jars
people out of a rigid story sense, away from an absolute sense of form
that isn't needed; at its best it can broaden a writer's framework by
showing what can be included in a story or a play. But I don't think that
formlessness itself is going to mean anything in the long run. Popularity, yes, the novelty of it, the temporary challenge. Plus the fact that
it can connect with the specially trained audience, the audience with a
very special interest in the progress of literature or the progress of
theater. But I don't think it connects with the basic humanity of the
general audience; they don't connect on that level. I've seen audiences
be polite and give their little pitterpat at the ends of the acts and go
backstage to do their raving, but I've never seen a theater really on fire
with one of these plays. And it's not a bad idea to set the theater on fire.

On the contemporary novel: to me the greatest living novelist that
has come to my attention is Carson McCullers. I think she is heaven on
wheels. It's a pity she doesn't have the physical strength to bear her
genius. She's the most neglected and abused writer. She's never won
any of those nice prizes they're always passing out. I don't understand
it. Another writer I always look forward to is Truman Capote. His new
book, *In Cold Blood*, will have to be brilliant; he's never done anything
that wasn't. After all this time it will have to be especially brilliant.
Imagine, almost *living* in Kansas?

Then there's Richard Yates. I believe it's Yates. He wrote *Revolutionary Road*—wonderful. Powerful, with a view of the contemporary scene,
contemporary life, particularly New York suburbia—an important
portrayal of failure. And the Australian, Sumner Locke Eliot—*Careful,
He Might Hear You* is superb. Ken Kesey I like; I read him with great
interest.

Joseph Heller, and *Catch 22*—I don't know. I appreciated the
zaniness of that book, and the kind of curve he had, a marvelous way of
bending what he saw to get at you, but it didn't happen to reach me. I
wish that more discipline had been involved in the writing of the book.

But lack of discipline has been a rather successful commodity, hasn't
it? All these ripples and fads that take four or five years to wear off.
They all have value, and I think that twenty years after ripples like the
beatniks, the Kerouac school, the Salinger people, someone comes along
with the synthesis of what they accomplished, plus his own great voice,

and we get what can be called literature. I think all is grist for the mill, and someday a cool cat will come along to grasp the essence of it and create a masterpiece. Look what happened not too long ago, when we went through all sorts of literary commotion asking ourselves whether Gertrude Stein was the mother or the daughter of Ernest Hemingway. I happen to think she's the mother of us all because she wrote, in 1909 I think, a fantastic book titled *Three Lives*. With it she taught this century what the American language actually was, and I think this had to be learned. I think we had to find it out. She sat over there in Paris and insisted upon this American language, not the English language in the sense of the nineteenth-century novel. She knew that nobody in America was about to write better English than Henry James had, and that we had to come into our own kind of a sense of literature, sense of language. America, after all, is not a stepchild of England; it's a great nation and it has a great tongue. But she's the one who insisted upon our identity, and I think that Hemingway, Faulkner, O'Hara — you name them — have been touched by it. All American writers who have a reverence for our idiom, our way of bending the language, have been directly affected by that old broad

Hemingway was a step, too. If we could just forget about his celebrity status and his lion hunting and fishing I think we'd think of him as one of the flurries like Salinger and Kerouac. He's just one of the steps forward. He didn't create a great or considerable body of literature, but he did something about acknowledging the American language that was important.

I hope the writers coming up are able to put a finger on the pulse of "now." That along with a finger on the pulse, they'll have skill with language, control of the American language, and the courage to write as they see life, to write their own observed truths. My hope is that there will be someone with a great eye and a great heart worthy of being given a great voice. I have no concept of what novel he'll write, or what play. I don't think it makes any difference what it will be about. I think it will make a difference, however, what the voice says in relationship to what is seen and felt. It can be about any particular layer or level of life, any part of the country, as long as it's written with the soul of now. It's a mistake to look for any particular form, any particular kind of material. Life pops up in the weirdest, most unexpected places.

"I think it's phony when authors say they write to please themselves. There is a fierce wanting in the writer; you want somebody else to read the book and like it . . . if your work is not going to communicate, what good is it?"

Laura Z. Hobson

Laura Z. Hobson

HOBSON: I don't remember that I ever had an ambition to be something other than a writer. My first ambition—as you'll note in *First Papers*, because so much of that novel is based on truth—was *not* to be a teacher. This was a negative ambition, but a teacher was the one thing my parents wanted me to be. And I was determined to have no part of it.

While I was at Jamaica High School I managed to become the assistant editor of *The Oracle*, our school paper. When I was fourteen, still in high school, I went in to New York to see a woman editor—Rita Child Door, I think, possibly Orr—on a newspaper called *The Daily Mail* (now extinct). I became the Jamaica High School correspondent for that paper, and nothing much more happened until I went to college. I spent two years at Hunter College, the city college for girls in New York, and I had a ghastly time. I couldn't bear it, in fact, so I transferred to Cornell. At Cornell I continued in my reportorial capacity, covering school news and school elections and school everything. Not sports. I did this for the *New York Globe*. I also wrote fashion notes for *Women's Wear Daily* on what college girls wore at football games, etc. So it's evident that I always wanted to write. When I got out of college I was determined not to teach, but I couldn't be just "a writer." So I got my first job; it was in advertising, but it was writing. So I can say that throughout my entire life—except for one summer, my nineteenth, when I was a mannequin (we call them models, now)—every dollar I've ever earned has come from writing. (That modeling bit, working for a fashion house, had rather an effect. I learned to wear expensive clothes, a major flaw in my character.) I didn't think of writing fiction until 1935, the year of my divorce. I wrote a short story and *Collier's* bought it, and from then on it was fiction, almost exclusively. But I didn't begin my first novel until 1941. Many people think that first novel was *Gentleman's Agreement*. It was not. It was a nice little success titled *The Trespassers*, which nobody remembers, now.

It was an interesting book I think, with many faults, but also many decent things in it. Dick Simon of Simon and Schuster urged me to take the big plunge and write a novel. He offered me a huge advance, five grand, and I think my vanity was such that I simply couldn't turn that down and then have to tell people, "Well, I was offered a big advance, but I just didn't want to write a novel." I had to do it. It sold very well, about 20,000 copies. It was at the bottom of the best-seller lists for weeks on end, but then, that was 1943. In 1947, when *Gentleman's Agreement* came out and was such a jackpot success, it acted like a screen for everything that had come before *(The Trespassers* was forgotten) and for quite a lot of things to come; people are forever saying, "Well, her third novel, *The Elder Father*, is good, but it isn't *Gentleman's Agreement*." It's all so ridiculous, but it's inevitable, and it never bothers me.

They want me to write *Gentleman's Agreement* again, and to write the sort of thing it was, again. In looking back at *Gentleman's Agreement* now —as the author of *First Papers*, which is a totally new experience for me in writing—I regard it with great pride. I'm deeply gratified and happy that I wrote it, but I do regard it as the "other" kind of novel I've written, the kind with an idea plot, a gimmick plot.

I think that one of the most encouraging, moving moments in the writing of *First Papers* came to me two days after Faulkner's death, at a time when I was still desperately struggling to get back to easy writing from the depths of my horrible writer's block. I was having lunch with my editor at Random House, a wonderful young man named Robert Loomis, and we talked about Faulkner and Faulkner's work. We finally got to the subject of my unfinished book (it wasn't even half done at the time) and Loomis said something to me about the difference between it and anything I had ever written. He said something that made such a difference, played such a great part in my courage to go on. It was this: "You know, Laura, whenever I think about *Gentleman's Agreement* I think, 'What a wonderful idea,' but when I think about *First Papers* I think, 'Gosh, what wonderful people.'"

The difference is so profound. I know that whatever stretch of time is left for me to write, and I hope it's a million years, I'm never going to write another book that has "a wonderful idea." It's got to have wonderful people.

I think a really good novel has to start with people. With *First Papers* I had the people, right from the beginning, but without a plot or story-line. This, indeed, was where the writer's block came up. Nothing is more dreadful than this. It isn't simply laziness; it's a disaster, like the blocking of an artery. I'll discuss it later, if you wish.

N: *By all means. Before we get too far away from* Gentleman's Agreement *I would like to ask you what you thought of it as a motion picture.*

HOBSON: I liked it very much. I really did. I admired it completely. They cut many things out of the book, of course. They had to. All the secondary threads involving the sister out in Detroit, the Grosse Pointe area, many other threads had to be cut out. Remember, the film was made in 1947. At the time, a movie about anti-Semitism seemed unthinkable, although Dore Schary did rush a picture about anti-Semitism to the screen that same year, something about a psychotic, so off-key the public would instantly say, "Well, I'm not like that."

Gentleman's Agreement was exactly the opposite. I used to say to people in a sort of gay, satiric mood, "Oh, it's about anti-Semitism among nice people." They would jump and say, "What do you mean, nice people?" and I'd reply, "Well, among people who think they are nice and free of it, but who really aren't."

I do think that Darryl Zanuck had great courage at that time, when the memories of the war were still very fresh. It won the Academy Award in 1948 as the best picture of the year. I think he really had great courage to put the word "Jew" on the screen as "Jew," and words like "Kike" and "Yid" and the opposite words, "Coon" and "Nigger" — all those filthy hate words were fed to the audience in a big, luscious theater from a great big screen. The public had never had that experience. Zanuck had guts. There were such pressures brought upon him not to make the picture, or to soften it. He told me that one of the antidefamation organizations we all admire so much, Jewish at that, put pressure on him to omit the anti-Semitic Jewish secretary, to leave her out. I can understand their anguish in a way, because I've had the experience over and over in my own life. One or two people with my publisher were very reluctant about this book and would say, "But Laura, you just make things worse by talking about it." And they were aghast at my putting in a Jew who concealed the fact that she was Jewish, who changed her name to Miss Whale, and talked about "those Kikes." What a loss that would have been, the omission of Miss Whale, both from the standpoint of honesty and the performance by June Havoc we'd have missed. She was marvelous.

But I don't think you want me to talk about *Gentleman's Agreement* all the time. I don't want to; I feel it rising up again, obscuring all that went before and all that has followed, and this is frightening. I can tell you in one sentence, the plot of each of the first four books I wrote. *The Trespassers* is the case history of an Austrian family, not Jewish, leaving Austria at the time of Auschwitz in protest against the Nazi persecution of the Jews, and what they were up against via the immigration laws and quota system when they tried to get into this country.

Gentleman's Agreement is about a guy who sets out to do a series of articles on anti-Semitism and doesn't know how to do his research until he realizes that all he has to say is, "I'm Jewish," even though he isn't.

The Other Father is about an Oedipus complex, done without the Freudian lingo, as though it had been written in 1848 instead of 1948. But the Oedipus complex has a two-way street; you can't have a father fixation in a family unless you've got a daughter fixation from the father.

The Celebrity—a steady but light satiric novel about phony celebrities; there are two brothers, one of whom has talent and writes a book that hits the jackpot, the other of whom becomes the celebrity, cashing in on it, becoming a big shot in Hollywood, New York, the lecture circuit, radio.

Now, I can't do the one sentence description with *First Papers*. When people ask me, "What is it about?" I'm in trouble. If I'm feeling sort of gay, I modestly say, "Oh, everything, just everything." If I feel more responsive, I say, "It's about a time in this country's history when you could be a radical without being subpoenaed the next morning." Tomatoed, yes, but not subpoenaed. When I go a little further I say, "It's about two families. Both are dissenters, the crusaders of the nation. One is foreign-born, one native-born." Or, "It's about the lives of people who know what total commitment means."

This is why I think the novel is so contemporary. The upset and conflict over civil rights would have most of my people in *First Papers* totally involved and committed. As I am. I didn't get into the racial issue in the book; it would have been phony. Besides, they had enough to feel committed about at that time. In those days—1911 through 1916—the great problems of the day were labor and labor unions, free speech and radicalism. In the book, when Evan denounces extremists ("extremist" had a rather archaic tone in 1953, when I began the novel), what was he denouncing as "extremist"? The anarchists and vigilantes in this country, the Bolsheviks in Russia. At that time in our history, and I've researched this very carefully, the nation was as concerned with those issues and extremes as it is about the civil rights movement, today.

N: *How much of* First Papers *is really autobiographical? This is normally beside the point with most novels, but with yours it has to dig to the heart of the matter since issues are involved.*

HOBSON: How much is true, how much invented?

I'll give you one perfect example of what happens between the time an absolutely true incident is chosen and then written for the novel.

Many people have told me that one of the sections of the book they find the most moving is when the house is draped in black after the Triangle fire, and there's this terrible scene in school when the little girl is badgered about it by her teacher, and she runs home to tell her parents about it and her father is upset and wants to go to school to protest this invasion of the inalienable rights of an American child. What was the actual event? My parents did drape our house in black, making it rather a standout in the small town, which was early Jamaica, Long Island; and my beloved teacher walked by our house, looked up at the black bunting, and with her beautiful face lifted in what could only have been a sneer, said to me and my sister, "Did your dog Shag die, girls?" And out of that little nugget came a fifty, sixty, and seventy page stretch in my novel.

But what is real—my father, my mother, that house, the father I now realize he was, and the one I wished he had been—these are inextricably intertwined. My father was the kind of man I present; his life went very differently, however. For many years I could hardly bear the thought of him; he was an awful man, in many ways, and in the book he is an awful man, in many ways. Unbearable. You know damned well from reading the book, how children eight and ten and seventeen would feel about him, but you can also see what was so great about him. I can too, now. When I was thirty-eight years old I was analyzed to get over my hatred for my father. Analysis must have worked, because I can now write of him with love.

Shag, the big sheep dog, a major character, is true—though it was my brother, not my father, who went to the dog pound to retrieve him. I had a brother who did have asthma and he did have a motorcycle, but he was nothing like Eli in the book. Everything is true and everything is invented. People say to me, "Were you ever an interior decorator? How do you know how that girl felt about beautiful furniture?" Well, one of the things this lovely apartment, this duplex on Fifth Avenue, is for, is to pay my father back for those unpainted walls and that God damned stairway going up backward. *My* stairway goes up at the front door, where it should. People say, "Why do you have a duplex when you don't even have a maid?" I take care of this place myself with a once-a-week cleaning woman, and I don't know why I have this big duplex, but I do know that I love these walls and that stairway—it's chic, so right, so proper. And so contrary to my father.

N: *Are you aware, as you write, of any specific obligation to yourself, the material, or the reader?*

HOBSON: I'm rather hung up on being accurate. I think it's dopey to make silly errors. I always hope I'm intelligent enough to check things; even the little facts you wouldn't think important. I don't want to be caught out in silly little errors that show sloppiness on my part.

More important, of course, is the responsibility of telling a story. I feel an immense responsibility to tell a story, but it's a responsibility that has changed a bit with this, my fifth novel. I think I've learned something from *First Papers* that will apply to all the novels I'm going to write, all the short stories I'm going to write, and this is to use real people instead of "pretend" people. There's an incredible gratification in writing about real people. I'm not saying that my previous four books were filled with "pretend" people—there were characters of stature in those too, but I think there's more warmth and believability in even the minor characters in *First Papers* than there is in the people I've worked with before. Even when they're totally invented they have such reality.

Perhaps the whole thing is a matter of the truth of your material. I've told youngsters not to write their autobiographical novel at the age of twenty-one; to save it for the time when they're fifty-one or sixty-one. They should write other novels first, to learn their craft; they shouldn't cut their teeth on the valuable material of childhood because they'll never have better material, ever, to work with.

N: *Louis Auchincloss says that childhood is the writer's whole capital.*

HOBSON: It is, and I never knew it. I had to be analyzed to find that out, and this was after I wrote four reasonably successful novels. I think here we come back to the question of responsibility, this time your responsibility to the reader, something you can't think of while you're writing. You can only wonder, "Is this right? Does this scene move me? Should I rewrite?" I rewrite everything, almost idiotically. I rewrite and work and work, and rewrite and rewrite some more. I could show you my first draft. I work on the typewriter, but there are pages with a paragraph pasted up twelve or eighteen times before I've gotten it right —and then it's apt to be torn up and typed fresh because I don't think it's properly developed.

Sometimes authors come up with cozy, pat answers, when they're asked who they write to please. I think it's phony when they say they write to please themselves. If I were writing and had the feeling that nobody would read my book except me and Bob Loomis at Random House, I would not be happy. There is a fierce wanting in the writer; you want somebody else to read the book and like it. It would be terrible I think, to *not* please yourself, to write falsely or write down, but if your work is not going to communicate, what good is it?

N: *You mentioned the extreme writer's block that afflicted you. Can you explain what happened?*

HOBSON: I think a writer's block is a gruesome disease, and I wouldn't wish it on my worst enemy. Writers talk about the agony of writing; I talk about the agony of not writing. It took me over nine years to finish *First Papers*. The knowledge that I was stumped for almost eight of those years made my life hell. External things contributed to it. The heart attack suffered by the editor I'd gone to work with at

Random House. When I try to explain it it sounds self-indulgent; believe me, self-indulgence was the last thing it was. Self-castigation became the order of the day, and of those years. The first six months I worked on the book I finished 146 pages. Pretty good; I moved along well. But I found it was harder to write then, and I was grinding to a halt, escaping into research. I wrote newspaper columns, book pages, filled in for Bennett Cerf on "Trade Winds" every year for five or six summers. I wrote short stories and one big novelette per year for rather handsome pay.

But I couldn't go forward on the novel. I went back to the public libraries in despair, reading old newspapers, searching for God-knows-what during the period which I at first thought was going to be 1911, and which it remained because I wanted to start with the Triangle fire, which was my own first strong memory. It was crazy; I did thorough research all the way through the end of the war in 1918 and the idiocies of censorship that followed, the deporting of the Reds in 1920, the rise of the Ku Klux Klan in the mid-twenties. My theory was that no matter what happens to us, no matter how many McCarthy eras there are, this is America. It's a free country, and it may take us time to get rid of our awful diseases, but we shake them off. This was my thesis.

The externalized part of my bogging down in the writer's block was that my research showed me that I was up against ten thousand novels; I didn't know where to stop or where to go. I could project from my 146 pages; I was still in the summer of 1911 with those, and here I was going to go through the mid-twenties. It would be a two- or three-million-word book, and who would read it? The block must have been something much deeper, a truly psychic thing, perhaps deeper than I know, certainly deeper than I'm willing to tell you. So I bogged down, helpless. I finally went back to trade promotion — I'm a very high-priced promotion writer, mostly for magazines — with a firm resolution to stick to the job or the book. No columns, no short stories, no novelettes, nothing, and I didn't write a thing. I even began to talk about the book as "my abandoned novel," yet I would go to the library and read old newspapers and think, "Well, I'll find out a little more about the strikes in Lawrence" or, "I'll find out about the Palmer raids," and I'd be off again in research that produced no writing. So from 1953 to April of 1960, nothing; then that month I wrote a three-page scene, later expanded to a four-page scene, and I began to have a glimmer of hope. I began to realize in a dim, vague way, why I had written the first pages.

In 1961 I began to work on the book quite hard again, but it was part-time work because I had my promotion job and some illnesses. That year I did one thing that was marvelous: I bought a clipboard and some ruled paper and a $17.00 fountain pen with real ink and went off on a vacation. It was a secret. I didn't tell anybody that I was trying to write again. I went to the Virgin Islands, had a cottage on the sea, and worked night after night. Even if I had a date I'd make it an early date, come back about eleven and write until three in the morning. This was the breakthrough—I was able to write easily again, with some authority, some knowledge of where I was going.

I came back to New York, endured a few more illnesses, then faced the big decision: Either I had to finish that book, or I would have to go back to making a living. The latter meant that it might take me ten years, working in the evenings, to finish it. I made the decision: the book. I was fortunate, in one way. The magazine I'd been working for as a consultant (this means you're too old to go on the payroll) gave me a farewell bonus. Perhaps they wanted to bribe me into not changing my mind, and coming back to them to be a problem. The bonus covered damned near a year's existence at very lofty levels, and I made that year stretch to a year and a half. I knew then that I'd write the book, and write it in 1963. And I did, working steadily, every day, every night. I had seven evening appointments in that year, and couldn't work at the time of Kennedy's assassination (but who could?), but otherwise I stayed solidly at it. It's a totality of work I'd never had, and it was glorious. I didn't even have an exhausted feeling at the end; in fact, I felt as though I could have gone on for five years.

I think only those writers who are blocked know what a writer's block is. I'm not talking about the lazy ones who say, "I'm going to write a novel," and do nothing about it for ten or fifteen years because they're too damned lazy. Hard-working, well-balanced writers get blocks. In a way I think it is a sort of menopausal loss of confidence and potency and everything else, and it afflicts men and women alike. The torture is incredible; it's as if you want to write to exist, but you can't write.

N: *How do you appraise the literary status of our time—in terms of things you favor or might disfavor?*

HOBSON: I'm almost forced to be glib, because there is so much that is good, and so much that is positively dismaying. I'm not making the usual objection and complaint, that the stuff Tennessee Williams writes is sick, sick, sick. I think he writes about life as much as anybody else who writes about unhappy and miserable people or problems. The one thing that does bore me in the novel and in the theater—and I read almost everything and see as much as I can—is the negative and existentialist outlook. I think one reason I like *First Papers* is that it is affirmative of life and love, belief and faith—faith in humanity and in a nation. My people are agnostics, but how they believe! I really don't think the negative and existentialist approaches serve our time. Now, I weep over what happens in the South, and in the North too, but the Negro revolution is on the march—it can't be stopped, it's moving affirmatively. So how can you ask me to believe a little pipsqueak novel that is just one long line about life being an empty nothingness, meaningless because of the atom bomb? I don't believe any part of that.

I don't get disturbed when the material is ugly, when drug addicts or homosexuals or neurotics are fawned upon—I am only bothered when there is a total loss of affirmatives. I'm not referring to optimism; a book or a play can strike total despair, and still grip me. In serious writing I think there must be affirmation. This is why I go back to read Dickens, Dostoevsky, Tolstoy—particularly after reading a book by some little pipsqueak squeaking. All the fuss and nonsense about the sexy book—let them be; I'm terribly against censorship. I think some of the sexy books are fun, some are filthy, some are hard-core, card-carrying pornography, but that's for the courts to worry about.

Affirmation—I think that's the key word. Not a Pollyanna complex or the Disney touch, but mere affirmation of the human spirit. We are not all bad, or lost.

N: *If you were to give advice to the younger writer—*

HOBSON: I have done this rather often. I think every author who loves youngsters gets a chance to be asked for advice by young writers. If it happens here in my duplex, I'll say, "Go over to my bookcase and take down any novel, any one you like." And they'll take down *Anna Karenina* or *The Brothers Karamazov* or *Main Street* or whatever. Then I'll say, "Don't open the book to the first or the final page, but open it at random and read it to me. One page." Chances are they will read a page that has no genius whatever, nothing very brilliant, nothing even beautifully written. When it happens this way I say, "When you look at a page you've just written and think 'Gosh, I just can't do it!' remember this page. It isn't a flash of lightning on every page you need; it is a total effect you're trying to get. These books have power. They are after something real and important, and you feel it all the way through, but at any given point there may be very ordinary paragraphs, and that ordinary paragraph you wrote yesterday shouldn't discourage you." This helps kids.

The other thing they must do, of course, is to decide what they really want to do, because a person does what he really wants to do. The guy who says, "I can't write the book because I've got to earn a living; I have a wife and child," doesn't want to write badly enough. If he did, he would give up everything else, earn a living, and then write.

There is time. No matter how pressed a person is, there is time. It's tougher, but as you get older you can concentrate only on your writing. You've simply got to make your way in the world, first. You'll never be a writer if you do the Gauguin trick and ignore all responsibilities, because good writing comes from good people.

"... There are honorable ways and dishonorable ways to review a book. The honorable way is to look at a thing and see what's good in it, to first of all say what's good and then land on what's bad. Do it like a gentleman. The reviewer is a literary mugger; he comes over and takes what is valuable and beats you up anyway."

Evan Hunter

Evan Hunter

HUNTER: I was born in New York City, October 15, 1926, which makes me forty. I lived in Italian Harlem until I was twelve, then we moved to The Bronx. My background is Italian-American. I was an art student, like Driscoll in *The Paper Dragon*. I won a scholarship, like Driscoll in *The Paper Dragon*. I went to Cooper Union, then into the Navy, and while I was in the Navy I decided I didn't want to pursue a career in art any more. So I began writing. I was encouraged by several officers aboard the ship. One, an instructor at the University of Wisconsin, would go over my stories with me and I would submit them to magazines. They were invariably rejected. When I got out of the Navy in 1946 I began school again, this time not in art, but as an English major at Hunter College in New York. It's a girl's school, you know, or was; they were taking veterans at the time. I was graduated in June, 1950, with a B.A. and a wife who is happily still my wife.

I taught for a short time. I had prepared for a career in teaching because I was fairly certain that I wouldn't immediately step out of college and make it as a writer. I taught for a very short time, student-teaching at one vocational high school here in New York and after graduation at another vocational high school. I didn't like teaching at all and I quit.

After that I held a series of wildly unrelated jobs. I sold lobsters on 72nd and Columbus Avenue; it was a wholesale lobster firm consisting of the boss, myself, and a Chinese girl who handled orders from Chinese restaurants. It was peculiar job. I called the restaurants in the morning, restaurants I'd never been in in my life, like the Chambord, and asked them if they'd like some nice, fresh lobsters that day. I'd quote prices and we would order them from Maine, where they had the plant or whatever it is that supplies lobsters.

Prior to that, another inspiring job — I answered telephones at the A.A.A. [American Automobile Association]. This was at night, and I could look for editorial work during the day. I thought the way to break into the writing field was to take an editorial job somewhere. So I'd work at the A.A.A. from three until midnight, then get up early the next morning to go looking for editorial work, which I never found.

After I was at the lobster place for a while I decided it was time to start looking for editorial work again, so I answered a blind ad in the *Times* for an editor. In my letter I said I had no experience, had been with the college newspaper, all the really unimportant background stuff employers are not too interested in hearing. When I went for an interview it turned out that it wasn't a magazine or a book house or anything like that, but a literary agency, and I almost didn't go in. I almost made the biggest mistake of my life by not going in. The man who was leaving the job they wanted to train me for was going because he had started selling so much of his own material through the agency, that it was no longer practical for him to stay there. It was the Scott Meredith Agency. I took the job, and I learned a great deal. I was handling excellent writers like P. G. Wodehouse, and talking to the top magazine editors every day of the week, and to book publishers. I learned what they wanted and how professional writers worked. I learned how much work was really involved in writing and in revisions. I learned how uncertain and insecure writers are; they would call three or four times a week to find out how their latest book was going, or what happened to the story they'd sent in. I enjoyed working there; it was exciting and educational.

After I'd been there a few months I brought in a few of my own short stories and showed them to Scott. He's an excellent editor in addition to being a top agent. He can tell you exactly what's wrong with a short story after reading it once and, if it's a novel, after reading it ten times. I think he's a better editor than any working in New York. In any case, he sold one of them. He turned back four, saying he thought two of them were all right and might sell. The one he sold went to a friend who was an editor of one of the pulp magazines.

I kept writing short stories, not for the little magazines, not for the literary publications. Most of them were very bad. They went to the pulps; they were mysteries, westerns, anything. The only thing I didn't write while I worked at the agency was confessions, and I think the only reason I didn't do those was because the author's name didn't go on them. Where I really learned to write was at the agency and for the pulp magazines, which is a different school of writing than most of the established writers of today have attended. The kind of stories I was taught to consider not good were the inconclusive slices of life, little character vignettes. They were not in my education. Eventually, when I stopped writing mysteries and westerns, the better stories I wrote were still what I consider to be stories. They had a beginning, middle, and end — the old-fashioned thing called a plot.

After I had been at the agency six months, Scott asked me how I would like to write a novel. I said, "I can't write a novel." He said, "Sure you can, it's easy." So I did two science-fiction novels, juvenile science-fiction novels, for the Winston Company. One under my own name and the other under a pseudonym, Richard Marsten. Ironically, the Marsten book was a Junior Literary Guild selection; the one under my own name went nowhere. Neither of them was very good. It's very hard to write for kids, I discovered. I also discovered it's very hard to write a novel, despite what Scott had said. By May of 1953 we had saved three thousand dollars, and though we had three kids by that time (not so miraculous; two of them were twins), we figured we had enough of a stake to carry us three months; so I decided to leave the agency, with Scott's blessing, and free-lance. And I came home to write. Before I left the agency I wrote a short story titled *To Break the Wall*. It was based partially on my experiences in the vocational high school in New York City. Vance Bourjaily, who at the time was coeditor of *Discovery* magazine, had bought it as my first "quality" sale.

After I left the agency I found I had a great deal of time to write — from whenever I got up in the morning to whatever hour I wanted to work at night. I turned out a great many short stories and an adult science-fiction novel which went to Simon and Schuster. Peter Schwed read the science-fiction book and liked it very much and recommended its purchase, but he was outvoted. He sent a very nice letter to Scott saying that if Hunter would care to show them any of his other work, they would be very kindly disposed toward him.

Suddenly all the magazines I had been writing for began folding. There was quite a bunch of men's magazines at the time, not of the *Playboy* variety. It was a little before *Playboy's* time. *Bluebook*, *Argosy*, *Real*, etc. were taking hairy-chested fiction, stories built around a character who is in some sort of danger, involved in or running from some escapade or another. Adventure stuff, very little sex. But I was left without any markets, so I had a discussion with my wife and I said, "I think I'll write a novel." Time was running out. I was afraid the gamble was not going to pay off and I'd have to begin looking for editorial work again in the fall. So I started *The Blackboard Jungle*, using the story that had been in *Discovery* as the springboard. It ultimately became the climactic story in the novel, not to me, but to everyone else. I wrote the book very quickly; it took me only two months. We showed the first hundred pages and an outline to Simon and Schuster, and they bought it from that.

Then strange things started happening. Very strange things. *Ladies' Home Journal* took it as a serial, which flabbergasted me, and MGM bought the film rights from galleys, which was also startling. It was published in October, 1954. The response was mild; it sold about 16,000 copies, which was excellent for a first novel but not enough to put it on any best-seller list, not enough to make any ripple.

I was in the strange position of having written a novel which I considered a good novel about a man doing his job against insurmountable odds. And it was being reviewed as a social document, and "exposé" of the schools. Hardly anybody said, "Gosh, this is well-written." They all said, "How terrible that such things can go on in our schools. We must do something about it." I was really disappointed in the reviews, even in the good ones.

There were some bad reviews, of course. *The New York Times Book Review* said it read with all the excitement of a social tract, a dissertation. They made it sound like a dull, boring book, which it wasn't. I considered that an unfair review. Whenever I went out for interviews or anything—I was only twenty-eight years old and terrified—everyone wanted me to be a knight on a white charger who was riding into the New York City school system, looking for heads to roll. All I wanted to be was a man who had written a book—hopefully, a good book

I wasn't clever enough or fake enough ("fake" is a better word) to realize I could have gotten a great deal of mileage out of the pose they were trying to force on me, and I refused to accept the pose. I said, "I'm not an expert on juvenile delinquency, nor am I an expert on the vocational high-school system." All I was an expert on was myself really, yet I had avoided the first-novel pitfall, the growing-up-and-going-to-your-first-whorehouse sort of thing. I had written about what had been the most meaningful experience in my life up to that time. Trying to teach these kids and not being able to. I refused to become an expert. Only much later when I wrote another book, I thought, "I think I'd better learn something about juvenile delinquency," and I did, more or less in self-defense.

Then the movie came out. They did a hell of a good job filming it. We were in Florida when it was released (the children were still preschoolers), so we missed all the hullabaloo that took place in New York. They had sound trucks blaring all over the city and signs in windows saying "Yes, We Have *The Blackboard Jungle*." It must have been very exciting, and I missed it. It was a genuine best seller in paperback; it sold several million copies, given the impetus of the film.

I had always assumed that if you wrote a big best seller your next book would automatically become a best seller. It wasn't, yet I think it was the second-best book I ever wrote. It was *Second Ending* about drug addiction.

I was strongly involved with that book. My closest friend as a boy had been a musician who became a drug addict. The novel was largely biographical, dealing with a time in my life when I played with a young band and toured around. The novel had truth, and the reviews upset me. You know, I feel there are honorable ways to review a book and dishonorable ways. I think the honorable way is to look at a thing and see what's good in it, to first of all say what's good and then land on what's bad if the reviewer thinks something is bad. Do it like a gentleman, you know. I think that too much reviewing makes fun of the work. The reviewer is a literary mugger; he comes over and takes what is valuable and beats you up anyway. It presupposes an intent that is not always there. So because *The Blackboard Jungle* had been a big hit movie, and the book was associated with the movie, a lot of reviewers assumed I had deliberately chosen a sensational theme for my second novel. I don't think writers deliberately choose anything. They choose something that's been in them for a long time, something they *have* to write about. When I chose to write about drug addiction I was really choosing to write about a dear friend of mine. I was terribly upset with what some of the reviewers said; they should have known better because at the time there was a stringent code against showing drug addiction on the screen, so I wasn't headed for a movie sale anyway. Nor has there been a movie sale to date.

It will be interesting to see what happens when the novel is rereleased, shortly. With the LSD business and pot and all being such an accepted form of entertainment, I wonder how it will fare.

I wrote *Strangers When We Meet* after that. Something happened along the line; I don't know where or when or how or why, but I have a feeling that the success of *The Blackboard Jungle* in the critical climate that existed in the late 1950's mitigated against things I wrote. It was disturbing. I don't know if it's worse to get a bad review than no review; I suppose every writer wonders at times. But I feel that I've been ignored over the years. I think I'm a pretty good writer, and I don't think I've written the same book twice, deliberately. And with the Ed McBain mysteries I have a climate of absolute acceptance from the critics. So I end up with the best in one possible world, the worst in another. I do know, from the McBains, what it's like to write when the climate is one of universal love and acceptance. "Do whatever you wish to do and we will examine your navel every time you come out and say how marvelous you are." On the other end of the scale, on the straight novels, the good reviews have come (almost universally) from the unimportant critics. I have never been really regarded as a serious writer, which I think I am.

It seems to me that there are cubbyholes in America that one gets thrown into, and once you're in that cubbyhole, you're stuck. Francis Brown of *The New York Times* will hold *The Paper Dragon* in his hands and say, "Back of the section." I don't know how he can tell that from the jacket; it's like a movie producer saying, "Cut ten minutes from it," without reading the script. And it annoys me. It annoys me because it would be very simple to write a cheap book, very simple to write a book aimed at motion pictures, but the fact that most of my books have sold to motion pictures doesn't mean that I have aimed them at the the screen. It means that I write books that have a plot and people moving and conflict of one type or another. As a matter of fact, the only book that was bought for the films before I wrote it was *Mothers and Daughters*, and they haven't yet been able to get a screenplay out of it because it was such an involuted, complex book. How the hell did I get on critics, anyway?

After I wrote *Strangers When We Meet* I went to the Coast to do the screenplay on *Strangers*. It was a terrible screenplay and a terrible movie. I really don't know what happened. It was the first screenplay I'd written (not that the next was any better), and it just didn't work out right. Doing a screenplay is like reading another man's book. There is a pattern to any man's book. It is probably in the speech pattern, I don't know, and it becomes his writing pattern. Some of us call it "style," but I think it's more than style. I think the books you don't finish reading are those where you can't attune yourself to the other man's pattern. For example, it took me a long while to get into Cozzens' pattern when I read *By Love Possessed*. Once I got into his pattern I could follow his complex sentences and his thoughts. Until then I was ready to put the book aside. I'm not talking about the scheme beneath the book, but the writer's fingerprints. When you're writing a film you have your pattern and fingerprints, and you hope, through some miracle, they will match the director's, that the director will fit into your pattern and see it your way. This doesn't always happen.

I worked with one of the best directors. I worked with Hitchcock on *The Birds*, which I don't think was a good film. Then, after *Strangers When We Meet*, I was approached by a man in Hollywood to do a screen treatment about Spanish Harlem. I had spent some time up there doing research for a play, and I started this treatment and it turned into a novel which I think is a very bad novel, *A Matter of Conviction*. I wasn't happy with that one, and I think the reason was that it didn't start out to be a novel. It started out to be something else and grew abortively into a novel. It's the one book I feel should not have been published. Then I wrote *Mothers and Daughters*. It was something of an exercise, and perhaps you shouldn't publish exercises. I wanted to learn about writing about women. I wanted never to be troubled writing about women again. Their viewpoints, feminine viewpoints, are virtually throughout the entire book. Different women at different ages; it was a complicated project. I can see why they can't make a movie out of it; it covered forty years and went on and on; the theme was that of life as a sort of repetitious moving of cycles. And I enjoyed writing the book.

After that, the best book I've ever written — *Buddwing*. The reviews on that were mixed. Some reviewers saw what I was trying to do, and they gave me good reviews. Unfortunately I remember only the bad ones; I don't know why that should be. And now *The Paper Dragon*, and it's too early to tell what the reception is going to play. In between these novels I did a play which was a big success at the Birmingham [England] Repertory Theater, and a failure here. It was called *The Easter Man* in England, and *A Race of Hairy Men* here. They didn't want to use the original title because they felt it had religious connotations; this eluded me. But it was a considerably different play here, with a shift in emphasis; now I'm writing another play.

N: *In reviewing* The Paper Dragon *I'm probably one of those reviewers who didn't please you because I felt that the sexual encounters were sort of larded-in, as though they were inserted to liven up the book at appropriate points. Do you use sex in this fashion?*

HUNTER: Not consciously, but it would be my fault if it seems that way. No one told me how to write the book. In truth, I think there's only one explicit sex scene in the book, and that's a rough one; I deliberately made it rough because it had to be, to justify what happens later in the story. I've always felt that this battle about sex was fought ages ago, and we don't have to worry about it any more; that sex is part of life and characters who are lawyers by day can be lovers by night and have relationships with women ranging from the healthy to the extremely unhealthy. I remember that one review of *Buddwing* said that the book is an excuse for a series of sex episodes. He had obviously taken the book literally and assumed it was really twenty-four hours in the life of a man instead of thiry-nine years of his life; so the sex episodes would seem to come with amazing regularity unless we inspect them to see that the first sexual encounter in the book is with a nineteen-year-old girl and is symbolic of young love, the next is with the woman he marries, and the last is with the woman she becomes. But I don't feel that there is a lot of sex in *The Paper Dragon*; if it's there the only thing I can say is I didn't decide that I needed a sex scene at this point or that point.

There are things about the novel that please me, things that displease me. But I don't feel that a book has to be perfect. Even before I publish it I don't feel it has to be perfect. I feel it has to be the most I can do then. I would rather send it out into the world as the best I can do at the time, move on to another book, and hope the next one is better, instead of keeping it and working on it for ten years.

The idea of working on a book for a year is tedious. There's no immediate goal. You work and work and work, and there's no end in sight. If I had to work seven years on a book or seventeen, as some writers do, I don't think I could be a writer. I'm not that kind of person. My attention span is not that long. I would rather move on to the next one because I always have an idea at the back of my mind of something I would like to explore. In much the same way, the Ed McBain 87th Precinct novels are like chapters in a long novel about crime and punishment. The characters are the same in each book. You meet different people, but the lead characters are the same, and it's like a long novel that's been going on for twenty-three chapters; there may be another twenty-three chapters before I die and that will be the end of the book.

So all of my other novels are actually like chapters of a life's work, and at the end of it all you should be able to look at it and say, "Oh, here's where he was lousy, and here's where he was good, here's where he grew, here's where he slipped back."

N: *In the same area, actually, could you define your objectives as a writer?*

HUNTER: That's a difficult question not to answer glibly. All writers say, "I want to illuminate a little section of life for people, blah, blah, blah." I don't think that is absolutely true. I have to tell you that I am fascinated with writing itself, with the whole idea of writing. I'm fascinated by the whole idea of technique, by the things that can be done with words and tried with words.

After *Buddwing*, for example, with its theme of identity (which may be important only to me because I'm never quite sure who I am, though I think it might be important to other people in America too), I wondered if I really did have anything to say in the book, or if I was so involved with the technique that it didn't matter what I was going to say. I still don't know the answer. I think it was a frustrating book for many readers because when they got to the end they still didn't know who Buddwing was, and neither did Buddwing. But that wasn't really my concern. My concern was something quite other than that, so to get back to your question, I guess my answer could not be "to illuminate something for the reader." I think it's to examine an experience I have, or a thought, to examine it so it becomes more understandable to me. Then, hopefully, it will be understandable to the reader as well.

When you're at work writing, the reader is a vaguely defined person. Sometimes you'll give him a personality so that you don't feel you're writing out to a void, so that you're writing to someone. You're trying to explain what something is about, you're trying to make him cry in that scene or laugh in another. I remember being at a party once with a motion picture critic and one of the writers in the Establishment. I was asked by the critic, "Why do you write?" and I said, "To be loved." I think this is why every writer really writes. He wants to be loved. He wants people, millions and millions and millions of people, to read his books and say, "You are marvelous, I love you." The writer from the Establishment disagreed with me. Now, maybe he doesn't write to be loved, but I do. Otherwise I would write a novel and put it in the desk drawer and start another one; the writing of it would be enough if all I were going for were personal catharsis. Obviously you're trying to communicate something to someone when you write, and I think the successful books in terms of being the realized books are those where you manage to reach that unknown person out there with what you were trying to say; the unsuccessful ones are those where you're so confused yourself about what you're trying to say that you don't reach anyone, least of all yourself.

Last night I picked up *Strangers When We Meet* from the shelf and thumbed through it to see if it was any good. I don't know if it is, any more. I know that I would write it differently now. But I like the idea; it seems healthy. If I were to look back at *Strangers* now and say, "I wish I could write that way now," or, "I wish I had that drive, that narrative power" or whatever, then something is wrong somewhere. If I can look at it and say, "I wouldn't write it that way now; I'd write it better," then I'm growing, and as long as I'm growing I'm not dead.

N: *You used the term "Establishment." What did you mean by it?*

HUNTER: I think there are six or seven writers in America who are considered *the* serious writers of our time, and anything they write, if not always well-received, will be given great attention and great respect. Again, it's this cubbyhole thing. It's almost foreordained that if a book by one of these writers comes out this week, it will be on the front cover of the *Book Review* section of *The New York Times*, the *Chicago Tribune*, or wherever. It will supplant Wouk or Michener.

I don't know what accounts for the Establishment. I think that the reputations of many of the writers in the Establishment are based on a collection of short stories and one novel, and it annoys me that there should be such worship of these people on the part of the reviewers — even fear, in many critical corners, when a new book comes out by one of these writers. I recognize that my attitude is a compound of jealousy and envy to some extent, something not very nice in myself.

I feel, and I think this is true, that writing is a very competitive business. All one has to do is to go into any bookstore and see the profusion of titles on those shelves to recognize how competitive it is. If a large measure of love and affection (getting back to what I said before about a writer writing for love) is going to one of your siblings, then you're being cheated somewhere along the line.

N: *In looking at what is happening in the novel today, which things do you find most and least encouraging?*

HUNTER: Another difficult question. I think I admire the writers who are refusing to fall into the trap of writing the same thing each time. For example, I saw a section of Joseph Heller's new book in *Esquire*, and it's as far from *Catch 22* as anyone can want it to be. I don't know if it will be a good novel or not because I only saw an excerpt. But even if it's a bad book it won't be the same book, and I imagine Heller is expected to write another black comedy. When Norman Mailer published *An American Dream*, which I thought dreadful, I at least admired the fact that he wrote what he wanted to write. Even if he wants to inspect smells, let him do it. He has a right to do it. It's what keeps the novel alive and keeps men moving.

On the other hand, when Salinger publishes *Franny and Zooey* and then *Seymour: An Introduction*, and then *Raise High the Roofbeam, Carpenter*, we're getting more and more involuted, more and more down to a minute inspection of the writer's own fingertips, and I think this is bad. I'm sure this is what he wants to write, but he's writing in the same narrow track all the time. He should loosen up, swing a bit. And it's sad, because *Catcher in the Rye* is such a marvelous book, and the nine stories are so marvelous. Now this—and what is worse is the way he's encouraged by the people who are reviewing the *Franny and Zooey* stuff.

N: *You touched on this area before, but could you elaborate on your views of reviewing and literary criticism in the U.S.?*

HUNTER: I have always felt that criticism today, the book review today, is aimed at the reader as a sort of consumer's guide, telling him what he should spend his money for. It almost relegates the book to the position of a camera or a washing machine. The thing reviewers forget is the fact that they could do a great service they are not doing: that they should have a duty to fulfill for the writer as well as for the reader. The writer, after all, is possibly the man most interested in what the reaction to his book is going to be—what the reaction of men who are professional reviewers and critics is going to be.

He can learn something from the critic, but—I guess I don't like critics. Most of the book reviews you read will have one or two lines either praising or vehemently denying the book and the rest will be a discussion of the plot. That's the review unless you get the front page, in which case every sentence will be examined. And *that's* of no real value. If you have a clipping service you get reviews from all over the country. You put them side by side on the table and discover that they're writing about twelve different books, none of which you wrote. Twelve different novels are being discussed, each from a different viewpoint of why it was good or why it was bad, but none of them will penetrate, will really try to understand what the writer intended.

It seems to me the first thing should be an assessment of the writer's intent. If he wanted to write a pornographic novel, did he succeed? If he wanted to write a comedy, is it funny? I feel that if a reviewer would treat a book with the same respect a writer treats a book—his own or someone else's—they would cease imposing an intent on a book that may not be there; they would make the field of literary criticism far more than the shabby thing it is.

Now, I think there are a lot of shabby books around, and I think that many of them are purposely shabby. But it's one thing for a book to be a bad book although it was written with serious intentions, and another thing for a book to be a bad book that was written with shabby intent; I don't think this distinction is often made by critics. Thus, if a man starts out to write a historical romance, it's not the same thing as a man who sets out to write about an Argentine prince screwing his way across the pampas. But they're treated the same.

N: *The final question: If you were advising the young writer, or hoping for him, what would the advice and hope consist of?*

HUNTER: The first advice I would give him would be to have him ask himself if he really wants to write, because it's not all that fun. Without going into the cliché of it being a lonely profession (I don't believe that; I think it's a very crowded and exciting profession. When you're working the room is full of settings and characters.) I must admit that it is a profession in which you are alone most of the time. Your contact with the outside world is by telephone, and it rarely rings during your working days, so you are alone and you must ask yourself if you want to be alone.

You must also ask yourself whether or not you really want to write— whether you feel egotistical enough and courageous enough and impervious enough to expose yourself every so often to the eyes of the world. It's considered very bad form to go over to someone at a party and say, "You know, I've been observing you for the past two hours, and I don't like the way you dress. I don't like your sense of humor and the stories you tell leave me cold and your eyes are the wrong color and

I think you're a pretty shitty person all around." But this is what happens to a writer when a book is published. You're exposing yourself to someone who comes over and says all those things. He may, on the other hand, love everything about you, but don't count on it. You've got to be ready to take it on the chin if you're going to commit yourself to paper.

So I would ask him if he wants that, and how much he wants what comes with writing. There are fringe benefits, you know, like fame. God knows what that is. But how much is he willing to pay for benefits from being what has become, in our society, a glamor figure—THE WRITER.

Then I would advise the poor bastard to write. Not to talk about writing or discuss the book he is going to write, but to write. Talkers don't work. Things talked out don't get written. If he wants to be a writer so he can say "I'm a writer" when someone asks him what he does, forget it. (He'll forget it too, sooner or later.) If he must be a writer with the same passion that a man wants to play music or sculpt or paint or play football, if he *must*, then he should be a writer. And if he must write he must then refuse to be discouraged by anyone who says, "Don't write; you're not good enough."

I can remember, in college, a C in a writing course. The instructor said, "What do you plan to do?" I said, "I plan to be a writer." He said, "Forget it."

As far as material is concerned I think just living is enough. I don't think he has to take a banana boat to South America and look for a revolution unless he's queer for bananas or revolutions. I think that right on his own street he'll find enough material for twenty novels, if he listens and observes and feels.

I don't know where material comes from. I know that much of it is things a writer has lived or has become so interested in he has explored it thoroughly enough to feel that he lived it.

All writers of fiction are really writing about life, and all you have to do is live, and if you're talented and hopeful and hard-working, things will work out.

"I don't think you should ever worry about what you're writing, about whether it's too strange, too personal, too limited. . . . One should never write down or up to people, but out of yourself."

Christopher Isherwood

Christopher Isherwood

ISHERWOOD: I was born in the North Midlands of England, in a place to be roughly associated with the *Wuthering Heights* country. In fact, looking out of the house on one side you saw the industrial plain and Manchester and Liverpool beyond in the far distance, and on the other side those moors which are really quite unspoiled because they've been made into a kind of national forest where people go hiking in the summer. (The moors are in Derbyshire.) If you followed those moors all the way into Yorkshire you'd get into the area where *Wuthering Heights* was set. The same atmosphere, old stone farms dating back to Elizabeth I. Everything is very miniature — the landscape, the small farms.

My home was partly Elizabethan. Curious mixture of things, that area. There's a bus line going to Manchester, which makes it all suburban, in a sense, yet you get just off the main road and you feel you're in the heart of country life that hasn't been disturbed for generations. Yet nearby Manchester is probably the most American city in England. There was a tremendous immigration from Manchester to the States, you know. When I went to New London, Connecticut, I was stunned between the resemblance of the old industrial structures standing in both cities. In Manchester you still see remnants of the terrible old mills, the ones where children were employed at the age of seven and fell into the machinery. They now have a sort of grandeur by virtue of stark horror.

I was born in a village so small that for years, when I gave my vital statistics, I never admitted it. I would say I was born in Stockport, which is miles away, or in Dizzley, a great deal nearer. Actually my birthplace was High Lane — just a straggle of houses along the road.

The name "Isherwood" belongs to the same group as "Sherwood," and it has to do with Sherwood Forest. I have no grounds for saying this, but I always think that the people were originally described as being "in the Sherwood" and then "Isherwood." I don't really know. The funny thing is that it wasn't the original family name. The family name was Bradshaw, and the only ancestor we have who made much of himself in the world was a Judge Bradshaw who presided at the trial of

Charles I and condemned him to death, and then became very interesting by defying Cromwell and reproving him for his military dictatorship.

George Fox, the Quaker, said that Bradshaw and one other judge were the only two judges who behaved decently toward the Quakers and gave them a break when they were brought up on charges of demonstrating against what they called the steeple-boxes of the churches. They said, "God is everywhere; why have a service in a box?"

In the middle of the eighteenth century the last Miss Bradshaw married an Isherwood. My whole name is Christopher William Bradshaw-Isherwood, but I don't like double-barreled names, so I dropped the two in the middle. But the Isherwood the Bradshaw girl married was a timber merchant; later the Isherwoods became shipbuilders, and some of them were quite wealthy and important in Liverpool. A branch of the family must have emigrated, because at Annapolis there is an Isherwood Hall, named for a ship designer named Benjamin Franklin Isherwood, who flourished at the time of the Civil War. And not so long ago I had a letter from a young officer on the U.S.S. *Isherwood*, a destroyer in the American Navy.

My father was a career soldier. In those days the oldest son inherited all the money and the next son went into the army or the church or one of the professions. He was a second son, and we traveled around with him, stationed in various places, ending up in Limerick, Ireland. Then he went off to France in the First World War and was killed, and I was raised by my mother.

I went to various boarding schools and ended up at Cambridge on a scholarship, a very good one. This came about through sheer persistence on the part of the history master at school who coached me so skillfully I gave all sorts of brilliant answers without knowing very much about history. When I had been there for two years I felt (as I describe in my autobiography, *Lions and Shadows*) that I really couldn't face academic life, so I wrote comic answers in one of the important examinations and was asked to leave.

I plunged into the London sort of bohemia and became secretary to a string quartet. I was one of the happiest boys alive. It was my idea of absolute bliss, going around in London, meeting fabulous people, even starting to write. But you never really avoid your destiny. I ended up three times as a Regents Professor at the University of California, and don't, to this day, have a degree. I hope someday I'll be given an honorary degree; it's the only way I'll ever get one.

Writing—I started very early. My parents were amazing. Both my mother and father painted (a strange thing for an army officer to do) and he also played the piano very well, was an excellent athlete — a particularly fine long-distance runner — and was quite a good ham actor. I remember him playing in *Charlie's Aunt* and that sort of thing in the regimental theatricals. So I was always encouraged to write and clown around and do anything I wanted. As a matter of fact, I don't remember a time when I didn't write. I had a toy theater and used to put on absurd plays when I was seven. I always thought in terms of writing. For a while I did consider being a magician. I was interested in conjuring, bought all kinds of apparatus, and did tricks — not very skillfully. I suppose I also wanted to be an actor; this ambition has been thoroughly fulfilled by giving lectures, really a more exciting art form, since you make things up as you go along. Nobody else can upstage you either.

But to go back, I was very serious about writing by the time I reached college. A strange thing had happened at the first school I went to. When I was ten, I met W. H. Auden, who was seven. At that time he had no intention of becoming a poet, but he did in his teens; then we met again after he had already written a body of verse which was quite remarkable. And I met Stephen Spender, a man considerably younger than I am. And there were other friends in school who wrote.

My first serious attempt at writing was an enormous novel — a childhood-adolescence novel which, I'm happy to say, is lost to the world. And I used to write a bit of verse. Some idea of what my verse was like can be gained by reading *Exhumations*, which came out this year. After my first ghastly novel I became absolutely engaged in trying to write a second, and I did variation after variation of it. I finally finished it when I was about twenty-four, and it was published. *All the Conspirators*, it was called. It didn't appear in this country until after World War II.

After that I wrote the usual sort of novel about one's family, titled *The Memorial*. That was published here in 1932. In 1929 I went to Berlin. I planned to go and stay with Auden, who was studying German there because he intended to be a schoolmaster, which he was for several years. I stayed on. In 1935 I published the first of two books about Berlin. One was called *Mr. Norris Changes Trains*, in England, and *The Last of Mr. Norris*, here.

The second book was to have been one gigantic, enormous novel about Berlin titled *The Lost*. It had so many characters and so many plots and subplots that I finally realized I'd better relax and throw the whole thing out and just write impressions of certain people without relating the pieces. Actually, the one called *Sally Bowles*, which was later used by John Van Druten as a base for his play, *I Am a Camera*, was published separately in England in 1937. After that, an early autobiography, *Lions and Shadows*. This really concludes the work I did when I was in England, or in Berlin feeling tied to home. I lived in Berlin until Hitler came into power, and wandered around Europe after that, coming back to stay with my mother for a few months at a time. But it seems I was always coming and going.

In 1938 Auden and I were offered some money to write a travel book, so we decided to go to China. Auden had gone to the Spanish Civil War; he wanted to go as an ambulance driver but they got him to make propaganda for the government. He found out that his broadcasts were being jammed, that they weren't being heard outside Spain, so it was completely frustrating. He left, and we agreed to go on one of those tours writers used to make. I think they impeded rather than helped the war effort, but a lot of us went. China had been invaded in 1937 by the Japanese, and we went in early 1938. We roved around, went up to the various fronts, and wrote a book titled *Journey to a War*. We came back via Vancouver, B.C., took the Canadian Pacific to Chicago, and then went on to New York.

In New York I ran into George Davis; I'd first met him on a trip he took to England. Davis had written one novel; later in life he married Lotte Lenya, then died. Davis was a great pioneer; he was one of the first editors to introduce fiction into fashion magazines. He was working on *Harper's Bazaar*, actually getting contributions from writers like Virginia Woolf. He met us in New York and showed us around in a most thrilling manner. It seemed as though one moment we were in the Rainbow Room, the next in Harlem at the Savoy, then in Coney Island, or we were meeting Orson Welles, Ruth Draper, or whomever, or touring the Bowery or riding ferries in the harbor. We were rather floored, and went back to England with the distinct intention of coming back. We did, early in 1939, and my home has been in the United States ever since.

It was not at all the way I planned it. I'm not a great planner of life. Things seem to happen to me, though it may be part of one's subconscious that makes the designs. At any rate, I didn't stay in New York, but came out here to California largely because, through the experience in China, I'd become a pacifist and was very anxious to discuss pacifism with Aldous Huxley, who lived here, and Gerald Heard, who still lives here.

N: *Many writers say they find Southern California a distracting place to work in.*

ISHERWOOD: Not for me. I find this the ideal place to write. The one thing that puts me off writing is extremes of weather, and this climate is really idyllic. Also, I've come to the conclusion that the ideal setting for my life is suburban. I don't want to be in the middle of the city and I don't want to be in the depths of the country. I want to be in a place where book shops, theaters, and stores are within reach, where I can see people and have some sort of social life. I find all this supplied here, along with the wonderful mountains and ocean and temperature. Furthermore, it's surprising how many creative people from England, not to mention New York, come out here. One meets everyone if one waits long enough.

N: *Many writers who do live here claim they aren't taken seriously, just because they live in California. Do you find this?*

ISHERWOOD: Heavens, yes. Just as New York used to be the whipping boy of Europe, California is the whipping boy of New York. I'm in a perpetual state of objecting to certain things about Los Angeles, and flaring up if anyone from out of town dares attack it. I remember once being back in London, and the people around me were attacking California, talking about how crazy it was, and I finally said, "Every word you say is true, and I wish I was back there this very moment." I get very chauvinistic about it.

From the critical standpoint I'm attacked for having taken up with ascetic interests in Hinduism as though I've taken up some kind of dishonest mumbo jumbo. People imagine it's connected with clairvoyance and crystal balls and heaven knows what. But whatever you do, you're going to be criticized in one way or another, whether you live in California or London. So I don't think you can take these things at all seriously.

N: *How did you become so interested in Hindu philosophies?*

ISHERWOOD: Through Huxley and Heard. You see, they had met this remarkable Hindu monk who lives out here, Swami Prabhavananda. I couldn't have been less interested in such matters until I met him, and then became fascinated. My approach to these things is what you would call extremely existentialist. I simply judged the whole thing on the basis of this individual, and as soon as I made up my mind that this individual wasn't any kind of a crook or a fake, I found myself in the awkward position of having to believe it if it applied to me.

It has become a very important part of my life and work. A pamphlet I wrote, *An Approach to Vidante* (actually rough material that will later go into an autobiography), describes how I got involved and why I feel as I do. Then the war came along, rather coincidentally, and I went to work for the Quakers in Philadelphia, where they operated a sort of hostel for refugees from Europe. The reason I did this was because I spoke German, incorrectly but fairly fluently, and all of the early refugees were German-speaking.

This was a peculiar period of the Nazi regime. Before the war broke out there were times when the Nazis went through variations in policy. Sometimes they would take the line, "Why not send the Jews out of the country, get rid of them that way," and certain people were able to get out quite officially. Then there were phases when Jews were imprisoned and later murdered. The refugees in Philadelphia had made their way out of Germany and Austria, mostly through Portugal, and they were largely very bright professional people in middle life. The function of the hostel was to provide a place where they could live, and get whatever training they might need. The location was perfect because of all the colleges and universities in the Philadelphia area. When America entered the war these people all got jobs because of the manpower shortage.

As a pacifist I had registered as a conscientious objector, I tried to get into ambulance units and couldn't because I was neither a citizen nor a qualified doctor nor an auto mechanic. About the time I was set to go to a forestry camp the age limit was lowered and I was suddenly overage. I was at loose ends, really not knowing what to do, when Swami Prabhavananda said, "I want to do a translation of one of the Hindu classics, *The Bhagavad Gita;* let's work on it together. Come and stay at our place." So for about two years I did that; we produced the translation, plus a lot of other work, and I edited their magazine for awhile.

N: *To go back to the period in Germany that produced those effective short stories which became the basis of* I Am a Camera. *It must have been a weird, almost unreal world to live in.*

ISHERWOOD: It was rather a traumatic place at the time. Germany itself, Berlin in particular, was on the edge of violent change. A great many of the best-informed and most acute foreign correspondents thought there'd be a Communist revolution. Few of them thought the Nazis would win out, but everyone was sure something drastic would happen. There were thirty political parties and splinter parties, all the way from extreme military conservatives to Communists. The Nazis played an ambiguous role, calling themselves National Socialists and posing as a worker's party. The Nazis were suspected by the army, leading to clashes which were never really resolved and which expressed themselves much later in the army conspiracies against the Nazis.

Berlin, at that time, had a shockingly high rate of unemployment. About a third of the population was undernourished, producing to-be-expected crime and prostitution. It was an uneasy, bizarre world, and I was deeply impressed by the poignancy and violence of it all.

N: *What is your opinion of the obligation of the author?*

ISHERWOOD: I think every writer has to do his best according to his standards as far as writing is concerned. This is a very general statement, but there are so many levels of writers and writing that the individual writer must establish standards at his level and try to live up to them.

I think too that as a halfway public figure of whatever degree of influence, the writer should use that influence. I find myself getting more and more involved in the American Civil Liberties Union, to me one form of political action; I always seem to approve of what they do. I'm a registered Democrat and have never voted otherwise, but it is all so amorphous. The Democrats do so many things I don't personally approve of, so I feel on much safer ground with the American Civil Liberties Union.

N: *As far as literary review and criticism as it is practiced in this country is concerned, what evaluation do you make?*

ISHERWOOD: It's very difficult to generalize. I come across startling examples of prejudice and equally astonishing generosity. In the old days in England, if you were a writer, critics backed their criticism with a view of the body of work you'd done. Even though your new book might not be so good, your shortcomings were held in some perspective.

I feel that here and now reviewing tends to be like show business in the sense that you're only as good as the last thing you wrote. Sometimes it's closer to prizefighting; you win or you're knocked out. Sometimes you're allowed to win on points. At any rate, it creates considerable insecurity for many writers.

N: *Does adverse criticism of your books bother you?*

ISHERWOOD: Only when I feel a personal malice. Occasionally — and I suppose it's inevitable — you feel that a critic (usually someone who doesn't know you at all) personally dislikes you. This is always distressing, because it's always a jolt to find oneself disliked by strangers (though God knows all my enemies, without exception, are people I've never met). It's bound to shake one up to be attacked in such a manner. But I can't complain. I've had very good treatment here. And in England I seem to be getting increasingly larger amounts of kindness. The last book, which, after all, was merely a collection, got extraordinarily good reviews almost without exception.

N: *In looking at American letters, in the contemporary sense, which elements, or writers, do you most admire?*

ISHERWOOD: One of my favorite writers, who has not had all the success I feel he deserves, is Calder Willingham. I find him extraordinary. He has such vitality and he's really a great serious comic writer. I'm an enormous admirer of two of his books: *Geraldine Bradshaw*, about a girl who was a pathological liar, and *Eternal Fire*, which was almost disregarded.

I'm also fond of Jack Kerouac's work. I like his wild, wandering style and his energy and his obsession with his world and all it implies.

I admire Truman Capote enormously. I do not feel he has yet written my type of Capote book, though he assures me that he is going to. I want him to write about the rich because he really understands them, profoundly. Truman is worldly-wise in a very good sense; he's an altogether unusual person.

Gore Vidal—a splendid writer. What I would like from him is a power novel; he has peculiar advantages in knowing about the inner workings of power. These two people, Truman and Gore, can't help but be interesting, personally. Gore's candidacy and Truman's adventures in Kansas are both fascinating things in themselves.

Of the older American writers I greatly admire Carson McCullers and Tennessee Williams. Also Thornton Wilder. There's no question that there is a tremendously high level of competency in this country.

N: *About things you dislike—*

ISHERWOOD: The word "competency" has a great deal to do with that, too. Novels about situations—mixtures of journalism and fiction. I'm the last person to criticize this in itself because I was written off, in my early work, as doing just this sort of thing: a producer of fictionalized reportage. So often there is a terrible slickness in the endings of these books, and I think this is one of the horrors of this country— everything is sweetened and the rough edges are taken off. I think Disney is responsible for much of our failure to see the other side of life.

We live in such an extraordinary world now. Created by advertising. A friend was in the hospital, terribly sick. I'd been away for a weekend, and I called the hospital to find out how he was, and the nurse said, "Oh, he isn't doing so well." I said, "I'm terribly sorry to hear that; have the pains come on again?" and she said, "No, the funeral is this afternoon." This is so typical of California, an endless turning the corner with everything.

N: *You have worked, and still work, with a large number of young writers. What have you observed as far as talent and development are concerned?*

ISHERWOOD: I always find a very high level of talent. I also find a certain tendency to think that it doesn't matter if one is sloppy. Sometimes I have to speak very strongly about the English language, opposing a general sort of carelessness they seem to feel is spontaneity. The "It doesn't matter if a sentence is finished or not; let's rush on to something else" approach.

But there is this remarkable level of talent and energy, and I really

believe that the present generation is in many ways the most remarkable one I've encountered in my life. Such marvelous and surprising
vitality is being displayed, so much of it impervious to mass media and
advertisements and all those forces that make for conformity and
prefabricated ideas.

It's natural, of course, that a certain amount of way-outness goes
with this. It must. I think we have to be prepared to see boys with their
hair down to their shoulders. They wore it this way in the seventeenth
century, after all, so what the hell!

One of the pleasantest constant surprises is the way today's students
are both learning the rules before breaking them, and even formulating
a new set of rules. A writer you regard as really way-out will say, "I
adore Ruskin," or Meredith's sonnet sequence, "Modern Love," or will
read something you thought was buried in the tombs. And I find them
hung up on, not *Ulysses* or *Finnegan's Wake*, but *Portrait of the Artist as a
Young Man* or early Gertrude Stein. They simply aren't terribly,
terribly anxious to be modern to the extent of reading only moderns.
I'm constantly surprised at the things they like and how far they dig
into the past.

It seems that my generation were great condemners of the past. I
remember how stunned I was when I got to college and sat in the calm
and read *Hamlet* and realized that it was really very good. We condemned everything, but I don't find this going on with university
students today.

The prodigious availability of paperbacks may be partially responsible for this. Almost everything can be obtained in paperback, and
apparently this has helped broaden interests.

N: *What advice, in a general way, would you offer the aspiring writer?*

ISHERWOOD: I always tell my students, or people in general who
ask for advice, this: "Don't spend a tremendous amount of time planning, saying 'I'm going to write.' Write." I very often suggest something
I myself do: keep a journal in which impressions of what happens are
written down. Later on these jottings can usually be introduced into
something else in another context. Even if they can't they serve to keep
the person writing. Only writing teaches you to write.

As far as reading is concerned, there's only one thing to do: read
what you like to read and as long as the appetite stays with you. Your
taste will change and you'll go on to something else.

I don't believe in a broad education for writers as far as the reading
diet is concerned. If one gets hung up on a particular writer I think he
should read everything that writer wrote until one gets perfectly sick of
him, or reacts in another way by building on that body of work. A

person must follow the lines of personal taste and not worry if he is following so-called classic tastes. The great thing is to get at it, to subject it to one's own standards as a human being.

I also don't accept the idea that a job prevents one from writing. I greatly admire the English writer, Henry Green. He had what in some respects was a terrible burden to bear. Great wealth, having to run an enormous family business, handsomeness, marriage to a marvelous woman. Everything was terrific, but he survived it all and wrote during the cocktail hour, the only time he could withdraw. Little by little he managed, in the cocktail hour, to produce a dozen novels. I really think anyone can make time to write. There is always time to do what one passionately wants to do.

As far as material is concerned, I think you have to start with yourself and your experiences and work from there. You'll bore yourself, ultimately, and go off to other things. But every writer draws deeply on his personal experiences. Some people transform them enormously, even turning them into historical novels or science fiction.

I don't think any life is so dull that it isn't the basis, potentially, for a masterpiece. People have written great work about solitary confinement in prison and about the most menial of jobs as well as about the most fascinating and brilliant lives of adventure. The one thing you have to ask yourself about what you're doing is this: "Is it depressing me to such an extent that I have absolutely no vitality?" You cannot write without that precious spark of vitality. Yet later on something can germinate from the rather sad experience of feeling utterly bored or drained.

There is, around us, an obvious wonderland of experience. Nothing happens that is not significant if you can only see the significance. However, nobody can be expected to see the significance in everything. People who are very unhappy or starving or mortally ill cannot be expected to look around and see everything as marvelous. Yet masterpieces have been written by the unhappy, the starving, the ill. It's a question of rising sufficiently above your environment to see something beyond it. But how the devil are you going to tell someone to do this? Everyone's life is an individual problem, set in a personal examination, as it were. Different people have different questions put to them.

N: *How would you yourself care to be appraised as a writer?*

ISHERWOOD: I believe in being a serious comic writer. To me, everything is described in those terms. Not in the terms of the unredeemably tragic view of life, but at the same time, not in terms of screwballism. Nor in terms of saying, "Oh, it's all lovely in the garden." I think the full horror of life must be depicted, but in the end there should be a comedy which is beyond both comedy and tragedy. The thing Gerald Heard calls "metacomedy."

Here, incidentally, you actually find the very greatest writers. Dostoevsky is screamingly funny in the midst of everything, but not for one moment (to me) unserious. I feel it very much in Forester, who is deeply involved in the struggles of his time but writes with a deceptive lightness. I'm opposed, I guess, to the "great novel" — the novel with the deadly seriousness that says, "Fasten your safety belts, we're entering the zone of the supreme tragedy." Another prime example of a writer who produced great comedy out of tragedy is Shakespeare. This combination is sublime in *Lear*, for example, my favorite Shakespearean play.

All I aspire to is to have something of this touch of "metacomedy." To give some description of life as it is lived now, and of what it has been like for me, personally, to have been alive. I don't think you should ever worry about what you're writing, about whether it's too strange, too personal, too limited; my experience has been again and again that whenever I've written what I thought to be the most secret and private truths, people have asked, "How did you know?" or, "That's exactly how I feel." You realize that you are much more kin to people than you realized. You don't have to hold your arms open and say, "My brothers and sisters." People are your brothers or sisters, whether you like it or not, and it comes out. One should never write down or up to people, but out of yourself. You commune at that level, even when you least expect to.

N: *Whether you are working through what might be called acute observa-tion, as in the Berlin stories, or in a situation more obviously associated with your life, as in* A Single Man, *your characterizations are extraordinarily thorough and believable. Are you aware of their synthesis?*

ISHERWOOD: It's terribly hard to say because so much of what one writes is written by the collaborator, the subconscious collaborator. I think the thing is that certain people I meet, the ones I eventually write about, are people who dwell on in my mind until I see them as more than themselves. I see them as poetic figures, symbolic figures express-ing something. My attempt, more and more, is to write about people who at first seem very ordinary, off in a corner somewhere; then through some process of the mind, "this" is confronting "that," and a tension builds that applies to everything around them — in optimum conditions, that is.

A great deal of *A Single Man* was autobiographical — the house I lived in, the college part; it's put together with bits and pieces of truth.

I actually started that novel with the woman as the central character; it was to be the story of a woman who married an American G.I. and came to this country. I started off with my usual stuff about Christopher Isherwood, a minor character who met her son in college, then met her and gradually became involved, but somehow or other I found that there were so many other things I wanted to say. Gradually, this other thing wove itself in so strongly that she became a minor character. In fact, I would like to write about her again and restore her to a major character.

It follows, of course, that if you are going to show a man who is bereaved because another man is dead, he must be a homosexual. If he loses his wife, everybody understands; it's something the neighbors go along with. I wanted a more secret kind of bereavement, a bereavement that people would understand in one way, but not in the innermost way. At the same time this aspect of the novel is much more fictitious, much more imagined. But I wanted somebody tremendously isolated, so it seemed necessary to work it this way.

You might never suppose there was any connection, but I was tremendously inspired by two works: Virginia Woolf's *Mrs. Dalloway*, which takes place in one day, and an Antonioni film, a great picture, that takes place through part of one day and all of one night. There was something about having a time limit in *A Single Man* which was very important. Also it was important that I invent quite a new way of writing, a sort of nonhuman observer watching this character, a sort of familiar. I though of the days when I was a medical student, of how the surgeon used to lecture during the operation to us students sitting around; I tried to strike that kind of note, observing everything, including the man's death (stolen, by the way, out of a book titled *Man's Presumptuous Brain*, a fascinating book about psychosomatic medicine). Yes, it's a very autobiographical novel, in a way; it's true. But I must say that if I lived the life of the principal character I would be a very unhappy person, which I'm not.

"As long as people take me seriously, I don't care whether they like a book I wrote or hate it. What I loathe is not being taken seriously. I don't like people thinking that I just turn things out for the movies."

Rona Jaffe

Rona Jaffe

N: The Best of Everything *established Rona Jaffe in spectacular fashion. The novel was a best seller, and its translation to the motion picture screen was successful. In fact, she seemed to become the spokesman for the career woman alone but not always lonely, the young American female superbly poised and groomed but (beneath it all) as bewildered as she is bewildering.*

It wasn't until after Mr. Right Is Dead *that I met Miss Jaffe and was charmed by her candor and her natural flair for individuality.*

I commented on the intriguing gallery of women who sauntered, slunk, or stumbled through such ubiquitous corridors in Mr. Right.

JAFFE: It's obvious that there aren't enough men to go around, and that the more successful career girl doesn't have too many chances to meet an attractive man who doesn't already have a wife and several children conveniently tucked away in the suburbs. Loneliness and need often make her settle for half a loaf or less, even though she knows damned well that Mr. Semi-Right may be able to leave his family for an occasional night but never for good.

N: *How much of your material is drawn from real life?*

JAFFE: Most of the things that happen in the book have happened to women I know. There's a great deal of locale-changing, of course, and I draw composites. The names are changed, of course, to protect the guilty.

N: *What happens to the girls we meet in your stories after the story has ended?*

JAFFE: I'm glad they seem that real. Actually, many of them do marry. Some go home to the boy next door they once thought a real square. At a certain stage in life the divorced man with enormous alimony payments comes along. Chances are, she'll keep working if she marries this particular Mr. Right. Then there are widowers and other happy accidents. I don't think the career woman's lot is really all bad.

Actually, if I have to ooze sympathy, I think the American male gets as much or more from me. Think of his confused version of womanhood. After he gets over the veneration of mother (if he does) he's got a choice of two symbols that represent the Absolute and Only Woman:

Elizabeth Taylor and Jacqueline Kennedy. One represents the epitome of sexual desire, the great lay he can't bring home to mother; the other is the utterly unobtainable version of dignity and purity and all that. Since we think in symbols he runs around with one hell of a complex.

I know that morals and mores and customs and all are at fault for this. But isn't it nice to meet an emotional man who wants you as you are, even though you might not be named Elizabeth or Jacqueline?

N: *How did you start writing?*

JAFFE: After I finished school I went to work for a publisher. I was an editor. This went on for an interminable period of time when it occurred to me that I was damned sick and tired of rewriting stuff turned out by other writers. I figured I could do as well writing my own fiction. And that's what I'm doing.

I hope I get better all the time, of course. I think I've improved from book to book, even though I started out cursed with a best seller

But I can't think of a time when I wasn't jotting things down. I think everyone does this—even people who don't turn into writers. It's a compulsion, a disease you don't get over.

N: *How do you feel about the reaction to your books?*

JAFFE: I don't want to be known exclusively as the spokesman for the unattached female. I want to grow into other areas. Yet I'm not complaining; I've got quite a built-in audience. There are so many of us who are bright and desirable and unattached.

Note: A little over a year elapsed before I saw Rona Jaffe again. This time the occasion was the short novel, The Cherry in the Martini, *getting strong play in a press that divided 90 percent for, 10 percent against.*

N: *There is a somewhat ambiguous separation of chapters in* The Cherry in the Martini. *In fact, the book is something of a series of related short stories, yet you staunchly claim it is a novel. Could you explain?*

JAFFE: This was written as a novel. My problem is that I like to give titles to everything. I'm a title freak. So I give every chapter a title because I love to give things titles. So when you say "something of a series," you scare hell out of me because it's got to hold together.

French novelists have been doing this—well, since long before Sagan. I mention Sagan because I'm not that intellectual. Actually, almost all American writers tend to overwrite, to tell too much. I get the disillusioned feeling that novels, today, are sold by the pound, like groceries. It actually takes a great deal more discipline to be able to leave out rather than to throw in everything. This means that you have to say in one sentence precisely what you mean, instead of saying sort of what you kind of mean in hundreds of sentences and hoping the sum total will add up.

In this particular book I wanted to leave things out because I felt they weren't necessary. Thus, as you say, there is a continuity even though it skips a period here and there. But I don't believe you should write a James Bond book in which you tell how he brushes his teeth with which toothpaste and what he ate for breakfast. I want to get down to the bare bones, to what is really important. In a way, my style has evolved in this manner since *The Best of Everything*.

N: *About the autobiographical content —*

JAFFE: As I say in the beginning of the book: "None of this may be the way it happened, but it's the way I remember it. I'm sure none of the people it happened to remember it right either, because people never do. Things are real because they seem that way. And so we live all our lives remembering it the way it seemed." I think this is true of everyone's life.

N: *The first chapter stands, I think, as a stunningly caustic look at the tendency, today, to overanalyze childhood.*

JAFFE: Thank you. I feel rather strongly about all that nonsense. The funny thing about that is the fact that the book took me a year and half to write, and about a year after I finished the first chapter I read a paperback entitled *Myself and I*, by a lady who had gone through sixteen LSD sessions with two psychiatrists to find out about herself. And I thought, "Good grief, all she ever found out about herself was precisely what I was able to write, without any drug, in my first chapter, which is really the truth about growing up." It seems a pity that someone has to take LSD to find out that she hates, or that she has any kind of animalistic instinct. I think everybody has these instincts. The funny thing is that when I wrote it I thought, "Well, I'm going to write this chapter and let everybody know that I was crazy." Then it came to Simon and Schuster; they read it aloud, and everybody at the place said it was them, that they identified. At first I was disappointed; one always likes to think one is the only maniac in the block, but afterward I was glad because I realized I had hit upon a truth without knowing it.

N: *Have you reacted to those criticisms that imply you're perhaps too truthful, too realistic, in the handling of sex?*

JAFFE: I've always been surprised when people say that I write sexy books or dirty books because my books aren't either. What I've always done is go beyond sex, because it's assumed that people have sex. It's also assumed that they enjoy it, unless I write a chapter that says they hate it.

What I'm primarily interested in is what goes on in their minds, the emotional attitude they have toward the relationship and toward themselves in the relationship. What are they doing there, why are they there, would they be better out of it. No "... so they went to bed and they liked it a lot."

N: *Considering the young career woman and her sexual involvements — are they inclined to occur because of a genuine emotional need or because of a sort of "status"? (The latter perhaps in her own eyes, as being "wanted.")*

JAFFE: It's both, in a rather odd way. I have a piece in the October, 1966, *Cosmopolitan* titled, "Why Nice Girls Get Hooked on Bad Guys." Now, you don't expect to get Freud in a magazine piece, but it is based upon the experiences of girls I know, one in particular, and to some extent on my life. It shows the relationship between a girl and a guy, neither of them are really too neurotic, who bring out the worst in each other. She makes him bad, and she shouldn't have chosen him because he is the kind of person who makes her act her worst. I've seen people involved in these relationships, relationships that would go on for years and years — a girl trying to hook a guy with whom she would only have misery and a "Virginia Woolf" marriage. They will even go to a psychiatrist to find out how to get him. I think it's the result of the way they were brought up; the pressures in life that demand they have "someone" around.

Very few people have the courage to be alone, even for a week. Consequently, even if a woman at a party excuses herself by saying, "Well, I'm alone here because I'm in love with a married man who's home with his wife," she has status. She can go out and cruise because everybody knows she has someone. It's even better to have a husband who lets her go out and fool around, or to be recently divorced. As long as there is someone in the background and she can prove she hasn't been alone she isn't a misfit. Yet so many people involved in relationships are with the wrong person, are misfits.

Now, there are very few people who will admit that they're divorced because they married too young and "didn't know what it was all about." They will say, "Oh, she was terrible!" or "He was rotten!" They won't just say, "We were too young." The trouble is that people who don't get married young have that young-marriage relationship in all their affairs, clear into their thirties. They go through that "Let's get married to get away from home because we're grown-ups and we know everything" business when they're grown-up.

Girls who live alone — lots of them — get involved with guys just because they don't want to be alone in their apartment. It's just like an eighteen-year-old saying, "I don't want to be with my parents so I'm going to go off with this guy and get married." And the thirty-year-old woman will say, "I don't want to be alone in my bachelor apartment; I'm going to go off with this guy." Both are trying to get away from something, and I think society definitely pushes them into it.

N: *Can you trace the evolvement of* The Cherry in the Martini?

JAFFE: At first I didn't even know it was going to be a book. I wrote the first two chapters because I had a desperate emotional need to write them. I didn't even think I would show them to anyone, and it took me a month before I had the courage to show them. The response was so overwhelmingly enthusiastic at Simon and Schuster that I was frightened to death, and it took me another six months before I had the courage to go on and do the third chapter.

During this time I resolved a lot of questions about the material. Like, was it necessary to sustain an emotional and perhaps even depressing tone in a book if it started out that way? I concluded no, it wasn't, because there are periods in a girl's life that are not emotional, periods of resting, periods of humor. (There definitely was a place in the book for humor.) I decided that since she had come through that time in her life when she was so frightened she was almost schizophrenic, and she was going to live, I would let her go through all the things I had gone through as an adolescent, including the period when a girl is still unformed sexually and can go either way, becomes Lesbian or heterosexual, depending upon who takes her over. And later in the story the girl goes on to other relationships, but she's still searching. Even in college she is involved in strange relationships she's not aware of. Like dating homosexuals and not knowing it.

N: *I've seen this happen often in college, and in very social sets, and again in groups of young career people. Is it a business of convenience or a matter of naïveté?*

JAFFE: It was so drilled into us in the 1940's to be "nice girls"; if you went out with a boy who was charming and attractive and socially adept, intelligent and a good dancer, and if he didn't try to tear your clothes off in the car after a date, you were delighted. You assumed he was a nice boy, well brought up.

It wasn't until ten years after I graduated from college that I discovered these boys were homosexuals. I continued to date them, after I got out of school, and I thought they all roomed together for economic reasons, that three or four of them lived together because they wanted a nicer apartment. (At that age people do have roommates.) I was also busy with romances with men who were not homosexual, but I still dated some of these "nice" boys. At home I caught hell from my parents about how these boys could never really be interested in me because they were society boys and I was Jewish. So I just assumed that I wasn't good enough for them, and consequently they didn't want to neck with me. I never thought for one minute that they were busy being queer. It wasn't necessarily being Jewish that mattered; it could as easily have been, "You're from the wrong side of the tracks, and that's why the stockbroker doesn't want you" and she says, "I guess I'm just a country girl." She doesn't know that she's pretty and he's queer.

N: *Has the matter of being Jewish posed problems for you?*

JAFFE: No, not at all. New York is a great place to be Jewish in; it's all very show business, and even very non-Jewish celebrities like Sammy Davis, Jr. and Elizabeth Taylor convert. It's just that my parents are a bit older than the parents of girls my age. My father is 72, my mother 66, and they were brought up in the early 1900's when people picked on you if you were a foreigner or an immigrant or of a different religion. Everybody got it. The Italians were the Mafia, the Jews were Chicken Flickers, the Irish were stupid. Everybody hated everybody. There was always prejudice somewhere. I spent a great deal of my childhood in Miami Beach, and I remember the terrible prejudices against Negroes. They had to have identification cards to be identified as household help to come into Miami Beach after sundown. Otherwise it was assumed that they were murderers or housebreakers. All of this seems very far away now, but if you hear things like "They'll hate you because you're different" as a child, it sticks with you when you get older.

Don't forget that a lot of girls from my background married nice boys and went off to live in Scarsdale, where everyone was from a similar background. They went to the same country club and never had a chance to see if the world was any different than they found it personally. I was lucky enough to become successful when quite young, and I met a lot of people I would not have met otherwise. But if people settle into a particular little community they get a rather restricted view of life. In fact, I'm sure there are little pockets of socialites still existing in this country where people sit and think about their own little world.

One of the woman's magazines had an interview with the man who married Anne Ford, and he said, "She was like a child she was so protected in Grosse Pointe." You'd think the Fords would have an interesting life, but she was the most innocent girl in the world. Every group keeps to itself to a certain extent; chances are, young people will get a broader view of life when they go to college. Yet if they go to the prep school type of college where they're confined to other boys and other girls from their own background, they'll never learn.

In a place like New York, where everybody comes from everywhere, people have a hard time staying in molds.

N: *In your novel you mentioned the heroine's difficulties in "being a writer"
—that the fact was resented by many men, even by girl friends. Has that
happened to you?*

JAFFE: It's quite true. Every once in a while someone will say,
"Why aren't you married?" and my answer is that all the people who
proposed to me would say either, "I like you even though I never read
anything you wrote," or, "I like you even though I hate everything
you've written." Or they would have the attitude that my being a
writer was a competitive and nasty thing. They were never glad that I
wrote. So if someone says he loves you and means it, yet resents the
fact that you do something which is terribly important to you, you
can't possibly love him. But these are basically insecure people, and
you'd be surprised at how many people who seem secure turn out to be
insecure when you get to know them well. I think that being a writer is
a threatening thing; so many men and women do the stereotyped, "Oh,
don't put me in a book!" or "Ho, ho, I'd better be careful or you'll
write about me." As if you're some kind of medium or gossip columnist.
I'm afraid that people who don't write think that writers live on some
higher level of perception in which they instinctively know all guilty
secrets. So when I get involved with a man he usually worries about
my seeing through him. He usually doesn't know that a woman usually
does, whether she's a writer or not.

N: *How have you reacted to reviews of your books—the more formal
estimation of you as a writer?*

JAFFE: As long as somebody takes me seriously I don't care whether
they like a book I wrote or hate it. What I loathe is not being taken
seriously. I don't like people thinking that I just turn things out for the
movies. *The Best of Everything* was my heart's blood. It was difficult for
me to write because it was a confession of everything going on at the
time, and it was embarrassing. Naturally, everyone identified with it
because they were doing the same things, and this embarrassed *them*.

The Best of Everything sold over two million copies and had a big
movie sale, but people didn't say, "It sold two million copies because
two million girls identified with it." They would say, when the next
books came out, "There she goes again, writing another best seller," as
though that was rotten. I have the feeling that if I had written a book
that sold two hundred copies I would now be looked upon as some
great literary light, and I think *that's* rotten.

At this point I think most people take me seriously. Certainly with
The Cherry in the Martini they do. I've come across one funny little review;

the reviewer was disappointed because I had written a serious book. They were waiting for another big old juicy sexy book. Actually, my other books weren't big old juicy sexy books at all. I think they should be glad this is a serious book—by serious I don't mean that it isn't funny. I think it is very funny, but if people think that my only function is to sit around and write stuff they can lick their lips over, I've got news for them: it's not.

My function is to write the things that come out of me as I develop as a human being, and to express the things I feel.

N: *How would you define your objectives as a writer?*

JAFFE: After *The Best of Everything* I had enough money so I'd never have to write again if I didn't want to. I was perfectly free to do anything I felt like doing. I wrote my second book, *Away From Home*, out of panic because I was afraid I was a "one book writer." When I had proved I wasn't a "one book writer," I waited five years to do another book; I wrote plays and short stories and wrote my children's book, *The Last of the Wizards*. Then the short stories were collected and published.

I fully realized I could do what I wanted to. I could go shopping all day, but how much shopping can you do? I could sleep late and have lunch with the girls—a deadly bore. I wanted to work, I had to work, and I wanted to write what turned out to be *The Cherry in the Martini*.

I think the great thing about having enough money is that you don't have to run scared. You can find out whether or not you really are a writer because you can write the things you care about.

Sometimes people who write bad things have the excuse, "Well, I had to pay the rent," and they never look at themselves and realize that they couldn't write anything other than bad things. You can also write good things and pay the rent. There are, fortunately, magazines in this country that will accept only good things.

N: *Do you feel that the writer has any responsibility?*

JAFFE: I don't think the writer has any more responsibility than the boy who delivers your groceries. His responsibility is to get the groceries where they're suppose to go, to see that the eggs aren't broken, to get them there on time. I think the responsibility of the writer is to get the goods there, to see that they aren't rotten, that he hasn't spoiled anything, and to get it there on time. That's his basic responsibility. From there on it's up to the individual writer. If someone decides that he just wants to write articles about a certain subject, that's his privilege; then he can decide whether he wants to be the best in that field or whether he wants to be tenth best. If someone wants to write books he can decide whether or not he wants to write garbage, or medium quality, or prestige books. Whatever he decides to do has equal validity. But then he must decide if he wants to write the best prestige books or just crummy little prestige books, or the best garbage in the world or the worst.

I'm afraid that people tend to think that just because we're artists we have some kind of ultra-super responsibility, like the President of the United States. I don't think this is true. The President has responsibilities because he was elected by a majority of people who put trust in him; he's the one who says whether or not we're going to get into a war, whether or not we're going to have a depression. The people who voted have given him the power to speak for them.

But a writer is an individual. That's why we're writers and don't have routine jobs. As individuals, why the hell should we have any responsibility to do anything except what we want to do?

"... we evolved from a literary magazine to one which was intensely involved and began to awaken to some of the enormous social issues that plague the United States today—the big issue, of course, being racism."

Edward Keating

Edward Keating

KEATING: I was born in New York City in 1925, raised in New Jersey until 1940, when my family moved out to the Coast. I went to Stanford, took three years out to be in the Navy, and came back to the university, where I met my wife. I graduated in 1950 and practiced law for several years and found that I didn't care for it, so I went into business. In 1954 I came into the Catholic Church. I had been raised a nominal Protestant — my father was a great admirer of Harry Emerson Fosdick. A very neutral sort of thing. My wife was Catholic, but what is known in the trade as a "bad" or "lapsed" Catholic.

After two of our children were born and baptized into the Catholic Church, the local priest said to my wife, "Come on, Helen, it's about time," and she came back. I've been asked many times about my conversion to Catholicism, and the only answer I can give is to turn to the person and say, "Are you married?" The man generally says, "Yes," and I say, "Well, why did you marry your wife?" These things are equally unexplainable, so it's impossible to ascertain the "why." I suspect it has something to do with grace; I don't know. At any rate, after I came into the Church I was still in business, but I taught at the University of Santa Clara for a year, which was an interesting experience — my first intimate relationship with the Jesuits. While I was there I got to know the Catholic publishing field, and I didn't think much of it.

In 1960 and 1961 the Catholic press was raising two questions: Where is the Catholic intellectual and where is the Catholic writer? Well, I was convinced they were on the scene, all right, but lacked a decent platform. Also, since most of the publishing in the Catholic community is done under clerical auspices, therefore subject to censorship, these people were not given freedom.

Take Ireland. When you realize that men like Frank O'Connor are censored, you get some idea of the problem. I would say that one of the great deterrents to creativity has been the suspiciousness on the part of what I call the "corporate structure" (the governing body of the Church) that creativity is a dangerous thing. It must be stifled because one never knows what's going to come out of it. As a matter of fact, it wasn't until just a few years ago that a young seminarian in one of our local seminaries could indulge in creative writing or anything similar, because that sort of thing was an act of pride. They are, fortunately, loosening up now on that score.

I decided to enter the field of Catholic publishing and the best way to describe the development of *Ramparts* is that, like Topsy, it just done growed. The original concept was to make it a Catholic literary quarterly. Unfortunately, there was a stigma attached to being a quarterly, so we became a fifthly, if you can imagine such a thing. And I did learn, very early in the game, that if I had to rely on nothing but Catholic writers, I would close down within two issues. There are some good Catholic writers, of course, but not enough to fill every issue of *Ramparts.*

Through getting to know men like Robert McAfee Brown, who is a Protestant minister acting as an observer at Rome in the second session of the Ecumenical Council, I began to walk, in effect, out of the Catholic intellectual ghetto. I don't think many people, even Catholics, realize how restrictive this ghetto is. We have over 120 diocesan newspapers published regularly in this country, the publishers of which are the local bishops. We have over 400 regularly published magazines – 90 percent of which nobody outside the Catholic community has ever heard of. Many of them are devotional and supporters of cults and societies. A few make a pretense at being what you might call a real magazine, but even most of those are pretty sad imitations of the real thing. There are also hundreds and hundreds of books published each year that are graced with the imprimatur, and therefore safe; Catholics can buy them and feel they're getting the true word. The reason I say this rather sarcastically is that when I converted to Catholicism I went way down into the ghetto and shopped at a Catholic bookstore and felt doubly secure when I saw the imprimatur. Incidentally, the owner of the bookstore told me that quite often the general publisher will put out two editions of a book, the only difference being that those copies headed for the Catholic bookstore will bear the imprimatur. A legitimate one, incidentally. But the general bookstore or the Protestant bookstore doesn't want it. I think the most important thing about *Ramparts* is that we have never had, nor will we ever have, an express or implied imprimatur. As a matter of fact, if the hierarchy had its way we'd be closed down.

Let me go into a brief outline of the evolution of *Ramparts.* As I said, it started as a fifthly, in the cultural and intellectual areas of interest: not particularly "Catholic" in the sense of religious limitation (one of the great problems faced by most Catholic publishing ventures, who have an odd sort of awe, a feeling that all roads lead to Rome, an attitude that Protestants can be decent fellows, but nevertheless) that sort of thing. They try to show, not only in terms of theology and philosophy, but in terms of culture, that that which is Catholic is doubly-blessed, doubly-better; and their creative writing is actually nothing but thinly-veiled sermons on deathbed conversions or why it's so marvelous to be a Roman Catholic. Clutching one's rosary beads, nuns teaching the roughneck boys how to play a good baseball game, the Loretta Young kick. This sort of nonsense. If a person isn't at all critical it gives them a wonderful sense of being very special, not only on the religious level, but in every other way. It's a very shabby business because it's so inferior.

It's interesting to note—and I think this is a direct consequence of the Catholic ghetto mentality—that the American "who's who" of literature is a list of ex-Catholics: Hemingway, Dreiser, O'Hara, James Farrell. Ireland's James Joyce. (People think that Synge and Carroll were Catholic because they were Irish, but they weren't. And O'Casey's not a Catholic, never was.) But after getting to know men like John Howard Griffin, Fielder, and Fowlie—liberated men, some of whom were Catholic—we evolved from a literary magazine to one which was intensely involved and began to awaken to some of the enormous social issues that plague the United States today—the big issue, of course, being racism. At times we have devoted almost entire issues to the subject, including one we put out on Mississippi, built on an eyewitness account of the murder of three civil rights workers. And we have published Thomas Merton's magnificent piece, "Black Revolution Led Us to a White Liberal." (This letter was addressed to me; I had conceived the idea of an exchange of letters between Merton and James Baldwin, and Merton was immediately excited by the idea, but I didn't get in touch directly with Baldwin. Baldwin's agent thought it was a good idea, but Birmingham exploded, and things somehow got sidetracked.) Anyway, Tom Merton wrote his piece as a massive letter. And you know, you discover that society and man are of a piece; if things are wrong in one community, one segment of society, you generally find that things are wrong in other segments of society, too. But as I said, I was raised outside the Church, then went into the Church, and I am still in the Church, but I am no longer in the Catholic cultural and intellectual ghetto.

N: *Could you define the Catholic ghetto in your own frame of reference?*

KEATING: The Catholic ghetto is of two types. One is, quite literally, a geographic one, clustered around the church building, the parish, the school. The old neighborhood-school principle. You want to be near your church, so you tend to gravitate to the proximity of church and school. But this is the minor ghetto.

The primary Catholic ghetto I refer to in my book, *The Scandal of Silence*, is essentially a state of mind: a highly-regimented state of mind, very subtly inculcated through the parochial school experience and through social activity. For example, before I became a Catholic, and before my wife went back to the Church, we had the world's worst time finding Catholics to be sponsors at the baptism of my first son. It took my wife's ancient aunt, and some person I didn't even know, living down in Southern California, to turn the trick. Then, four or five years ago, I suddenly realized that all of our friends were Catholic. The people we went with to cocktail parties, the people we had over for dinner — all were Catholic. Not that we're anti-Protestant or anti-Jewish in any way; it's just that there are all the institutions at hand to place you firmly in a Catholic environment.

For instance, once a year, through the bishop, everybody is solicited at mass to subscribe to the local diocesan newspaper. There is a proliferation of organizations involved in fund-raising projects for the Church. There are Catholic Boy Scouts, a Catholic All-American football team, Catholic athletic leagues all over the country. There is a Catholic Press Association. And the entire Catholic school system perpetuates the ghetto — particularly the mentality of the ghetto, or the ghetto of the mentality, whichever way it fits best.

Primitive math is still taught like this: "If John says five Hail Marys and Judy says three Hail Marys, how many Hail Marys did they say together?" That teaches you how to add. Then, of course, there is the practice of nuns teaching the children, frankly indoctrinating them into what I call the Catholic mentality. I haven't been through the Catholic school system, but my children have, and associates of mine at the magazine have. And the daily little — what I can only call — "atrocity tales" are continuous. It's like the endless beads of the rosary. My wife has forbidden my children to relate these stories to me anymore because I get so damned mad.

I'll tell you a few of them. They had the practice of encouraging good little boys and good little girls to go to mass every morning before school. So, in class, all those good little boys and good little girls who went to mass that morning put up their hands. Those who didn't put up their hands were embarrassed. (Some of the masses the children attended regularly were masses for the basketball team.) Then there's a form of competitive spirituality. They have a crèche during the Christmas season with baby Jesus in it, and about thirty-five little lambs, each with a child's name on it. The child who went to mass that morning and said a novena or made some sort of extra sacrifice or did something extra-devotional has his little lamb placed closer to Jesus. By the time Christmas comes, he whose lamb is closest to Jesus is really *the* chosen one. And there is this other barbarism: the buying of pagan babies. It used to be done the way war stamps were sold—fill a book, you know, and get a bond. A pagan baby used to cost five dollars and, if a child got an allowance, he'd save, say, ten cents a week and when he'd saved his five dollars it went to the missionaries in Africa or Asia where they hooked some kid by the scruff of the neck and baptized him and gave him the donor's name. If you want verification of this sort of thing I would recommend reading certain Catholic magazines: *St. Anthony's Messenger*, *Extension*, *Ave Maria*, etc. They are abominable, but they pass for culture, and you don't realize how many Catholics subscribe to these things.

N: *Does a large portion of the Catholic population of the U.S. fall into this control pattern?*

KEATING: It isn't something that is specifically entered into. As I said before, the Catholic ghetto is a way of life, a perspective one acquires. I've known highly commendable Catholics, clerical and lay, who drop little things in conversation that make it clear how they feel about Protestants. There is a conceit and, as I say in my book, I think they protest too much, and I think that by protesting too much they reveal a basic uncertainty underneath it all.

The whole process of education is at the root of it. The statement of answers without questions. I understand you went to a Jesuit school— you can fill in a certain section of this, yourself.

In *America* magazine, a number of years ago, appeared an article by a Jesuit on fallout shelter morality. He did a beautiful job, through syllogistic reasoning, to explain why it would be perfectly all right, in defense of your space in your fallout shelter, to shoot your neighbor's child. I'm sorry; it won't wash. You could shoot this child?

N: *I remember that; it caused quite a fuss.*

KEATING: You're damned right it caused a fuss, and it should have. But these fellows can somehow comfort themselves and assure themselves that they're intellectually right, and this is where something is wrong. I think this is where the Church has gotten itself into bad trouble: why it's in the mess it's in now, the mess it has been in for over four hundred years. Somehow they managed to compartmentalize man into the rational man who is (at best) a theoretical being, and the living man, who is the living and suffering man.

Now, can you rationalize love? Can you quantify it? In seminary teaching I think they've got something like twenty-four categories of charity, with the obvious corollary that if a particular instance of potential charity doesn't fit one of those twenty-four categories it cannot be called charity. How can you quantify that which is qualitative? Yet, up here in the mind, they try to do something which creates a complete divorce from reality.

This is what the Catholic intellectual and cultural ghetto is.

N: *In your book,* The Scandal of Silence, *you bring out the fact that there seems to be an intellectual front in the Catholic Church today, which is demanding — or at least asking — that the Church modify certain positions and stands it takes. Did I misread or misinterpret?*

KEATING: No, you didn't, and I like the way you phrase it. You said "demand," and then softened the word to "ask." This is significant, because the popular image of the Church, historically and factually, has been one of rigid authoritarianism, and in such a structure one does not demand, one asks — generally as a supplicant, because of the power with which one is confronted.

I think "demand" is now the appropriate word. There is a tremendous ferment going on inside the Church, but its rumblings are very seldom heard outside of the Catholic community. Even within the Catholic community it is generally conducted behind closed doors, limited to select groups, because of the power of censorship and the career-destroying tendencies of power politics. I'm one of the few voices that can be heard without censorship. A high percentage of the things I say and the things I write actually originate with nuns and priests who can't talk, simply because they can't voice their thoughts and opinions.

I'm considered by some to be a radical. Here, I mean, within the social spectrum. I'm nothing of a radical compared to some of the Catholics I talk to, but they simply cannot speak — they'd be destroyed. And the Church has all the ways and means of destroying them.

The point is that there is this ferment and it's deep and impassioned, but don't be misled: it is not involved with a large segment of the Church. It is very, very small in terms of numbers and in terms of influence.

The question is, "Will the Vatican Council come out with what we consider to be a significant statement?" And I suggest that we defer discussion of the Vatican Council until after the fourth session. Then we defer discussion of the future of the Church until about ten years afterward, to see whether or not the stuff is passed and if it is implemented in reality — not just legislation on the books, like in the Reconstruction states after the Civil War.

The four pivotal issues in this fourth session are these: first, the statement on the Jews which I would like to see them scrap. This is the most presumptuous statement the Catholic Church has tentatively planned to promulgate in a long, long time. Pope John said, in essence, "Look, we've been guilty of anti-Semitism for two thousand years and it's about time we ended it." That's what he intended. So what happens: the computer mentality of the old cardinals got hold of it and, with one eye on the Arab states and another on the Jewish population of this country, they came out with the most coldly judicial statement in the world. They should have come out with a very simple statement: "We have been guilty of anti-Semitism for two thousand years. Forgive us." Not, "We're going to absolve you."

Secondly, religious liberty. This is extremely significant because what's good for the goose is good for the gander and, if the Church comes out and says something about religious liberty, it not only affects you cats, you see. The primacy of conscience is reinserted in the Catholic Church. Under canon law it's there but never promulgated. It's what Holy Mother Church says, regardless of your conscience. This is heresy.

The third, thermonuclear war.

The fourth, artificial birth control. And, incidentally, we'll get all four of them or we won't get any of them, except watered-down versions that would be meaningless. If these things go through, the ferment latent in many Catholics will come into being, and we will see one of the most exciting periods in the history of the Church. It will be like a man who's been held down by a press, suddenly springing up onto his feet. Potentially, this is a very exciting thing. On the other hand, we have Pope Paul. Somebody said that John opened the windows and the windows can never be completely closed again. This is not true in an authoritarian organization. Incidentally, if they do pass the religious liberty resolution, and it has teeth in it, the Catholic Church is going to lose its authoritarian power over the people and the superstitions that go with it; it will have to lead through love and not fear. Because of the legalistic approach to life in the Catholic Church, the Catholic who eats meat on Friday or misses mass on Sunday is committing a far more serious sin than the sin of racism or the sin of sharp business practice. I feel strongly about this because of my own experience in the Church and the experiences of hundreds of Catholics I've talked to over the years. Instead of the church of love, which it was destined to be, it is the church of legalism. Trying to see how close you can come to sin without actually sinning.

This, in turn, develops a morbidity of guilt.

Let's talk about sex. Now, we don't practice artificial birth control in the Catholic Church, but the fact is that a large percentage of Catholics do. One of the hallmarks of being a Catholic is having a large family.

But if there's one thing Catholics are really hung up on, it's sex. I remember a book on homosexuality written by a Catholic priest in England; he purported to write a scientific work, and in the introduction, before the subject had even been explored, a moral judgment was made. This is where you have a prior conclusion that must be reached. And everything will be twisted to reach that point.

Catholics have that problem. Prior conclusions that have to be reached, then the morbid guilt, then the thing called scrupulosity: "Have I made a good confession? If I haven't, I must go back to the confessional again before I can receive Holy Communion."

What's missing is the joy of life. Imperfect as it is, painful as it is, the very fact of being is the most exciting thing in the world and we're here by the grace of God and we should take great joy in that fact—but we don't. We spend half of our lifetime lining up at the confessional, most of the time confessing things that are absolutely inane. "I have said something uncharitable about my neighbor," or "I ate meat on Friday," or "I missed mass." Never for once thinking of the horrendous sins we commit every day when we make some snide remark about a "Yid" or a "Nigger" or drop bombs on women and children.

We have segregated dioceses in the South where Negroes have to go to one church, whites to another. We have segregated parochial schools. And in those communities in the South where they have a so-called integrated church, the Negroes sit in one set of pews, the whites in another. The whites go up to the communion rail to receive Christ, then the Negroes can go up. And if that Negro goes up before he's supposed to, he'll be passed up at the communion rail.

Yet they're hung up on this matter of meat on Friday. Incidentally, I had meat this morning, a Friday morning, for breakfast. I forgot the day and had sausage. I know Catholics who would get absolutely hung up on this. It's so phony. The average Catholic would go to the confessional and confess, knowing damned well that he hadn't done anything wrong, just so he could go in there and appear to be a good Catholic. Priests have told me they get so tired of this nonsense they feel nauseated by these people. Yet, in a perverse way, they like people toadying up to them. Father knows everything, you know, whether it's a political issue, a baseball score, or whether or not you should read *Ramparts*.

Incidentally, the answer to that last question depends upon the individual priest.

N: *In some parishes isn't the matter of artificial birth control now up to the individual priest?*

KEATING: And it's none of his damned business, if you want to know the truth. This is based on theology. A great debate is going on in the Church regarding this matter. Anything involving what we call faith and morals that is caught up in doubt and confusion and debate is left up to the individual conscience. Nobody knows for sure, so it is up to the individual conscience, not to the individual priest. The point is this: the priest cannot form the conscience of another person, just as I cannot form the conscience of another person.

Now, I'm not referring to matters of confession; I'm talking only about the "conscience which doth make cowards of us all," but it is the one thing I have that is mine, given to me by God, and it is a most precious thing. This is why canon law says that if a superior gives an order that is against your conscience, that order must not be obeyed. Conscience I'm referring to—not whim or caprice. And when they try to take our consciences away from us, the Church becomes sterile.

N: *The final question: Could you explain your objectives, as found both in your book and in the publication of* Ramparts?

KEATING: The answer is very simple. An old children's story about "The Emperor's Clothes." The tailors made clothes for the emperor, or presumed to, but there were no clothes, so the emperor appeared naked. But all the courtiers and bystanders, knowing he was their ruler, admired his clothes until one child came along and pointed out the truth: that the emperor was as naked as a jaybird.

The point is this. If the emperor went around long enough without any clothes on, he would catch pneumonia and die. So when the child points out the fact that he hasn't any clothes on he'll put some on, if he's wise. He'll stop paying attention to the phony adulation and hypocrisy of the people standing around. (Privately I know priests and nuns who agree; publicly, none.)

The charade continues.

I use the word "Scandal" in the title of my book not in the popular sense, as it's used today, but in its more theological sense. This scandal does harm to the Church. By being silent you do harm to the Church, just as speaking out can cause another form of scandal. It's like a lot of people having ideas and thinking and suffering and living, but never saying something they want desperately to say. Then somebody says it and others get courage to say it. We have failed miserably in many areas of the Church. We have something to offer and we're not offering it to the world or to ourselves.

And I'm trying to get us to do this.

Note: Since this interview was recorded, the magazine Ramparts *has ceased to be a Roman Catholic periodical of liberal persuasion and has become a protest publication sans religious affiliation. The change is not a drastic one, since the primary topics to which* Ramparts *has always been devoted — civil rights, the war in Vietnam, and the threat posed by ultraconservatives of the right wing — continue to dominate the contents.*

"I simply want to write good books. It isn't that I'm naïve, that I'm trying to divorce myself from the racial struggle, but I don't think it should enter into my art in such a way that my writing becomes propagandistic. I want my books to have reason to exist."

William Melvin Kelley

William Melvin Kelley

KELLEY: I'm a New York City boy, and I think you can hear it. Born 1937, attended a private school, went on to Harvard. I was in the class of 1960, but never finished—I have only a half year to go.

I started to write—honestly—because I was looking for something that would give me as much satisfaction as the shot-put. I mean that. I haven't the real physical attributes to be able to shot-put well, but I decided to do it, worked very hard at it, and finally broke the record at my high school. This was the first time I ever worked hard at something, and in this case the rewards were internal rather than external because nobody comes out to watch a high school shot-putter. They watch football and baseball and track, but nobody comes out to cheer the shot-putter. But it did force me to internalize my goals, and gave me great satisfaction.

At Harvard I majored in four things—economics, architecture, government, and English. I tried some painting, some acting. I began to write just before I got to English, which was a shame; a writer reads books quite differently than other readers, but I've tried to bridge the gaps. I discovered, as soon as I began to write, that it made me so happy I wasn't going to do anything else, and I haven't. I've been very lucky that way.

In June, 1962, I finished my first book, *A Different Drummer*, which came out the next year. Then a book of short stories—I finally put enough of them together to make a book. In 1965, my second novel, *A Drop of Patience*.

A Drop of Patience has an interesting genesis. It goes back to the first teacher I had when I began to write—a writer named John Hawkes, nominated for the National Book Award for his novel, *Second Skin*. Unlike most writing teachers, Hawkes used to say to us—to me, especially—"Don't write about what you know; make it all up." He believed that if you created fiction almost entirely out of your imagination you could manipulate it and control it much better. I think that what is missing from a great deal of modern fiction is this matter of writer-control.

Anyway, I became interested in jazz musicians. I'd been thinking very much about the death of Clifford Brown, a jazz trumpeter who was killed in an automobile accident. That was probably when I decided that I wanted to write something about the jazz musician. That particular accident affected a great many lives, because Bud Towles' brother was also in the accident. I decided it was about time a Negro wrote a really good novel about a jazz musician, but as I went along I began to put more and more things into it. I decided that I would use no visual imagery—this is something most of the reviewers have not caught. I try to do some type of technical "trick" with each novel because I feel that it makes me stretch. I don't want to write the same book over and over again. I used only the four senses, and told the story that way. I also decided, arbitrarily, that I would not use the verb "to hear," but I broke down and used it five times. You see, since I was going to rely so heavily upon sound, I was afraid that if I began to use the verb "to hear" I would end up using it a million times, and I didn't want to clutter up the story with all those repetitions. I also got very interested in the idea of a Negro who had no concept of color. A blind man would have no concept of color, naturally, but a Negro without one...!

I suppose that certain characters in the novel are drawn from people I know, but in terms of the central character, Ludlow Washington, I had no particular jazz musician in mind, but a great many great ones in mind, ranging from Bessie Smith to Lester Young to Charlie Parker and, of course, Ray Charles, because he was blind. But I don't think anyone should read a book and say, "I wonder who this is?" I think fiction should create its own world, and my heroes in fiction—John Hawkes, Nathanael West, Emily Brontë included—are all people who have managed to created their own world in fiction. It doesn't amount to plugging, either—this kind of car, that brand of cigarette, this make of suit, and all. I don't want my fiction to be dated. I don't want it to be tied to the time. This is very difficult for me because most reviewers see my Negro face on the jacket and say, "Aha! Negro problem!" I want my stuff to be able to be read by anyone in the world, to be read a thousand years from now; if it's too much within the confines of any current problem, it's not going to last. And I want it to last. Of course, it must have a great deal to do with the current problem, but I hope it is in terms of the universals rather than the particulars. I don't think that I have too many specific objectives as a novelist beyond the fact that I want to continue to stretch myself. I want to bring new things to the novel if I possibly can. I have seen my novels get more and more experimental as I've gone along. Not for the sake of experiment, but for the sake of dimension.

Another thing I'm doing is tying things together. *A Different Drummer* has some characters in it that are connected to people in short stories; the wife of the central character in *A Different Drummer* appears in *A Drop of Patience* as a baby, the daughter of Ludlow Washington. Perhaps I'm trying to follow the Faulknerian pattern — although I guess it's really Balzacian when you connect everything. I'd like to be eighty years old and look up at the shelf and see that all of my books are really one big book.

I'll change, of course. There are things I see in *A Drop of Patience* I would already like to rewrite. I won't bother; I'll just write another book.

N: *You mentioned the reviewer who sees your Negro face on the jacket and assumes the novel will be about racial problems. What is your consciousness, as a writer, of the Negro problem?*

KELLEY: I'm not conscious of the problem as I write. I simply want to try to write good books. It isn't that I'm naïve, that I'm trying to divorce myself from the racial struggle, but I don't think it should enter into my art in such a way that my writing becomes propagandistic. If my novels are so strongly tied to the times the book would have no reason to live once the present struggles are over — if, indeed, they ever will be over. I want my books to have reason to exist.

I frankly think that half the reason for the existence of what I call the Negro literary ghetto is the attitude of white reviewers. *A Drop of Patience* was reviewed in *Newsweek*. It was a fairly good review, and I'm not complaining about it, but I didn't think it was quite right for *Newsweek* to take an African writer, a West Indian writer, and two American Negro writers, lump them together and treat them sociologically. The matter of art is superseded.

The other half of the reason for the Negro literary ghetto seems to involve the Negro public. If Negroes judge fiction only on the basis of whether or not the writer makes a strong statement to The Man, or whether or not he tells about things as they are, that becomes a disservice to Negro writers, too. I frankly do not want to be compared exclusively to Negro writers. A comparable situation would exist if Saul Bellow, Philip Roth, and Bernard Malamud were lumped together and treated exclusively as Jews. I think it would be a great disservice to them. A writer is such an individual. I can't even speak for the Negro writer. I don't know how many of the Negro writers feel. I prefer to stay to myself and write as much as I can. This is my individual view of the world. This view is colored, of course, by my Negro experience here in the United States. My skin, all the things that flesh is heir to, especially brown flesh, gives you a certain set of experiences. But it is up to the individual to make these experiences his own individual work of art, not a reflection of generalities. Who speaks for the Negro? Nobody does.

When I was working as a newspaperman I used to interview Negroes about various problems. Each one had something different to say, and I think both white and Negro people do a great disservice by categorically saying, "Well, they all feel like this . . ." because they don't. Maybe they should, but they don't.

I think we must understand that James Baldwin speaks for himself, and Ralph Ellison, and me, and any Negro writer you name. That's the point; nobody speaks for all Negroes

I would like to get some things straight, however. I'm terribly angry about many things. I'm angry about our policy in Vietnam, I'm angry about our policy concerning Cuba, I'm angry about our huge load of poverty. I think they are connected. And I was a great admirer of Malcolm X. These are my *personal* feelings. I can't say that people all over the country feel the same way I do.

The racial problems — to a great extent you have to blame them on the white people of this country. They had a stereotype of the Negro — all Negroes were lazy, shiftless, undependable, etc. Now they *want* to feel that all Negroes are this way; it helps to keep them from admitting the possibility that Negroes are human beings, each Negro a different human being. They want to lump them together as Negroes. Now, Negroes have not put James Baldwin on the cover of *Time*. White people have — because they want to listen to him. Unfortunately, a great many whites in this country want to believe that most Negroes are homosexuals because that is a convenient way to deal with them. You don't have to face them as men. You don't have to worry about whether one of them wants to marry your daughter because he obviously doesn't. But you have to watch out for your son.

I don't want to diminish Baldwin's achievements. I think he's a lousy novelist, and I would tell him that. As an essayist, however, I think he's the greatest in this country. He's no playwright. But he has done a great deal, and I think the earlier essays, when he spoke as James Baldwin, senior citizen, bringing something to the attention of America, are superb.

I also think that to a certain extent American society controls people — especially people who are in some kind of rebellion. They choose their leaders for them, they say who speaks for the Negro. They choose a Baldwin, or another man, and say, "He is the leader and I will concern myself with him and no one else." It's a very effective way to control people and situations.

This not only happens to Negroes, it happens to many types of people, many groups. There's a question of whether or not George Meany speaks for the laborer, the rank and file of laborers.

To get back to the Negro, I think that the middle class has been effectively cut off from the lower classes by giving them an investment in the American system as it exists today. I have an uncle who, can I say, "benefited from?" segregation in the South because he had a taxi service, and his taxis would pick up only Negroes. There were five taxi companies in this town, but the other four were all white cab services, so he had a monopoly of the Negro market. Under integration he would be in competition with the other cab companies. Naturally, he will stand against integration to some extent; this has happened in many, many other areas. I don't know if this is relevant, but it's part of the problem.

Another, just another, reason why no one person speaks for the Negro, and no one should assume that one person speaks for us.

N: *In surveying the American scene in general, perhaps with specific impressions of the arts, what are the things that impress you most — favorably and unfavorably?*

KELLEY: I'm full of impressions. Negative ones, at that. First of all, there is this terrible development in the art world of pop art and op art. There's the cult of the seventeen-year-old virginal girl — thirty-five-year-old women dressing like seventeen-year-olds. I like women. But the people who rule the fashion industry don't want to deal with women — it's easier to cope with the virginal seventeen-year-old. The new man is rather a mess, too. The man who selects his perfumes with care, buys unguents for the skin, wears his hair tossibly long. And tosses it.

Things I like — Malamud, especially in short stories. J. D. Salinger, sitting up there wherever he sits, has never knuckled under, never written anything people would want him to write. Never sold his novels to the movies. Perhaps what is happening to the arts in America is the by-product of the publishers' discovery that you can write down to people instead of writing up to them. Salinger, thank God, stands aside.

Publishing — look at it this way. To me, the greatest innovations of the novel are short, running from fifty to two hundred and fifty pages. Faulkner wrote naturally in a form which ran between fifty and seventy-five pages, Hemingway's novels were never too long. Look at the really great short novels — *Heart of Darkness, Secret Sharer, Turn of the Screw, Gatsby.* The fact is, it is no longer economical to publish a short novel. A publisher can't produce any novel for under a certain given price, but the more pages he adds, the more he can charge. His costs don't go up nearly as fast as the price. For example, if I write a novel two hundred pages long, it can't be sold for less than $4.50, but if it's a hundred pages long, it can't be sold for much less. Let's say costs are a minimum of three dollars. A seven-hundred page novel probably boosts costs to $4.00, but they can charge $7.50 for the book. I think that publishers very often encourage writers to produce long novels. And if the writer turns out a seven-hundred page novel, and works on it for a year, he can't have real control over the fiction; he can't pay the attention he should to prose rhythm, the close attention to the words that Hemingway or even Faulkner did. Thus I think that we are developing what can't be called a non-book or a non-novel, but a big, sloppy novel with lots of plots, lots of characters, but very little artistry. Such novels do not make any revelations of the human being, the way he lives and thinks; they skim over life at a superficial level.

It is my belief that the novel should educate men's hearts. Ever since time began we've been educating our minds — the caveman first used his fist, then found out he could make a hammer, then a hatchet; the cavewoman began to wash her clothes by beating them on rocks, and today's woman has an automatic washing machine. But our emotional education is far behind. We haven't begun to learn how to cope with our technological innovations. I think it's the role of the artist to begin educating the hearts of people, which means that he must reveal things that human beings have never been exposed to in the novel, before. I try to do this a little in *A Drop of Patience*. The first chapter is very traumatic, and I wrote it so that the reader will have a bit of sympathy for Ludlow no matter what happens to him afterward. He will realize that this kid has gone through something, at the age of five, that nothing will ever smooth over. No matter how embittered he gets, *this* has happened to him, and the reader understands.

I also like to create a character as a villain, and show something about him which will arouse sympathy. I tell my kids that it is very easy to have sympathy for a boy and his dog, and if the dog is killed by a wolf, everyone will cry. The really great writer is the one who can make you feel sympathy for the wolf, because the wolf has somehow been put into the position where he has to kill the dog. This is what writers are not doing. They merely reinforce our prejudices, back up the things we believe in, when they should be revealing new things. Very few writers in America even attempt to do so. Mailer tries, but he doesn't succeed very well. You never know about Salinger. But he's a great craftsman, and you can never give up on him; there's no telling what a man, as young as he is, with his talent, will be able to do; he's got a lot of time.

I haven't much hope for a writer who hasn't developed a craft in writing by the age of fifty. This may be the trouble; we don't think of it as a craft. America en masse, being basically anti-intellectual doesn't like to think that it takes any special sort of talent to be a writer. Most of our writers have come to us out of something else—trauma, you know. Someone feels something, has something terrible happen to them, and sits down to write a novel about it. The novel may be good, but then he writes a second novel.

This is a catastrophe. He has no more idea of what goes into the making of the novel than (to quote Mencken) an archbishop knows about religion. He just doesn't know. Why is it that most of the great novels by American writers are written by these writers when they're young—and then these writers peter out? I think the answer is the fact that the American writer very often has no idea of what goes into the making of good fiction, the elements of craft—the tricks, if you want to call them that. Conversely, a great European novelist is able to write better and better novels as he grows older. But in Europe a man will school himself to be a writer; he will read and study the worthwhile writings, and consciously acquire the crafts of writing. Hemingway, whose education as a writer was basically European, produced well-written novels that hung together as novels. He may not always have had good ideas, and he wasn't particularly bright. (If I had a problem I would rather take it to Faulkner than Hemingway.) But Hemingway knew the craft of writing, and he could always write at a dependable level.

I don't think it relates necessarily to the writer's growth as a person —it's the matter of craft. I don't think Hemingway grew as a person; he suffered the trauma of his father's suicide, and he never grew beyond that. But he did grow in his knowledge of fiction, his sense of prose rhythm, the knowledge of what words could do. His style continued to develop; I think *The Moveable Feast* proves that. At the end of his life he could write a book with the same sort of precision and clarity with which he could write at the beginning.

It's a matter of craft. A doctor has to go to school to learn about this muscle and that ventricle and all; a plumber has to learn about pipes and water pressure. But what does the American writer think he has to do? The concept, here, of the writer, is of a guy with a bottle in one hand and a pen in the other who sits down and writes through the night and comes up with The Great American Novel. It's not so. *A Drop of Patience* is 237 pages long and it took me two years to write it. This means I was in there doing something. Trying to get the prose right, the text, each nuance of thought and characterization and movement. In two years most American writers would have turned out at least five hundred pages. I think the writer can control the short novel because every word means something. Most American writers seem to have forgotten that fact.

When you read *Heart of Darkness*, which I've just finished teaching, you realize that this novel is one hundred pages long and that every word in it is a conscious choice. Now, Conrad couldn't speak English until he was twenty-one years old, and perhaps he came to the language with the intelligent precision of Nabokov, perhaps when one *learns* the language correctly that way. (I still use Bronx colloquialisms in my writing that I don't catch.) But I do think that American writers can learn a great deal about the English language by reading Conrad. He didn't pour out torrents of words for no discernible purpose.

It's interesting to note that Hemingway wrote only six hundred words a day, no more, no less. If he was going fishing the next day he would write twelve hundred so that he wouldn't lose the day. Robert Graves writes only three hundred words every day. I haven't been this disciplined, since I miss some days and then follow up by writing in a torrent, but I do try to give words a tight control.

How much American fiction can be read aloud? A writer like Agee can be—"We are talking now about summer nights in Knoxville, Tennessee, and the time that I lived there so successfully disguised to myself as a child." Beautiful words, by a man who knew something about words. But would you like to read Herman Wouk aloud for prose rhythm? I can't take everything away from him, because he and his type often have something that serious writers miss; they know how to tell a story.

Something has happened to American writing which has separated it into two distinct types of writing. We have the serious, highbrow writer who produces quality but has no idea of how to tell a story. And we have the middlebrow writer who has no idea of how to write in terms of the craft and the prose itself. But when we look at writers like Hemingway, Faulkner, Fitzgerald or Nathanael West, then reach further back to Dickens and Emily Brontë, we find that the stories are good and the writing is good, too.

Perhaps this schism occurred when publishers began to realize that people no longer wanted to educate themselves to read good books. They could pander. In Dickens' time the reading public educated itself so that it would be able to read Dickens; of course, no one cared whether the people at the lower social levels read or not. I do think publishers realize that all that has to be done to sell one hundred thousand copies of a book is to keep that book simple; people who are ignorant will eat it up.

I think this goes back to the educational system — to the fact that we don't pay our teachers enough and overwork them. And perhaps Shaw was right to some extent — a great many people consider teaching better than working in a post office, so they go into teaching. It shouldn't be that way. In our society the teacher is an important person, and he should be paid on a scale that reflects his importance. But the greatest compliment anyone can pay you is to say, "Hey, you're too smart to be a teacher." Or, "Why are you teaching? You could be in industry!" That's a terrible situation. Our kids are going to decide upon whether or not we survive as a nation; they're our most important investment, so we put the money into a World's Fair. Crosstown bussing isn't the real issue in education; the issue is good education for everyone, but somebody has to fight to get new books into the school, and fight to raise teachers' salaries. What kind of system is this? Then we have the presumption, the gall, to feel that we are smarter than everyone. We look with shock at the Russians and say, "How come they got that thing up there so fast?" It's because they're spending millions on education, and honoring the educational system.

I spent a year in Italy. A teacher in Italy is called, with respect, "professor." A teacher is respected. He is an important person in the society.

Here a teacher is some sort of a kook if he likes what he is doing. I think our work-play concept is at the evil heart of the matter. In America there is either work or play. Play is what you want to do, and work is what you have to do. Someone said to Humphrey, "You enjoy your work so much, you shouldn't be paid for it." What a puerile attitude. We should enjoy our work; it's the only way we do good work. I enjoy my work, and I think it has a great deal to do with how I am as a person. If I enjoy my work, then I have a good life.

Now, it seems as though I've criticized everyone and everything. But it seems to me that the writer's job is to raise questions and to criticize in a constructive way. If pushed farther, I'll criticize Mao, Johnson, Wallace, Bellow, everyone. I think this is my role. And I don't feel that, as a Negro, I have the right to criticize American society without turning around to criticize the whole Negro movement. I'm not ever going to give up my right to speak. Prevalent now among Negroes is the feeling that we must have unity, unity, unity, at all costs. I don't think this is true. I think there are things that are wrong with the way the civil rights struggle is going, things wrong with American foreign policy, things wrong with China's foreign policy, and I think my job is to be able to criticize whatever I feel is wrong, to remain free. Without this freedom one cannot be a writer, much less a person.

"My advice to the young writer is this: Write for the reader, not for the critic. Write a damned good story and pray that it means something more than a good story. Trust yourself . . . accept the influence of people who really have something to say to you. Live, grow, be a *mensch*. That's all I can say."

Robert R. Kirsch

Robert R. Kirsch

KIRSCH: I was born and brought up at Coney Island, and was graduated from high school in 1939, at the tail end of the Depression when it was virtually impossible to get any sort of decent work. I didn't want to go to college in New York. In fact, I didn't like any part of New York with the exception of Coney Island, which was a very isolated town with an identity all its own, totally different from the popular image of the crowded, garish little strip along Surf Avenue, the board-walk, and the beach. The interior of the town was virtually a microcosm of this country. At the very tip a place called Sea Gate had fences and guards at the gates; very wealthy people lived there. Middle-class people also lived in Coney Island, and there were large communities of Jews, Italians, Irish, and at that time Negroes were beginning to move in. We had what you might call "horizontal segregation." In the three-family houses the Negroes would invariably have the basement flat and Jews would live on the first and second floors, yet there was no particular sense of conflict between Jews and Negroes. I don't know why I go into this, except for the fact that I have always been fascinated by the contrast between the real and illusory Coney Island, and a large part of my early fiction is centered there. There was a warm and almost mysterious aspect of this town edged by water on three sides. We enjoyed an outdoor life totally unlike the sort of life imagined for New Yorkers. We swam and fished and played football on the beach, played all sorts of games in the streets, and it was a long time before I left Coney Island. My life was there.

I didn't go into Manhattan until after I was fourteen years old, and I knew I didn't want to go there after I graduated from high school. So I hitchhiked across the country and ended up in Los Angeles. As I traveled across the United States, the West opened up for me. I remember staying over in Cheyenne, Wyoming, loving it; it was such a clean, open, almost stark and shining town. I suppose if I had gone to San Francisco then I would have stayed there; nobody who sees San Francisco first would possibly choose Los Angeles. But I came to Los Angeles and attended Los Angeles City College; I worked in the public library as a page and in a bakery at night. I managed to support myself through the first few semesters, then decided to go to Davis to study soil science and agronomy. I was fixed on that.

As I hitchhiked up to Davis I stopped in a little town named Merced. It's in the center of the San Joaquin Valley and for some reason it appealed to me, so I got a job selling shoes at Montgomery Ward. A few weeks after I started working, a girl came in and asked for a pair of shoes. We talked, and she told me there was an opening on the *Merced Sun-Star*, the daily paper. I went over there on my lunch hour and was hired as a reporter. I remained there until the war started; I enlisted, served overseas, and came back in 1946 to Los Angeles, to work for the City News Service, then for United Press. I went back to school, completed my bachelor's and did graduate work for my master's, both degrees in English and American literature. My goal then was to go into full-time teaching; in fact, in 1951 I was appointed as an Instructor and began to teach while I worked for my doctorate. But I found that I couldn't support my family by teaching, so I went back to the copy desk of the *Los Angeles Times*, working at night to support my teaching habit.

Gradually, I reversed this. Dr. Joseph Henry Jackson died, and I was offered a daily column in the *Los Angeles Times*. After Paul Jordan Smith retired, I became the book editor as well. This was in 1957, and I've been book editor ever since.

In addition, (I don't think anyone is solely a book editor), I've written a lot of fiction: four novels under my own name, six novels under two pen names, many short stories, some novellas, lots of articles, lots of reviews. I've done a bit of everything; I wouldn't say any of it with great success. I think this is very good for a critic. It has certainly given me a sense of respect and appreciation for the act of professional writing. I don't, for example, share the veiled contempt so many literary people have for screenwriters and television writers. In fact, the only contempt I have for any writer is for the true hack, and I define "true hack" as a man who has contempt for what he is doing. I don't care if he writes greeting-card verse; if he does the best job he's capable of doing and has a professional attitude toward his work; if he has self-imposed standards and a sense of what it is he wants to accomplish, then I have respect for him. Having tried my hand at many different kinds of writing, knowing how difficult writing is, I'm often irritated by the people who put down screenwriters just as novelists were put down in the eighteenth century and through a considerable part of the nineteenth.

I am, for example, excited by motion pictures. I think the really great work of its genre is being done in film and not in the novel, at least not in what I see of the novel. I think this is something we must recognize. I think it is part of an audiovisual revolution. I don't believe that people are evolving through another stage because of McLuhan's electric revolution, but I think there is always a tendency to deprecate the popular art, the mass art. Actually, today's popular expression is the soil from which tomorrow's great art grows. Consequently my position has always been what I suppose many critics would call "middlebrow." Actually, I don't accept the gradations "highbrow," "middlebrow," and "lowbrow." I simply have great confidence in the intuitive response, the experimental response, even the untutored response, of ordinary, intelligent people. I value those responses over the intellectualized self-conscious response which is so much a part of the culture in which we live.

As a writer, I write the kind of books I would like to read. When I have written a book I think the critics would like to read, I have been dissatisfied with myself. As a critic I find that I want first to enjoy the reading experience. It doesn't matter to me whether I'm reading a mystery, an espionage novel, a book of poetry, a biography, or a history. At the core there must be a self-rewarding quality in the experience of reading. It's the thing I strive to reflect in my reviewing. I suppose that all reviewers go through periods of shell shock — I know I do — when one is suddenly depressed by the vastness of the product, has a desperate feeling of wanting to cover all that is going on, and is cowed by the obligations associated with literary activity; but I try to avoid being worried or intimidated by those things. I don't really care what goes on in the literary world. I'm not concerned with the arguments of critics or the critical concensus. I am concerned with finding what might be called the "experiential mode" in reading.

By this I mean that I believe I must attain a kind of balance, yet have a willingness to venture and risk, to go outside the ordinary required activities. I don't have many things to boast about, but one of the things I can be proud of is that I was the first reviewer in the United States to regularly review paperbacks. This happened long before anybody reviewed them, and in the face of tremendous opposition from booksellers. I reviewed paperback originals, paperback reprints, books that came out originally a century ago and were brought back to life in paperback, Library of Congress publications, and anything which I felt deserved attention and notice and compelled a response from me.

I found, very early, those things a reviewer must have as opposed to a critic's qualifications.

A reviewer works; let's call him equivalent to the handicapper in the newspaper. He tells you a good bet for tomorrow. A critic is a man who might be writing for *Thoroughbred* magazine, saying, "This bloodline will win the derby in twenty-five or thirty years." American reviewing falls short, it seems to me, in its failure to adopt and embrace some of the criteria, a portion of the erudition, we associate with criticism. In other words, American reviewing tends to be overenthusiastic or overly negative. When it doesn't fall into either of these traps, it falls into the trap Elizabeth Hardwick wrote about, where a certain kind of jargon has been evolved that makes a review like every other review. You find the same adjectives, the same descriptions, the same sort of careful charade in which a little is praised, a little negated, a little built, a little broken down.

I don't believe in all this. I think that the reviewer's first obligation is to read the book. By reading the book I don't mean just a matter of going through it from the first page to the last; this is only the first step in the process of reading. Reading is a process of interaction. You must then respond to the matter of the book, but you have to bring something to it; thus the reviewer has the special obligation of the reporter as well as that of the critic. He stands between the two functions.

In other words, he should give the reader a fair statement of the *news* of the book. What it is about, what it covers, a sampling. I'm not afraid of a synopsis in a review; I do resent reviews which give no idea of what the book is about.

The reviewer must have identity. He must have a stance and a position, and it must be one that is judicial and judicious. His judgments should be informed judgments, taking into account the literature of the past, the relationships between the book reviewed and what has transpired in literature. He must also balance his presentation. Wherever possible, the evidence should be drawn from the book itself. When I write a review I try, whenever and wherever possible, to buttress any positive or negative statement with the material, with some quotation from the book. In other words, many people are going to trust my judgments because they've known me over the years as a reviewer. But these people comprise only a portion of the reading public. I want the people who disagree with me, who may feel that I am wrong, to have a chance to make their own decision. In other words, I would hesitate to make final, ringing judgments about the work at hand.

I'm afraid this tentative approach is missing in much of the reviewing now being done. I'll put it another way; in fact, I'll give you an example to illustrate. I dissented on James Gould Cozzens' *By Love Possessed.* I wanted to praise the book because I appreciated Cozzens' work in the 1930's. I read *By Love Possessed* very carefully, twice, before I wrote my review. My review ran completely against the majority of extravagant praise. Then, Dwight Macdonald did his piece for *Commen-*

tary. A whole reaction set in, but I had felt it was necessary, from the beginning, to place this book in its perspective. It was not a new gospel, as Brendan Gill seemed to suggest. The book itself could not sustain the excitement generated for it by the Establishment.

I did give a fair statement of the book, and paid considerable attention to its style, so that people who might differ would have some sense of the book beyond my opinion. I felt vindicated in that particular review, largely by the response of English critics and reviewers whose work I follow closely because I believe that the English reviewers, on the whole, are superior to our reviewers. They write in a language which is lucid and imaginative and meaningful. They have a deeper sense of the rhetoric and the elements of literary form, and they tend to be more judicious and more aware of the ultimate decision. American reviewers tend to get very excited by newness or novelty.

Ship of Fools was another novel which I wanted to be a great novel. I'm an admirer of Katherine Anne Porter. I know her stories and I know her work; but it was not a great novel. It was only a long novel with some moving and meaningful parts; it could have provided what I think most people want out of a novel.

I must admit that there are whole areas in which I find the great praise given certain writers totally incomprehensible. I cannot understand the excitement and enthusiasm for Wright Morris, nor for Herbert Gold whom I consider a very imaginative, shrewd and cunning literary ward heeler. If he can do it, fine. He has managed to live on grants and subsidies for a great many years on a very slender reputation, a very slender body of work.

On the other hand, I believe that there are many neglected and underrated writers. Some of them function in areas which have not been given the proper attention.

I think one thing the reviewer must do, in all fairness, is to admit areas of prejudice — to disqualify himself, so to speak, if he can't be fair. I could not read beyond page seventeen in Reynolds Price's first novel, and I said so in my column; I wrote, "Look, this is my blind spot and prejudice. I simply cannot swallow another novel about the South that is written in this style." I thought it fair to give the reader this information; the reviewer cannot emerge from his corner giving the impression that he is without prejudice, without irritation, without all sorts of eccentricities. For example, I can't stand novels set in Florida. I shudder to think of what will happen when a great novel comes along with a Florida setting. I won't recognize it. When I first started reviewing, Robert Nathan told me that I was making a mistake because I was too temperate in my reviews. I was really trying to be fair. He said, "If you want to make a reputation, do it in six months. And you'll do it in six months if you kick hell out of everything that comes across your desk." He told me that there are twenty words in the English language of negation and deprecation—pejorative words—to every ameliorative, complimentary word, and it's more forceful to use them.

I couldn't take his advice. I think he was half-kidding. Certainly he would not want me to apply that as a standard to his own novels. I simply realized that all I have to offer as a reviewer is my particular personality, my particular tastes, the gathering of traits and qualities and interests which I am. In other words, I had to speak with my authentic voice, for better or for worse.

I've had lots of advice. At the beginning the booksellers said I wasn't doing a good job for them in selling books because I often avoided the puffed book, the book the department stores had ordered heavily. To this day, whenever I walk into a bookstore, a clerk will say something like, "Where did you dig up that thing published in South Africa twenty-three years ago and reissued by that outfit up in San Francisco?" Well, I dug it out.

There was a marvelous Library of Congress account of a poetry conference which I found to be the funniest thing published all last year —a great gathering of poets from the hinterlands, some well-known, some not so well-known, all crowding into an auditorium with manuscripts under their arms. The Library of Congress reported on the affair in a transcript, and I read it and it broke me up, so I reviewed that publication. I review many Library of Congress publications, but this doesn't serve the bookseller.

I don't serve authors, either. I don't serve anybody except the reader. My job is to inform him, to make a judgment which is relevant and fair. People used to tell me that I wrote for a small number of intellectuals, that ordinary people couldn't understand me. I would reply, "Well, I can't write any other way. I can't write down to people." I believe in that aphorism by Goethe: "If you talk to a man as he is, he will remain as he is. If you talk to him as he should be, he will find out what he should be." A very rough quotation. Most people in communication— newspaper, television, motion pictures—tend to underestimate their audiences.

Five or six years ago Randall Jarrell made a speech at the National Book Award ceremony and mocked the impulse for self-improvement. He questioned the cultural explosion. Well, I don't question it because I know there is a palpable increase in intellectual and cultural interest and experience. Carried too far, however, where people want to "belong" by buying the right painting or seeing the right shows, is a symptom of another disease—the outer-directedness Riesman talks about. But for me, I believe the old *consensus gentium* of Aristotle. I think that anything large numbers of people voluntarily accept and appreciate over a long period of time has some merit in it. This is why I'm interested in the mass forms. I want to know why they capture an audience. Invariably, a novel or motion picture or television show in which large numbers of people are interested has some element which is worthy of their interest, which compels and entertains them. If you're talking about art in terms of absolutes it's very easy, of course, to indict this position because it is a compromised position, but I don't live in an atmosphere of art in its absolute greatness. I think a truly classic work of art, a truly great work of art, is a rare accident in any age. Great pieces of work come very rarely. I think it was a priest in Massachusetts who was teaching at a Catholic university and, after studying television programming, said in effect, "Okay, what would *you* program for eighteen hours a day on seven channels?" You would soon run out of classics and great plays and lectures and all the other quality programs. I think that this is where Susan Sontag makes her most important point in *Against Interpretation*. A lot of things she has said may be challenged, but she did point out that there is an increasing tendency to be insulated against art as an experience, to regard it instead as some sort of intellectual problem, to seek always between the lines for subtleties and nuances. There are certain experiences in which you cannot do this, when you simply have to accept the experience for itself.

In my own work I think that what keeps me fresh is my unwillingness to isolate myself, to become the typical book reviewer, to play the role of the bookish person. (Tempting, in a town like this, which is ready to lionize anybody who is connected with the world of writing, the world of painting, the world of music.) I try to keep myself balanced. I try not to turn away from the range of experiences necessary to stabilize, to give context to literary judgments.

After all, this form of expression is an illusion. Fiction is an illusion designed to compel some sort of belief. Motion pictures are an illusion. All of the art forms are constructions and reorganizations placed upon materials of life, but what makes the ultimate judgment possible is not something you learn from books alone; it is something based at least partially upon intuition, upon the interaction between you and the event. I think much of this is lost in our tendency to over-instruct people—particularly those who are in the humanities and liberal arts— to make them specialized, to separate them, as intellectuals and cultured people, from the rest of the world. Not merely the separation C. P. Snow talks about as existing between the humanities and science, but the feeling that if you don't know what's going on you're not "in"; if you can't define Kant, if you can't do this or that, you're left out.

I am concerned with the quality of the individual experience. I'm concerned with people seeing, touching, tasting, allowing themselves to have pleasure. I thought that Walter Kerr made this point well in his *The Decline of Pleasure.*

I go after it; I walk on the beach, coach a little league team, go to baseball and football and basketball games. I try to surf. I try to keep myself challenged and stimulated, to keep my experience in some sort of contact with the total world. I do not believe in the intellectual as a separate and distinct type who is alienated and exiled from all the rest of the people in the world, the technicians and scientists, etc. I think everyone is capable of the kind of intellectual activity, the kind of perception, the kind of judgment, the kind of critical response, that counts—whether their vocation or profession has anything to do with teaching, writing, or criticism.

When I talk to groups, as I occasionally do—I'm very big with the American Association of University Women, now—I know they're ready for a desiccated, dryly witty, sarcastic performance as given by the stereotyped book reviewer. I start off by saying, "You've invited a book reviewer to speak, but I look more like a bookie. I don't feel like an ordinary book reviewer. I believe that books are only a part of life, and I think that the kind of interaction which takes place between people in books must involve the current experience." I think that a sort of separation accompanies the intense worship of books. Years ago when I was a boy, there were always some kids in the neighborhood who were sickly and nervous and liked to read a lot. They were bookish kids, and they wore thick glasses and never played handball and never went swimming. They got all the scholarships and fellowships and prizes, and felt that all the rest of us were the clods of the world—the unthinking, the unfeeling. I believe this sort of separation is wrong and dangerous and puts a burden on books which books were never designed to carry. It endows books with a kind of mystery, a kind of potency, a kind of magic; therefore the tendency for people is to be afraid of them.

The reason we get these surges of censorship, these urges to suppress books in a library, is because people think that a book like *The Communist Manifesto* or *Mein Kampf* or *Lady Chatterley's Lover* is capable, by itself, of contriving to change a person in an insidious way. But the book as it sits on a shelf is a dead thing; it does not take on life until a human reads it. Until we have people who are able to maintain their poise under the pressure of good books and bad books, saintly books and evil books, books for pleasure and books for functional need, we are not really approaching a decent level of education. We are literate, but most of us are only half-educated, because education involves the ability to make value judgments, to suspend judgments, to be poised in a condition of ambivalence, and to tolerate ambiguities and uncertainties. This state comes, I think, from being able to live as well as to read, and to bring life to the books you read, and to take from the books for your own life. This, I think, is what we seek from books. Another by-product of all this which interests me in teaching, is the tendency for students to have an almost scriptural respect for the printed word. They don't believe there can be an error, an outrageous lie, or illogical and mis-guided thinking in a book.

The state of ambiguity and ambivalence, the reader's perspective of what he is and what he reads, is essential to a cultivated and cultured society. I think it is coming. I don't think that people are now as prone to accept uncritically everything that is handed to them. During the McCarthy period we had a terrifying crisis of courage, and we seem to by reacting to that. People are resisting being manipulated.

In the long run I suppose I am primarily concerned with education. I want to teach, not merely instruct; to somehow convey in my own style, through my own approach to things. through my own example, what it means to be educated. It doesn't necessarily mean being happy, it doesn't necessarily mean being successful, it doesn't mean being a prodigy. It means being able to live a thoughtful, completely-sensed life in any situation in which a person finds himself. And it involves the capacity to act. It involves character as well as mind. These things concern me as a reviewer.

As a writer—I won't go into the novels I've done, or most of the books I'm planning to do, but there is one I'll be working on soon that I would like to mention. This will be a description of the work I've been doing at U.C.L.A. in the teaching of writing. I became interested in it about ten years ago, when I started teaching what some people call "creative writing"—a term which makes other people ill. I don't really think there are orders of creative writing, but I don't think that creative writing is limited to fiction, poetry, and drama. I think that, in at least one sense, the striving for precision and felicity, the attempt to write something effectively and perhaps gracefully and beautifully, is pretty much a continuum of action.

Anyway, I've been interested in it from the point of view of whether people *have* anything to say, in ways of helping them reestablish some sort of meaningful contact with the world—not in the formalities of language, which I think are well-handled in the conventional, rhetorical ways. I have noticed—particularly among the adults I have taught in our extension division, but also in undergraduate and graduate courses —the fact that there is some sort of relationship between the ability to sense and perceive the world about, and the ability to express, in language, these tangible and intangible experiences.

It never surprises me that painters, sculptors, and musicians are often fine writers. It is rare, in fact, to find one who is not capable of writing effectively and sometimes originally and sometimes, as in the case of Van Gogh, beautifully. I began to explore areas involving awareness—of how people sense the world or how they can restore their sense of the world. I began to examine what has been said about this by philosophers of the past, by artists and writers—particularly those I call the self-conscious writers. Certain writers, and certain painters and musicians, have this dual awareness—can do something and also know why and how they do it. It's rare, but not as rare as we might think. Challenging work has been done in psychology on awareness perception and creativity. I took all sorts of things from all sorts of places to bring together a succession of experiences, exercises, or experiments, which the students do and which they can relate to language because they are really exploring the vocabulary which informs language. In other words, if they were to come into this room, they would have to know the room before they could describe it. They would have to study all of the textures and the whole sum or gestalt, all the details. I've been going on with this for some years now, and I'm beginning to see some results in the performance of students who have had this course as opposed to others who have not.

Now, for the writer coming up—not necessarily in my classes, but about to come on the scene as, say, a novelist. I hope that we are about to obtain an appreciation or a recapitulation of those things which make fiction compelling: story, plot, and character. Not in the limited sense of psychological analysis, but in the sense of persons in contention with each other and with the world about them. I think that the really important quality a writer must have is a willingness to attempt to hypnotize his reader, to be part musician, part seer, part prophet. To do what after all is the initial primal function of the storyteller. I'm borrowing from and paraphrasing Sir Philip Sidney, but the writer must have the capacity to take children away from their play and old men away from their chimney corners. This is the obligation of the writer. If he wants to be a philosopher, a psychologist, a minister, or a teacher, then he should go out and get the lectern or pulpit from which to teach or preach. But the storyteller has a basic obligation to compel the attention of the reader.

I can't go into the mystery of talent because we can't legislate talent. Certainly critics and reviewers can't legislate talent, but I see the young writer in America as being particularly vulnerable, more vulnerable than he has ever been, because most of our emerging writers in the past have come from the periphery, the more isolated areas, not the center. They've had a chance to respond to the challenge of their craft and their art by themselves, away from an establishment.

A Thomas Wolfe comes from North Carolina, a James Jones from Illinois via Hawaii, even a Hemingway from Oak Park, a Howells from Ohio to New York, a Faulkner from the rural South. In James Jones' *Some Came Running*, which I thought a vastly underrated book, you find an illustration of the point I'm trying to make. The book may have had its faults, but it was a beautiful study of the disappearance of the small town. Now, because of mass communication, because of television and radio and motion pictures and the paperback revolution, everyone in every part of the country is in immediate contact with the literary environment. In other words, the young writer who once had only access to a public library, who imitated Stevenson or Scott or whomever, started with an individual experience, then blended his native experience with the more sophisticated world of the successful writer. Today that doesn't happen because most of our writers are put through the experience of higher education, which is basically a homogenization. They all read the same books, have the same galleries of teachers — rebels, conformists, neo-classicists, etc. — and tend to deal with the literary experience in abstractions and generalities and critical constructs. I would hope to see in a young writer — and it is there, to some extent, in Elliott Baker and Joseph Heller, among others — the strength to be his own man. He must expect to be the servant of the reader. He has to want to earn the right to tell stories. Then, if he has it in him and he grows, he can add wisdom and maturity and depth.

What bothers me is the fact that so many of our young writers are praised for poor, derivative books, and are given a completely distorted idea of the nature of success. They get into this extraordinary role of celebrity in the publicity mill. The kind of thing Mailer, consciously or unconsciously, is captured by. He is, in my opinion, the saddest example of this kind of waste; ironically, he is both at odds with the system and the absolute serf of the system. In *Advertisements for Myself*, for example, he says that if the book sells X number of copies it will be a success, he will be vindicated. If it sells less than X number of copies, he will have failed.

We don't give our writers a chance to serve an apprenticeship. This is an important deprivation. I don't believe that the creative writing programs, in general, produce the kind of independent, solitary, discernible, identifiable voice. I think the *Times Book Review*, in referring to the anthology of Iowa writers (I'm generalizing), said something to the effect that the manner was fine, that all of them were good writers, masters of the craft, they knew language, could handle techniques, but that their subject matter was deficient and this matter could only come from experience. (I've overstated this; I believe that Iowa is one of the better centers of creative writing because they do take a variety of students and do not make an effort to force them into a mold.) But the fact remains: Where does the young writer go, what does he do, to assert individuality? In a symposium Granville Hicks edited on the novel, Mark Harris said, "I write; let the reader learn to read." I submit that this is an arrogant statement because the reader with equal justice can say, "I read; let the writer learn to write." Both points are valid. But I think we also must stop worrying about the disparity of audiences; everyone cannot like everything. Some of the best writers in this country communicate to relatively small audiences.

I don't know how you convince young writers that solitude and independence and obligation to craft and obligation to reader are important. There are too many people in the "Look-Ma-I'm-writing!" school. Words are put together, somebody publishes them, and they assume they have accomplished something. Simply having a novel published doesn't mean very much. Critical praise can be cheap.

I've been reviewing for a dozen years or more, and when I think back over all the young writers who came along who were hailed and praised and given front-page reviews in various papers, who were extravagantly welcomed — many of them went nowhere. Not that there aren't personal tragedies and misfortunes among these failures, but a very large percentage went nowhere because they didn't deserve the rousing welcome they got.

My advice to the young writer is this: Write for the reader, not for the critic. Write a damned good story and pray that it means something more than a good story. Trust yourself. Write a book you would enjoy reading, accept the influence of people who really have something to say to you, not the ones you're supposed to like. Live, grow, be a *mensch*. That's all I can say.

"We're afraid to say what we really want to say. We're afraid to communicate because by doing so we become vulnerable ... take off your armor, do violence to jargon and platitudes and make yourself vulnerable. Talk and write about the things that matter, even if people think you're silly. This is the only thing that will give language back its dignity and joy."

Madeleine L'Engle

Madeleine L'Engle

L'ENGLE: My husband claims that I've used my early life in so many books that I no longer know fact from fiction, so I'll have to admit that I may have things somewhat confused. Yet what I'll say is more or less true.

I was born shortly after the First World War. My father was a foreign correspondent and a writer of all sorts. He was gassed during the war, so I never knew him as the volatile, fascinating, attractive person he must have been. I saw him dying for eighteen years; the gas just went on eating. My mother had studied to be a pianist until she married, and for a while, when we lived in New York, my father was drama and music critic for the *Herald-Evening Sun*. The house was full of peculiar people.

I always wanted to write, but I wasn't encouraged at home because my father was a writer. (I certainly would not encourage my children to write. None of them show any tendency to do so, thank God.) My early teachers didn't encourage me to write either.

I was well into adolescence when I started really doing something about writing. This was when I attended a perfectly ghastly school. I was quite lame, and at this school they placed a tremendous emphasis on prowess in the gym. It was also faintly social. A really repulsive New York-type school. I remember coming home and saying, "All right, so I'm the unpopular one," and I began a life purely of the imagination. I wrote to keep myself company, to make myself happy. The homeroom teacher went along with the kids in labeling me the lame and unpopular one, and she also decided I wasn't very bright. Her name was Miss Pepper or Miss Salt, I forget which, and she was dreadful. I probably didn't change her opinion by the way I didn't study. The last year I was there they had a poetry contest in the spring that was to be judged by the head of the English department. The submissions went right to her without screening; otherwise, I wouldn't have had an entry. I won it, and there was great sound and fury because my homeroom teacher said, "Madeleine isn't bright. She couldn't have written that poem; she must have copied it." So my mother had to go to school with the mass of poems, novels, and stories I'd written, and they finally had to allow that I probably had written the winning poem.

Also at school (and this I put into *Camilla*) I had to go to the bathroom, and the teacher wouldn't let me go, so I wet my pants. My mother went to the principal about it, but the teacher denied what she'd done and was believed. I learned about adult perfidy from her.

I was twelve when it became apparent that my father couldn't stand living in the city any more. He adored London, he adored Paris, he adored New York, but the fumes were just too much for his lungs. It was cheaper for us to go to live in Europe than for him to be ill in America, so we moved to France. My parents stayed in the French Alps and I was sent to a boarding school in England. After the completely solitary life I'd led in New York, I was suddenly in a dormitory with twelve other girls. The only American, the foreigner. It was absolutely splendidly horrible. I still get books out of it, but I honestly learned all sorts of valuable things. I learned to concentrate anywhere; consequently, I wrote my first book when I was on tour with a play, wrote it in railway stations, on trains, in dressing rooms. I remember saying once, "No, no, I can't talk quite yet; I'm in the middle of a seduction scene. Wait."

While at this school, I also resolved, after deciding I would not die of anquish, that I would show them. This is not really good motivation, but quite a lot can come from it. When I graduated I was president of student government and everything else you can be president of.

I wrote my first novel when I was twelve. I still think it quite splendid. All about triplets; one was great at sports, one a great intellect, one marvelous socially. So they pretended to be one person, and were very successful as one great person. Then one of them fell in love and he had to confess to the girl that he was only one-third of himself. The last line as she left him was, "He said nothing. What was there to say?" I suppose that twelve is the classic age to write the first novel.

I went on writing reams of poetry and reams of short stories and did nothing about them; I think this was wise. I simply wrote them to pile up experiences. I went to Smith and was graduated with honors. I'm probably the only Smith graduate who lost Phi Beta Kappa for misbehavior.

After I got out of college I decided it was time that I get published. All the magazines that paid turned me down with not-surprising regularity. I began, however, to get things into little magazines. I didn't know then that publishers read little magazines and contact writers they think might show promise. So I did get letters from several publishers. Bernard Perry, now the head of Indiana University Press, was then with Vanguard, and he wrote and asked if I had a novel. I told them I was in the middle of one. They said, "Show it to us when you finish it." I did. It was very rough. (I must always do a great deal of rewriting, but I don't mind doing it.) They offered what seemed to be a fabulous sum of money—a hundred dollars. And I spent the entire summer sitting alone in an apartment in the village rewriting *The Small Rain*, which they bought with some trepidation; it surprised them by doing very well. (It was good, in other ways, to sit that summer out; I was recuperating from my first wild love affair.)

Vanguard then published my second novel exactly as I wrote it. It was a damned good first draft, but it had no business being published.

Then, at Bernard's suggestion, I wrote my first so-called children's book. In *The Small Rain* I wrote about the dark side of the English boarding school; in the children's book I touched the slightly brighter side of it. It's still doing very well.

Then came the phase when nobody would publish me. The decade of the 1930's was absolutely ghastly. I had married Hugh by then, and he had decided to leave the theater because it wasn't fair for children to have a father whose profession was so precarious. He left, and we decided that if I got pregnant within a month we'd settle in the country. So I got pregnant, and then what do you do? He thought that thirty-five was a young enough age to start a new career. Well, it's not—not when you have only a degree from Northwestern in Speech. Fortunately, we had bought a house the first spring we were married, an absolutely marvelous old white farmhouse in the northwestern corner of Connecticut, for $6,300. So we went there to put roots down. There was a town nearby, and he went to see about getting jobs in various factories. He didn't have an engineering degree so they couldn't use him in a white-collar job. He said he would just as soon work on a machine, so they gave him tests and he came out rated "Genius." They said he'd disrupt the men, so he was just plain unemployable.

I took the baby to visit mother in South Carolina; I hadn't been there long when Hugh called me and said, "I bought the Goshen general store." This was a completely dead general store in the center of town, and he had mortgaged us to the hilt to buy it. He had no experience in this sort of thing. He comes from a family of lawyers, and being an actor is strange enough, but a general store operator! Yet we ran that store for many years. He built it from a completely dead store to a flourishing business; it reached the point where the only thing to do would be to buy more stores. One night, when we were sitting in front of the fire having a drink, I said, "Hugh, are you still happy with the store?" and he said, "No." I said, "Sell it."

We lived there nine years. The children were little, the house was drafty, and there were days in winter when we couldn't get the kitchen above 45 degrees. I was struggling with diapers. I was in the store for three hours every day so Hugh could come home for lunch and have the kids nap. I wrote at night after the kids fell asleep. Frequently I fell asleep over the typewriter. I learned a tremendous amount during that decade, and I wouldn't give it up for anything, but I hope never to live through anything like it again.

The only thing I was selling during this decade was stuff from the store, and I was fairly successful in talking people into buying things they didn't want. I have a splendid imagination.

I do remember, with fondness, the carnival people. They had a real old-fashioned country fair in Goshen, and during the winter they rented the fair buildings to carnival men. They're basic, dirty-clean, marvelous people, and most of the town stood off from them a bit, but I wasn't afraid of them. I always came to the store at noon, and one day the carnival men were there and one of them said to Hugh, "Where's the boss?" Hugh said, "What do you mean?" and he said, "Ah, come on now, you know who the boss is!" and Hugh said, "I'm the boss." At that point I walked in, and Hugh raised his finger and said, "Madeleine! Down on your knees!" Naturally I dropped to my knees as any good wife would, and the carnival men thought this was the loveliest thing they'd ever seen, and they treated me like a queen after that.

During this decade I was looking forward to my fortieth birthday. Instead of dreading it I was dying to have it, because it seemed to me that things would have to change; somebody would have to buy something I'd written. I had a book out at Simon and Schuster, and I knew that three editors were very strong for it, one hated it, and a fifth had to be heard from. They'd had it for three months and I was hopeful. But on that longed-for day Hugh called me from the store and said, "I'm sorry, I know it's your birthday, but the answer is no." That almost finished me.

During that decade it seemed I had two alternatives. Once in a while I would come very close to doing a Gauguin, just leaving diapers and washing machines that froze, the whole household bit. The other—and because I do have a strong conscience it popped up more often—"It's not fair to Hugh and the children. I'm not selling, I'm not pulling my weight financially, I don't sweep in the corners, I can't bake pies. I should stop writing and be a proper housewife and mother."

So Hugh's call seemed that the message had gotten through, and this was it; I should stop. Each time a book got rejected I had to go off somewhere and bawl, and it was hard on the family because the mother

sets the tone of the house, and if I wasn't gay nobody was gay. So I
went to the typewriter and covered it with a great gesture of renuncia-
tion, vowing that I would learn to bake a cherry pie. I bawled at the top
of my lungs as though I was four, not forty (thank God the kids were at
school), when all of a sudden I realized what my subconscious was
doing. My subconscious was very busy writing a book on failure, so I
went to the typewriter, took off the cover, and said, "Okay, this is it. If
nobody ever publishes anything I write again, it is nevertheless what I
am." When Hugh asked me to marry him it was, "Yes, I too want a
family and would be as good a wife and mother as I could, but I am first
and foremost a writer." And I'm forever grateful that I made my
sweeping decision in a moment of absolute failure, when I really
believed I'd never be published again. But during that fortieth year
things did change. I began to sell what I wrote, and things have gone
considerably better ever since.

Meet the Austins was taken that year by Vanguard. It was turned
down by most publishers because it begins with a death, and we
mustn't let children know about death. It is also a book about things
that happened in our family, and I wrote it purely as a love letter to my
husband. But I don't believe that children should be cushioned from the
darker things. A clergyman friend and his wife once attended a seminar
conducted by a very famous child psychologist. It was a question-and-
answer affair, and she asked him, "Why is it that everything in the
household falls apart around dinnertime?" He said, "The obvious
reason is that it's the time of day when children are tired, they want
their dinner. You're tired too; you've been struggling with diapers and
formula and all the household routine. Your husband comes home at
the end of his day and he's tired too. But the real reason—and you'll
probably contradict me—is that we're all afraid of the dark."

They all did contradict him, and he said, "The very violence of your
reaction proves the truth of my words." This hit home because I think
we all are afraid of the dark. Part of the reason for this is because in the
child-centered life of the average American home children aren't
allowed to know that there is such a thing as the dark, or that it's
perfectly all right to be afraid of the dark. It's *fine* to be afraid of the
dark. You're afraid of existing evil, and you look for the light instead. If
we try to cushion our children we are really pushing them into the
dark, denying them a chance to find a light to see by.

We have never had a child-centered household. We adore the
children, but Hugh is first. In every family there has to be an apex, and
I'm dead against the matriarchal setup which usually goes with a child-
centered household. When we came back to New York the kids were

seven, ten, and twelve, and Hugh went back to the theater. We ran into a problem because I was trying to get up with the kids and get them off to school, then stay up with Hugh when he came home from the theater at night. I think he has a right to expect a wife ready to sit and eat with him and talk to him. It just didn't work; I ended up in the hospital.

So we called a family conference and I said to the kids, "You don't need me in the morning as much as Daddy needs me at night. You're old enough to get yourselves off to school, and when you get home from school, from then until you go to bed at night, I'm wholeheartedly yours. But you're on your own in the morning. Get up and make your own sandwiches, get yourselves decently dressed and off." I don't think they suffered abominably from it.

We do have a good family relationship. The kids think I'm a nice kind of moron. They like my books, and they like my cooking, but they do think I'm a nut. I was so determined not to get in the girls' hair when they got into their early teens that when it was time to get clothes I'd say, "All right, we have just this much that you can spend; here you are. Go buy what you want." Finally they came to me and said, "Look, Mother, we know the other girls all gripe because their mothers go out and choose all their clothes, but won't you come with us just once?" and I said, "No. You all have very good taste and if I go you'll just waste my time and yours." And I held off until this spring when our 18-year-old finished her second year at Smith, had exams, and planned a June 8 wedding. I told her to get her clothes in Northampton so things wouldn't be so rushed, and she said, "No. I'm not going to get one single thing without you this time." So we shopped when she got back.

Back to books. After *Meet the Austins* I wrote *A Wrinkle in Time*, which got rejected by everybody. It was turned down for about the twentieth time just before Christmas, when I was sitting on the bed wrapping Christmas presents, and I thought, "Madeleine, you've really grown up; you're being terribly brave about all this." I didn't realize until later that I had sent a necktie to a three-year-old girl, some perfume to a bachelor friend. So I called Theron, my agent, and said, "Theron, it's not fair to you or my family because this is such a peculiar book that nobody will buy it. Just send it back. I love it, but forget it." So he sent it back.

My mother was up for Christmas, and after Christmas I had a small party for her, and one of my friends said, "You must meet John Farrar." I said, "Yeah," because I was down on publishers at that point, but she insisted on setting up an appointment and I took the book when I went to keep it. What did I have to lose?

John Farrar had read my first book, *The Small Rain*, and liked it, and

asked if I had anything else. I said, "Yes, here's a book nobody likes."
He asked if he could read it, and two weeks later I signed the contract.
They said, "Now, don't be disappointed if it doesn't do well; we're
publishing it because we love it." And it did very well indeed. It is still
doing very well, and with it things certainly changed.

Farrar, Straus and Giroux have been wonderful for me — perfectly
willing to let me write a different book every time. I don't have to do the
same thing in a different color, which was my problem before, which
must be a problem for most writers. I've done five books for Farrar,
Straus and Giroux, and each has been completely different from the
others, and they don't mind. They're wonderful.

Now, I feel a bit strongly about this categorizing of "children's
books." All of the so-called children's books I care about passionately
are not children's books. I don't write children's books. I think anybody
who writes for children is being intolerable to children. I don't think
they read children's books except as they read comic books, and this is a
stage they outgrow, we hope. The real children's books are those they
go on reading all their lives, books that come to terms with man's place
in the universe. They are written because the writer is trying to work
something out, and the only way the finite can say anything about the
infinite is through paradox, through telling a story. I don't think it's any
coincidence that, with the exception of the Sermon on the Mount,
Christ taught entirely by telling stories. Anything lasting that has been
said about man's relationship to creation has always been in the form of
what is now called "fantastic fiction." It is the only possible way we
have of doing it. And children who haven't been taught that they must
be terrified of this, love it.

Perhaps I'm being unfair to many parents and teachers because I'm
generalizing, but as children are taught by parents and teachers they are
apt to lose their concept of imagination. In schools today they're taught
only the material things. They're taken on field trips. They're taught
only the provable because people are afraid that anything which isn't
provable isn't true. Thus what children are being denied are vital areas
of real truth. Is Shakespeare's *The Tempest* true? Is Dante's *Inferno* true?
What is truth? It's more than provable fact. And in imaginative fiction
writers are usually groping, in one form or another, trying to come to
terms with proof.

I think that even the funniest of books in this field usually come out
of tremendous personal anguish. *Alice in Wonderland* is the classic
example. Lewis Carroll was an Anglican clergyman and a mathematician, but what he really wanted to say he said in *Alice*. His excuse was to
write it for a little girl, but he obviously wrote it for himself. George
MacDonald, a Congregational pastor, wrote hundreds of books of

sermons that nobody reads, but his fairy tales are read over and over again by children and adults. The same is true of C. S. Lewis. He wrote theology and fiction simultaneously, both dealing with the same theological problem. The most challenging thing in writing stories is to absolutely avoid showing the bones of the problem you're dealing with. If you show them, you're not being a storyteller. You write beyond what you actually are at that time, beyond what you are capable of knowing in the field.

I find that when I'm writing poetry or fantasy I'll make progress in my subconscious thinking. My subconscious works far ahead of my conscious, freeing it.

This kind of book is always written on many levels. Children will respond to some of them; they will always respond to the story. In fact, it must be, first and foremost, a good story. If you are a storyteller, not a theologian or philologist or whatever, you are successful at the most important level. Then, beneath that story, come the subterranean currents, the things you are really writing about. Without these currents there would be no writing, no music, no painting, no art of any form. This is our attempt to make order out of chaos, to see all of the seeming confusion of the world and put it into a pattern so that life becomes not only bearable, but joyous. You can't have joy in carelessness or lack of discipline or disorder; there is only confusion, which leads to sickness.

Writing is a way of our being healthy, I suppose. And there's always a paradox, always contradictions of pain and happiness, of opposites. I find that when I'm teaching I will frequently contradict myself and I will have to say, "The contradictions stand because of these things that are true."

To bring things up to date: *The Love Letters* has a strange history. I have to call it a totally adult book, and this kills me, because here I am, making this division again. In one way or another I've been working on it for almost six years, but it started as a play based purely on the tiny bit that is known of the seventeenth-century nun, Maryana Alcoforado, who was seduced by a French soldier of fortune. When he abandoned her she wrote him five wild love letters, and he allowed them to be pirated and published. They became what we might call the first best seller.

We know, from the letters, that she was not thrown out of the convent. She was demoted to sister portress, which was far more drastic a thing in those days than it would be today, because in the convents the choir sisters were the nobility, and the sister portress was a lay nun who could have been a peasant.

The only other thing we know about her is from her death notice, which discloses that she was made abbess of the convent after thirty years of penance.

There are more or less two things you can do with this story. You can write a nasty, scandalous, blasphemous shocker. I knew I didn't want to do this, but I also knew I was going to have to come to terms with love (in both upper and lower case) and with sin, repentance, and regeneration. I had to do a great deal of theological thinking about this which I hadn't anticipated.

The play I wrote was read by several people, and finally George Shaffer, who does the Compass productions, read it and got quite excited. But I told him that there were problems with the third act I couldn't resolve. He agreed and thought it would make a much better movie than it would a play, and would I like to try a film treatment? I'm usually willing to tackle almost anything anyone suggests. I knew this would be difficult because it meant a completely new medium, thinking in completely new terms, but I went into high gear and had a marvelous time until my body gave up and put me in the hospital. (My body does this to me.) The film treatment worked, probably because I was in a semicomatose state, and George liked it; then, because it is a ticklish subject, I took it to Father Harold Gardner, the Jesuit who was editor of *America* and was at that time on leave of absence from Catholic University. He liked it and said that he would be interested in advising if it were made into a movie.

So then I wrote a scenario, but before I wrote the scenario I went to Portugal because I realized I had to see the actual places where the story occurred. Hugh was in a soap opera at the time, and they wrote him out of it for ten days, and we left for Portugal the day after Christmas. We couldn't land at Lisbon because of fog, so we went on to Madrid. It was cold in Portugal, terribly cold, and we weren't prepared for it. We had some language problems. They thought Hugh was English and I was his French concubine, but we loved it. I saw the convent where Maryana had lived, and the curator was delighted because I was the only author who had ever dealt with Maryana who'd come to see the convent. We also found how little was known about her, and how some people don't even think she existed.

I came away untrammeled by fact. I could never write a historical novel; I'm uncomfortable if my imagination isn't free to do what it wants. If you write a historical novel you're stuck with what happened, with what people actually did. The exciting thing in writing a book is to have your characters do what you didn't expect of them. Anyway, I finished the scenario, and everybody promptly got worried about it as the subject for a movie.

Simultaneously everyone involved thought it would be a great idea if I wrote it as a novel, and if Farrar, Straus and Giroux did it, this would help us past any real or implied censure. (FS&G simply would not publish a blasphemous book.) But I wanted to do it as a novel anyway, but I had trouble switching mediums and turned out one treatment after another instead of a novel, until it finally (I don't know how) came out in the form it's in. Theron Raines, my agent, read it and said, "Thank God you didn't tell me what you were going to do because I would have told you not to do it, it couldn't be done." But it's done, and people at FS&G call it "ambitious," but to me — well, what I've done is to write from two places in time. I start with a young American woman whose marriage has broken up. She flees to Portugal and discovers Maryana's love letters. I move back and forth in time between Charlotte, the American, having to learn what love means, what marriage is, and Maryana having to learn what love means, what faithfulness is. In some places it isn't even clear whether it's Maryana or Charlotte I'm talking about, which is deliberate. So I suppose it is ambitious, but if I'd thought of it that way I'd have scared myself off.

But it's done. Rewritten, cut, edited, cut again, enhanced by a good editor, a good copy editor, all sorts of nice people.

I don't think my objectives as a writer have anything to do with the size of my talent, be that talent small, medium-size or whatever. *Being a writer* is the premise upon which I have always based my life. It's what I am. So I suppose it is not only a profession, and I care very much about being professional, but it is also a vocation.

I feel that no matter what I do, whether it's a little tiny book or something in which I am (knowingly or not) being ambitious, I have a responsibility to the reader. Now there is a tendency in some writing, some by tremendous writers, at that, to use the reader as a psychiatric couch and the book as a self-indulgence. But this is what you should do in your first draft. An awful lot of first drafts are getting published. But you should take the book beyond the self-indulgence of the first draft and write it for your readers.

I'll use acting as an example. If an actor cries onstage, the audience may be impressed by it, but the audience will not cry. If a comedian laughs at his own jokes, the audience won't laugh. All of this "onstage indulgence" must be weeded out in rehearsal. In rehearsing a tragic part the actor will probably bawl his head off, but this is necessary. But when he performs for an audience he has to pattern his performance to wring emotion from the audience, not put on a mere display. When all you give your audience, either onstage or from a book, is a slice of life, what's the point of going to the theater or reading a book? They might as well sit in the middle of Broadway and watch people.

A piece of art, no matter what it is, is discipline. It's got pattern; it fakes chaos. It says something about our place in the world, even if it's a very tiny thing. You don't have to be very ambitious to interpret the meanings of life. Or you can be ambitious beyond your capacity, which is an extremely good thing—I think you expand your capacity only by trying to do things that are more than you can do.

In last Sunday's *Times* there was a fascinating article by a historian who said that things were accomplished only by people who acted "as if." England, during the blitz, acted "as if" it could overcome Germany. You "as if" the impossibles, then you do them. I think this is the premise upon which all real writers write. We write as if we could write a better book than we can, and it may not be the book we want to write, but it's probably better than the book would be if we were willing to stay within the limitations of our talent.

Then there's an English poet who said that poetry is like ice cream. Tremendous heat is needed in the generating of it, but in the actual writing there has to be ice, for otherwise the ice cream will melt. This is true. The more emotional a scene is, the cooler I am when I write it. This is not intentional; perhaps it's another part of the subconscious working as a guide. You can call it your subconscious or unconscious or (I'm still thinking in theological terms) grace or whatever.

I think also that a writer has a tremendous responsibility to his work, to make his instrument as good as it can possibly be so that it can be kept constantly fit for playing. I know writers who write only when inspiration comes. How would Isaac Stern play if he played the violin only when he felt like it? He would be lousy. Perhaps every concert he gives isn't as great as every other concert, but if he didn't practice and work constantly he wouldn't have an instrument for the great work when the time came to perform it. The same is true for art of every type. It may be that what we do in practice, what we throw away, is almost as important as what we keep. I know that for each page I keep I've probably thrown away a hundred.

As I said before, I resent the book as a self-indulgence. I don't think this is fair to the writer's talent or to the reader's time. I'm always a number of years behind reading current books, because I usually wait to see if they're still around in five years. I'm not going to live long enough to read everything, so I've got to do a certain amount of sifting. I find, after my plunge into theology while writing *The Love Letters*, that I'm reading more philosophy. Oddly enough, I also read a lot of physics; I get very excited by physics. I was terrible in that area at school, but in reading physics, I get more of a sense of theology than I do in reading many theologians. One of the books that to me was most filled with God was *Limitations of Science* by Sullivan, which never once mentioned the word "God." And I read science fiction in the bathtub; I love it, but it doesn't matter if it falls in.

In fact, I discovered science fiction when I was eight years old; I read Oscar Wilde's fairy tales along with H. G. Wells. *Happy Prince* and *The War of the Worlds* go beautifully together.

I do regret that I sound pompous when I talk about myself as a writer, but maybe it can't be helped. I have to regard being a writer as the most important thing in the world; otherwise, there is no point to my life. I also have to constantly balance "being a writer" with being a wife and a mother. It's a matter of putting two different things first, simultaneously. This obviously makes for some frustrations, tensions, and conflicts, but that's fine — out of them comes creativity in what I write and in family relationships. I get terribly excited about things and passionately enjoy things. I enjoy life tremendously. Last spring I was going on about one of my great enthusiasms to my eldest daughter when she threw her arms around me and said, "Oh, Mother, you are such a child!" I must have looked appalled, so she very quickly said, "But we love you this way. We wouldn't want you to be any different."

I'm afraid the children think I am rather immodest both in conversation and behavior. We will talk about absolutely anything. And if I'm taking a bath, and I suddenly have an idea, I'll plop right out and sit down at the typewriter and they'll say, "Mother, really!"

This summer our young son, fourteen, was about to go away to boarding school for the first time. He said, "I want to have an embarrassing conversation with you, Mother," and I said, "Fine, what about?" He said, "What do fourteen-year-olds usually have on their minds?" I said, "Sex," and he said, "Yup," so we went through the whole thing. He said, "All the other boys are going to know all the words, and I want to know all the words, too." So we just went through all the words.

No wonder the kids think I'm sweet but nuts.

I know I'm regarded as a happy person, and I think I am. But I think that being happy (again we come to contradictions) involves pain and anguish as well as laughter and good feeling. Only the contented moron can have joy without pain, night without day. Light means nothing unless there is dark. A candle is useless if there's no night.

I'm not very bright; I'm not an intellectual. I got through college with honors on the gift of gab because I could write things that appealed to professors. But as far as having an intellectual mind, I don't; I have an instinctual mind. Without my husband's patience and tolerance, heaven only knows where I'd be. Not only that, but he is an absolutely magnificent editor, and when he reads something of mine and criticizes it I know that he's right and that I'm going to have a tremendous amount of rewriting to do. I get absolutely furious and behave abominably; I scream at him, I defend what I've done, I shriek, I yell. I don't know why he puts up with it. Then I go back and do what he says.

With *The Arm of the Starfish* he was out of town with a play, but my agent read it, was excited by it, and thought it the best thing I'd done. Hugh read it and said, "No, no. It's good, but you left strings untied here, you left strings untied there. The plot isn't tight enough. The book isn't nearly good enough." I got really furious with him, because I knew this meant rewriting the whole book.

I did. I rewrote the whole thing, and the last third was completely changed. The strings he pointed out meant that I had to change the whole resolution, and it was a much better book because of him.

The next thing he does which is absolutely invaluable, and saves both Theron and my publishers a great deal of time, is the way he goes over a manuscript with me word for word, cutting. "You don't need this word," or even "You don't need this comma." I scream, "You want me to cut the whole thing, you don't want anything left!" But it ends up tighter and tidier because of his vigilance. I always put in too much overcerebration, and he takes it right out. And he's right. It doesn't belong in a novel; it belongs in an essay. The world has lost a good editor in having him a great actor.

Finally, in this matter of advising the young writer, hoping for him, I suppose I have to assume that he shares my aims: to be published, to be read, to communicate. The only school for this is reading other writers—the great writers, over and over. Some writers say no—that you become derivative, but in the great writers you find the right things done the way they must be done, and certain things that are never done, and you can learn from these.

I think you must also write constantly, whether you feel like it or not. I have kept copious, unpublishable journals since I was eight; they are my self-indulgence, my safety valve. When I'm miserable I let it all out in there, not in published first drafts. Into the journals go everything I see, any ideas I have, pictures and anecdotes of the children (which have been invaluable material for the Austin books). I copied down, for example, Chekhov's letters to his wife, great reams of his advice on acting, because it applied to what I felt was true about writing.

In college I majored in English, but most of my friends majored in theater, and I spent most of my time in the theater making them put on my plays. This was terribly good experience, so when I came to New York to make my fortune I went into the theater for two reasons: to get over my horrible shyness, and to gain experience as a writer, to see what happened to words night after night on the stage. I have a flair as an actress, but I'm much too tall to have ever been serious about it. My flair was for the comic, but I was perfectly happy to get understudy jobs. I did learn most of the things about words I hoped to learn, and I did get over being shy. Also, working in the Goshen general store helped me in overcoming my shyness. I had to pay attention to the person on the other side of the counter. I can't advise every young writer to go into the theater, but it could be a great help.

I think the journal is important, both to absorb self-indulgence and furnish source material. Experimentation with all forms of writing is important.

At dinner once my new son-in-law talked about some theologians who claim that God is not dead, as some theologists are claiming, but that language is dead, and that if we are to revive language so that it will have any meaning, then violence must be done to it. I got very upset. I felt very threatened by this, because if language is dead, so is my profession. Then I began to realize that doing violence to language didn't mean at all what I thought he'd meant at first. It didn't mean doing anything different with the words or reversing the order of words or of doing anything strange with words. What it meant was not being afraid to use words directly to communicate with each other. This applies very much to writing, just as it does to our personal relationships. In today's world what we've done is to cushion language so that we don't communicate with each other; we retreat into jargon. We talk about things being relevant and meaningful in order to avoid relevance and meaning. We're afraid to say what we really want to say. We're afraid to communicate because by doing so we become vulnerable. I'm being vulnerable, right now, because I'm being very open. Yet I realize more and more that you cannot be creative in any way—in personal relationships or in work—unless you completely take off your armor, do violence to jargon and platitudes and make yourself vulnerable. Talk about the things that matter, and write about the things that matter, even if people think you're silly.

This is the only thing that will give language back its dignity and joy.

"I do feel a deep responsibility to the truth, and I am very glad that I've rarely been caught off-base in this regard... nothing has been perverted or distorted or cheapened. I've never been improperly materialistic in using things for sensation or shock value."

James Michener

James Michener

MICHENER: Not long ago a history of the Michener family was written in my home town and published in, of all places, Tokyo. The Micheners are a very distinguished family of farmers who came from England to settle in rural Pennsylvania. A conservative, prolific family, men with a genuine touch of the soil; delightful, cautious rural Englishmen who came to Pennsylvania and didn't modify their behavior at all. This history was immensely interesting to me because I have never known exactly what my background is. It's been very clouded, and the history makes it clear that I am not a Michener, that I was taken in by the Michener clan when I was very young from a background which is totally unknown. I was brought up by a wonderful widowed woman who gave me a great education and a place in her home. She did the same for a great many other youngsters. In fact, one of the experiences in my life that is far more dramatic than anything I've written about is the performance of this wonderful woman in taking care of homeless children, providing educations, even sending some of them, like me, through college. She made her living by taking in washing and sewing shirtwaists, and she could never have earned more than six or seven dollars a week throughout her entire life. She was helped by the community and from such social service agencies as existed in those days, but the bulk of the work was hers.

It was from that background that I sprang and acquired the attitudes I have. Fortunately, I grew up in America rather than elsewhere, because in some other countries (which I know well) I would have been totally cut off from any higher education or any opportunity to advance. But in our system we have always looked out for the bright boy, for a kid who might profit from being given some degree of help and privilege. At the time I was a boy a very wealthy store owner in Philadelphia had just given a large sum of money to a nearby college for the identification of just such youngsters. The scouts, luckily, came to my small town, observed that I was something of an athlete and never got less than "A" in my classes, and thought I was exactly the type of person they were looking for. So from no background at all I was picked up (this was in 1925) as one of the scholars, and from that year on everything was roses. I went to a great school in Pennsylvania, got a scholarship that took me to Europe, knocked around in Europe for a few years and came back home. I got more scholarships; I attended nine or ten different universities, none at my expense. (Even in my adult life all the travel I've done has been at someone else's expense.) The reason I mention all this is that it amounts to a case in point proving that the American system, properly applied, has safeguards in it for the identification of kids who cannot pay their own way but who are good risks.

If I were to start over at, say, the age of twelve, which was the point at which my intelligence began to make itself obvious to me, and when I began to realize that I must do well in school, I would rather be a Negro than a member of any other race because every good school would be looking for me; in fact, they're begging young Negroes of promise to come. They pick you up at 12 or 13, pay your way through graduate school, and when you're done corporations bid for you, and if they don't get you the federal government does.

At any rate, I have lived off the public treasury from the time I was about 14 years old, and I think I have more than repaid any sums that were invested in me through taxation and through what the government has received from the things I've done. I suppose that in Russia, China, and Israel, efforts are made to identify boys and girls of aptitude, but I don't find this in France or Germany, England or Italy. I do find it in the Arab countries where they are trying desperately to modernize, to broaden their base. In those nations that aren't so progressive I would hate to be myself in 1925.

I'm a freak in the field of writing because of the fact that I didn't do any creative writing until I was almost forty. There's a saying in our profession that if you don't write your first book before the age of thirty-five you probably never will. I believe this is a sound doctrine, and it applies even in my case, though obliquely, because even though I didn't start writing for general publication until I was forty, I was a college professor, writing papers and preparing learned materials on history, so that I was learning my profession. I had a long background and long training with very good editors on the matter of putting sentences together. In any event I was a college professor of history and loved it, worked hard, and had a long, happy life ahead of me. But all that was taken away from me by a New York publishing firm that needed a man of my age to step into a vacancy they had. So I became an editor at the age of thirty-five and was an editor for about ten years. I was very happy at that, and would have been quite content to continue, but the war intervened and I was thrown into the Pacific theater with very little to do. It was there that I started to write, very late in life, but with a great deal of drive.

Tales of the South Pacific was written on a little island virtually in the middle of that ocean. I did have the advantage of being able to go to many different islands; the kind of work I did necessitated that, so I saw a great deal of the Pacific, but by and large the stories were done on one little island after working hours. I wrote it all at night, none during the daylight hours because I had a full-time job. How I've switched from a night to a day writer I don't know; now I'm disciplined to work during the day almost exclusively. Perhaps, if I had my choice, I'd have written *Tales* during the day.

Tales of the South Pacific was never a best seller. It had tiny, wonderful lives, and I could not wish more for any beginning writer. It was published by Macmillan, and if you ever have a chance to see a first edition, by all means do. It was printed on blind paper, horrible paper, and it is one of the ugliest books ever turned out. They didn't even begin each chapter at the top of a page. One, in fact, begins two lines from the bottom of the page. I never saw a book this dreadfully printed, but there were wartime restrictions on the use of paper, and mine wasn't a very important book. Nobody thought much would happen to it.

They sold a few copies, but not very many. But apparently the right people got hold of some of them, because one New York critic gave it a glorious, glowing review. All of the good fortune stemmed from that beginning; the major magazines of the day didn't even notice it. I think that of the ten major book-reviewing agencies, nine ignored it completely. *Saturday Review, Time, Newsweek* — they didn't even notice it. I had no occasion whatever to get a swelled head. That one review did attract the attention of people who should read a book, and that saved it. It was published, and it died, with that one epitaph.

A year later *Tales of the South Pacific* won the Pulitzer Prize, and it got a second life, as it were. But on the day the prize was announced the paperback edition came out and completely killed any further hardcover sale, so not much happened saleswise after the Pulitzer. There were editorials that declared it was the least-deserving book in recent years to win the Pulitzer; it was by no means the popular choice. In fact, it was an insulting choice to many. At least two other books had been definitely favored to win; I believe the *Saturday Review* ran a preview of Pulitzer selections, discussing about fifteen books as possible winners, and I was not even included on that list. Again I had no occasion to develop a swelled head.

The Pulitzer Prize was rather a shock to me. I think it was a very valiant choice on the part of the judges. I don't know who they were, but they had a lot of guts to choose my book. Over the years I think the choice has proved to be far from disappointing. The book has gained increasing stature and is much more widely read now than when it was published. Then, after the Pulitzer had created no stir whatsoever, Rodgers and Hammerstein came along with their musical a year later. I must admit this *did* rather establish it.

South Pacific thus had three lives: the critical reception and lack of reception when the book came out, the Pulitzer Prize, and the play, all spaced over a period extending from three to four years. This gave the book a tremendous, long period of vital life, and I think this is what a young writer should aspire to. Too many young fellows I see write one book, everything happens to them all at once, the money and the acclaim, and they face a difficult problem of keeping a balance. I think this is why so many of them never do a second or a third book, or if they do a second one, it's pretty bad and they quit. The spacing out was a godsend in my case — the best possible thing that could have happened. By the time the Pulitzer Prize came along I knew this wasn't the greatest book in the world, and by the time Rodgers and Hammerstein came along I knew that my book had been out there a long time and had created no excitement whatsoever. Yet it had always provided a solid base so there was never a sharp feeling of regret, of time wasted.

I could not wish the young writer a better break. Let a book be published, let it fall flat on its face, and let it find its own honorable level. Never give him too much money to live on, but enough to encourage him to spend money on the things he ought to — travel, books, and more books.

Oddly enough, *South Pacific* made so little splash, even in paperback, that I get about the same royalty from it today as I did when it was published.

N: *And after that,* Hawaii, *an immense job from the standpoint of the time and research that must have gone into it.*

MICHENER: *Hawaii* is rather a strange case history of producing a novel, if only because it deals with four or five different areas of the world, and I think it fair to assume that I am the only man (let alone writer) who was rather closely acquainted with all five areas involved.

Now, many men have been in rural New England, and a great number of writers; virtually anyone could have written that portion of *Hawaii.*

Hawaii, itself — well, it seems that most of the writers of the world have stopped there at one time or another, so almost anyone could have written that part.

Southern Japan—that begins to eliminate some people, most writers.

Rural China—that knocks out a lot more. And Tahiti and Bora Bora, which eliminates just about everyone except me. It was an accident that I had spent time in all these places and had vivid memories of them. I returned to each to make certain my memories were correct and to gather more pertinent information before I started writing.

I would say that the basic structure of *Hawaii* was an accident of my adult experience as a professor in New England, as a citizen in Hawaii, as a man from the Korean War vacationing in southern Japan, as a man from World War II flying into China at the end of that war, and as an adventurer knocking around the remote parts of the South Pacific.

I think all this is a good case-in-point: that the life a man leads prepares him to write certain things and not to write other things. I don't mean this exclusively in terms of geography, but in terms of experience or insight or knowledge or professional and technical acquaintance. A writer is limited to his base of cognizance. It doesn't have to be physical cognition; I don't think he has to go to all places and engage in all occupations, but I think he must have experiences into which he can inject himself. It can be as simple as hearing a vivid story in a bar; it can be extensive reading; it can be pure imagination; but somewhere, somehow, he must go through the basic emotional experience. I can easily visualize taking a brilliant young man who is better at raw writing than I am, and presenting him with the problems of writing the novel, *Hawaii*. After a certain number of years he might very possibly come up with a much better job than I did, using a different approach to the experience. These things are possible, but not for me. I am a very tactile writer. I must have the experience visually, emotionally, historically, geographically, economically, every which way, or I can't do it. Yet I do visualize a situation in which a smart young man could do any of the things I've done.

As a matter of fact, I'm rather inclined toward the Henry James approach of digging within oneself, rather than the Jack London approach of believing that you have to be on the ship before you can write about it. I think the James approach is better, but for those of us who have a more limited artistic experience, the experience is an essential and legitimate way to operate. Thus, in writing *Hawaii*, in building upon the experiences I had had, I wanted to construct a long and vivid and intricate book utilizing all the strands of experience. I did this very consciously because I foresaw the fact that the spirit of Hawaii was going to be a major factor in the world for the next few decades, the matter of how races and people and contrasting cultures can coalesce.

To an extent I was fortunate in my timing, in that I think that a great many people have read *Hawaii* with that problem in mind and find it a solution, in its own small way, to the greater problems that heckle us today. I certainly think that *Hawaii* is as good a statement on the race question as has been provided in America during the last ten years. It is nonhysterical, descriptive, and it is possible to identify with it. I must qualify this by saying that it is, unfortunately, an oblique approach to the great problem of Negro and white, but I was not writing about Negroes and whites; I was working off to one side in order to illuminate that problem without the hysteria of the American situation. It would have been a much better book had it tangled head-on with the Negro-white problem, but I wasn't capable of doing that. Somebody else must do that. But within the limits that an oblique approach always imposes, I think *Hawaii* is a very strong statement on our race problems.

N: *To bring you up-to-date, and here again it's a matter of tackling a very large novel with the tremendous amount of research that had to be involved, could you talk about* The Source?

MICHENER: I spent more than two years overseas, primarily in Israel, though I did find occasions to make long excursions into the surrounding Arab countries. This time was spent collecting material for *The Source*—exploration, research, discussion. It was one of the most intensive periods of work I've ever undergone. I got up every morning about seven-thirty and worked until one o'clock. I don't believe I allowed any interruptions during those two years of mornings, except for certain field trips I wanted to take. Then I would put in a comparable time working in the afternoon or evening, though not writing. Since *South Pacific* I've never been able to write at any time of day other than in the morning, from 7:30 to about 12:30. If I get in three hours of writing a day I have done rather well; after that I find I'm just writing words.

The concept of a writer who sits and writes around the clock does not apply to me at all. I have known some people who can do it, and with great distinction, but I'm not one of them. In the afternoon I almost never put pen to paper; I read, check things, go over what I've done. Often I just conk out. In the evening I unwind and read or do research on what I want to write the next day. I've found that the great-est asset a writer can have is the feeling that at 12:30 on a bright, sunny day, he's got something great at hand that he wants to write the next sunny morning.

But with *The Source* this regime went on for two wonderful, fruitful, memorable years. I can't recall a day — Saturday, Sunday, or holiday — when I allowed anything to consciously intrude.

I suppose *The Source* is of the genre which claims *Hawaii*. It's a long novel, but really a short novel. Let me explain this contradiction because I've had trouble explaining it to myself. I've actually written a novel that could be published in about 280 pages if the paper were thick. (You know how publishers work. If you write a short novel they use thick paper to make it look big; if you write a long novel they print it on thin paper to make it look manageable.) At any rate, I've written a short novel, and I think it's pretty good.

It deals with a group of archaeologists who come to an imaginary site in the Holy Land and excavate it. They are people of diverse character, diverse interests, and certainly diverse religions. There's an American Catholic—a wonderful man, of whom I've grown quite fond over the past few years. He's the American archaeologist in charge of it all; he comes from Chicago. Chicago is an important focus in this novel; several people from Chicago become important in it. Anyway, he leaves Chicago to conduct a regular investigation of the site, vaguely remembered as being of some potential importance. He works with the assistance of some people from England, an Arab, and two Jewish scholars. He doesn't know what he's going to find, nor does he know what relationships he's going to establish with these people. So in this relatively short, intense novel, he and his international colleagues dig an exploratory trench from the top to the bottom of the mound.

As they dig they uncover certain artifacts of importance and many of no real significance at all: a coin, a spearhead, a hammer, a tombstone. They go through fifteen layers of these civilizations, digging up items which appear in the first chapter of the novel. They have philosophical discussions, minor adventures; they have picnics together. It's somewhat in the mood, one might say, of Jane Austen—just a group of people.

In the last chapter of the book they reach two additional levels which are of great significance historically. They wind up the digging, pay the workmen, close down the holes, and go their separate ways. Certain things have happened to them relating to beauty, triumph, disappointment, but the year is at an end and the characters disperse.

This novel, by itself, would attract a good many readers. I think they would find it amiable, reasonably intelligent, and some of the characters quite attractive. I would be satisfied to publish this short novel as it is. With some modifications it would stand.

However, when the archaeologists have uncovered fifteen layers of civilization by the end of the first chapter, a series of fifteen flashbacks in reverse order begins. These are glimpses of man, of what has happened to man, in the Holy Land, and it comprises the bulk of the novel—nearly a half-million words. The flashbacks look at society in terms of profound problems, built upon incidents that are implied by what the archaeologists uncover. Thus we have a novel somewhat in the form of a César Franck symphony—a theme at the beginning, a return to the theme at the end, and discursions and excursions during the body, with the theme repeated. This is what gives the book its character, and will either allure or repel the individual reader. It's a complicated and sometimes beautiful and sometimes difficult ebb and flow of time and history; my gamble is in being able to make it interesting enough so that the reader will try to stay with it to the very end.

As to the fifteen episodes which form the heart of the book, they range from 10,000 B.C. to 1948. One sees the Babylonians coming to the Holy Land, the soldiers of Mohammed making their appearance, King Herod at the end of his reign, Solomon, a man trying to grow wheat at the beginning of history, a man digging a well. I have obviously tried to avoid the central figures of known history. No King Saul listening to David play his harp, no Elijah or Moses—it isn't that kind of a book. I've worked along the edges of history in order to use people who would have a vitality of their own and provide a certain illumination, and I think I may have succeeded. It's a tough job, and I'm glad I did it this way. I hope the public will be able to, willing to, follow the construction.

N: *What obligation do you feel as a novelist?*

MICHENER: I've had to do a great deal of thinking about this in the past months because I've been under some pressure to respond to the question of what's happening in publishing today, with the paperback houses playing the increasing role they do, and I have come to the conclusion that I do have certain responsibilities. I haven't thought about them in the orderly way your question implies, but let me state what I think they are.

First of all, I have a responsibility to the reading public to lure people into a manuscript which they might not normally read, and to make it so proficient that they will be carried along by it and introduced to new ideas, new concepts, perhaps new experiences they might not obtain otherwise. I take this quite seriously. For example, in *The Source*, despite the fact that it is complex in its construction, every device I know that will carry the story and the reader forward is used. Perhaps this does account, in some measure, for the success of *Hawaii;* this was an ambitious novel too, and complex, and required a great deal of conscious skill on my part to keep it in motion and interrelationship.

I feel no responsibility to subject matter that I can think of; I have about fifteen marvelous novels I would like to write. I think this is true of a great many writers: what we have is an inner drive, an inner compulsion, which could be spent on any variety of subject matter.

I do, however, feel a deep responsibility to the truth, and I am very glad that I've rarely been caught off-base in this regard. Sometimes I may have deviated on matters of psychological truth, but one can do only what one's own insights permit. Certainly nothing has been perverted or distorted or cheapened. I've never been improperly materialistic in using things for sensation or shock value.

So it adds up to a great responsibility to the reading public, virtually none to choice of subject matter, and grave responsibility to truth. I would hate to get caught off-base; it's as simple as that.

There is another responsibility which I feel very strongly, and it is difficult to explain, but it is a responsibility to keep the artistic system moving. By this I mean that I have always been willing, in the years when my books have been widely read, to give the hardback publisher a big cut of whatever I make on paperback, movie rights, and so on, because I want to see him stay in business. I want to see him stay in business because he performs a most useful function in selecting material, in carrying new writers along, in developing new writers, in paying the way for them during the years when they're not making much money. He encourages fifteen new writers when he knows that possibly only two or three are going to make a profit for him. He doesn't know which two or three they'll be, but for his own well-being, and for the literary world as a whole, he has to back all fifteen.

I presume I will always continue to be very willing for the hardcover publisher to make the maximum dollar out of me. I don't find this at all repugnant. I encourage it because it's better to scatter the income around during the years of the big best sellers. I prefer to be with a house that is plowing back a large percentage of its profits in the unprofitable business of uncovering new writers. I doubt that a contract could be written that would take me to a publisher that merely rode the best seller waves, unless the contract stipulated that a certain percentage of his profits, and of mine, were spent on the encouragement of new writers. It's as simple as this: Who the hell is going to keep the new William Faulkner alive through his first six books?

N: *If you were to offer advice to the young writer, or hope for paths or principles he'd follow, what would that be?*

MICHENER: That's a tough question, because the only way I can answer it is with the assumption that the youngster on the other end is interested in wanting to write the way I write. So with that restriction, here goes.

At the end of a book I wrote titled *The Voice of Asia,* I said that I had been asked to write a similar book about Africa, but declined because I thought I simply didn't have the human energy to become proficient in that field. My eyes aren't good, there are only so many hours in the day, and I have only so much spiritual reserve.

Talent is very common in the United States. There must be fifty or sixty young writers who can write as well as James Jones and Morris West and me. But what these young men should do is to stake out some area of acute experience. In my case it was a geographical setting — I ought to be more universal, but I'm not.

The young writer should learn one or two languages — Spanish, if Latin America will be his sphere, one of the Arabic languages if he's going to Africa, perhaps French in any event. He should certainly spend four or five years studying the history, geography, geology, philosophy, certainly the literature of the area he chooses, and build himself a base of travel and experience. Perhaps he should work for a company in the area, for the State Department, or as a teacher in one of the Army schools, but he should make himself proficient in the best sense of the word. Then he can say, "I'm going to be as good a writer in this field as can be provided by any country in the world." At the end of a five- or ten-year apprenticeship he should be an invaluable asset to this country, perhaps to the world.

And there are at least a dozen areas, not tactile, but human, that are calling for the attention of a Malamud, a Cozzens, a Roth. Areas of important human interest where the young writer who dug in could win all the value and monetary reward and fame he could possibly want.

I know that in my life, because I have established a reputation as a hard worker and an honest worker who performs his contract, I am probably asked every week to do things that would keep me busy for the next two or three years. They don't need me because I couldn't do those things nearly as well as someone else would, but the other fellows haven't presented themselves.

Therefore, to the young writer I can only say, train yourself extensively and intensively, learn to write, travel, study, read. The beauty of it all is that the best fields don't demand that you leave your chair to do the intensive preparation — the Henry James field, the Jane Austen field, the George Eliot field. You can spend your day at home in your chair and say, "I'm going to be the world's leading authority on what happens when there's a divorce in New York State." Write a big novel about this and it would make anything that skirts the subject seem trivial.

It's specialization to some extent, I guess — but artistic, not mechanical, and therein lies a profound difference in the meaning of that overused word. No one person can know everything. But because man's knowledge of everything is now so vast, it behooves any one person to know virtually everything about at least one thing.

Merle Miller
and
Evan Rhodes

If you have suspected that most television situation comedies and dramas are produced by a number of monkeys locked in a room with an equal number of typewriters, you are wrong. Not too far wrong, however, since the mob-action antics that create these shows are somewhat simian.

And it's shown in all its comic and horrifying aspects in *Only You, Dick Daring*, by Merle Miller and Evan Rhodes, the book that has reportedly upped the tranquilizer intake on Madison Avenue.

"Unfortunately, every word in the book is true," Miller explained. "I was asked by United Artists and CBS and various others to write a pilot for a TV series about a County Agent, to be played by Jackie Cooper, and a Home Agent, to be played by Barbara Stanwyck.

"The work these people do, in every county in the United States, is terribly important, and I thought we could produce a valid and realistic show. This thought was utter nonsense."

What went awry?

"Everything." Rhodes shook his head. "Absolutely everything. Merle started working from an eighty-one-page outline, supposedly approved. Then Hennessey-type gag lines were written in for Cooper, and tough-tender lines for Stanwyck, then realism was abandoned for more climax and violence. Everyone rewrote the script—I think even the office boy tossed in a few deathless lines."

"It's as if Laurel and Hardy, the Marx Brothers, and Abbott and Costello were all playing television executives," Miller added. "When we finally saw the monstrosity which had been shot at $1,000 per minute I debated killing myself, but decided no—it wasn't worth it. Television is simply in the hands of men who are paranoid, terrified, and stupid."

"Let me hasten to explain," Rhodes interrupted, "the book is not serious although it is utterly truthful. It's satirical and funny and it may even be a textbook for eager young writers who want to know what to do and (specifically) what not to do."

Whose fault is it that television has ended up in its untalented, untidy state?

"It's a two-way street, isn't it? The public has a right to demand better stuff, and the producers haven't taste enough to give it to them."

"Mercifully," Miller said, "our show was so bad that even the network wouldn't use it. "Calhoun"—that was what we named it— ended in a projection booth."

Is there a chance that the book, devastating as it is to actual people controlling the industry, will have an effect?

"It's possible," Miller nodded. "After he read the book, David Susskind—as you know, he's one of the people in the book—called and said that the book has moved him to renew the crusade for better programming. Since he's one of the very good and strong men in the industry, perhaps there's hope."

"Right now we have a school of writing, mostly in fiction, which is the self-pity school. . . . I think we ought to be able to express some kind of exuberance and jubilation over the good things in life that are left to us, even if it is light-hearted mockery of the things that beset or besiege us."

Ogden Nash

Ogden Nash

NASH: I was born in 1902 in Rye, New York, and raised in a back-and-forth way between Rye and Savannah, Georgia, until I was fourteen. My father was a North Carolinian who, as a boy eleven or twelve years old toward the end of the Civil War, patrolled the grounds of the family estate with a shotgun to protect his mother and sisters from stragglers and looters. He came North as a young man, and got into the naval stores business — rosin and turpentine — and he had dual headquarters, New York and Savannah; that was why we spent winters in the South and summers at Rye.

At that time Rye was a small country town with dirt roads. One of the main roads ran right outside our place, and my brother and I used to sit on the wall and count the number of cars traveling on the Boston Post Road. If we counted eight or ten we had a very high mark to be chalked up on the calendar.

My education was rather varied. My mother came from a very scholarly family. Her father, Jason Chenault, of Louisville, Kentucky, had been a professor of classics — Greek and Latin — and his high principles regarding the "right" education had been passed along. The family's intent was to send me to very good boarding schools, but when I was twelve or thirteen my father's business began to rock due to a series of lawsuits brought by the government, so our lives were disturbed as the financial situation changed. I was too young to realize exactly what was going on, but I knew that things were not as they used to be or should be. I went to day school in Rye, for a bit, and there was one short period — I was about ten and my family had gone abroad — when I was sent to a small boy's boarding school. When I say small I *mean* small. The capacity was eight boys, and it was outside Groton, Massachusetts. Presumably it was a preparatory school for Groton itself. At any rate, I spent a year there; the first half of it I was very homesick, but I got over that. I learned some Latin — began my rather serious study of Latin, a language I've found very useful — and I spent a good deal of time riding a bicycle through the New England countryside.

After that my eyes got very bad. My mother was quite disturbed about this and thought they were going to grow progressively worse, so two things of some significance resulted. She had me take a course in touch-typing which proved invaluable until my fingers curled up on me in later life. And she took me out of school and had me study at home. I did a great deal of reading with her; she was very widely read, a scholarly woman, and I think that most of my real education was gained in those years she tutored me.

Later on, when I was fifteen, the family fortunes had recouped sufficiently to send me off to boarding school again, so I went to St. George's in Newport, Rhode Island, where I spent three very happy years. I was lucky enough to encounter a few good masters who were extremely stimulating, particularly in history, Latin, and English. I can't value Latin enough in view of what it has given me in later life. Nor, for that matter, can I value the whole experience of boarding school enough. A boy gains so much, not only in the matter of a better education, but in self-reliance and the disciplines and the individualities needed to cope with life.

After St. George's I entered Harvard, where I spent only a freshman year. By this time I knew the family finances were again in very bad shape, and I'm afraid that I didn't have enough intellectual curiosity, nor enough physical vigor and ambition, to work my way through the remaining three years, so at the end of my freshman year I left and attempted to make myself self-supporting.

I bounced through a variety of jobs. In 1921 I went, as all young men of that day around New York seemed to do, down into Wall Street. Not willingly, but because there were friends of the family who could give me a job, and I spent a year in the mailroom of Dillon, Read and Company, working from four o'clock in the afternoon to twelve or one in the morning. I discovered what the downtown financial district looks like at midnight, with no one in the streets and cats prowling around the garbage cans. It was a lot like Don Marquis' *Mehitabel*. I also developed a deeper interest in writing. I always had been interested in writing; I started jotting down verse as a small child. When I was six or seven I started turning out verses, jingles, rhymes. Now, on Wall Street, I knew that I wanted to write, and I found myself trying to get closer to it. But I did not know at the time what or how I wanted to write.

I must say for myself that I did not write to established authors to ask them how I should go about being a writer. The saddest mail I get, and I get a great many of these letters every day, comes from the ambitious young who want to be writers and ask me how to write. The minute I get one of these letters I immediately know that whoever

wrote it is not going to be a writer; you simply don't write to someone
to ask "how." I think the only two roads to becoming a writer are heavy
reading and doing as much writing as possible, then seeing what editors
have to say about what you're doing.

I was thoroughly sick of Wall Street in short order, and began to try
seriously to get a writing job. I got one — writing advertising copy for
streetcar ads. There were still streetcars running on trolley tracks in
cities and towns, and I worked for a firm that sold poster space. I did
this for two or three years, but I followed in good footsteps: Scott
Fitzgerald had worked for the same firm some ten years before me, and
John Held, Jr., had been one of the artists on the staff. While I did this I
roomed with three or four other young men in a gas-heated cold-water
flat in the sixties, under the Elevated on Third Avenue in New York.
One of my roommates, a fellow named Joe Alger, had been two years
ahead of me at prep school, and had been very prominent at Harvard in
the Hasty Pudding and on the *Lampoon*. He was a brilliant fellow, and he
and I decided to write a book. We thought that the easiest book to turn
out would be a juvenile, so we did it, *The Cricket of Carador*. It was
accepted for publication by Doubleday, Page and Company. During
the process of publication, I met the head of the advertising department,
Dan Longwell, who had just lost his assistant, Frank Chapman, who at
the time was married to Irvin Cobb's daughter. Chapman had ambitions to become a singer, so he left the publishing business and took
some singing lessons, later did some concert work and married Gladys
Swarthout. At any rate, Longwell hired me.

Now, after two years in the streetcar advertising business I was
getting $100.00 a month. Doubleday offered me $90.00 a month, and I
netted rather less than that because I was living in New York City and
Doubleday's offices were out in Garden City, Long Island, so I had to
buy a commutation ticket out of my $90.00. But I wanted so badly to
get into the publishing field, to become associated with writers in one
way or another, that I jumped at the opportunity. I spent seven or eight
years in publishing, almost as happy as anyone could be, working in the
editorial and advertising departments.

To me it was the exciting sort of job a young man would grab and
work on eagerly, twelve and fourteen hours a day. I used to get up at six
o'clock to catch the Long Island out to Garden City, and I wouldn't get
back to New York until eleven-thirty or twelve-thirty at night. Along
about this time I began to stumble into the sort of thing I've been doing
virtually ever since. As I said, I'd written a great deal of verse throughout my youth; I like to think of it as poetry, and it certainly was
serious in conception and execution, but sometimes I was writing like

Swinburne, sometimes like Browning, then like Kipling, then like Tennyson. But I finally realized that my imitations were not very good, and that I simply couldn't qualify as a serious poet. There was a ludicrous aspect to what I was trying to do; my emotional and naked-beauty stuff just didn't turn out as I intended.

So I began to poke a little bit of fun at myself and these attempts, turning them upside down and accentuating the ludicrous side of which, at first, had been attempts at serious poetry. I kept working on these things at night after I got home from work, and eventually summoned up enough courage to send one of them to *The New Yorker*. To my great surprise and joy they liked it and asked for more. So I wrote more, at the same time keeping my job in editorial and advertising, and by 1931 enough of them had been assembled to encourage Simon and Schuster to ask me to make a book out of them. I did, and they published it, and it was extremely successful for a book of light verse. I think it sold about 40,000 copies rather quickly.

I was launched. I still had no idea of devoting my life to being a writer; it was to be a sideline while publishing was my mainstay. But along came the Depression.

The Depression hit after I'd left Doubleday to do a three-month stint as managing editor of *The New Yorker* magazine. Harold Ross hired me under two misapprehensions: first, that he wanted a managing editor, and second, that I would be a good one. At that time the job of managing editor of that magazine was like being caught briefly in a revolving door. In my case the revolution of the door took ninety days which was, I believe, the usual period of tenure at the time.

Ross was an astonishing man, worthy of all that has been written about him. He had superb taste, taste of an extremely sophisticated sort, yet he took great pains to present himself as an awkward, vulgar hick. I don't know if it was performance he enjoyed, or whether he was really a shy man hiding behind this facade; he certainly made a deplorable personal appearance. But his energy and taste made *The New Yorker* a great magazine.

After my brief stay with Ross I went back into the publishing business, this time with a smaller firm, one that was just starting out. This was in 1933, and the Depression had hit, and it was particularly rough for a young publishing house. Therefore my salary got cut and cut and cut until it was finally down to $25.00 a week. I was literally back to the $100.00 a month I'd earned in the streetcar advertising business eight or ten years before, and in the meantime I'd acquired a wife and one child and had another child on the way. Thus the new firm didn't seem to offer too bright a prospect. Fortunately, I knew most of the literary agents in New York through my job, and I approached one of them, a particularly good agent and also a dear and helpful friend. I asked him if he thought I could make a go of it as a free lance, and he scouted around amongst some magazine editors and finally said yes, he thought I could. The first thing he produced was a contract with *The Saturday Evening Post* for twenty-six verses a year during the next year, for which they would pay $100 each. That gave me a backbone of $2,600 a year that I could count on, so I packed up my family and we moved out of New York and came down here to Baltimore, really as a temporary expedient. (As it turned out we stayed for twenty years.) And with that I became a free-lance writer.

I supported myself completely by what I was writing, but at that time there were a great many more magazine and newspaper markets and even types of markets that don't exist anymore. I was extremely fortunate that I came along at a time when my sort of work had some novelty appeal and when there was a demand for it. In looking over my records I find that I sold 157 verses in 1935. A lot of them were very ephemeral stuff, some brief and topical, others done on assignment, but a good many of them seemed to qualify, in my own eyes, for inclusion in books. In fact, I can read them today without visibly flinching or wincing, and that says a great deal. A poet, whether he be serious or "light," often has a rough time reading his own stuff.

This went on for a great many years until I made the mistake of going out to Hollywood, where I had the sort of experiences other writers have complained bitterly about, but which are no less bitter because they're duplicated. I was out there for two and one-half years under option, with my option being picked up every six months at a slight raise in salary, and I really had no work to do at all. I don't think I had more than four weeks of real work in that entire period and this was not good for me. Anything I could work on—well, I'd find myself engaged with four or five or six or seven other writers. Often you didn't even know that other writers were working on the job that had been assigned to you, so any sense of individuality, any sense of pride in what you were doing, was destroyed. Toward the end of that dreadful period I would often awaken in the night, then wake my wife to ask her who I was. I felt that I had become so merged in this vast conglomeration of writers that I didn't know whether I was me or somebody else or perhaps six other people. I had been used to being a sort of lone wolf.

At any rate, it took me quite a while to recover from Hollywood. It wasn't until about a year and one-half after I'd come back East that I was able to stand on my own feet again. Since that time I've done some work in the theater, some on television, some on radio, but I made sure that writing was my main prop, my primary activity. I enjoy doing it. It comes a little harder now than it did thirty years ago; the ideas don't bubble up as fast.

On the other hand, I think I've developed a little more discipline. Perhaps a more interesting point of view. I don't know — but I should like to think that my experiences, both in life and in writing, have contributed somewhat to the improvement of my attempts. So here I am at the age of sixty-three, living between Baltimore and New Hampshire, doing as much writing as I can.

As I said, the markets have dwindled, but I still find some people who will buy what I turn out. I'm happy to say that I have thirteen or fourteen books in print that still sell moderately well. As old age approaches I find myself supported, to some extent, by the young man who was me twenty-five or thirty years ago, and I am very grateful to him for his energy.

So here I sit saying things that might have interested my mother. Poets, particularly the lighter variety, might well be more interesting read than heard.

N: *You mentioned before that Latin has been particularly valuable to your career. Could you explain that?*

NASH: Unfortunately, in recent years I haven't kept up with Latin as I should have, but the one thing that has stuck to me is the roots, the word roots. It's trite to say it, but so many of our English words are based on Latin, and the derivations of words have always been of great interest to me.

Now, to some extent I make a habit of distorting words, of distorting the language, but you cannot distort it or play with it successfully unless you know what it is you are tampering with. You can't break the rules until you know what the rules are. Otherwise it would simply be anarchy and chaos. The form I use happens to be suited to me, and it is one I was able to adapt myself to. Fortunately, I was able to persuade a number of readers to adapt themselves to it, also.

However, my own rules are very strict. I'm very conscientious about the liberties I take. But the knowledge of Latin and the roots of English words has remained with me, although the surface, the flowers of the field of Latin, have more or less vanished from my memory.

N: *Have you found any marked changes in the taste for poetry, or the appreciation of poetry, on the part of the public, during the course of your career?*

NASH: I spent some fifteen years doing something I had sworn I would never do. With the narrowing of markets I discovered I could not exist on verse alone, so I succumbed to the blandishments of a lecture bureau and spent about fifteen years giving thirty to forty talks a year in all parts of the country. I've been in all the continental states, and have moved from the largest of colleges and universities to the very smallest.

Now, I always managed to find wonderful audiences – and I don't think it was simply because people came to be entertained by light verse or by what is loosely, sometimes falsely, termed "humor." I think these people were interested in poetry in whatever form it took; I could tell this from the questions they asked and the books they carried. The growth of distinguished paperbacks now available to students has made a great difference. I think there's a tremendous wave of interest in poetry. It isn't always the type of poetry I'm interested in, but nevertheless it is stimulating, and I think a great deal of poetry reading is being done. It's still difficult, of course, for a good poet to make a living as a poet, and I think most of our poets now also teach. They're associated with universities or have grants. It's a very rare book of poems that sells more than two or three thousand copies, and those sales don't pay for much in the way of breakfast food.

I think that poetry is swinging back a little from the crooked verse of the late 1920's and thirties. It's becoming more communicative than it was at that time, less of a secret between the poet and his soul. The lyric element is coming back and I think that the prospects are very bright.

N: *Whom do you regard as our major poets?*

NASH: I've always avoided discussing my contemporaries. I can speak a little about the field of light verse, and in that area, unfortunately, most of the practitioners I regard most highly are doing very little. Phyllis McGinley seems to be writing no more light verse, and she was magnificent. Morris Bishop and David McCord are doing very little, and they were absolutely at the top of the tree. Samuel Hoffenstein, from whom I learned a great deal and from whom I'm afraid I stole a great deal in the manner of approach and view, died fifteen years ago. Another who is dead and will probably never receive the appreciation he deserves is Arthur Guiterman, who was a beautiful poet and versifier.

I see occasional bits of good light verse now and then in magazines, but before I become familiar with the names of the poets the names simply disappear. It seems that a lot of people write one or two delightful bits of light verse and then are heard from no more. I think it's much the same as the fate of what we used to call the "casuals" at *The New Yorker*. The prose pieces of the kind that Benchley and Frank Sullivan used to do. They simply don't exist anymore. The trend, the mood of the times, seems to be against them, and all of these brilliant young writers who come along are very serious-minded, rather moody and gloomy. I suppose they have every right to be, but I nonetheless find the results rather depressing as continuous reading.

I do think the light point of view is in a bad way at the moment. Most of our comedy is mechanical drag comedy, the kind that is created by five writers in a smoke-filled room. It's all very much formula, rather mechanized, and I think it eventually can be done by computers.

I would like to think that this is just a temporary eclipse, and that the jubilation of the human spirit will burst forth once more, regardless of world conditions.

Right now we have a school of writing, mostly in fiction, which is the self-pity school; most of these young men have the distinct feeling that nothing awful has ever happened except to them. I don't think this is true. I think the human race has always been in one hell of a mess, whether we've been chased by saber-toothed tigers or dinosaurs, whether we've been struck down by the black death or bubonic plague, having our cottages overrun by Visigoths and Vandals, going through fires and earthquakes. Human life is a perilous proposition. We might as well realize that we are born to die and that there are many different ways of dying. I suppose some ways are more agreeable than others, but I think that humanity has always been on the brink; yet a lot of us regard this as a condition that has never before existed.

I think that we ought to be able, at least some of us ought to be able, to express some kind of exuberance and jubilation over the good things of life that are left to us, even if it is some kind of lighthearted mockery of the things that beset or besiege us. I find this spirit awfully lacking at the moment.

Another thing I find rather dreary is the incessant, repetitious accent on sex. There are only certain ways you can couple, after all; the variations are not infinite, though I expect any day to read a novel in which they perform while swinging on a chandelier. The whole business lacks grace and taste and can't even provide much titillation for the subnormal types who read such things for kicks. It might be a good idea at that, to have some writer resort to the chandelier. The ultimate would have been reached and we could put an end to the whole silly business.

N: *To turn to your own work — in this case the question of paternity, to an extent — Dorothy Parker once remarked that many of the things she is reputed to have said actually came from you.*

NASH: I can return the compliment. On my lecture trips I was frequently approached by sweet, well-intentioned people who told me how much they had enjoyed such-and-such a two- or four-line or eight-line verse, a verse not written by me at all, but by Dorothy Parker. The first few times this happened I would correct them politely, but I found that this only served to embarrass them and probably didn't

change their conviction that I had written it. It was much easier to
thank them and let it go. It wasn't about to hurt Dorothy Parker and it
wasn't going to help or hurt me.

I've had the damndest things attributed to me; I still get credit for
"The Purple Cow," which was written by Gelett Burgess in 1902, the
year I was born. And there are some attributed to me that I distinctly
wish to disavow the authorship thereof. Like that famous, witty, nasty
thing, "How odd/of God/to choose/the Jews." It is often attributed to
me and I cannot renounce it or denounce it vigorously enough; somehow it's apt to turn up hanging around my neck. As a matter of fact, it
was written by an Englishman whose name I forget. It keeps appearing
in anthologies, but I do wish his name would be appended to it every
time it appears or is quoted.

N: *You mentioned an indebtedness to Samuel Hoffenstein.*

NASH: I cannot tell you how much I owe Sam Hoffenstein. I only
met him toward the end of his life, when I was out in Hollywood. He
had gone there after the success of *Poems in Praise of Practically Nothing*.
He remained, to the end of his life, a very highly paid and excellent
screenwriter. Obviously it was not the traumatic thing for him that it
was for me.

It seemed that any picture which cost more than a million dollars,
which was a great deal of money in those days, was very apt to have
Samuel Hoffenstein's name on it. But we're talking about Sam as a poet.

I think that Sam actually liberated light verse. I don't take much
interest in early light verse, except for the work of a real genius like
Gilbert, because I think most of it was done as parlor tricks. It was
exercise in verse writing and it was graceful, facile, and said nothing. It
was inoffensive, like wax flowers under the bell on the mantlepiece.
Then Sam Hoffenstein came along in 1925 or '26 with this absolutely
irreverent human approach, and he took light verse out from under the
glass bell and took it into the kitchen and the bedroom and onto the side
street, into the human experience of living human beings, with a
slightly cynical "this is the way it is" approach which opened the doors
wide for me.

I know that I could not have done what I did if Sam Hoffenstein
hadn't gotten there first. I was never quite guilty of actually plagiarizing
him or actually stealing from him, but his influence was so great that I
cannot overestimate it.

N: *Does the poet have a duty, an obligation, an objective that underlies his
art? Or should he have?*

NASH: I can only speak from a personal point of view because I
think each writer has his own degree or manner of involvement. I know

from experience what I can and cannot do. As far as the deeper social and political questions are concerned, I know I should leave them alone; every time I try to cope with them I find myself writing bathos, and the side I'm trying to benefit would be better off without this twelfth man on the field. This has happened in working for the Treasury during the war, and on bond tours; it's happened when I've occasionally been moved to violent indignation by some atrocious outrage. I just can't do it. It comes off very badly, so I simply have to go on dealing with subjects that are permanent.

I'm primarily concerned with human relations, human nature, particularly the relationships between men and women, the relationships of humans to the world in which they live and their attempts to cope with it. This is the body of what I have done, and on the fringes of it is the pure nonsense sort of thing which has no basis in anything except fun. I think there are poets who feel very deeply and are able to express themselves on social or political injustices and evils, and I envy them. But I'm not one of them and it's wrong for a pussycat to get mixed up with tigers.

N: *You've written a great many books for children. Has there been any particular pleasure on your part in doing them?*

NASH: Oh, yes. Always. I started writing verses for children many years ago when I did them for my own. I had no intention of making books out of them, but some did appear in one magazine or another and I found that certain verses I'd written twenty or twenty-five years previous still drew letters from schoolchildren. So my publishers and I started doing children's books. They took some of the verses I'd written long ago, made them into very handsome books and the books did surprisingly well. I found that I appreciated them, so it seemed logical to plan intervals here and there, between my other books when I needed a change of pace, to try my hand at writing new verse for children. So I've done quite a few books for youngsters; they've given me pleasure and they sell nicely. It's not a millionaire's investment, but the books sell year after year. The royalties are never high at any one time, but oddly enough, a book even ten or fifteen years old will bring in pleasant royalties, and with six or seven going you end up with a little steady income.

Now, the main thing I find in writing for children is to absolutely avoid the tendency to write down to them. I'm violently opposed to the trend in education today of trying to suit the books to the little mind instead of letting the little mind grow as it tackles the books. I think one of the reasons for the greatness of Churchill's oratory was that he would use a four- or six-syllable word or a Latin quotation if he wanted to, and it suited his purpose. He wasn't thinking about whether the trash man or the beggar understood it or not; he simply swept them along with him through the power and grandeur of what he was saying. If they didn't understand the particular word they still got the idea; the context gave that to them.

I think that's the way children learn; I do not think you can teach them by simply repeating hat, cat, rat, mat, vat. I think you have to sneak a few words in on them, and if they don't know them they'll either look them up or learn what they are from the context.

I also think they love rhythm. I am much more careful about my rhythm and meter when I'm writing for children; I see that it has rollick and dance to it because I think they have a very keen ear, a deep appreciation of rhythm.

N: *Do you think that poetry has a definite place in their development?*

NASH: Definitely. Some of the things going on now in education horrify me. A few years ago we did a great deal of reading during the summer, reading aloud to one of my granddaughters and having her read to us. Well, she read a certain book — I forget whether it was *Lorna Doone* or *Treasure Island* — and her teacher was absolutely horrified to learn she had read it. She said, "If you've read that now, what are you going to write your book report on next year?" Where are we when that kind of nonsense goes on?

N: *Hilary Knight illustrated your most recent children's book, didn't he?*

NASH: Yes, *The Animal Garden*, and it's one of my favorites. What Hilary Knight did for it was beyond my wildest hopes. I think he made a beautiful book out of it and the combination of verse and art seemed very successful. Sometimes I'm not too happy with what happens to my books when I get them, either because I don't care for my contribution or what the publisher has done or what the illustrator has done. I don't work with the artist; he simply gets the manuscript and has his own conception. I wouldn't attempt to dictate to him what he should do. As a rule, preliminary sketches are submitted to me by the publisher when they're choosing the artist and I will say, "Well, I think this man's style is awfully good, but it's not right for what we're doing. Let's see something else." Or if it's right, "Fine, let's go ahead with him," and then the artist does it on his own.

N: *From all your poetry, adult and children's, can you choose favorites?*

NASH: That's rather hard. I've done so many and I like to think of it as a virtue that I can't remember anything I've written unless I see it. I can recognize a verse I wrote twenty years ago and even recall the exact circumstances under which it was written, but I couldn't quote it to you. I might remember an occasional two-liner or four-liner, but that's all. But choosing a favorite would be like trying to pick out a favorite child.

N: *How does the genesis generally work?*

NASH: They come about in several ways. One group is the result of observation, of noting human traits and characteristics you might see in an elevator, at the dinner table, at a party or a bridge game. Some trait, some idiosyncrasy, will lend itself to being written about; that generally is the beginning and it works from there to some conclusion, although the beginning usually ends up in the middle and the first part has to be written.

Another group, which includes the nonsense poems, are just flash ideas built around a silly joke or a preposterous pun. Then the framework has to be erected upon which the joke or pun can be displayed.

Occasionally something drops in my lap; one of my favorite verses, because it's quite a triumph to be able to read it, is sort of an exercise in sibilance. There was a small newspaper heading a few years ago about "Soviet Assistance Helps Cyprus Citrus Surplus" and in two hours I turned it into a fairly amusing verse in which nearly every word began with an *s*. You could hiss your way through it, spraying the first two rows of the audience at the same time. Some poems do come that way — there'll be a strange running together of words, combinations of words that strike something in the mind.

But now you're driving me into self-analysis, which is a very dangerous thing because it leads to self-consciousness which is ultimately stultifying. It is also apt to turn you into a stuffed shirt.

If I had to figure out what has happened to me and how, and why I've been able to get away with what I've been doing for the last thirty-odd years, I'd have to say that I'm something of a freak with a knack. The knack is there in the sense of thinking in terms of rhyme. It's always been easier for me to write verse than prose. Prose terrifies me. There's something naked about it, and in the verse I have a sort of disguise I can assume so that I'm not so vulnerable. And it comes to me much more easily; I'm more at home in it. Just as I assume the mathematician naturally thinks in terms of formulae or whatever mathematicians do, my mind works in rhymes, and in all of my reading, even in overhearing other people's conversations, I always hear the possible rhymes, those that could be made through slight distortion and become a bit more flavorful.

The most important thing — aside from the knack that has enabled me to survive in this perilous, ephemeral field of humor, a field where tastes change fast and without warning — is the fact that most of what I do deals with human nature, which is always with us; consequently there's a point of view built in. I can't really find out what the point of view is, myself, but I think it is highly individualistic, and I think that individualism is a very important quality for a writer. The work you do —good, bad, or indifferent—should be individualistic enough so that it could not have been written by someone else. Regardless of what it is, it's yours, as individual as your fingerprints.

I might say, I guess, that human nature has been my bedrock, and the rest of it mere trimmings. When I used the word "freak" a minute ago it's because I did stumble onto this method—which has been used by other people before me, not to the extent I've used it—which provided me with a disguise. I had attempted to write very seriously indeed, and had the good sense to discover that such writing was not for me. Therefore I was able to hide behind this mask, keeping people from knowing whether I'm ignorant or just fooling around. It gives me a protection that enables me to operate; I wouldn't have this in the nakedness of prose.

N: *To turn from humorous verse to humor in general, what writers have you regarded as the best in the field over the course of your career?*

NASH: I'd have to put two or three together on the top rung to begin with. Robert Benchley, Perelman who is still writing, and James Thurber. Frank Sullivan, in his heyday, was a magnificent humorist, but he's doing very little now. Oddly enough, most of the great humorists of our time were to be found at work in the early twenties and thirties and at *The New Yorker*. I don't know when there has been such an amassment of high and rare talent. E. B. White was there; he has great humor and writes superb light verse, but far too little of it.

I think that Thurber will outlast every other humorous writer—better, writer of humorous material; many are rather grim characters in person, contrary to their work—because he worked with human nature, not just with things on the surface. He was very funny on the surface, but underneath one finds the people; I think that Thurber is the greatest since Mark Twain.

The joke itself, remember, is never enough for survival. There has to be something underlying it and you find this in Thurber. The others are great, but I don't feel that they're as deeply rooted in human nature. You recognize everyone in Thurber. You know your uncle, or you know your aunt, or your wife's great aunt, or yourself. And despite all the fantasy he could construct about them, they remain human beings who were alive yesterday and are alive today and will be alive tomorrow.

N: *Do you find humor a different commodity today?*

NASH: I don't know. My circulation is not wide enough now. I haven't been well for the last few years and I haven't been out in the great world. I've only seen my own little circles, so I'm in no position to make pronouncements. I think that editors are hungry for humor and I would assume the public is. I think they take an awful lot of ersatz humor when they can't get the real stuff. So I do think that anyone with a gift for humor will find that he's welcomed with open arms.

Wodehouse is still writing; I think he's one of the great masters. And Peter De Vries is not only a friend, but someone I admire greatly. I think he sometimes stretches a bit too far to drag the pun in, but he's a very funny, wry, sardonic writer. One of the good ones.

And there are others, so I don't think there's a total absence of real humor. There's a shortage, but not a complete lack.

N: *You mentioned the mail from young people asking you how to become a writer. How much of this do you get?*

NASH: I get a lot of such depressing mail. I think anybody whose name has ever been in print gets it. Philip Wylie has written some rather vigorous articles on the subject. They can best be characterized by the letter I got last year from a young man in high school saying, "Dear Mr. Nash: My teacher has told me to write a paper on your works. Please send me your works."

There is a tendency, and I'm afraid that teachers have encouraged it, to have the kids get somebody else to do their homework for them. I used to try to answer these letters, but I found that I could not do it because it takes twenty minutes or a half hour per letter. Now I try to answer any halfway intelligent letter with a postcard. The others go in the wastebasket. There's no use trying to fool around with them; it wouldn't leave time for anything else. For awhile, in New York, I attempted to cope with them with a part-time secretary, and discovered that it cost me about ninety cents per letter to answer some idiot. This was more than the purse would stand.

I do get some wonderful letters which I take great joy in answering. Sometimes, especially with teachers, I develop a continuing correspondence. These are the ones who are bright enough not to get their kids to have someone else do their homework.

But too large a proportion of the letters are abominably illiterate. It's frightening where such handwriting and grammar are concerned, to realize that they're considered at least partially educated. I've had two or three letters from senior students in teacher's colleges that have given me something to think about. To imagine them going out into the world to teach the young!

N: *You also mentioned the fact that the only preparation for writing was a heavy diet of writing and reading.*

NASH: It's the only advice I can give. To read and to write. Again, though I speak from personal experience, I recommend that the youngster try different forms of writing. I know that I was an imitator. I tried to write like Swinburne, like Tennyson, like the Elizabethans. None of it worked, but it was all experience. It gave me fluidity and facility. Good reading can't help but make an impression on the mind and give the youngster some idea of good taste and bad taste, what is fine and what is meretricious. Reading has to play a big part. It will send the young writer through phases; today he may be Hemingway, tomorrow Fitzgerald, the next day Mailer, the next Kerouac. But I think he'll go through all this until he finds something he's at home with, that fits him, that *is* him. It can't be done just by sitting down and saying, "I want to be a writer." Sounds lovely. They're probably thinking in terms of these package deals whereby they write a synopsis and the reprint is sold for five hundred thousand dollars before the manuscript is in, and the movie packet is included, and it all looks like the quick route to the James Bond automobiles and blondes. But I don't think they're the ones who are going to be writers. It's those who sweat it out by themselves and spend more hours working than dreaming that will make it.

N: *What about your own working and reading schedule?*

NASH: I don't do as much of either as I should. I find myself getting a bit lazier and other things take up the time that used to be spent reading. But then, most of my reading was done at the time when it should have been. Perhaps I should have continued stronger than I have, but I don't know.

Between the ages of eight and twenty-five is when a person should gobble every book in sight. There are things you should read and enjoy when you're young that you just can't bear when you're older — Cooper, Walter Scott, most of George Eliot.

Reading lists are another thing I have a tremendous quarrel with. The kind I see being brought home from school by my grandchildren make me think that teachers have gone completely mad in their idea of what is going to be of use, what will form tastes and bring experience.

But I don't have required reading lists now. Just some required work I go at all too slowly.

"Humor in its simplest form, is the unexpected ... it is the sudden disruption of thought, the conjoining of unlikely elements. It's the nostalgic reference that pleases or delights people."

S. J. Perelman

S. J. Perelman

PERELMAN: I was born in New York in 1904 and reared in Rhode Island, where I attended Brown University. Simply stated, I became interested in the life creative because I was a comic artist at college. I was more interested in working for the college humor magazine, *The Brown Jug*, than I was in trigonometry and all those necessary adjuncts. Eventually, in my senior year, I became editor of the magazine and subsequently went professional in New York as a comic artist. This lasted for six or seven years, when I drifted into writing, principally because my cartoon captions became longer and longer and longer. Finally, having become somewhat schizophrenic, I decided I'd better become a writer rather than a comic artist. And in 1931 I ran afoul of the Marx Brothers and did a hitch or two for them — *Monkey Business* and *Horse Feathers*.

After that, a sortie into the theater. The first show I did was a review for Beatrice Lillie and Bobby Clark titled *Walk a Little Faster*. It didn't move in as spritely a fashion as the title might indicate. It had a very moderate success, indeed, which we all ascribed to the great Depression. Its most notable feature was a song, now famous — "April in Paris." Music by Vernon Duke, lyrics by E. Y. Harburg. Forgive me for sounding like a catalog of names, but we were all neophytes; this was the first Broadway attempt by all of us.

Shortly after I should have walked a little faster I began working for *The New Yorker* and have worked for it rather steadily ever since, interspersing with bouts on Broadway and in Hollywood.

I started off under Harold Ross, of course. It's difficult to describe him in light of Jim Thurber's book about him because that book is so all-enveloping. I don't agree with all of it, but Ross was actually an inspired man. The magazine was his entire life, and properly so, because he conceived it originally as a magazine for metropolitan New York. He started it in 1925, when there was no such animal, and *The New Yorker* actually displaced a number of comic magazines that had existed until then, including the old *Life* magazine, *Judge*, and (prior to both of them) *Puck*. What *The New Yorker* did was to create an urbane and well-edited magazine that didn't cater to the level of the barbershop mentality. It tried to appeal to literate people, and it's always been my view that it is extremely well-edited, civilized, and intelligent. I have great admiration for it.

Nor has *The New Yorker* changed appreciably from the day of Ross to the present editorship of William Shawn. Some of the articles have become longer. Whether it's become more serious a magazine I don't know. I think it was a serious magazine during the 1930's; it couldn't help but be. After all, the times were so terribly out of joint. *The New Yorker* has always carried a great deal of extremely good reportage; the excellence of people like Janet Flanner and John Hersey goes without saying, and Robert Chaplain, now reporting on Southeast Asia, has been great. And in book reviewing men like Edmund Wilson and V. S. Pritchett have the finest critical minds in the business.

N: *What were the advantages of your long association with* The New Yorker?

PERELMAN: I consider myself purely as a contributor, you know. I have no staff connection, nor has Updike or Cheever or virtually anyone you can mention. The magazine doesn't have a great masthead, like *Time*, where you find literally thousands of names of editors and subeditors and researchers. (This, to me, is pretentious behavior.) *The New Yorker* has a small and very efficient staff. The emphasis is placed entirely on good writing, on clear and concise lettering. There's a notable lack of phony showmanship.

The personal advantages in working for both Ross and William Shawn lie in the fact that I've found people who do their best to comprehend what I write, and who give me as much latitude as I can possibly have. I've been able, in the type of writing I do, to go off the deep end if I felt like doing so, yet be condoned and understood. That is enormously important to a writer. I have done considerable work for some of the big, slick, popular magazines, and almost every word I've turned in has been questioned. They seem to feel that certain words are beyond the comprehension of their readers. This seems, to me, a patronizing attitude. I prefer to feel that if I take off at right angles or go off in a flight of fancy, the reader should be given the privilege of being allowed to follow me without being given a crutch by the editor.

N: *Are there significant changes in the field of humor that have taken place during your career?*

PERELMAN: You have just handed me a license to pontificate. You see, I consider myself purely traditional, a descendant of people like George Ade, Ring Lardner, Stephen Leacock, Robert Benchley, and Frank Sullivan—people who have worked in the field of free association. That school extends all the way back to the Midwestern humorists, including Twain, who gave us a tradition in humor—at least, of sorts.

What seems to be happening now in the field is a rather dreary emphasis on the sadder aspects of life, less emphasis on what is funny. I suppose it's our reflection of the Depression of the thirties, the World War following that, then the Korean War, and so on. Perhaps young people are no longer interested in doing the sort of free association humor I do; consequently there are very few people plying this particular craft. Yet I'm constantly told that there's a crying need for humor in times as depressing as these, and that people need to laugh. But I don't see many people making the effort. Among newspaper humorists you have Art Buchwald and Russell Baker, both extremely able and talented men. In the magazines there is a remarkable dearth of new people. I can't really account for the lack; perhaps the increasing conformity of American life places real humor at a disadvantage.

You see, a rise in conformity is attended by a decline in eccentricity. I notice this very much. You have only to go to England, for example, to see a country that still nourishes and appreciates her eccentrics. This isn't true here. We're not interested in the eccentric or the old person. Everything is beamed toward youth and spring and bounce, whereas in England the individual who doesn't conform is accepted with some degree of sympathy and rather liked. I don't think that American life condones, much less fosters, eccentricity, and I'm afraid we've descended to a dead level, to a thoroughly uninteresting kind of person who reads certain things, wears certain clothes, drives in certain automobiles, etc. (I shan't mention the sort of thing he reads because I might begin insulting a few periodicals and authors of my acquaintance.)

N: *What are the things you find significant in the culture of conformity?*

PERELMAN: I shall start with the theater and work backward. It's no news to anyone that the theater is in a lamentable state in this country. The approaching theatrical season has only three or four plays one would want to go to see, and they're all imports from England. There does seem to be a great deal of vitality and humor in the English theater, but our own native theater seems entirely concerned with transcriptions and reworkings of old material. For example, the new show *Holly Golightly* is only a redo of Capote's *Breakfast at Tiffany's*, and there are at least four or five other shows coming which are variations or adaptations of old material. A strange sort of flaccidity seems to have overtaken our playwrights. And the theater has to start with the playwright. That's where the trouble is. We keep hearing about the lamentable state of health of "the fabulous invalid," and the rascality and venality and homosexuality of the theater, but we've got to start with plays and, in my view, the plays are simply not being written.

As far as books are concerned, we seem to be having an absolute blizzard of ethnic novels about Negroes and Jews. This is all very well, very encouraging to social progress, I presume, but the eyelids tend to droop at the vast number of books written about Jews and Negroes. I can't say what books *should* be written about; if I knew, I'd probably be writing one of them. All I know is that when I go into the bookstore I really have to hold on to a buxom saleslady for support when I see the crop of dreary books on the shelves.

As far as movies (I'm beginning to sound like Jeremiah here), I ask any fair-minded person whether or not the best pictures he's seen in the last few years haven't been European films. The fact is that movies as we all knew them during the thirties and forties, Hollywood at its best, have disappeared. Now all we get out of Hollywood is something with Rock Hudson and Doris Day, a tired, dreary, stereotype. The best movies come from Italy, Sweden, France, Poland. All this may be a consequence of the fragmentation of Hollywood. When the great big studios like Twentieth Century-Fox and MGM and Paramount fell apart, production became an individualized matter. Small companies and directors and writers started joining together to make pictures, but for some unaccountable reason they chose to imitate the worst features of the big studio movie instead of picking up the good features. In recent years pictures have become truly international, and I think there's been a notable improvement.

During the so-called "Golden Age" in Hollywood, around 1935, really interesting pictures were produced — *The Thin Man*, the films of Carole Lombard, the MGM and Paramount specialization in swift, witty pictures. Then came the best work of people like Billy Wilder, pictures like *Double Indemnity* which he made with Charles Brackett. And the early melodramas of James Cagney, like *The Public Enemy*. They were first-rate. They had vitality and jump and timeliness. But Hollywood lost out.

N: You worked out there quite a bit. What were your impressions of the screenwriter's life?

PERELMAN: I worked out there over a period that can best be circumscribed as 1931 to 1942, and certainly not all the time. I went out there from time to time to replenish the larder, and most of my Hollywood experiences were dismal and unrewarding because the screenwriter in Hollywood (and there were 1,275 of us at the peak of the movie business!) was subject to all the stress and strain of supply and demand. He was in the position of a man who works on a shoe lathe in a place like Lynn, Massachusetts. There were good times and bad times. Consequently, as a free-lance screenwriter I was thrown into all sorts of curious ventures.

Once, for example, I worked with Ogden Nash, collaborating on an attempt to write a screenplay of *How to Win Friends and Influence People*, which sounds grisly and was, except for the fact that Nash and I got to know each other well and subsequently collaborated in the theater on a musical for Mary Martin titled *One Touch of Venus*. We enjoyed doing that; Mary Martin was sublime to work with. But the original screen hitch was a matter of sitting in an office trying to scratch out something for the needs of the producer at that moment. We spent the time profitably at that by inventing a Sherlock Holmes quiz. We did not attend strictly to our knitting.

I also worked on an attempt to do a musical comedy movie based upon a successful British musical, *Nymph Errant*. I was on that for twenty-two weeks, and had three sets of collaborators. The first two sets were gangland experts and spent all their time trying to insert bits about arson and mayhem and violence of all sorts. They were followed by an earnest young radical who kept trying to get social consciousness into the script. This nightmare lasted twenty-two weeks. True, I was getting paid every Wednesday. But the whole film aborted, nothing came of it, and I was left with some of what Dorothy Parker called "fairy money." Hollywood money had a strange way of evaporating. You knew it wasn't real money; unless you spent it fast it had no validity. I used to try to spend it fast by fleeing to Europe, where it seemed to purchase a lot of satisfaction, something it didn't do in Los Angeles.

N: *But wasn't your experience with* Around the World in 80 Days *quite satisfying?*

PERELMAN: That was sort of a blood bath too at the time. It brought me into contact with that notable personality, Mike Todd, who was made of the stuff they usually put on the points of fountain pens, iridium, the hardest metal known. Mike did the whole picture, of course, on a shoestring, parlaying his luck throughout, borrowing money left and right, constantly being told by older and wiser heads that the whole thing would be a disaster. I must say that he had a lot of guts. He was a man with an *idée fixee;* he was convinced that *Around the World in 80 Days* was a good property, and he stuck to this project through thick and thin. And it did come out right side up as far as he was concerned.

N: *Most of the script was yours, wasn't it?*

PERELMAN: Let's not forget a man named Jules Verne, who thought the whole thing up in the first place. It's awfully hard, when you talk about a screenplay, to tell whose lines are whose. So many situations arise during production when a gaffer or a grip on the set suddenly says to the director, "Hey, wouldn't it be a good idea if she said such-and-such," and they say, "Fine, print it."

In the main I think I can say that a lot of the lines were mine, but to chemically assay the whole thing is very difficult. It's a corporate venture, a cooperative venture, you know. It's written or originated by one person, or by fifteen who rewrite each other, and then it's produced in a building the size of an armory with a whole flock of people holding lights and sound booms and moving things. It's distinctly a community project.

N: *You mentioned taking your fairy money to Europe. In considering the body of your work I find a great deal concerned with both the pleasures and the vicissitudes of travel. How did your nomadic tendencies come about?*

PERELMAN: I've been going to France with some degree of regularity since 1927. But the first ambitious tour I took was in 1947 when I made a trip around the world with Hirschfeld, the *New York Times* caricaturist, for *Holiday* magazine. That really set me off, and I made a second world tour a few years later, with family intact, and wrote about that in a book titled *Swiss Family Perelman*. (The first was *Westward Ha.*) After all this the vagabond instinct became rooted. I dashed off to East Africa in 1953 and was able to revisit that area a few years ago; since then I've been in Eastern Europe. I really love to travel, and I find, as far as copy is concerned, that the stresses and strains one encounters with customs officials and hotel capers and all that sort of thing is highly productive of the kind of situation I can write about. In other words, misery breeds copy.

N: *What is your family status?*

PERELMAN: I was married in 1929 and have two children, a boy and a girl. They're grown up, of course. My base today is Pennsylvania. We have a farm there, a farm we've had since the early thirties. I bought that farm originally with my wife's brother, Nathanael West. West and I had known each other at Brown University, and we remained friends after that, then through the thick and thin of in-law association. West, you know, went into the hotel business in New York, managing a hotel and concurrently writing his first novel, *Miss Lonelyhearts.* Then he drifted out to Hollywood and lived there for some years while he wrote a succession of books.

N: *You mentioned a fling in theater that actually came quite early in your career, and then, again, later. Could you single out those that were the most satisfying?*

PERELMAN: My wife and I wrote a couple of plays together. One called *All Good Americans* in 1934, a comedy about Americans in Paris, an expatriate sort of thing. Another, in 1940, titled *The Night Before Christmas* that dealt with hoodlums who bought a luggage shop on Sixth Avenue in New York in order to drill into the vault of a bank adjoining their cellar. Both of these were subsequently made into movies, and I must say that we had a lot of fun with both experiences.

I also enjoyed working on the musical I spoke of, *One Touch of Venus*, with Ogden Nash. Following that I did another musical, *Sweet Bye and Bye*, which dealt with the future. I've always thought about that show in terms of a remark made by Lincoln Steffens, the great muckraking journalist. When he returned from Russia after seeing the Russian experiment he was besieged by journalists who wanted to hear his impressions, and he said, "I've seen the future and it works." Well, we saw the future, and it didn't work.

The Marx Brothers, earlier in the game, were such jolly good fellows. Our first experience was the movie *Monkey Business*, when they were really feeling their way. This was the first thing that had actually been written for them for the screen. Prior to that they had made *Coconuts* and *Animal Crackers* as transcriptions into film from their stage work, but *Monkey Business* was their first screen original.

Like all first-rate comedians, and I've learned this by working with other blithe spirits, they were extremely insecure. I think all comedians are far more insecure than "straight" actors; it seems to be part and parcel of their natures. They're in constant fret about whether or not the audience is going to laugh, perhaps because without laughter the comedian is utterly lost. But at our first point of contact they were venturing into a world they didn't know at all well—Hollywood. Consequently, there was no relaxed attitude, and the writers bore the brunt, so to speak. When that picture was released and was successful, and we came to work on *Horse Feathers*, they were much more relaxed because they had more confidence. My particular friend was Groucho, and I've happily been able to remain great friends with him ever since. I have great esteem for Groucho Marx. He has a very quick and civilized mind. However, this shouldn't be news to anyone.

As you probably know, there were originally five Marx Brothers. The fifth, the unknown, was Gummo, who is in the lady's underwear business and has never participated in a theatrical career.

But I do love the theater—the pleasure of working with so many first-rate people, and the response, that immediate response, of the audience.

N: *In a different vein, concerning the upcoming writer who would be a writer of humor, what advice would you give him? What would you hope for him?*

PERELMAN: I should think, first of all, that he ought to be an omnivorous reader. He should acquaint himself with everything that's been done. Then, frankly, I would counsel him to be imitative. We hear a great deal, it seems to me, about the necessity for avoiding imitation, but I don't feel that way at all. I feel the young writer has to model himself upon standards they admire, and I base this upon my own experience. I was a slavish admirer of Stephen Leacock and Ring Lardner, and when I now look back upon my early work I find whole chunks that seem to have been lifted out of their works. I think that the more the writer continues and perseveres, the imitative bits tend to drop away. They eventually begin to develop qualities that are idiosyncratic, true to the self, rather apart from the image of whatever hero was in mind.

I do think it is vital to read as much as possible. There is such a great volume of stuff to go on.

As far as opportunities are concerned, I fear that the printed page is going to become less and less valuable. This is an awkward way of saying that the mass communication media are going to take over. Obviously, television and radio have usurped so much of the attention of people that I believe that someone who wants to be a humorous writer is going to have to be thrown into fields like television. I deplore this because the level of most television is so terribly low that I hate to see anyone get involved in the business. I'm sure you've read Merle Miller's very funny book, *Only You, Dick Daring*, in which the horrors of what a writer in television goes through are so wonderfully cataloged. But every writer in television is bound to go through this sort of thing because it is a community business if ever there was one.

If someone is really, truly devoted to putting words on paper, and is willing to endure the struggle and make the effort, I would remind him that there are still some places where his work can be printed. *The New Yorker* is one of them, and there are some English magazines, too. Then, of course, some of the smaller magazines, staid and respectable ones like *Harper's*, occasionally do use humor.

But the road is rough and the commitment is long.

N: *If you were to look back over your own life and career and pick out those persons who were influential, who would they be?*

PERELMAN: To mention just a few names. The first would be Robert Benchley, with whom I was fortunate enough to be friends during a good portion of my career. Dorothy Parker is another person. Both of these exercised a role in my life which is difficult to put into words. I had great admiration for both as individuals and as artists. I think their standards were very high, indeed, and that just knowing them meant a great deal to me. I'm also sure that knowing Groucho Marx has meant a great deal. To a lesser degree there are people like Somerset Maugham and T. S. Eliot, both of whom I knew. I always had the greatest possible esteem for Maugham's work and read it from childhood on. Eliot I knew since 1944 or 1945 and saw him frequently in America and in England. There are also more obscure individuals who exercised a beneficent effect on my writing and on my personal behavior.

N: *We've referred to changes in humor and tastes. I was wondering if you think public preference has had an effect in supporting or enforcing changes.*

PERELMAN: I don't know if I'll answer your question directly, but from the mail I receive as a consequence of what I write, I should say that people are very alert. I am constantly pleased to find a public that reads my work, and they do exercise a regulatory and corrective influence. I'm able to judge from them how and to what degree they appreciate what I've written.

Naturally, all writers receive mail. I'm constantly impressed by the quality of the letters I get. In those moments of self-doubt, which are legion in the life of every writer, when you wonder just who you're writing for when you sit in your hot little room stringing those beads together, if those flights of fancy are going to be too obscure for any reader, you are happily surprised to find yourself appreciated at what you thought might be your most obtuse level. Their alacrity and appreciation makes me seriously doubt that the public lacks in appetite.

N: *What, to you, is the nature of humor?*

PERELMAN: That's the roughest question of all. If you look in Fowler's *Modern English Usage* at the definitions of wit, humor, satire, and all (he has them all separated), you can become so confused you don't know which end is up.

Humor, in its simplest form, is the unexpected. Let's not go into those dreary definitions concerning a man sliding on a banana peel. Humor is the sudden disruption of thought, the conjoining of unlikely elements. It's the nostalgic reference that pleases or delights people. In my case, it is frequently a word that unlatches the past or creates a sudden picture of a past era. This is one of the reasons for choosing *Chicken Inspector No. 23* as the title for my most recent book. It's a reference to the sort of badge sporty young men used to wear on the lapel to flash at a girl to indicate they were pretty civilized fellows, ready for a lark. Now, I don't think anybody has mentioned those badges since I was about fifteen; they're associated with the era

following the First World War. Yet I discovered in the course of writing
a rather extended series for *The New Yorker* titled "Cloudland Revisited,"
in which I covered a lot of the books of that epoch as well as the silent
films, that I was constantly amazed and gratified by the memories of
readers who communicated with me after the pieces came out—the
sharp images they retained of these movies and of their youths; it just
needed a catalytic agent to awaken them.

N: *In terms of your own sense of achievement and satisfaction, which
experiences stand out as the most satisfying to you?*

PERELMAN: One of the reasons I've worked in the theater in
preference to movies or television is the fact that the theater provides
the keenest distilled satisfaction a writer can get. It's immediate. I admit
that the writing of a play is obviously arduous, often a bitter experience.
It entails a great deal of very hard work; the writing is even more
tedious and dismal. The rehearsal period is normally difficult. You
rehearse in drafty, badly-lighted places, you live on cardboard cups of
coffee. It's all very provisional. And what you're doing throughout this
whole period of writing the play, casting it, rehearsing it, and all, can be
compared to a ride on a roller coaster. You're approaching that high
point on the track just before the sickening plunge. The high point is, of
course, opening night. You're going up and up, and the excitement
comes the morning after when you pick up those first newspapers to
find out whether you've given birth to a monster or an absolutely
beautiful and profitable baby. But I think the keenest satisfaction one
can have is that moment of uncertainty just before you learn your fate.
A first night is a very exciting thing for author and playwright. The
experience of working in movies doesn't compare, because when a
movie you've worked on is finally released in a whole series of theaters,
you're not there to judge any effect upon the audience; it's just a lot of
film.

Television seems eminently unsatisfactory. I don't see how any
writer can gain any benefit out of seeing his name on the television
screen, particularly since it's flanked by people rubbing floor wax into—
I was about to say the ceiling; it might as well be, I guess, the floor, or
becoming absolutely unglued over a deodorant, or leering over that
fragrant wash. There is great satisfaction, too, in seeing a majority of
your words emerge on paper, and this gets back to *The New Yorker*. I've
found that the maximum of my words emerge in that one place without
being butchered or manhandled or rewritten or pawed over, prayed
over, or jolly well mistreated.

Now, to try to look farther, to attempt to find something in my work
that is important or enduring, is frightfully difficult. I know some artists

who constantly do that, and I've been exposed to their maunderings as they talk of themselves as historical figures in their own lifetimes, as Thomas Babington Macaulay. Presumptuous, isn't it?

My sole ambition is to write as well as I can in the form of the short comic essay. I've written some longer things, but I think that my shorter pieces stand the best chance of maintaining some swiftness and pace and sharpness after a few years. If a piece still stands up after four or five years, it is rather miraculous; humor does tend to date. If you look back now at the work of Artemus Ward and Josh Billings, your extremities are all a-twitch with nostalgia. Time has a corrosive effect on humor, but there is an extraordinary way in which types of humor come in and out of vogue. I get great pleasure personally from rereading the fables and slang of George Ade; he went through a curious process of becoming rather stale and démodé. But today they have a new freshness because all the slang of the early 1900's becomes fresh as you reread them.

I strayed off the point here, but what I'm trying to say is that I think it's a creditable motive for anyone who works in the vein I explore to simply hope that his work will retain some degree of freshness after a very few years. And I want to go on improving the form if I can — which amounts to a rather modest ambition.

"... there is great beauty in life, too. The wonder of friends, the wonder of life, the capacity for laughter. Above all, the ability as a human being to live with some measure of grace, some measure of vitality, to enjoy that which we have ... that each day becomes a way of enriching another part of you, supplying another means of fulfillment."

Harry Mark Petrakis

Harry Mark Petrakis

PETRAKIS: Born—St. Louis, Missouri, 1923. My father was a Greek Orthodox priest. We moved to Chicago when I was six months old, and I've lived in Chicago ever since, except for a couple of brief interludes.

My basic interest in writing came about through illness. As a child I spent a couple of years in bed and during this confinement I became a voracious reader. I went through the general run of pulp magazines and when I finished those off I moved to books, any books that could be gotten into the house. It was also during this period of time that the introversion which seems to characterize so many writers came into full bloom for me. I remember lying in my room, flat on the bed, listening to the children playing outside. To try to shut them out I created people of my own in my room to talk to, mythical people out of stories my father had told me of Greece.

The writing itself didn't start until I was in my early twenties. I had been through a series of jobs, moving with the terrible restlessness that characterizes people who don't know exactly what it is they want to do. I was aware of a formless feeling for writing, but kept thrusting it aside. I did make some attempts at poetry, but I was horrified at what I put down on paper. But in my twenties, I started writing with some encouragement from a magazine editor who saw the first of my work.

Success did not spoil Harry Mark Petrakis. I began sending off material in a serious, somewhat systematic way, taking time off between jobs, moving from job to job. I thought it would be a matter of months before I sold something and could make a living as a writer, but it was actually ten years before I sold my first story. Those were ten incredibly dry years and yet there was progress, if only because I moved from the standard printed rejection slip to the small note to the small letter.

Certain editors of certain magazines stand out naturally from this drought. George Wiswell at *Esquire* gave me some marvelous criticism. Several editors at *The Atlantic*—a woman named Esther Shiverick, in particular, and Ed Weeks—gave me astute encouragement. It was all so agonizing and yet the move from the printed slip to the letter was so encouraging.

I remember a rejection slip from *Harper's;* it was the standard one, kindly reading "... we are forced to reject stories which are ably written and publishable..." but an anonymous editor underlined the "ably written and publishable." I went back to study that rejection slip at least a half-dozen times, feeding on the fact that some human hand had touched that printed slip and had underlined that type-frozen phrase. *The Atlantic* was the first to buy one of my stories. It was just before Christmas in 1956. I was selling real estate. They had had stories of mine for a few months and I had a certain queasy feeling about one of them as though something might really be cooking, so in the early part of December I sent off a wire to Ed Weeks—it is not good practice to plague editors with wires! I said that my blood pressure was rising, and were they considering my story? Four days before Christmas, Ed Weeks sent me a wire saying, "Yes, your story is going to make a splendid *Atlantic* 'first.' Merry Christmas!"

It was an incredible Christmas. No great amount of money rolling in, no real change in my situation, but that first promise of publication, that first acceptance. It's a wonderful moment for a writer. It's as though he's been struggling along in a dark and impenetrable forest for several years, and suddenly the trees part over his head and he gets a blinding view of the sky. It's unmatched.

I've published thirty-five to forty stories now, and the publications in the U.S. range from *The Atlantic* to *Harper's Bazaar, Country Beautiful, The Saturday Evening Post, Playboy, Cavalier, U.S. Catholic, Chicago Review.* In Europe some of the stories have sold in as many as twelve countries, small magazines for the most part.

N: *I'd like to turn to your latest novel,* A Dream of Kings. *What are its traceable origins?*

PETRAKIS: Looking back on it I suppose the idea for the novel came through my acquaintance with the type of man Leonidas Matsoukas, the hero of this novel, really is.

As a young man part of my development took place in gambling houses. I spent a great deal of time in bookie joints playing the horses, playing poker at night, and it seemed to me there were uncommonly large numbers of Greeks hanging around, little grocery men, sweet store operators, restaurant owners. Now, the Greek gambler has always held a strong fascination for me, and I suppose I came to Matsoukas before I had any idea of the story. A wonderful and terrible man, really; wild, vibrant, zestful, blind in one sense yet acutely sensitive and perceptive in another. I think this must have been the beginning.

Like a great many other writers, I wanted to write a contemporary tragedy that would have the resonances of the old Greek tragedies, the

Greek past. I wanted a man who would commit the sin of avarice, the sin of arrogance, of pride, the sin of daring the gods. I wanted to put him in conflict with the old pantheon of gods, the gods of Homer's *Iliad*, the gods who would take strange shapes and who would in strange, ironic, sadistic ways join the battles of men, now for one side, now for another—not just in conflict with the one Christian God of our age.

Then, of course, it became a case of resolving other situations, resolving the people with whom he came in conflict, establish the work he did to make a living. It was out of this combination of pomposity and sensitivity that the Pindar Master Counseling Service was born, with Leonidas Matsoukas, President, Doctor of Wisdom and Inspiration, as the title on his door indicates, "Specialist in Astrology, Palmistry, Hypnosis and Inspiration to overcome Bedwetting and Impotence, Wrestling Instruction, Real Estate Bought and Sold." So when you have a man as marvelously rich and fruitful as this, it then becomes a problem of setting up a series of conflicts. And I wanted to really try to shatter him, to see if in some strange way, again with the overtones of the Greek tragedies, I could end with a note of affirmation, because life does go on. Individual men are stricken down, but life in some distorted and absurd and oblique way manages to continue.

N: *For the greater part, your work has adhered very closely to the Greek community. Why has this been?*

PETRAKIS: I was raised in the Greek community of my father's church, and when you're reared in a city and live on urban concrete you find no tradition into which you can pattern yourself. It isn't like being born in the South where a tradition is ready-made for you. There is a great facelessness to city pavements, to city neighborhoods. You know your part of the city, yet for all intents and purposes you live and exist in a little world of your own. You read the history of the country, the movement and activity of the government, yet it really has nothing to do with you. Thus there is no definable tradition with which you, as the son of immigrants, can identify. So what becomes most real is the little world in which you live and make immediate contact, and for me this was the world of Greek immigrants, the world of my father's parish. From an early age I went with my father to church on Sundays, standing in the pews beside leathery-cheeked men and women with dark mantillas on their heads; they might have been figures from an Attic chorus. As I grew older I danced at Greek weddings and baptisms, always feeling an affinity with these people, a commingling of the blood.

I suppose too, that as I grew older it became more than a matter of identifying with them as people. I also sensed a great sadness in many of them, a sadness because what they said about their lives and about the old country seemed to me to be untrue; that they had a particular set of phrases they used about the greatness and the glory of Greece, the ways in which they represented that greatness and the glory in their grocery stores and sweet shops. And it was a sadness, almost a fear of the truth, a bit like whistling in a graveyard. They talked of a greatness that no longer existed, as though they sought to bolster and reinforce their own egos and stifle their feelings of inadequacy in this new land, overlooking their inability to adapt swiftly to the mores and the rhythm of America. So they talked about the old country as though it were some kind of golden place, never letting on for a moment that if it had been so marvelous, a land of golden serenity and grandeur, why did they leave? So it occurred to me that these people were a great source of dramatic material. Not just the Greek, but the Greek looking back, remembering not the barrenness of land which could not sustain them and therefore caused their departure, but a golden land suffused in myth and legend and the mists of the past. There's nobility and beauty and sadness in this because there actually was some glory in that past that cannot be applied to the new situation.

N: *Yet for all your play upon tragic themes your work has a vigor, an affirmation of life so many American novelists more or less deny.*

PETRAKIS: This isn't something that is imposed upon my work. I think you used the key word when you said "vigor"; for me this has been a saving grace. Basically, I have a rather tragic vision of life. I think that any sensitive person—writer, artist, or musician, any human who examines life—must be aware of its tragic aspects. It's tragic if only because nothing endures. The sun rises in the morning and sets at night and in the space of that day you've grown a day older. Love, which is so consuming and overwhelming, is going to pass. The young girl, lithe, slim-hipped, bouncing along the street with a lovely, unlined face, will, through the passage of time, become a worn and red-faced old woman. I think that anyone looking at daily life with any degree of awareness must recognize that in this transient quality there is tragedy.

Yet I feel—and this is something so strong and inherent that it comes out in the material—that there is great beauty in life, too. The wonder of friends, the wonder of love, the capacity for laughter. Above all, the ability as a human being to live with some measure of grace, some measure of vitality, to enjoy that which we have. To try to live in such a way that each day becomes a way of enriching another part of you, supplying another means of fulfillment. It's hard to define the affirmation of life because it's deeply felt and simply *there*.

I also know it works hand in hand with the aspect of tragedy.

Perhaps this, too, relates in some strange way to the Greek. If anything characterized the classical Greek it was a sort of vigor and vitality, not a romanticism that obliterated the fact that the earth was a savage place on which to live, but an ability to accept the harshness of reality and go on to soar above it. The harshness was a starting point, not a reason for distress or despair, but a reason to go on, to catch the savagery and ugliness if need be, but to show ways in which people can overcome these. Then, too, in all aspects of life, everyone reaches out in one way or another to touch other people; sometimes the connection is made, sometimes it isn't. I think all these elements have become underlying factors in my treatment.

N: *To turn to the rudiments, what are your working habits?*

PETRAKIS: I've read journals and interviews with other writers, and I know that there are as many ways of working as there are writers. So each writer sets his own pattern.

I think there are certain basic things you've got to recognize. In the same way that we can acquire numerous bad habits we can cultivate good ones. A good habit for a writer is to attempt to establish a regular time for his work. I am forty-three years old and fight the battle each day. I write in the morning; I don't start off as early as I did when I wrote my first novel, because as I've grown older it has become more difficult to get up at six or seven o'clock. Little by little time has been chiseled away and now I start at nine.

But there are so many things that try to grab you away from writing. It's so much nicer to sit and read someone else's work than to grind out your own. Or to pay too much attention to the family or friends.

I would say that the regularity of the writing schedule is the most important thing. To make working hours a firm habit. I have to do this. I'm an emotional writer and write emotional stories and books, but I must discipline myself. Sometimes, if the words have difficulty in coming, I read aloud parts of the Old Testament or Thomas Wolfe or some lyrical writer who has a flowing use of language; this, in some strange way, lubricates my own juices. I even fill pages with absurd material just to get myself started. The regular start is so important, and it's been said much better by many other writers, and it is admittedly elemental. Perhaps the real difference between the professional and the novice is the professional's awareness that if his work is not turned out he will get no checks and thus not be able to live. A great amount of work can be turned out through regularity and necessity.

N: *What obligation do you feel, to whatever quarter, as a writer?*

PETRAKIS: As a starting point, I feel that I have a great responsibility to myself. I felt as a very young man that there was something a little different about me. Many people in many walks of life must feel this. The child who cries out and is inarticulate must feel in some way that he is different. It is the "I" shrieking in the face of the universe. Along with this difference comes a feeling that I have a responsibility to communicate the different things I feel; my particular vision of life must be reflected in my writings.

I must communicate this vision to others. I know that there are poets and other writers who feel that it is enough to express what they want to say. If nobody is able to understand it, their expression is nonetheless sufficient for them. It isn't for me. I have to be able to know that people are reading what I write and understanding it to some degree. I want to make the reader feel the emotions I am trying to generate. I want to make them laugh at particular scenes and cry at others. But I feel an even larger responsibility than that.

When I go to college campuses and work with young people in seminars or lecture or read my stories, I find that they quiver and tremble with fantastic emotional reaction, and I know that I'm in the presence of young men and young women who are able to feel life as strongly and as intensely as I feel it. The difference is the fact that I'm a professional writer who has now given almost twenty years to my craft. I am able to articulate the emotion and they are not yet able to. This is the only difference between us as far as the eye on life is concerned. They see and feel what I see and feel. I feel a responsibility to them in the sense that I am articulating through my years of apprenticeship and published writing, articulating that which they cannot.

N: *To look at the state of contemporary letters, considering the past few decades as well as the present day, what facets do you find most encouraging or conversely, most discouraging?*

PETRAKIS: There is a great deal of talk about the savage nihilism of the contemporary novel, yet I find in so many of them, even among the black humor, elements of vigor. Perhaps the contemporary writer is much more involved with an individual search than he was twenty or thirty years ago. One questions the value of any particular book you write today in face of all the great tides and forces that assault us. One can't help thinking at times, "Does it make any difference what I write? Will it be noted among the deluge of books and among the crucial tides at work?"

But I find reason for optimism in books by Mailer or Heller and books of the black humorists. I find vigor in the contemporary novel because I think that many of the old boundaries that men like Joyce and Lawrence fought against are gone. We're in an era now when almost anything can be printed and published. This means that there will be movement into areas that have heretofore been forbidden to us. This cannot help but be important.

What I find in the contemporary novel that makes me unhappy, is the trend in the novel as represented by some of those that have come from France, the influences they seem to have generated. I can't speak with any authority because, as a free-lancer, I'm so involved with writing my own books, with lecturing, with all the sundry things I must do to make a living and feed my family, that I have little time to keep up with the other gladiators who are probably bleeding as badly, at times, as I am; I concentrate on keeping out of the pit myself. I don't like the academic influence; by "academic influence" I mean the theory that we no longer need the conventional form of the novel. It's as though young writers want to knock out all of the pasts. To me, one must learn what the past has supplied and use it as a starting point and move on, but *not* discard the past simply because it is easier to formulate a style and vision totally spontaneously. To use the example of an artist, it's like painting cows knee-deep in grass to avoid learning the anatomy of a cow's leg.

There are traditions. There are things that have to be done in the novel. There are things that have to be done with language, and though a writer may not want to write like the men who have come before, he should have some awareness of the traditions.

He should read the stylists. Jeremy Taylor, the seventeenth-century English bishop, Joyce, Lawrence, Thomas Wolfe. If, after comprehending what these men tried to do, he then moves radically away from their concepts of the novel, that's fine. But it can't be done as a shortcut, by ignoring the traditions without knowing what these traditions are.

N: *You have partially answered the next question, which concerns the advice you would give the fledgling writer or the hopes you might have for him.*

PETRAKIS: I've been asked this question in most of the writing classes I've taught. Instead of going into the usual sort of response I'd like to tell a very brief story.

A few years ago when I was on the faculty of the Writers' Conference at Indiana University, I had a woman eighty years old in one of my classes in the short story. Out of the twenty-five people I had, she was certainly the oldest, you might say the most unusual. At the end of the session a small award is given to the outstanding student in the class. I was overwhelmed by her story, as rough and undisciplined as it was. It was one of her first attempts at writing and it was savagely powerful.

Now, if I were to have given the prize legitimately, it would have gone to one of the nineteen- or twenty-year-old students in the class, who was brilliant and would undoubtedly go on to do great things in writing. But I gave her the award because I was so overwhelmed by the story. I had an opportunity, in a personal session, to talk to her. She told me that she had always wanted to write, but for one reason or another had never allowed herself the time or set any routine. On a number of occasions during her life she had decided to write an hour each day and read in preparation for it, but somehow or other the years passed ever more swiftly as she grew older. Now she had begun to write because she had a feeling that death was near. And I had the awful, overwhelming feeling that it was too late. Not that she wouldn't be able to publish; in the years she had left she certainly could. But it was too late for her to learn everything she should learn about writing, those things that can only be learned by the act of writing itself. I thought, "What a terrible thing it must be to want to write, to have this feeling inside yourself, and to procrastinate because you think you've got all the time in the world. Then time gets away, and someday you're faced with the infirmities of age and the ills of the body and the wounds of the spirit which accumulate, and you realize that there is no longer time to do that which you wanted to do." What a bitterness this must be.

I often had a feeling, during the ten dry years when I could not publish, of wanting to quit, thinking, "To hell with them; if they don't want my material I'll make a living doing something else." Yet I always had a terror of someday opening a book by another writer and finding my words, my ideas, in his book; words and ideas that in some strange way belonged to me.

Along with a sensitive eye, a capacity to hear and smell, there has to be a drive. The drive has to be virtually overwhelming because you're going against what appear to be overwhelming odds. The important thing is to write. It is also important to expand. I've seen people in writing classes work on one novel for years and years, carrying that one novel around, beating a dead dog. You've got to be able, if you're a novelist, to do at least one novel and discard it; in those ninety thousand words you may well learn what not to do in the second novel which becomes the publishable one.

Do you want to write short stories? I must have discarded seventy short stories that were not publishable before I wrote *Pericles on 31st Street*. I didn't write a publishable story overnight. There was a gradual development that came from the process of writing, from the capacity to drive myself, from the awareness that time was getting away. There could be no graver moment for an adult than to wake in the dark, silent hours of the night, to hear the breathing of your family in the rooms around you and the stirrings of the city outside your window, and have a terrible sense of unrest because there were so many things you wanted to do when you were young and vigorous that you have not done, so many hopes still unfulfilled.

The young cannot understand that when you are young you are rich with time to be spent lavishly, never realizing that the day will come when you don't rise from the bed in the morning with bounce and zest.

This is probably a deluge of an answer to your question, but as you can tell, it's something I feel strongly about.

N: *How do you regard criticism and review as performed at present?*

PETRAKIS: The disqualification I offered a few minutes ago, when I said that I am not a student of the contemporary novel as such, would apply even more graphically to criticism. I really don't know the various schools of criticism and what they represent. I catch from some of the journals a feeling that there is one kind of school here, another there, and that some warfare goes on between them. This is occupational infighting and I have nothing to do with it.

When I myself read a review or criticism, I like to see it done in some depth. From what I see in general of the state of reviewing, it seems rather pallid and weak. So often, in picking up reviews published here and there across the country, I find that many of them are little more than a mishmash of the material on the jacket and the biographical stuff the publisher sends out; little attempt is made to grasp the significance of the book.

Sometimes, too, there seems to be a necessity to pull off a clever phrase. Or a case of revealing the reviewer's erudition as opposed to the comprehension of the book. An example: George Eliot is a fine novelist. I read a review he did of Malamud's *The Fixer* in *The New York Times*. It's a brilliant review in all that it reveals of Eliot's scholarship, but by the time he traces Judaic and Christian traditions and involves himself in many types of scholarship, I lost track of the form and substance of the book he was reviewing. So when I say, "a little more depth," perhaps I mean that the reviewer should have some credentials in order to review, the same way a writer has to fight his way to publication, but he shouldn't obscure the book he is covering. Perhaps it should be mandatory that a reviewer have published a book or two himself in order to review other books, to have some awareness of the work of the writer, and to approach it on a basis of some understanding.

N: *Who are those writers you regard as "giants" in American letters? And why do you hold them in high esteem?*

PETRAKIS: I find the works of Hemingway and Faulkner very rich and fertile for me as a writer. I count them as giants, but since both won the Nobel Prize this is hardly a startling or original view.

I've always read Scott Fitzgerald with a feeling of ambivalence. I enjoy some of his work but I get a feeling of waste, a feeling that here was a man who never really did the work he might have done.

A man for me — and this is very personal, because I'm talking about a man who has had a great deal to say to me personally — is Thomas Wolfe. God knows I've had to defend him on college campuses where English professors have a habit of parroting the line about Wolfe being an overgrown adolescent who never really learned to compose a sentence. Yet when we think of all the pallid, weak, anemic, and inadequate novels that have been produced in this country, I think we can forgive Wolfe some of his excesses.

More than any other novelist, Wolfe has given me some sense of the complexity and size and grandeur and culture and cruelty of America as a nation. I'm fully aware of his excesses and faults, yet I don't think they're as important as his incomparable vision of this country. They speak of Whitman as being the great American poet, but I think that Wolfe was an immeasurably greater and better poet than Whitman, the way he moved across the country, zeroing in on the way people thought and talked and moved, the way Americans themselves move restlessly from pole to pole.

To move to contemporary novelists, there are a few writers, somewhat neglected, who are giants to me. Take Gladys Schmitt in Pittsburgh. Her last books have been historical novels, but if you go back to her earlier work, you'll find magnificent books like the *The Gates of Aulis*. In fact, whenever I begin feeling too good about a flattering review or a check coming or someone praising my work, and I want to attain proper perspective, I go back and read Gladys Schmitt and wonder if I shouldn't burn my books.

The short-story writers who've had great influence on me and stand as giants, writers I read with admiration and affection: Liam O'Flaherty, Sean O'Faolain, Frank O'Connor, Bernard Malamud, Isaac Bashevitz Singer, Isaac Babel, Sholom Aleichem. I find an intensity in writers who work in the Jewish or Irish traditions, a kinship to my own background, perhaps my own awareness of tradition.

N: *Come to think of it, there's a great literary affinity between the Irish, the Greeks, and the Jews.*

PETRAKIS: That's interesting. It hasn't occurred to me, so I'm thinking on the hoof, but there must be; I've felt it between the Jews and the Greeks, but the Irish must share it. Perhaps it's a sort of ambivalence; one weary eye cocked at the tragedy of life, a sparkling eye catching the fun of it. Zorba can dance in the face of disaster; the Jews can dance and laugh in the face of catastrophe. The Irish writer must have traditions too; along with realism there is a tendency to hang on to lost causes. The I.R.A. can go on fighting long after everyone thinks they should give up.

N: *Three frequently defeated peoples who are never beaten —*

PETRAKIS: — never able to swallow that sad plate of porridge.

N: *Could you pick catalytic moments out of your life? Events that, if they had not occurred, might well mean that you wouldn't be sitting here now?*

PETRAKIS: I think the most obvious catalytic moment was the publication of my first short story. Before that, in a literary sense, there was the encouragement of those particular editors I mentioned before. They seemed to catch me just as the waters were closing over me for the third time, and somehow or other picked me up enough to keep me struggling.

I remember one extremely pivotal moment. It was while I was finishing my second novel, *The Odyssey of Kostas Volakis*. A marvelous editor was then at *The Saturday Evening Post* — Merrill Pollack, now at Norton. He had bought several of my short stories and kept me alive. I wanted desperately to finish *Odyssey* before going back to some kind of regular employment, and Merrill had one short story he had asked me to revise. All my hopes lay on this because the *Post* paid me a very good rate at the time, and an acceptance would mean that I'd have several more months in which to finish the book. He passed through Chicago and called. I was away but my wife asked him about the story and Merrill told her that while he thought I had done a good job on it, he was sorry that others hadn't agreed. So I called several employment agencies the next morning and made appointments. Pollack got back to Philadelphia where the *Post* was headquartered, and discovered that he was talking about the original version of the story. While he had been on the road he had not been able to see the revision I had done and they were now buying my story and paying me my $2,000. Again I was snapped out of the shark's mouth. An incredible moment. And there was another time; I was all set to go to work as a copywriter for an advertising agency when I got a call from the Coast to work on the adaptation of *Pericles*. Since that time I've managed to stay afloat. Each year things are correspondingly better, with the growing reputation of the writing, the lecturing.

Other catalysts — the reactions of people around me. My father died thirteen years ago and never lived to see any of my work printed, yet he used to keep old manuscripts of mine in the drawer of his desk at church and when a visitor came into his office he'd take them out and say, "My son is going to be a good writer some day." He couldn't read

English that well because Greek was his language, but he left me a legacy: I can never become unduly arrogant over the fact that I love words because he was a man who loved life. I think this was a very formative influence because it made me understand that the man who loves life is always to be admired more than the man who loves words.

N: Speaking of legacies, what would you like to leave behind?

PETRAKIS: This is extremely hard to answer. I know that we say to ourselves as writers that it may be necessary to wait. We need this as consolation sometimes. To wait for the evaluation of posterity to give you your proper due. But in the meantime it would be nice to be recognized. Read. Appreciated.

I would like to think that seventy-five years from now—if we can speak in such a measure of time in this fantastic day when we seem to be moving so rapidly toward nuclear destruction—that the young people in colleges and libraries might take down one of my books from the shelf and read it. I'd like them to think that Petrakis was a great writer, but if not a great writer, at least a writer who had lived in the city long ago and had briefly and beautifully caught some of the truth and motion and pattern of people's lives. I suppose that is a moderate expectation.

I want my books to live. I think any writer does, and this may seem absurd because we know that books can be burned and places destroyed. Someone may someday decide to abolish all Jewish and Greek literature. It's not an impossibility. Yet I'd like the books to have a life of their own. I don't think I'm at the point where I can think of my work as a body; they're individual books. Although I think all of them are good books, *A Dream of Kings* is probably my best because of the pendulum-swings of emotion I felt in writing it. Laughing with the humorous scenes, crying with the tragic ones. With this book—my third novel, the fourth if I consider a ninety-thousand word job I did that was never published—I think I've become a novelist. Up to this time I've been a good short-story writer and my novels have been little more than expanded short stories. But this is a novel with a life and dimension of its own. Having written it, I walk the earth with a great deal more serenity. This may not last, but at least I ride airplanes with a sense of fulfillment. I hope, naturally, to do even better books, but if *A Dream of Kings* alone survives, this would garner for me, wherever I am at the time, some degree of consolation.

"We've had dark times before, times that seemed just as dark to previous generations as our age seems to us. But we'll come through; even if we have to fight for every breath forever, we don't have to be destroyed. What we do need is endless courage."

Katherine Anne Porter

Katherine Anne Porter

PORTER: I really don't care what I say; that is, I'm not in the least afraid of saying what I think. But I am often misquoted in the most appalling way by people who don't seem able to understand even the plainest speech, much less any idea it might be trying to convey. I get transcripts back with whole pages so utterly muddled I can't even straighten them out myself. I have to rewrite the whole thing. And then there are the ones who wish to edit other people's notions and change the sense to suit their own.

Not long ago this happened rather comically. I was talking at a convent, a highly accredited, elegant school for girls, and I remarked, "Slander is something that should be talked only privately between friends about their other friends who are not there." The young girl who was taking notes changed it to "gossip" and explained that Mother Superior had advised her that "slander" was too strong a word. It is a strong word for a nasty vice and "slander" was what I meant.

You can imagine what it is like, trouping around the country in girls' schools and boys' schools, though some of them are pretty well grown up. The young are very smart and quick; they amaze me sometimes until I remember that I have now known many generations of students, and they were all bright and inquiring and skeptical and ran rings around their parents and other elders, and I remember too that my generation did the same and so back through the ages. Yet I do feel that the last half-dozen classes, surely as intelligent as any, are not as well educated in many ways as the older ones. They are more superficial, yet quicker, and I feel they could take much more education than they're getting. A different kind, you know. I don't care if I ever see another student. It was nice, all this traipsing about the country in universities and colleges, but I wonder if they gained anything from it. I know I did. It gave me a living, and fresh glimpses of the changing fashions in students, and I expect that's not to be despised.

But let's start and I hope I don't ramble. If I do, give me a chance to come back to the point.

N: *The first question up is the standard query regarding birth and education.*

PORTER: That tale is neither sad nor long. I was born on May 15, 1890, in Indian Creek, Texas, near Austin—I should say sixty-five miles away. This was in central Texas, blackland farming country, but I didn't stay there long. Until I was eleven I lived mostly in either San Antonio or in a small town named Kyle that was about five miles from my grandmother's farm. She had quite a large landholding there; little by little she dispersed it by giving it to her children and by the time she died she had a very small farm, a few hundred acres.

After that I was in San Antonio and New Orleans. I went to girls' schools and convents and had quite a classical and ornamental education, the kind girls got then, and I don't think it took very well. I seem to have spent most of my time "bootlegging" literature. When they were trying to make us read St. Thomas Aquinas I was reading *Confessions of St. Augustine*. I read and read and read. I got most of my education from books. We had a good collection at home; most old-fashioned literate families had. I think mine was the very last generation with a certain sort of upbringing. After Grandmother died everything was scattered— the books, furniture, the family life and all—and the next two generations were brought up on radio and records and cars, no books at all, nothing that we would have called education. It seemed an extraordinarily savage kind of upbringing, but they didn't seem to miss anything so I suppose it was all right for them. It was very disappointing for me.

I remember once telling somebody who asked me about my education that by academic standards I was an illiterate. My father read this and his feelings were hurt and he said, "Well, we did our best to educate you but you were proof against it." He was right. I really was proof against the kind of education they wanted to give me and I never went to college.

I left school when I was about sixteen and never set foot in a university until I went there to teach. Since I came back from Europe I have spent thirty-odd years traveling about this country, teaching and lecturing and running classes for would-be writers. The kind of class I liked best did not involve teaching them how to write; rather, it was how to read. In recent years students have the idea that you don't have to know how to read in order to write. This kind of illiteracy hasn't appealed to me at all. In very large colleges where I've gone as guest writer or lecturer, they have enormous classes of little people who were going to learn to write and it turned out that they had never read a good book. Over and over again you would find them studying *Gone with the Wind* or Daphne du Maurier's romances. Some of them had never read anything but whodunits and I used to look at them and think, "I wonder where one begins." It was like being in a house with a whole set of very bright baboons. You expected them to burst into human speech at any minute, but they never did, not on the subject of writing anyhow. It used to distress me a great deal. Yet was it always their fault? In a California university where I spent a year persuading my class to read the work of masters in order to know what the standard of excellence is, there was another teacher who ridiculed my work and my ideas to these same students, assuring them there had been only two good short-story writers in this country—Bret Harte and O. Henry.

Well, you asked my about my education, and I can't draw a line because I'm still picking up an education. You see and hear certain things and you want to know more so you find out more.

I can't imagine deliberately going out to get material for a book. I suppose if you were writing a travel book you'd have to, but the writer doesn't really need to look for material for anything. It's there. You soak it up as you go along; it belongs to you, will come to you. Wasn't it Molière who said, "I take my own where I find it"? A great waste of energy. If you sit still it comes to you.

Yet I've been out of the country a great deal, in Mexico and in Europe. I stayed in Mexico and Europe about seven years at one time without returning, and when I came back all sorts of things had changed. For example, there was a vogue for bus travel. It was the latest thing to do. I believe Thomas Wolfe did it first, and suddenly it seemed that you just had to take a bus trip from Coast to Coast or some such uncomfortable distance or, as the saying was, you hadn't lived. I tried it, not that far, and it was enough. They had what they called "tourist camps," the things that finally became, with the death of language and the deterioration of the vocabulary, "motels." I found the whole business appalling. Everybody was eating hamburgers and hot dogs. I was brought up in the South where we had perfectly wonderful food. I think they're right when they say that our restaurants are bad; all the good food is at home. Anyway, I thought that getting things out of tins was perfectly savage and that bus travel was just plain hell, but I suppose it added to my education.

Another digression: I remember, in Europe, the way the American embassy people would celebrate the Fourth of July by sending back here for canned pork and beans; they'd buy hot dogs, which are Vienna sausages (Austrian origin) and, of course, hamburgers (German). All of these things are European, you know—not particularly American. It's just that Americans pick up all the worst things from Europe, just as the Europeans pick up all the worst things from us. This cultural exchange starts in the basement; it may work its way up to the ground floor someday, but it doesn't seem to be going there very fast. We exchange everything frightful. The yea-yea, the jazz, the hoodlum manners, the tight jeans, all the dreadful little girls who go about looking like Cinderella ten minutes before she was hauled out of the ashes. They were all over France and Italy when I was there in 1963, with boys to match. You want to tell them, "For God's sake, go comb your hair."

I probably sound like an old fuddy-duddy but I wonder about these little creatures. I know how bright they are really, and how good-looking—taller, in better health, in every way better off than we were—and I don't understand how they consent to be so ugly and, worse than that, like tramps. But this is not only of today I am speaking; I'm referring to things I began to notice thirty-five years ago when I gave up wearing slacks because of the kind of women I saw wearing them then. It isn't any newer than this pornographic literature thing.

Heaven knows pornography isn't new. The first person I knew personally who wrote that kind of thing was Henry Miller. He gave me a copy of his *Tropic of Cancer* the day it came off the press. That was in Paris. I have it yet, dated 1934, and the funny thing is that nobody has ever gone further in plain or fancy nastiness than he did. Several years ago I was called upon to go over to Maryland to testify for Henry—I've done this several times—and I thought, "I wonder if I'm ever going to be called upon to testify in defense of a good book? Why must it always be a bad book with a few dirty words and scenes that don't interest me?"

Actually, these silly words are dull, show a lack of imagination, a lack of vocabulary. When you write like a green boy just being broken into the Army, you're not even pretending to turn out literature. You're forgetting your language. And anyway, this verbal riot of mud, blood, latrine smells, and sex has about run its course. It's high time writers got their minds above their belly buttons. Some very exciting and entertaining things happen from there *up* too!

There is a natural human speech which is the speech of literature, of human beings, of poetry. It isn't from the gutter and it isn't exalted. It isn't Pentagonese or Madison Avenue or Bronx Yiddish or Freudian jargon or Harlem Congo or any dialect or the steerage-bilge school of criticism. It is the daily human speech of those who love and respect their mother tongue and learn to speak it clearly. I can't understand why people think they can get through life on a vocabulary of 350 words—we have such a marvelous, rich language, and I don't know why we are so tolerant of the dull minds who try to destroy it. Hearing this ugly patois, this language that isn't my language, is a fairly unpleasant part of my recent education.

N: *What do you think is responsible for the deterioration of vocabulary and pronunciation?*

PORTER: I think it comes from the popular lowering in standards of education. We have the mistaken notion that everybody in the world has to go to college. If he doesn't go to college he won't be able to get a job. The colleges are already crowded with people who never in this world will absorb more than a rudimentary education, and we dilute everything to meet this low standard instead of giving the 10 percent of students who can take higher education a chance to use all their powers. It's really true that the forces of inertia seem to be prevailing and are strong enough to bring everything down to the level of the slowest mind.

Picasso—he's an awful bore, but he does know another painter when he sees one—said about Matisse that when Matisse put three colors together the viewer would see a fourth. It's the same with language and poetry; it's the artists who hear the overtones that say something with layers and layers of meaning and shades of feeling and sound. Matisse said in effect, "You must be very careful to keep your colors on your palette separate and pure, put them together carefully, lay them side by side carefully; if you mix all the colors on your palette, you'll have mud." And this is exactly what we're getting—apparently what the great common world wants—the mud where they feel at home. They want mud, they are mud, they're at home in mud, and they will have mud, and refuse everything beautiful that grows out of it.

This nature totally lacks the faculty of respect for excellence. There is a homely old saying that everyone must eat a peck of dirt in his lifetime. Maybe, but the important thing is to know what you are eating and call it by its right name. So often in Europe I would feel humiliated by the awful things, the parodies of our national character we had sent to represent American culture. I'd think, "I don't know who you're representing, but I know you're not representing me, and I don't think you're really representing my country, either." They would have these international festivals where every country in the world would send something, presumably the best it had, whether the art was theater, dance, music, painting, the beautiful things would come. I'm thinking most about Paris in 1952 because I was there and took a great interest; I was one of our delegates.

What did we send? *Four Saints in Three Acts*—or are the numbers the other way around? —with a Negro company. Can you imagine this as representing the American arts? I think Virgil Thomson is a very good composer, but this strange little trifle appalled me. And Gertrude Stein was American-born, but got back to Europe as fast as she could and stayed there. She was an interesting phenomenon in her own right, but representative of anything American? I think not. The Negroes were extremely good singers and dancers, and it was an amusing little show, but was that the best we could send? And I thought, "Oh, God, this is terrible; let me live to get away."

I suppose this is more of my education, whether I like it or not. At one time I thought we had a fairly good literature and art established, and that it was going to grow, but I'm not so sure anymore.

N: *You've done quite a few things for the State Department, haven't you?*

PORTER: It seems like more than it is. These excursions are laborious. I've only been on what they call a cultural mission three times. These are the forays one of the cultural attachés in Mexico calls "committing cultural relations."

N: *How do you do that?*

PORTER: I'm sure I don't know. Yes, I really do know because I've done it. Twice I've been to Mexico because I know Mexico, and then I've done these other things, like the International Festival where I went as one of the six representatives of American literature. Then I went abroad as a Fulbright lecturer and landed, of all places, in the university at Liège and was there for about six months. I later toured Europe; I was booked everywhere from Salamanca to Barcelona, from Rome to Bologna, three lectures at the Sorbonne, all across Europe to the great universities, but I had to get back to Liège every Thursday afternoon. It was awfully hard work and I became exhausted and fell on my face and had to come home, with a magnificent winter completely wasted. Just plain bad management on somebody's part.

Actually, I've been trying not to do much of that sort of thing, but it's hard to break away. I don't know why they presume you should go on until you drop in your tracks. I don't feel like doing it now and I'd like to stop. What use was it anyhow?

I don't think the arts should ever be tied up with officialdom. ("Officialdom" isn't a word; it's a terrible slip of the tongue, like "normalcy.") I don't think the arts should be tied up with politics or government in any way at all. The politicians and the elected officials should look after the running of the country and let the artists run art. The minute the cold hand of the State is clamped down upon anything human, that thing is apt to die. The arts are tougher than people are willing to believe, but they can be blighted from time to time. The people who do the official interfering are never artists; they scarcely know one art from another. That's why these cultural attaché departments that are now blooming in all the embassies of the world have nothing in the world to do with the arts. It's like the Gertrude Stein thing: a play that was supposed to be representative of the American arts was presented and it wasn't representative at all. Another example: in the summer of 1963, I was in Paris and I met the very nice young people who run the cultural attaché business in France and I said, "Why in the world don't you bring in something American?" And they said, "Why, we have some things wonderfully American." And they thought I was being terribly unjust.

What had they brought? That little musical *Play of Daniel*, the twelfth-century thing — wonderful, lovely, and I saw it at the Cloisters and bought the recording — but would you call it typically American?

Perhaps it's a waste of time because it gets to be a cabal; the really fine young writers and playwrights, at least the ones I think are fine, are never heard of in Europe. They get the sensational people, the self-advertisers, and the cabals, the little cliques and huddles get together and tout each other. I was pleased and surprised to find that Flannery O'Connor had been translated. I saw several books in a shop and I asked the proprietor if people liked her, if she was selling. He said, "She's not selling greatly, but she has her readers," and I thought that was lovely. But are our finest people exported — Eudora Welty, Peter Taylor, Andrew Lytle, J. F. Powers, Caroline Gordon, Walter Clemens, and this remarkable young man named William Humphrey who's just published *The Ordways*? Of course, some of these are fully recognized in our own country. It's a shame that their books go out of print so quickly. I find *that* a calamity too. I don't know why it happens unless it's because they're not self-seeking people. They don't look for publicity; they don't want it. In former times they didn't need it because people read them, but now the large sale goes to writers who perform better on television than they do on paper. And these people *are* an unholy cabal, very organized, like a gang coming out of a dark alley. They're thugs. This is a new thing in the arts, and it's alarming.

N: *In painting it's worse, isn't it?*

PORTER: Painting doesn't exist anymore. The gang has taken over. I never knew Jackson Pollock, but I've seen pictures of him dribbling paint, you know, like a little boy building very sloppy mud pies, and recently he came to a full and deserved cycle: I saw a jigsaw puzzle of a Jackson Pollock painting. This is beyond comment.

I've always been a hopeful person and despite some of these calamities I'm hopeful now. I can't live without it, and I cannot believe that the good and fine things, the real art, can be utterly destroyed.

Remember Einstein's statement, after having helped with the formula for the atomic bomb? I'll never forget him heading a committee trying to raise a million dollars to fight the planetary disasters that might come from his bomb; a million dollars, imagine, against a billion invested in destruction! Such childish sweetness, such imbecile immorality. Anyway, he figured it out very carefully in his scientific way and said that the most powerful bomb they could make, used to do the most damage they could do, couldn't kill more than two-thirds of the people on earth. There'd be enough left, like a little piece of yeast or sour-dough, to start another human race.

And start it we would.

We've had dark times before, times that seemed just as dark to previous generations as our age seems to us. But we'll come through; even if we have to fight for every breath forever, we don't have to be destroyed. What we do need is endless courage.

N: *And intelligence.*

PORTER: Yes, because courage without intelligence is brute non-sense. But I have to be hopeful; we have artists in every medium at present who possess very high degrees of talent. We can't see them too clearly because we have to let our age recede into some measure of the past before the great figures really stand out.

I was brought up in the generation that Miss Stein described as "lost," but I'll be damned if ever I was lost. I always knew where I was. I sometimes wondered how I was going to get out of it, but I knew where I was and how I had got there. I don't think we were lost, straying off somewhere like witless children in the woods; we merely had to work at finding our right way.

Perhaps we represented the real break with the nineteenth century. That century in very important ways was an appalling fraud. We were nurtured on the Victorians and it took us awhile (with what strange giant geniuses, like civic monuments!) to realize what stuffed shirts they were on the whole, and to recognize our own world and our own talents. Look back now at the giants of our age, starting with Henry James and Hardy, then Yeats and Joyce and T. S. Eliot, then our whole group of wonderful poets like Robert Penn Warren and John Crowe Ransom, Wallace Stevens, Allen Tate, Marianne Moore—oh, many! People like that were very grand, and I see some others coming up now, that are going to last. But we're not the future, we can't judge. We'll have to judge as well as we can, however, to see that the splendid talents of our day aren't neglected or crushed or driven to the wall. All this is a long way from committing cultural relations, the State Department view of the arts; but unless, by some miracle, government officials and cultural attachés learn what should be presented and what should be preserved, it's up to those of this day with knowledge and talent and judgment to make sure the best survives.

N: *When did you start writing? How did it all begin and how did you emerge in print?*

PORTER: I suppose that is a question that has to be asked, about how you started to write, but there isn't any answer; I don't think any writer knows. A child can't be told to start walking, you know; he crawls till he's ready, then he just gets up and starts.

I began writing when I was a child. All children, if you leave them in a room with crayon and paper and books, blocks with letters on them, will start making things. I started to write and I also illustrated what I wrote; this was when I was about six years old.

You see, we had this old-fashioned home education—the place was full of books and music and very literate grown-ups who tried to bring us out, to teach us; and a young governess, who lived with us for several years. I don't remember learning to read and write; it seemed I could always sing the scales and count to ten and read, "The cat is on the mat," or something similarly profound.

When I was six I wrote what I called a novel—I spelled it "nobble" —but I knew what I was talking about. The title was *The Hermit of Halifax Cave*. The cave itself was about ten miles out in the country near a roaring river; we used to go there for picnics and summer holidays. I don't know where I invented the hermit; perhaps it came from Peter the Hermit who got up the Children's Crusade. At any rate I wrote my "nobble" very carefully and illustrated it with crayon and sewed it together like a book. Then I passed it around to the family, and far from cradling and coddling me and looking upon me as a prodigy or budding genius they just laughed their heads off and passed it around to the neighbors, and the neighbors laughed *their* heads off.

I got to be such a laughingstock that I learned something: to keep things to myself. No child had less encouragement, but I suppose the "nobble" was funny and I wish I had the thing now. So that was my start in literature. Oddly enough I went right on with it; I couldn't help writing and they couldn't teach me anything in school. I couldn't learn arithmetic for one thing. They dragged me through all stages of mathematics by the hair, and I don't know to this day what they were talking about. I was mad about history, grammar, world geography, music, poetry, painting; I'd put books on subjects that enchanted me inside textbooks and read, read, read.

I found, at home, all the things I really needed to learn. We had all of the classics; we started with Homer and came all the way to the moderns, like Thackeray and Dickens, of whom my grandmother didn't quite approve. She thought that Dickens was a bit coarse and Thackeray frivolous. But I was allowed to read *Wuthering Heights*. She didn't stop me from reading anything I wanted to read, but she made her disapproval very obvious. Perhaps she was right about Thackeray; he bores me to this day. As years went by it became obvious that I really was trying to write. My family's attitude was, "What do you expect to add to Homer and Dante and Chaucer and Shakespeare, to say nothing of Henry James?" They didn't realize that if young people felt that way they wouldn't turn a hand to anything; they'd vegetate. Those literary heroes gave me a foundation.

I don't know why I kept writing. I didn't particularly want to and I said a hundred times that I would never write another line. Yet I wrote all the time. I kept notebooks, and I'd write things down on pieces of paper and throw the paper into a basket. I've got all the baskets and they haven't been opened for years.

I think that a real bent, a genuine vocation, comes so naturally to a person that one simply performs. I've been kept from writing for long stretches, making tours and lecturing for a living, and all my energy went into these secondary things, but nothing could stop me for good. I always went back to writing or, more precisely, I had never really left it.

You asked me about my first published work. Oddly enough, a professional career or "getting published" never occurred to me. I felt I wasn't good enough, didn't know enough, and didn't have any business trying to get published. I was literally trying to learn to write, as a pianist runs scales. I practiced, I imitated, I parodied—wasn't it Stevenson who said he played the sedulous ape? Incidentally, I can write very good parodies of Dr. Johnson, Montaigne, and Gertrude Stein. But for a long time I did nothing of my own. When I did branch out to try to see if I couldn't do more than imitate I discovered that I had acquired a very good vocabulary, a feel for the language. I wrote a couple of novels and had the sense to throw them away, but I have most of my early stuff around somewhere; every once in awhile I run into some of it and I'm astonished at how good two lines will be and how horrible the rest of it is. Evidently I was the world's worst when I started and I don't know what kept me at it.

You see, one has so many little talents. If you have one talent, one simple little interest, you're apt to have other interests and talents too. I loved music. I wanted to play the piano, the violin. I sang, I danced, I drew. One year I spent painting in egg tempera on cedar panels, just to see what that was like. I'm a Sunday poet, even now, but I know better than to publish the output.

Once—I don't know why—I decided that I had to finish a story. My life was going along and I had been writing and there I was, twenty-eight as I recall, just doing magazine stuff; editing, not writing, with all sorts of jobs behind me. I think my first trip to Mexico by myself set me off. I ran into things, heard things, saw people. One might think my New York experiences would have been the catalyst, but New York never impressed me particularly. I never had any mysterious fear or a feeling that it offered challenge. But I went back to Mexico and began to be really interested in motives and to make stories. When I came again to New York I used to tell these stories, and by then I'd met all kinds of writers and publishers and editors who would say, "Why don't you write these things?" One evening I was talking to a man who said, "Oh, I wish you would stop telling your stories and letting them go into the air. Why don't you put them down." I told him I *was* putting them down. He said, "I want you to finish *this* story and let me see it."

I thought it was a good idea and I actually did finish the story. I didn't have very much money — I lived at the edge of starvation for the next fifteen years, in fact — but I thought that was part of the business. But after I got started I never thought that having or lacking money had anything to do with me particularly, excepting when I was really hungry.

But I finished this story. I worked on it for seventeen days and nights. I had paid for my room and breakfast — cups of wonderful black coffee and a bunch of grapes and a big crusty roll with butter went with the room. It was run by a French-Swiss woman on Washington Square South. The house is gone now, and the land is part of New York University. I lived on peanuts and bananas in addition to the food my landlady furnished and at night I'd go around the corner to a little place that had sawdust on the floor to buy one hamburger. With onion. That was my supper. Then I'd go back to my room and keep working.

Oh, I wanted to quit writing it, but I finished it, finally, and called it *Maria Concepción*. The next day I called my editor friend, the one who'd goaded me into doing it, and said, "I've got the story." He didn't wait for me to bring it down; he came over and took it away with him. Three days later his magazine sent me a check for $600.00. It was the old *Century* magazine, and the editor, of course, the literary editor, was Carl Van Doren. My young friend was the art editor; I had never thought of this young man as anything in the world except a good dancing partner and someone who could be totally depended upon to take me out occasionally for a very nice dinner in some very nice place. He turned out to be the man who launched me into professional life. I don't think I've ever had the occasion to tell this story, but it was Carl Van Doren who accepted my first short story, and it was this casually friendly young man who took it to him to read.

N: *I'm not trying to be gossipy, but I vaguely remember the fact that you've been married and I have really read nothing about your marriage.*

PORTER: I have no *hidden* marriages. They just sort of escape my mind, and I think other people forget about them too. They caused me great trouble, but they are over. I've never had any secrets; there's always somebody, somewhere, still living, who knows all there is to know about me. I mean many people, each of whom knows a part, at whatever time of my life I was near them.

As for marriage, there's probably nothing more public than getting a license and going before a notary public. Now I won't say I was unlucky, but with the best will in the world I didn't make a success of any marriage. I've been divorced three times and that's enough. I don't know if the subject is worth talking about; there was nothing scandalous about any of it. I was just a little ahead of my time. After the first divorce they all said, "Well, go right ahead; be cast into outer darkness." It was a very disreputable thing to do at the time.

N: *You were Roman Catholic*—

PORTER: It wasn't exactly that. I suppose Catholicism was part of it, but the whole society took a dim view of divorce. It was just as disgraceful for a Presbyterian to get a divorce as for a Catholic. So I did break with my family and with my part of the country; I'm sure they all thought I was just leaving home to lead a disreputable life. Of course, years after I did reconcile with my family, and we became good friends.

N: *But to be divorced, and to be writing*—

PORTER: My father once said, "If you want to write you can write just as well here at home. Besides, what business has a lady writing? Why not write letters to your friends? Look at Madam de Sévigné!"

I had no intention of sitting in my little two-by-four bedroom in the old family house writing letters to people. I had to get out to see the world, and my idea of seeing the world was really rather innocent. I realize now, how extraordinarily innocent a generation we were. We were guarded and cared for and watched and we had about as much chance of being seduced as learning to fly by flapping our arms. I never got nearer than arm's-length to a boy until I ran away and got married when I was just past sixteen. Mrs. Treadwell's instructions from her dancing teacher in *Ship of Fools* is a literal transcript of the instructions we were given for dancing. You put your arm like this and kept your young man this far away and if he tried to impinge—well, you lengthened your separateness again and if he was a gentleman he took the hint. If he didn't take the hint, he didn't get back in that group. The innocence and credulity were astonishing.

I think today's youngsters know far too much about sex far too early, and it has destroyed something that was rather nice. God knows I'm not for all moonlight and roses, though youngsters naturally have a lot of this in their makeup. But when I was a girl, a girl and a boy together at a party didn't take their minds off each other for one split second, yet all we could do was look at each other. But oh, what a lot we got from those looks. Then, too, the fact that I was instructed to hold off this wild man gave him such importance. He was *dangerous*, don't you see, and it set him up no end. But they have destroyed something that ought to exist in sex. God knows it's an animal instinct, but we are not four-footed creatures, and when it's debased we're destroying something profound in human nature. Today's children know so much about sex they can dance without touching each other, narcissistically, by themselves, a ritual that has nothing to do with real dancing. Dancing should provide great pleasure, based on sexual attraction, not on boredom; on attention to another, not preoccupation with self. But let's get back to my marriages.

My first one was a plain disaster. I was so terribly young and it took all my resources to get me out of the scrape, but I got out of it and I've forgotten about it, really. He went off and married somebody else and seems to have done very nicely; he was several years older than I and he'd be a very old man by now. He is dead. He was from the Deep South. There was nothing wrong with him; he just wasn't the man for me and I had no business bolting off with him. He was rather a nice man — I know that now — but I didn't like him, and that's no foundation for marriage.

He wasn't the most composed of men, come to think of it, but it was a typical thing on my part because I've always loved men like that, high-strung, moody, fickle — impossible, in a word. Once when I was in a very bad state, having great trouble with life, just trying to exist, to survive, I said to a doctor, "Do you know I attract insane people?" — and I do, the hysterical, lost people, often quite clinically mad, who come to fasten themselves around my neck, and I have to deal with them. So I said to the doctor, "Do you suppose it's deep calling to deep? That they know I'm just as crazy as they are if I would only break down and admit it?" And he said, "No, on the contrary. They're looking for sanity, a stable sort of relation, a person who stands firm." So I've been certified as hopelessly sane, and I can't get out of anything.

I used to get fits and leap up and down and tear my hair and say to my second husband, when we were traveling about in Europe and we'd have to pull up stakes and go somewhere else — he was with the foreign service — "I'm going to wind up in Bellevue if this goes on!" And he'd say, "Don't be silly; you're never going to enjoy the advantages of Bellevue." Sure enough, I never have, and I've sometimes longed for it.

At any rate, I've been married to three very passable men and couldn't make any of the marriages work. I suppose the contrary demands of career, my husbands' and mine, got in the way. But we're kaffeeklatsching now; interviews always degenerate into this sort of thing, don't they?

People are always asking me questions, and the letters I get—you should see them. I get an enormous number of letters from students.

N: *Quite a few writers I've met complain about this.*

PORTER: Well, I think we should complain. Teachers, apparently, are bored stiff with literature, especially the teachers that teach literature and English. They can't or don't want to answer the questions their students ask, so they sic the student onto the poor, hapless author. "We have been assigned a topic," you know, or, "We were to choose an author and I chose you," and they never have my name spelled correctly, and they never, even by accident, mention a book I wrote. They don't seem to know a thing, yet the questions they ask are wonderful. I've now got into the habit of writing back, "Ask your teacher about how one goes about researching an author or any public figure you want to learn about. If your teacher doesn't know or is unwilling to tell you, follow these instructions. Go to the library and look up my card. Just do that and you'll know how to spell my name, at least."

As I said, they ask the most incredible questions, especially those concerned with writing, and I would like to answer them but there's nothing to discuss and nothing to explain. Anything really important about writing is as mysterious to me as it is to anyone else. I don't know why I have the bent in the first place. I don't know why it held on to me so hard that I couldn't get rid of it. Yet I'm totally unable to imagine a life without writing; it gives meaning to everything I do, everything I am, everything that ever happened to me, everything I have. And I never set out to get money; I never set out to have things. When *Ship of Fools* became a best seller nobody was more surprised than I, although I think my publishers were almost as surprised; they were caught with 35- or 40,000 copies and suddenly had to print a great many more. I was terribly in debt to them and all I thought was, "God, let the book sell well enough to get me out of debt." And the Book-of-the-Month Club got me out of debt at one blow.

This is an odd way to end my diatribe on student letters and teachers, but what does one do to elaborate on the obvious or explain the unexplainable?

N: *I'd like to turn to* Ship of Fools *now. Recently Mark Van Doren told me that the success of that novel "proves there's a God in his Heaven."*

PORTER: He's one of the sweetest men who ever lived. I haven't seen him for years, but we used to be on a radio program together, now and then. I met him when he was young; he was one of the most delightfully good-looking men you could hope to see. He's a good poet and has such a gentle and beautiful mind. Of course, Carl was the one I knew first; Carl was sort of a hearty, hefty person, totally outgoing. He was the one who thought of introducing Gypsy Rose Lee into social and literary circles, for example. He gave a party for her and invited all his highbrow friends who wondered what they'd been missing all those years. He helped her write her book, and somebody asked her what she was doing and she said, "I'm making with the book words." Gypsy talked like that, naturally; she had never learned English and did not really need it.

I've had some strange things happen with *Ship of Fools*. The half-young set—the set the old ones of my time helped establish, helped them get their Guggenheims, got their first stories published—have grabbed up the literary quarterlies and are now slashing up poor old Granny and Gaffer with pruning hooks. One of them, a man I've always been so friendly to and helped, has gone back to take in even my short stories and is trying to undermine them, to bulldoze me out of the landscape from the beginning.

I don't blame them if they don't like *Ship of Fools*. But isn't it odd that they can read Burroughs' *Naked Lunch*, they can read Hawkes' scene in *The Lime Twig* about that man in the dark cellar beating a woman to death with a sandbag, they can read and applaud all the horrors in the world from Norman Mailer to James Bond, but they hate *Ship of Fools*. Nobody's going to identify with that man in the cellar; that's all sexual daydreaming. They know it doesn't apply to them. However, *Ship of Fools* is about live people, and if they don't take care they're going to see themselves.

About *Ship of Fools* they say—"no nobility." Of course, there's nobility and there's goodness and love and tenderness and feeling and emotion but, with the instability of the human heart and the uneasiness of the human mind and the terrible stress and strain of human relations, these qualities are tempered and strained and frayed and aborted.

They can't stand *Ship of Fools* because the people in it are alive and real. Not one of them would beat anybody to death in a dark cellar with a sandbag, with the double meaning of a beastly sexual act. But in the most civilized houses the best people in the world do the most horrible things to each other, sometimes not knowing what they're doing, and when they find their lives approaching some sort of disaster, they don't know what happened. This is the true human predicament, and it's there on every page of *Ship of Fools*. It's life as it's lived, not detached insanity—though we must recognize insanity for what it is.

Nor are all of my people commonplace. There are two painters and some dancers, a doctor who is really a good man of noble intention —

N: *And that unfortunate dog.*

PORTER: Yes, that unhappy dog. And they said, "That revolting dog." What's revolting about the poor darling; God bless him, he was seasick. I think Jenny was rather a good girl, wayward, misled —

N: *Sometimes she irritated me.*

PORTER: Sometimes she annoyed David, remember? David could irritate a reader too, and very rightly, and he was quite annoying at times. Yet David had his qualities. I don't understand why people can't see that people are all very much like the people in *Ship of Fools*. We're all capable of doing virtually anything. We hurt each other and injure each other and are cruel to each other in small, cowardly ways. Just like my people. The only real crime is when the children throw the dog overboard. The Spanish people beat up their children, but only once; come to think of it, I've known one of the most talented writers of our time to beat his small daughter with a razor strap.

I can't know this absolutely, of course, because I can't go all the way into their minds, but I do think the critics and the writers, the enemies and the friends, who disliked *Ship of Fools* the most and protested so much, were really protesting the glimpses they caught of themselves.

N: *In* Ship of Fools *and in so many other writings, you seem to have such a wonderful affinity with Mexico and all things Mexican. How did this come about?*

PORTER: I was born in Texas and Texas used to be part of Mexico. Some of my very earliest memories — pleasant and unpleasant, but *vivid* memories — are of San Antonio which was a Mexican town. It's the third-oldest city in this country, and I heard more Spanish and Mexican than English when I was there. It still is a Mexican town to a great extent and still has a number of those houses with red tile roofs and patios.

My father took me to Mexico when I was about ten, when Díaz was still president, and I was impressed with those wonderful, wide streets and the painted carriages and the horses with silver bridle reins and silver shells on the harnesses, and the music was really unforgettable.

Do you remember, in *Old Mortality*, when Harry takes a shot at Raymond who came over and danced with his sister? Well, my father was the one who took that shot, and he had to go to Mexico while the thing blew over. Most of his letters, while he was courting my mother — they were already engaged, and why she didn't break it off I'll never know, but she was a patient woman, I imagine — came from Mexico. He stayed there almost a year; I still have the packs of love letters he wrote in which he described his life down there. He tried to make her jealous by telling her about the dances he went to and the beautiful dark-eyed señoritas he danced with, and so on. At any rate I had a true feeling for Mexico. I was there, you know, during most of the twenties when everybody was hauling off for Europe; I went to Mexico rather than across the Atlantic. I had nothing to go to Europe for; I never did travel just to go someplace, to see the scenery. Besides, I always had a job.

When I came to New York, incidentally, what did I run into? A whole knot of young Mexican artists and musicians and writers. I told them at one point that I was going to Spain and they said, "Why Spain? Go to Mexico; something wonderful is going to happen there." So I went to Mexico while all these exiles — they were virtually exiles because of the revolution going on — sat in Greenwich Village. They gave me letters and notes, and wrote letters about me to their friends, influential people in the National Museum, people in the arts, archaeologists, just everyone. I remember standing on the sidewalk with great crowds, all throwing confetti and yelling, "*Viva!*" after General Obregon, later president, had taken the city.

I felt at home in Mexico. I didn't have any business in Europe. So I missed more than half of the twenties in Greenwich Village, I missed the Hemingway epoch in Paris, and I think these are two of the luckiest misses I ever made. Paris in the twenties, I suppose, was Hemingway's time and place, but that had nothing to do with me. I have never been drawn into a group; I cannot join a circle, a crowd, the thing I call a "huddle." Mexico was wonderful; a crowd of us were there, perfectly free of each other yet happily knit together by our interest in Mexican art. The one person who tried to make a thing out of us was Diego Rivera, but he came later. I was there before his time, and he was the fraud of frauds with his syndication of painters and his false Communism and his totally shameless pursuit of publicity.

Mexico has meant something else to me, and I can't explain it anymore than I can explain how you fall in love. I hear all the analyses and theories, and I can rationalize and give you a dozen reasons, but not one of them would be right because there are no reasons. If there are, they're so hidden in my experience, so much a part of imagination and feeling, that they can't be isolated. So *my* 1920's were spent in Mexico, not in Paris, not really in New York, and I didn't miss a thing.

N: *Why did it take you so long to write* Ship of Fools?

PORTER: In the first place I didn't know how to write it. I looked upon myself as a short-story writer. I started with short stories and gradually expanded them; whatever a story took, I gave it its own head, so to speak, and gradually went from little things like *Magic*, all of 1,400 words, to *Flowering Judas*, five or six thousand words, to *The Cracked*

Looking Glass, which is thirteen thousand. As I became more practiced
and worked easier with length, the publishers kept shouting for a novel.
When I took *The Leaning Tower*, the third collection of short stories, to
Donald Brace, he said, "Oh, we can't publish any more short stories." I
somehow emerged with three short novels. They are not novellas; they
are not novelettes; they are short novels. Every time I see the word
"novella" my hair stands on end. I have tried so hard to keep that
pretentious, slack, boneless word out of the language. The other day a
man wrote and said he'd liked my novella, whichever one it was, very
much, and I replied by saying, "The first thing I want to tell you is that
it is not a novella. If you would look on the cover you will see that it is
one of three short novels, and I think that the least you can do for a
writer is (1) get his name spelled properly and (2) call his work by the
name he uses." I haven't heard from him since.

I say we have four classifications and they're good enough: short
story, long story, short novel and novel. Who needs something cute and
tricky and horrid like "novella"? But back to *Ship of Fools*. While I was
living in Basel, after my first trip to Europe, I made some notes. Then
there was a sort of log, or long letter, that I'd kept on my first trip,
sailing from Veracruz to Bremerhaven. I sent it to Caroline Gordon and
she sent it back saying she thought I'd need it someday. I read it over,
began thinking, and what I believed would be a short novel began
forming in my mind. So when I came back to the United States in 1936,
I had several things all ready to go. I went to a publisher and made a
contract for four short novels, the titles to be *Noon Wine*, *Old Mortality*,
Pale Horse, Pale Rider, and *Ship of Fools*.

I wrote *Noon Wine* in one week, from Saturday to Saturday, and that
very evening I started *Old Mortality* and wrote that in a week. Then I
got interrupted somehow; I'd gone up into the country and had taken a
room in an inn and in fourteen days had written those two short novels;
but the interruption finished that. The thing that is death to me is to
have my time frittered away; I must have absolute concentration, no
breaks until the vein is worked out. So I went to New Orleans and
found another hidey-hole (an old Scotch word). It took me nine days to
produce *Pale Horse, Pale Rider*, and I rolled up my sleeves and said,
"Here goes the big voyage," because I knew it couldn't be a short novel.
I worked and worked, month after month, and the notes piled up
incredibly.

Oddly enough, everything you see in the book was there at the start,
except that the novel itself is five or six times as long as I'd intended it to
be. Not a character has been taken out. But as I tried to write it I realized
that I was up against something I probably couldn't handle, so I wrote

to the publisher and asked him if he'd let me off this fourth one. He was happy to have the three and let me off, so I kept working on *Ship of Fools*. There were interruptions — I had to go to Reno to get a divorce, I broke up a household in Louisiana, and I had to take to the road, though perhaps I never had left the road. I always lectured when I came back to the United States and took jobs in universities. That may have been one reason why the marriages didn't last, but I had to work at these things to make a living.

There came a reprieve when I could sit down, and in six weeks I wrote the first forty-eight pages and the novel was started. I realized from the slow pace it had started with, that it was going to be a very long novel and I didn't want to write it. But I had painted myself into a corner, committed myself to it, and I had to go on. I'd work on it and push it away. I separated myself from it for two or three years at a time; I'd quit in the middle of a paragraph and start again months or years later, and I thought it was going to look like a piece of restored pottery dug out of a prehistoric midden. Yet I would come back and finish the dangling sentence where I'd left it, and little by little I decided that I was just being obstinate, cutting off my nose to spite my face, and that I was going to write a long book no matter what it might take. For the deepest truth is that I loved the book and the times I worked on it were the happiest, most exciting days I have ever known.

At last I relaxed, but I still went along thinking, "You don't *have* to write it, you know," and they offered me everything. My professional pride was at stake; I wanted those publishers to admit my *right* to be a short-story writer. I was like the poor donkey; they put carrots in front of my nose, they beat me with sticks, they lit a fire under my belly, they walked ahead of me playing flutes, and nothing worked. They offered me a fortune; goodness, how they gave me money. Year after year after year they poured money into it, but even this didn't spur me because I have no respect for money as such. Money is only to spend as far as I'm concerned, and I spend quite a lot. I spend all I can get my hands on as a matter of fact. I enjoy the things I buy with my money. Now I've made a small fortune but they've got it stashed away in a big lump in the bank and I can't get my hands on it; I suspect it's just as well that I can't. I have a yearly income until I die, and unless I live to be 120 years old my family will receive some good sums. So I get by on my measly little income. I shouldn't say that; it's really very good and I'm glad to have it. Until *Ship of Fools* I couldn't see any future for me except sleeping under bridges; I certainly wasn't going to any old ladies' home, and I figured that as soon as I wasn't able to totter about on platforms any more I was finished. And boy, at that point I was tottering — I was so tired I thought I would die.

Back to *Ship of Fools*. I was determined to finish that book so I went into the country and leased a house, an inexpensive country house on a hill, and I lived there for three years and every single blessed day I worked on that murderous, entrancing book. Then the lease ran out so I had to do something else; I went to the University of Virginia, then to Washington and Lee University, and tried to write in the hours I didn't face amiable shiny faces, but I couldn't. To me the situation was getting ridiculous; they'd started advertising the book and set up a false clamor.

Somebody told me that when the book came out I'd get a *Time* magazine cover. I had always heard that a *Time* cover is the kiss of death, but by the time the book came out they were so crashingly bored with the whole subject they hardly mentioned it, at first. I got what they called a "take-out" but it was the most casual, superficial treatment imaginable.

In the meantime I had left Harcourt, Brace; they were tired of me and I was certainly good and tired of them. Seymour Lawrence came along and said he was going to *Atlantic Monthly* and Little, Brown, and asked me to come with him, so I went along. Little, Brown, took me on with magnificence. They bailed me out of Harcourt, Brace, gave me an advance, and I was $35,000 in debt to them by the time *Ship of Fools* was published. Very few publishers will do all that. But Book-of-the-Month Club in turn bailed me out and erased all the deficits.

At any rate, with all the clamor about the book going on, I decided that I couldn't put off finishing it any longer so I went to an expensive (I didn't know how expensive at the time) place on Cape Ann overlooking the sea. I had a great glass wall, a stunning view, and I sat there for three months. They'd send me my breakfast on a tray, and when I didn't skip lunch I'd walk a few steps for it. Nobody came near me, and when the girls came to sweep the room I'd just move into a corner and let them work around me. No telephone calls, no visitors, no telegrams, nothing. And I finished the thing, but I think I sprained my soul. I've got rid of that large problem but other troubles began.

Ship of Fools was like Mark Twain's tight shoes; he was having an argument with a friend, I think it was William Dean Howells, who said, "Say something in favor of tight shoes." And Mark Twain replied, "Well, they make you forget all your other troubles." This was my book, you know. As long as I had it to worry over I couldn't have other troubles, but now a sea full of other things has washed up to haunt me.

N: *Where did you get the title?*

PORTER: It's explained in the book, but nobody looks at it. *Ship of Fools* is a satiric poem by Sebastian Brant with wood-block cuts, published in Basel in (I think) 1494. I spent a great deal of time in Basel; my husband was in Geneva at what they used to call a "peace conference," and I hated Geneva so I stayed in Basel and he came down on weekends and we walked in the Black Forest. I spent most of my time in the great Basel library or walking about with my camera or making notes. This was when I made most of the notes on the short novels and began piling up the preliminary work on *Ship of Fools*, though I didn't call the novel that at the time because Donald Brace, my editor and publisher, objected deeply to it—he said it was "stacking the cards." I didn't agree then and I still don't. When *Atlantic Monthly* asked for the title, I said firmly, "*Ship of Fools*," and so it was. At any rate, I ran into the book, this delightful book, written, I believe, first in German, then translated into Latin. I read it in both languages, and the woodcuts were so marvelous I rather suspected the signature "Brant" so I asked to see the first edition of Erasmus of Rotterdam's *In Praise of Folly*, illustrated by Hans Holbein and all those wonderful Basel painters, kids sixteen to nineteen years old, Urs Graf, Manuel Nicholas Deutsch, Ambrosius Holbein, Hans' younger brother who died young. They sat on a bench in Froben's printing press and drew pictures in the margins. I studied these drawings with a magnifying glass. I think they did the woodcuts for *Ship of Fools*, too. The day I found *Ship of Fools* I decided that my book was to be the story of a ship setting out for eternity, stopping at all the ports where people leave—the deaths, you know. Very few of us arrive at the last port, the far part of very old age. I'm one of them. It looks as if I'm going to live forever, a chilling prospect. No, it's not that bad; I enjoy living and I intend to do so as long as I can, but I do not accept silently some of the conditions of living and wonder why I should put up with them.

But *that's* where I found the title.

N: *A final question: If you were to give advice to the young writer just starting the voyage, what would that advice be?*

PORTER: Art is not a religion, it's not a substitute for religion, and though it can be a friend of religion, or an enemy, it's strictly of this world. But you have to be sure of your vocation. You can't just say, "I'm going to be a painter," or "I'm going to be a writer," without being so sure of yourself you can't be thrown off. You've got to have a certainty beyond rationalization or question. Nobody can help you and nobody can promise you anything. You've got to take your life in your own hands, and you can't go showing manuscripts to other people and asking advice. You've got to work on your own without letting anyone else touch your work.

I suppose, like all advice, this is not to be taken. I told a friend not long ago that I will never again attempt to tell any young person what to do—the really gifted don't need advice and the others can't take it.

I remember Robert Lowell. I knew him when he was very young, nineteen, more or less, when he came to a writers' conference in his blessed innocence. I was there, along with John Peale Bishop, Allen Tate and Caroline Gordon, Sherwood Anderson, who knows who else? We were all enjoying a vacation, showing off a bit, having fun, and this solitary, strange, gifted child came among us so we all took turns reading his poetry and talking to him. Finally I said, "I'm not a poet and I'm not a critic, but I think your poetry is wonderful and you are going to be a poet, so why not go to Allen Tate?"

Well, he followed the Tates, went to their country place in Tennessee in a battered little jeep. The Tates didn't have any room — people were always streaming in and out of their lives — so Lowell erected a little tent of some sort on their lawn and lived out there a whole summer, sitting at Allen Tate's feet, so to speak. Allen was wonderful in instructing him in techniques, shifts, and stratagems. This is what a good poet can do for one who is going to be good. But the funny thing is that there's not one echo of Tate in Lowell now, yet what he needed was to see that the life of the artist can be real.

Life is short and art is long and what is needed is a living touch with reality, a tangible proof in a way, which an older artist can sometimes give to a young one. But I'm the last person who should give advice; I'm anywhere from fifteen to twenty years older than my contemporaries — or so-called contemporaries — because I was a late starter. The others started out to go their way — they knew something of what they wanted; they saw writing as an active way of life in which you advance from one point to another — and I never saw it that way at all. I still don't even when it seems as if I've lived forever. I've stayed with the ship, and heaven only knows what glorious islands I'd have found if I'd got off somewhere along the route.

But perhaps every young artist has to do it one way, his way, and the hell with patterns. Remember who you are and where you are and what you're doing. Nobody else can do anything for you and you really wouldn't want them to, anyway. And never take advice, including this.

Won't you have a drink?

Cornelius Ryan

The Last Battle, is not only a superbly constructed book, moving as it does among those Berliners who survived the holocaust and the city's conquerors, but it clears away the last of the confusing mysteries surrounding the city's capture and immediate occupation. Since much of this material appears for the first time in the book, I asked Ryan a few of the basic questions that would probably occur to anyone who recalled those dramatic days when Berlin fell.

How did he gain access to facts held secret by the Russians for two decades?

"I was fortunate that when the Russians decided to invite me they were ready to talk. You can imagine the frustrations their historians and generals felt; because the Soviet government had never officially announced Hitler's death they could not complete their own World War II histories.

"It was like a dam breaking when Hitler's suicide was made official, and the Russians could really talk. One of the interesting things I uncovered during personal interviews was the depth of rivalry and bitterness between the two generals whose armies took Berlin — Zhukov and Koniev — and the undying enmity both of these men felt toward Stalin, who played them against each other and denied clear title to the biggest prize of the war [Berlin] to each.

"Now, when the Russians first entered Berlin they announced Hitler's death. Then three bodies were discovered that could have been Hitler's, so they hedged on their statement and said that Hitler could have escaped Berlin by plane. By the time positive identification of the body was made, enough friction had grown between East and West to give Stalin a certain advantage in not proclaiming Hitler dead. Khrushchev held the line as long as he could — thus it wasn't until eighteen years after the fact that the Soviet admitted Hitler had indeed died in the bunker."

How did Hitler die?

"His aide described waiting in the foyer, watching a large white clock, waiting for the shot from Hitler's room. Magda Goebbels rushed up to him while he was waiting and wanted to see Hitler—she apparently realized that the Führer's suicide was imminent, and that since she and her husband had promised to kill their children and die with him, they were doomed.

"Hitler wouldn't see her. The adjutant heard Eva Braun washing her hands in the bathroom, and he went back into the hall. When the shot came (by this time the Russians were only forty yards away), he rushed in, saw Hitler dead—he'd blown the back of his head off, firing a revolver through the roof of his mouth—and Eva lying dead on the sofa, a smell of almonds in the air, her lips blue from cyanide. Oddly enough, she had taken off her shoes and arranged them neatly at the end of the couch."

Why didn't the Western Allies take Berlin?

"The story is complex—pressures were brought to bear on Eisenhower to race the Russians for the city, but other larger pressures were brought to let the Russians get there first. We've got to remember that Russia lost 17 million soldiers and civilians in the war—dead, not just total casualties.

"Also, remember that we were still fighting in the Pacific, and wanted to pull troops out of Europe as quickly as possible. It is estimated that if we had pushed on to Berlin our casualties would have numbered 100,000 men. How would the American and British publics have accepted that loss in the final days of the war? There are so many things to consider..."

Why did the Germans fight on even after their defeat was clinched by the Battle of the Bulge?

"A copy of the detailed occupation plan, called Operation Eclipse, was captured from Montgomery's headquarters by the Germans. When they saw the plan they knew that the demand for unconditional surrender was a hard fact, that Germany was to be partitioned. So they fought on in desperation, knowing they could salvage nothing. (I'm referring to the German general staff.) Thus it took the final virtual destruction of Berlin to end the war."

How does Ryan regard the style of documentary reportage he has put to use in assembling his book?

"Regardless of all the talk about this being a new style, it is not. It's being rarified, redefined—but we're doing no more today than fine historians and crime reporters have always done, beginning with Thucydides in his history of the Peloponnesian Wars. Take Stendahl's magnificent description of the Battle of Waterloo — when asked why he did it that way he said, 'I simply wanted to know what happened.'

"I felt this way about the battle for Berlin — I wanted to know what happened, so I talked to hundreds upon hundreds of persons who were there, or encircling the city, or waiting in the Western Allied camp in their private frustration. A single bit of fiction would have destroyed the book; that is why the documentation is so complete.

"It is not a new style or form. But it is a wonderful way to say to the reader, 'You are there. This is what occurred.'"

"I think that the tragedy of America is that we're covered with so many layers of fat, literally and figuratively, that we don't feel anything. We've polluted the air so that we can't breathe it, and we've lost our sense of smell. We have obliterated our landscape with billboards and ugliness . . . we make such noises that we can't hear anything."

Robert St. John

Robert St. John

ST. JOHN: I was born in what is now perhaps the most horrible slum area anywhere in the world, the near West Side of Chicago. When I was a small boy the family moved from there to Oak Park. Ernest Hemingway's father was our family physician, and the Hemingway children attended the same high school I did. Both Ernest and I had the identical experience with one particular teacher, who told us that we could never become writers. (Ernest at that time decided to become a famous doctor like his father, and I don't quite know what I decided.) I was three years behind Ernest, but the last time I saw him, before his death, we compared stories and discovered that both of us were assured we could not become writers, despite the fact that this is often denied by people connected with the Oak Park-River Forest High School. Ernest said it happened, and I know it happened to me, with the same teacher.

We shared another experience. In our boyhood days there was a huge reservoir on Oak Park Avenue, close beside the Chicago and Northwestern Railroad tracks—a reservoir a city block square in size from which Oak Park drew its drinking water. (Ultimately when Oak Park hooked onto the Chicago water system and drew its water from Lake Michigan, this reservoir was drained, and there are now a number of buildings on its site.) When they drained the water they discovered that the bottom was covered with fish, and the *Chicago Tribune* and other papers ran a number of speculative articles about how the fish could have gotten into this reservoir. One theory, printed in the *Tribune*, came from a scientist who advanced the theory that the fish had been carried from Lake Michigan ten miles away, by high winds.

But Ernest and I and a few others knew the real answer. We used to go fishing in the Des Plaines River, some distance west of Oak Park. We would fish until dusk, then start home with catches of four or five little fish. They seemed quite big when we caught them, but the more the fish began to smell, and the more we thought of what our parents were going to say, the smaller the fish seemed to get. So we would get as far as the reservoir on Oak Park Avenue (in our separate times, of course; we never fished together), and since it was dark by then and we had to get rid of the stinking fish, we'd toss them over the eight-foot fence into the reservoir. Apparently some of those fish were not dead, but lived and propagated, and as the years went by quite a colony thrived in what Oak Park thought was its pure drinking water. That was the only fishing I've ever done, but with Ernest, as you know, it was only the beginning.

Back to high school — I did drop the writing course on the advice of the teacher who told me (and had told Ernest) that writing wasn't in the cards. I not only dropped the course, but I dropped out of school at the age of sixteen, ate a lot of bananas, and went to France during World War I as an enlisted man in the U.S. Navy. I was in the war just long enough to acquire an undying feeling about the horror of war, a feeling which has colored my life ever since. I also learned a few things about the inherent ugliness of mankind.

After coming back from the war I went to St. Alban's, a boarding school in Sycamore, Illinois. Then on to Trinity College in Hartford, Connecticut where, in my sophomore year, I had my first fight with censors.

I was the college correspondent for the oldest newspaper in America, the *Hartford Courant*, and the president of the college was a fiery, young, red-haired Episcopal clergyman. The college was one hundred years old and was trying to raise a million-dollar centennial fund. The most distinguished member of the faculty was a former Chicago newspaperman by the name of Odell Shepard, Pulitzer prizewinner with the Bronson Alcott biography titled *Pedlar's Progress*. He was a great Shakespearean scholar, but he hadn't gotten the newspaperman out of his blood. He had the good reporter's instincts for a good story.

I was taking three or four courses under him, and he knew I was the college correspondent for the *Courant*. One day he called me up to his rooms on the campus and said: "I get many, many requests to speak in public — women's clubs, civic clubs, all that sort of thing. I turn them all down. I refuse to waste my time that way, but I have just been invited to do a series of ten lectures for the Hartford Grade Teachers Association, hundreds of teachers, and I've accepted for one reason. I think that grade-school teachers are in more of an intellectual rut than any other group in the community, and I'm going to jar them out of it.

"In the course of doing this," he continued, "I'm going to make a lot of exaggerated statements, a lot of sensational statements. Each lecture will be worth a newspaper story, and the lectures are not open to the public. They are strictly for the members of this teachers' association, but students of Trinity College will be admitted, and since you are a student, you have an opportunity to get in."

I'll never forget the headline in the *Hartford Courant* the day after the first lecture. It read, "Walt Whitman Wrote On Prohibition While Sipping Gin Cocktails." After the story appeared the president of the college called me in and told me that I had a grave decision to make. I had to decide whether I was going to serve God or mammon. I knew what he meant, but I was a sophomore, literally and figuratively, so I snapped back, "And which is God, and which is mammon?" He said, "You know very well which is which; God is your college and mammon is this newspaper you're working for."

I promptly went to tell my managing editor, Emil Govero, what had happened. (He was the first and most celebrated tabloid editor in America, by the way; he later became the editor of the *New York Mirror*, and wrote a book on tabloid journalism.) He was a short, tiny man with a terrible inferiority complex; he walked with a limp due to some physical handicap. Govero was a little Napoleon, and he hated this college president with a great passion because the president had several times complained to him about his editorials and the way he was running the paper. So when I told him I was being censored, he let forth with a lot of expletives about that redheaded so-and-so.

I forget what headline appeared on the second day, but again the story was on page one, and again the college president called me in. He said, "As long as you refuse to listen to reason I am going to impose active censorship. Next week after the lecture I want you to bring the story to this office and I shall eliminate those things I do not want to appear." I told Govero of the demand, and he told me to comply, but added with a wicked, satisfied grin, "We'll fix him."

When I went to the lecture the next week I took another young reporter from the paper with me. He looked enough like a college student so I could smuggle him into the hall. We both took notes. He went back to the office to write his story, and I went back to the campus to write mine. I took it to the president, and he blue-penciled it quite thoroughly. I wrote the lead on the story with my own by-line; when the story appeared it said, right under my by-line, "President R——last night imposed strict censorship on news emanating from Trinity College. He personally blue-penciled a report of a lecture by Odell Shepard, and about all he left of the report was the fact that Odell Shepard spoke. Thus the *Hartford Courant* regrets that it is unable to present to its readers, this morning, an authorized censored version. However, in the following story by John Jones is a complete account of everything he did say."

That was the end of my formal education. Not only was I expelled from college, but when I tried to transfer to several other colleges I was unable to get my credits or any account of the fact that I had completed almost two years of college. So I became a newspaperman. I told Emil Govero that he had gotten me into this fix and that he had to get me out of it, so he said, "I'll make a newspaperman out of you."

I got my first training on that very conservative newspaper under a very unconservative managing editor. I went on from there, back home to Chicago, to become the youngest newspaper publisher in America at that time. My brother and I were joint publishers of three newspapers in the Chicago suburbs. The principal newspaper, in Cicero, Illinois, was the *Cicero Tribune*, and our editorial policy was to try to drive scarfaced Al Capone out of business. He had made Cicero his headquarters, supplied some eighty or ninety speakeasies with liquor and beer, and owned several big gambling joints and a tremendous whorehouse.

I heard of the opening of this house of prostitution near Stickney, near the Hawthorne race track—it was so big that somewhere between two and three hundred girls were employed. I went down and spent a night in the place, equipped with a big wad of twenty-dollar bills. I handed out the bills to the girls to talk to me and pass me on to the next one. Along about five o'clock in the morning one of the girls came running upstairs from the bar to tell me that Ralph Capone was downstairs, that he knew I was up there and he was waiting for me. There was only one staircase, the one I'd come up, so I jumped out of a second-story window onto a small lean-to and got away. I then acquired what I used to boast was my principal distinction in life: I wrote the most complete journalistic exposé of a house of prostitution that, to my knowledge, had ever been published in an American newspaper. It was not quite a *Moll Flanders*, but it was quite a sixteen-column story.

Several days after this exposé appeared, I was walking to my newspaper office in Cicero when a car, a big, black touring car stopped beside me with the traditional screeching brakes. Four men jumped out, and I found myself on the floor of the car. I was taken for a "ride." They gave me the usual treatment; in those days they wrapped a cake of Fels Naphtha yellow laundry soap in a heavy, knitted, woolen man's sock, and clipped you at the base of the brain; if it was properly done it left no mark, death was instantaneous, and the body was dumped into a ditch to be found several days later, bearing no signs of violence. Unfortunately, they didn't hit the right mark, probably because they were quite drunk. They gave me a good working-over before they clipped me with the cake of soap, and I ended up with my left leg quite badly banged up. I was thrown into the ditch and found some hours later.

I spent a considerable length of time in a hospital. As I lay there I thought of all the charges I could place against these men. When I left

my bed I went to Ted Svoboda, who was then the Chief of Police; he
was later killed by the Capone mob because he hadn't played square
with them. I asked Svoboda for four warrants for the arrest of the men.
Ralph Capone was one; the second man in the car was Pete Pizzo, and
there were two John Doe warrants for the men I couldn't identify.
I wanted to charge assault and battery, assault with intent to kill,
kidnapping, and one thing or another. Svoboda patted me on the back
and said, "Kid" (the most insulting part of all; I was twenty-one years
old and considered myself a man), "Al is never going to let his brother
be arrested. You know that. You got out of it lucky. Just go your way."
I insisted, so he told me to come back the next day. I thought he had
changed his mind and I'd get my warrants.

I came back the next morning at nine o'clock. He said, "Go up to my
office." I went up. As I was standing at the window, looking down into
the street, I heard the office door open and close. I turned around, and
there was Scarface Al, a very pleasant man — a pleasant, kindly gangster,
but who might have become the head of a steel or automobile company
if he had gone in a different direction. He had tremendous ability and a
charming personality, contrary to the image given on certain television
shows that have characterized him as a stereotype. (He actually did
have a rather pronounced scar on one side of his face, however. He was
conscious of this and hated to have people refer to it.) Al patted me on
the back, put his arm around my shoulder, and told me he was very
sorry about what had happened. "The boys had gotten a little drunk."
His instructions to them were never to bother a newspaperman. He
said, "We all have our rackets, you know. You have yours, I have mine.
As a matter of fact, you did me a big favor. I couldn't advertise my
whorehouse. I couldn't take a full-page ad in the *Chicago Tribune*. My
business has doubled since your exposé, and I'm very grateful to you. I
regret that the boys gave you a working-over. They were a little drunk
or they wouldn't have done it. They violated my orders. You know, I
paid your hospital bill." (When I left the hospital they told me at the
desk that my bill had been paid. I told them that was impossible, but
from their description of the man who paid it I began to feel that
Capone had done it.)

At this point he pulled out a big roll of bills (this *was* the stereotype,
with the fat bankroll) and started counting. He said, "You lost your hat,"
and pulled off a hundred-dollar bill, "and you must have torn your
clothes," and he peeled off another hundred-dollar bill, and so on. He
must have peeled off ten or fifteen hundred-dollar bills.

But I walked out. There were certain times later, in the lean years,
when I thought of those hundred-dollar bills, but I walked out. I was
a crusading young editor.

Al Capone drove me out of Cicero eventually. I kept trying to drive him out, but he was just a little bit stronger. It's too long a story to go into, but I left and went East to such papers as the *Philadelphia Record*, the *New Jersey Courier*, and finally to the AP in New York as city editor. I covered Roosevelt's campaign in 1932, and such murder cases as the "Star Faithful" case out on Long Island, and a weird and fantastic murder trial called "the Bluebeard Powers case" down in West Virginia, involving a man who advertised for wives and hacked them up into small pieces as soon as they arrived. He didn't hide some of the pieces too well.

Finally, in 1932, after the election of Roosevelt, I decided that I had covered all the stories there were to cover. I felt very blasé about it all and decided to retire without waiting until I was sixty-five or seventy and would be relegated to some croquet course in Florida. I was all of thirty. I bought a two hundred-acre farm in New Hampshire for $3,000, raised turnips, raised chickens, and carved copies of an antique snuffbox. There were thirteen stars and thirteen stripes on each and every snuffbox, and I carved a thousand of them. The boxes were carved out of solid blocks of pine, held a package of cigarettes, and I sold them for $2.00 each. I made my living for two years that way, a thousand dollars a year. But oh, how I came to hate stars. I couldn't even look at them in the sky for years to come without remembering the thousands of five-pointed stars I'd carved.

For six years I saw no newspapers; I was really in the backwoods. Late in 1938, an old, old friend from my Philadelphia newspaper days, Frank Gervasi, who had been head of the Hearst bureau in Rome while I'd been on my farm, came to visit me. He thought it was a wonderful idea for me to retire at the age of thirty, but he said that I ought to cover one more story before I really quit. I said, "What's the story?" He said, "The war." I said, "What war?" He said, "My God, don't you know about Hitler and Mussolini?" I said, "No, I don't know about Hitler and Mussolini." He didn't really believe me, and nobody really believes the story to this day. But I was really isolated up there.

He predicted that the war would start on the first day of September, 1939, which was a fantastic prediction because it was on that exact day that it started. Gervasi was a very good foreign correspondent in those days, so good he convinced me that war was coming. I trusted his depth of knowledge. So I went down to New York to the Associated Press. I told them I was a former employee and that I wanted to go abroad as a war correspondent. They said, "There's no war," and I said, "Yes, it's going to start on the first of September." They said, "Who told you that?" and I said, "Frank Gervasi." They replied, "Oh, Frank Gervasi— we fired him long ago. What does he know about it? Besides, even if

there is going to be a war, you're much too old to be a war correspondent." So I decided I would go to Europe on my own and hope that
Gervasi was right, and that I'd be able to pick up a job over there. I
didn't have any money.

I borrowed a thousand dollars from a bank and bought a bookshop
in Concord, New Hampshire—the Apple Tree Bookshop. It was going
out of business. It was located in a basement and had a stock of a few
thousand dusty old books. Six or eight months later I sold the shop at a
profit of $2,000. I took that money and bought steamship tickets for
myself and my wife and had a thousand-dollar nest egg to live on. We
got to Paris and found Paris full of such people as John Gunther and
Dorothy Thompson—all the big names. Half of them were predicting
that the crisis was just another Munich; half thought something would
happen. This was now August, 1939. My thousand dollars was going
pretty fast, so I bought railroad tickets to Bucharest, Romania, with the
idea that there, at least, I wouldn't run into so many John Gunthers and
Dorothy Thompsons. My competition wouldn't be so overpowering.
Also, in case the "positive" half of the correspondents were right, and
war would be averted, I'd be able to write a book about the love life of
King Carol and Madame Lupescu, his red-haired mistress. I've often
regretted that I didn't.

War came. We had to change trains in Budapest, and we had to lay
over for eight hours. The Orient Express ran, in those days, through
Budapest on the way to Bucharest. There hadn't been any food on the
train between Paris and Budapest; Europe was in a rather hysterical
state at the moment, and somehow we ended up without a diner. So we
headed for a restaurant. The menu was in two languages, German and
Hungarian, neither of which I knew. The waiters spoke only German
and Hungarian, so in desperation my wife pointed at something on the
menu and said, "Zwei," German for "two," and the waiter went off and
came back fifteen minutes later with two dill pickles. I decided that
drastic action was called for, so I told my wife to sit and wait; I'd call for
help and come back. I went to a telephone booth, looked up the
Associated Press in the directory, and by sign language learned from
the headwaiter that the office was only a few blocks away. So I dashed
down the street, hoping to get an AP man to come and help us get a
meal. I opened the door to a little office about ten feet square. In it were
two or three men and a few women acting like maniacs, screaming,
yelling, picking up telephones, throwing down telephones, banging
typewriters. I stood in the doorway for a long time, and finally a man,
the bureau chief, said, "Shut that goddam door." I said, "Oh, excuse
me." He said, "My God, you speak English?" I said, "Yes, a little." He

said, "You're not a newspaperman, by any chance?" I said, "Former city editor, Associated Press, New York." He said, "My God, come in, take your coat off." I said, "What's the matter?" He said, "Don't you know? Warsaw is being bombed. Germany has invaded Poland, and World War II has started." This had happened while we were on the train. Forty-eight hours later I remembered my wife sitting in the restaurant.

In about two or three weeks, things quieted down a bit and I said, "How about some money? Am I employed?" He said, "I'll send a cable to New York." So he sent a cable to Associated Press in New York and they said they had a rule that they could not hire American foreign correspondents abroad. If I would pay my own transportation from Budapest to New York, they would hire me and then pay my transportation back. But I wasn't about to take a chance on not being able to get back to Europe, so the bureau chief (a very astute young man) solved the problem by remembering that he could hire natives of the country as stringers. The maximum he could pay them was $100 a month, so I was hired and went on the payroll as John Unesco at $100 a month. I worked that way, under that name, until the Balkans fell. It wasn't much money but I was *there*.

Eventually, when things really started to break and the Nazis swept into Romania, I was sent there. I got some wonderful beats. It always seemed that the minute I would phone a story to the AP in Switzerland for transmission to America, the Romanians would close down the telephone lines, and my competition—the United Press, INS, and the rest—would be beaten by forty-eight hours. Finally AP in New York got suspicious about this fellow Unesco. They wanted to know more about their correspondent in Romania. When they learned the truth they began putting my own name on by-lines, so if you look back at 1940 and 1941 newspapers you'll see by-lines by Robert St. John, even though I was still on the payroll as John Unesco at $100 a month. Finally, of course, I had to flee. This escape resulted in the book, *From the Land of Silent People*, a hundred-thousand word account that doesn't seem appropriate to repeat here.

I was probably the first American war correspondent wounded. This happened on a troop train in Greece when we were trying to get to Athens to restore some communication after the fall of Belgrade and most of Greece. I got three Nazi machine-gun bullets in my right leg, almost twenty years after Capone's mobsters messed up the left leg. I still carry the scars; the Capone marks have rather well disappeared, but Hitler's marks are still there, complete with bullets. Every once in a while they hurt; the bullets move around, and when they hit a nerve, it's hell. Once one hit a nerve just as I was crossing Fifth Avenue against the lights, and I nearly got mowed down by a taxi. But I like to have the bullets there to hit a nerve once in a while. I like to remember.

Those three Nazi machine-gun bullets remind me of a little Greek girl. After this train was shot up one of our fellow pressmen, Lee White of CBS, was badly banged up. He had ten or fifteen slugs in his derrière, and we were trying to find a hospital for him. We finally found one, but there were no beds. There was one nurse for three or four hundred Greeks in the hospital. (There had been an air raid that day on the town, Corinth.) We were lying on the floor, and everything was quiet except for the whimpering of this little girl. As the nurse came by, I said, "What is the whimpering?" She didn't say anything but just turned her torch on a child of six or seven. Her left arm had been blown off at the elbow and hung in tattered shreds of dirty black flesh. I said, "Why don't you bandage it?" She said, "We have no bandages." "Why don't you give her a narcotic of some kind? She's in terrible pain." She said, "We have no narcotics." I said, "Has a doctor seen her?" and she said, "We have no doctors. Now go back to sleep."

This is why I'm glad I still have the bullets in my leg. The mind is a forgetting instrument as well as a remembering instrument.

I have had a lot to do with the state of Israel. I've been there thirteen times, and I'm going back again very soon. I've written several books about that country and its people; Israel is a country of people who are alive only because the mind is a forgetting instrument. Over half of the two million Jews in Israel have had horrible war experiences. Many of them were in concentration camps. Actually there's hardly an adult in Israel who didn't have some close contact with the horrors of war, yet they've been able to go on because they've been able to forget. For them it's good to be able to forget. But I think it's a tragedy that we forget as readily as we do, because if we remembered perhaps it wouldn't happen again. But we've all forgotten.

I think that the tragedy of America is that we're covered with so many layers of fat, literally and figuratively, that we don't feel anything. We've polluted the air so that we can't breathe it, and we've lost our sense of smell. We cover ourselves with so many deodorants and perfumes that we no longer smell the good odors of human beings. We have obliterated our landscape with billboards and ugliness until we can't see anything. And we make such noises that we can't hear anything anymore.

A friend of mine, a New York doctor named Rosen, went to Africa with a tape recorder like yours and found a tribe of Africans with beautiful hearing—beautiful because they had never heard an ugly sound. They live in an area where there are no huge wild animals, an area that has never had airplanes, automobiles, tractors or sirens, just the gentle chirping of birds, the sounds of small animals, their own voices. He found that these people had the acute hearing at the ages of sixty and seventy that we have when we're small children, before our ears start going to pot.

At any rate, I got back to America. Even though I was still John Unesco on the payroll, AP gave a great banquet and handed out some publicity. We had been all reported dead, all of us who'd left Greece on a little boat — an Englishman, three Americans, and a Serb, so there was a bit of a stir. An editor at Doubleday called me up one day and asked me if I would write a book about my experiences. I was completely flabbergasted and said, "Oh, I'm not a writer, I'm a newspaperman." He said, "Well, yes, but will you try?" At that time I really thought (and still do, to some extent) that books should be written by authors, but they twisted my wrist finally, and I agreed.

But I had something to say. I had something burning inside me, a protest against the horror of war. The funny thing is that that first book, *From the Land of Silent People*, was made compulsory reading by several pacifist societies, yet Goebbels listed it as one of the twenty books that got America into the war. I wasn't trying to play both sides of the street at all. The book was a diatribe against war, but it was also a diatribe against American complacency, and I guess the latter is what Goebbels singled out.

As strange as it seems, AP had a rule in those days that no correspondent could write a book or a magazine article, or lecture or earn money from any source other than writing AP dispatches. They wanted him to be a devoted AP employee and have no mistresses. When I told them I had signed a contract to write a book, they told me I must cancel the contract or leave AP. So I left. Several years later Walter Winchell wrote a little piece in one of his columns in which he gave me credit for breaking this rule; several years after I left, AP set up a bureau within its organization to encourage employees to write books and give lectures, which is a policy they continue to this day.

But about *From the Land of Silent People* — in the flight from the Balkans in a twenty-foot sardine boat I had lost everything. I lost most of my belongings in the bombing of my hotel in Belgrade, the Srpskyk-rajl Hotel, which was bombed and burned to the ground during the Palm Sunday burning of Belgrade. I lost the manuscript of a novel, the only copy I had. I lost the only six tailor-made shirts I ever had in my life, and a tuxedo made by King Carol's tailor (after Carol had left, of course, and the tailor was reduced to making clothes for ordinary mortals). Then we went down through the Balkans and kept losing things in Serbia and on Corfu and so on. I came out of the Balkans clutching a portable typewriter in one hand and, in the other, a bundle of hotel vouchers and other expense account items I knew AP would have to have if they were to pay me the thousands of dollars they owed me for telephone bills, hotel bills, etc. That was all I saved, so there I was in New York, and Doubleday wanted a hundred-thousand-word book. I said that I didn't have any notes, so they said, "Just write your impressions." So I decided to write a book about the twenty-eight days between the bombing of Belgrade and the day we got to Cairo, Egypt, in that damned boat. In those twenty-eight days we had almost no sleep, never had our clothes off, were machine-gunned and bombed, and had very little food. All those experiences, and no notes.

I rented a room on the top floor of the Hotel Roosevelt, a tiny room, the simplest I could get. I had them take out all the furniture except a bare wooden table, a chair, and a cot. I brought my typewriter, some copy paper, and a case of Scotch whiskey. Stupidly, I bought no carbon paper, so the novel was produced without a carbon copy.

I would start to work at dusk. In those days the airliners went right over the top of the Roosevelt, so this gave me some of the sound effects of war. I drank anywhere between a pint and a quart of Scotch at night, and that helped take me back. I worked from dusk to dawn; at dawn I'd generally have a chapter finished, and I would take my single copy of it, put it in a long envelope, stamp it, walk out to the mailbox for a constitutional, and send it off to Doubleday. The Doubleday office was only a few blocks down the street, but by mailing it early in the morning they'd get it in the afternoon.

It took me twenty-eight nights to write the book. One very interesting thing about it was this: On the day I got shot, when the troop train was strafed and hundreds of men were killed, the narcotic of excitement and sleeplessness and taut nerves was so powerful that I did not know I had been shot until five days later. When I tried to take my trousers off in Cairo I found that they were stuck to my leg, clotted with blood. So the trousers were cut off, somebody washed my leg, and we discovered that there were three holes in it. I went to a hospital in Cairo and had my leg X-rayed; they found three sizable machine-gun slugs. I didn't even know I had been shot. But the night at the Roosevelt Hotel when I wrote about this I seemed to have total recall, and I suffered the tortures of the damned. Then I really felt the pain of the strafing.

At any rate, the book was published. I was offered a job by the director of news and special events for NBC. Abe Schechter, now the head of a public relations firm in New York, was one of the pioneers in this "international" type of radio. He decided to send me to London, and he said, "I have just two pieces of advice. When you get over there and start broadcasting to America, none of this chi-chi 'Syngyn' like the British say it, or 'Synjohn' as I hear you say it. Your name is 'Saint John' when you're with NBC. The other is this: If a bomb falls when you're on the air, keep broadcasting as long as you can, at least as long as you're conscious. And don't worry. If anything really happens to you, we'll send a replacement as soon as possible."

Those were the days when every time the German air force sent a wave of planes over England, no matter what the target was, London or another area, one plane always tried to drop its bombs on Broadcasting House. This was because the Germans thought they knew the British mentality well enough (and they were right) to assume that if they could knock out Broadcasting House, thus forcing the British to broadcast from Liverpool or Manchester or from any of their other transmitters, they would do great damage to British morale, because the British would be so honest they'd say, "This is Liverpool calling." The "This is London calling" buoyed up the British and also irritated the Nazis, so they tried to knock the building out. They never hit it once as far as I know. I remember walking up Regent Street one day and seeing a land mine in the days when they were parachuting land mines down — colossal bombs attached to parachutes — and this bomb was coming right straight at Broadcasting House. I ducked into a doorway, put my fingers in my ears, and said, "This is it." The bomb got somewhere between ten and twenty feet from the roof and a gust of wind took and landed it over on a nearby hotel, where it took out a block of buildings.

We were actually broadcasting from rooms three stories below ground level. Ed Murrow, from CBS, would be on one side of the table, and I would be on the other side. Our broadcasts were within fifteen minutes of each other, so we were always in the studio at the same time — Murrow, myself, a censor, and a British engineer. I'd get on the air and say, "This is Robert St. John in London," and the Englishmen would cringe. Finally one night the censor said to me, "Look, Mr. Syngyn, I can't censor you, I can't force you to say it, but if you can't say 'Syngyn' at least say 'Sin John.'" But I had to stick to the NBC pronunciation.

During the rest of the war I broadcast from various places. I did one of the first broadcasts from liberated Paris. I broadcast Roosevelt's death over the network. I covered the creation of the United Nations in San Francisco. And I was convinced that the time to retire from broadcasting would be on VJ-Day. I felt that because of nuclear bombing we could never have another big war. I am still convinced of this; if we do, there'll be one big broadcast, then curtains for all.

Thus I was determined to broadcast the end of the last major war in history. Many of us have forgotten, but there was an on-again-off-again situation at the time of VJ-Day. Have the Japs signed or haven't they? This went on for seventy-two hours, and during those hours the other NBC men like Kaltenborn, Lowell Thomas, John Vandercook, Don Hollenbeck, and Don Goddard came and went; they'd stay eight or ten hours and then go get some sleep. But just as I gambled when I climbed into the little sardine boat and pushed out onto the Adriatic, I gambled here in a lesser way. I stayed at a microphone for seventy-two hours, and so determined was I to be the one to do this "final" broadcast that I got the reward. I was the one who finally said over the NBC network, "Ladies and gentlemen: The war has ended. The Japanese have signed." And that was the last big broadcast I ever did. It was the last big broadcast I'll ever do. It's the end of that chapter of my life. Over there is a picture of the empty booth in which I said the war was over. In this building we are now, here in Milwaukee, I re-posed the picture twenty years later, almost to the minute. If I could take some of the wrinkles out of the second picture they'd be quite alike.

Now, as to books—first there was *From the Land of Silent People*. Then, when I was in London for NBC I wrote a little novel titled *It's Always Tomorrow*, a war novel set in London. Everybody's forgotten it, but it had the largest circulation of any book I've ever written. It was not an important book, not even a good one.

After that I went back to Yugoslavia and retraced my steps, revisiting all that went into *Silent People*. Incidentally, the Yugoslavs were furious when they heard the title of this book. "Why did you call us silent people? Didn't you hear about the partisans, Tito, Mikhailovich, and all the rest? Why did you call us silent people?" Stupidly, in the front of the book I omitted to credit the title, which came from a speech made by Roosevelt when Greece and Yugoslavia fell. In this famous address he said, "All of Europe is now a land of silent people. We must go to their aid." This was at the point when we were giving lend-lease aid to Britain.

I hadn't meant to imply that the Yugoslavs were silent—of course I knew that the Yugoslavs fought in the hills, so I went back and tried to make up for that title by titling the sequel *The Silent People Speak*. This was a book about the new Yugoslavia. I had a most unfortunate time-break with this book because it came out just before Yugoslavia broke with Russia. If it had been released three months later, I wouldn't have been called such ugly names by some critics and some publications.

After this I became intensely interested in the Middle East. I guess it was the old fire-horse, war-horse correspondent in me. In 1948, war broke out after the UN partitioned Palestine. Israel was invaded by four Arab armies, and I went to cover the war. In the process I fell in love with the area and with the people. I go to some of the Arab countries, and always to Israel, each year. It's an area with terrific problems — one of the most feudal sections of the world.

Incidentally, I'm often asked by people in lecture audiences (not unkindly) what the real problem *is* in the Middle East, what crime Israel has committed that they are so hated by the Arabs. The answer is very simple, and yet I think it's profound. The crime the Jews have committed in the Middle East is to introduce the twentieth century and our concept of democracy to this feudal region. The oil barons of the Middle East who have their money in numbered accounts in Swiss banks loathe the introduction of Western democracy. This is one aspect of the Middle East that fascinates me, to see feudalism crumbling before your eyes.

I've written most of my books, actually, on that part of the world. First, *Shalom Means Peace*, which came out of the 1948 experience of covering that war. Then I became interested in the only man in the world who had single-handedly created a language. This language is modern Hebrew. (Ancient Hebrew had been dead for more than two thousand years. Many people think Christ spoke Hebrew, but he didn't; he spoke Aramaic. Hebrew had already started to die out at the time of Christ.)

In the latter part of the nineteenth century one Eliezer Ben Yehuda, a Lithuanian Jew living in Palestine and a truly prophetic man, decided that some day there would be a return of his people to their ancient home, and he knew they couldn't have a country without a language. Ancient Hebrew had remained a language only to pray in. You couldn't curse the camel or order groceries. You could make love in ancient Hebrew — there was the "Song of Solomon." But the only surviving Hebrew was in religious works.

Ben Yehuda spent a lifetime looking for lost words. He knew, for example, that the word for "tomato" had once existed because they had this vegetable in biblical times, so he searched throughout the world for old manuscripts to obtain these lost words. And he had to invent words, of course, for things that did not exist in biblical times — "radio," "telephone," "psychoanalysis," and so on. *Tongue of the Prophets* was the biography of Ben Yehuda.

Then I went to South Africa and lived for a year in another feudalistic nation and wrote *Through Malan's Africa*, a very unfortunate title for a number of reasons. After I'd been in South Africa for a few weeks, I cabled my publishers that it was going to take me many months, perhaps a year, before I would have material for the book, but that I did have the title. (It is always a problem for authors and publishers to get or agree on a title. Sometimes the author has what he thinks is a good one and the publisher doesn't like it, or vice versa. It takes time to reach agreement.) But I knew I had a title—*Land of Fear*. It *was* a land of fear, and still is. Everybody is afraid of everybody else. The Indians are afraid of the Africans, the Africans are afraid of the whites, the Afrikaners are afraid of the English-speaking whites, and so on. My editor wrote back and said, "Wonderful, fine title, short, tells the story." Just before publication the title was submitted to the sales force, and they decided that it was a very bad title because of the political climate in America at the time. They thought that anyone seeing that title in a bookstore window would think it was a book about Russia. So they cabled me (I was back in Switzerland by that time) to submit a substitute title. I did and they didn't like it; they submitted one to me I didn't like, and we went back and forth. They wanted a three-word title if possible, and one of the words would have to be "Africa" because they thought that was salable. It should also pinpoint what part of Africa, and it should imply that I had been there, so I finally told them to choose the title. They came up with *Through Malan's Africa*. But while the book was being manufactured Malan died, and the few people who had ever heard about the man promptly forgot him. Malan was the inventor of the horrible thing called *apartheid*, which is quite properly pronounced as though it were spelled "apart-hate." That's the way it is pronounced in South Africa, and that is precisely what it means. A wonderful story about Dr. Malan is this one. In a Johannesburg paper at the time of his death the obituary read ". . . Dr. Malan was a predicant of the Dutch Reformed Church, he was a very abstemious man who did not drink, did not smoke, and he had three adopted children."

Other books—*This Was My World*, an autobiography that focused on the old newspaper days in Chicago. I continued the autobiography with *Foreign Correspondent*, taking my life from the beginning to the end of World War II. After that I went off and wrote the biography of David Ben-Gurion. You know, during the thirty-five years or so that I have been wandering around the world interviewing people, reporting on persons and events, sometimes for radio, sometimes for television, sometimes for books, I have felt myself in the presence of greatness five times. By "greatness" I mean, first of all, a man with such a pervasive personality that if he entered the room and you were blindfolded you'd know he came in. But my definition also, of course, implies that the person has a great goal, a great concept, a great ambition, a great ideal. This is why such men as Churchill and Roosevelt are not on my list. You can't name any great principle that dominated the life of Winston Churchill, though he was a very fine prime minister in wartime. Even Roosevelt's life was not dominated from boyhood by a great intention. But my five choices — Ben-Gurion, of course, and Gandhi, Einstein, Schweitzer, plus Helen Keller.

I have a wonderful story about Helen. I gave a luncheon for her some years ago in a secluded outdoor restaurant in Paris. She arrived with her companion, Polly, and through tapping on Polly's palm said to me, "Do you mind if Polly and I walk around the garden before we sit down?" They went for their walk, and when they came back Helen said to me through Polly, "Lovely garden. lovely white lilacs." I replied, through Polly again, "I can understand how you knew they were lilacs, but how could you know they're white lilacs?" and she said, "Oh, you poor people with your undeveloped sense of smell. White lilacs smell different from purple lilacs."

Of all my great people, David Ben-Gurion has been the most fortunate. Einstein died a bitter man; Gandhi died before his goal was realized, before India became free. Schweitzer was a sad man because he's famous for the wrong thing, and he knew it. The great thing about Schweitzer was "reverence for life," those three words, yet he lived in an age that has shown less reverence for life than almost any other age in the history of man. Six million exterminated in Europe. The two big powers with enough of a nuclear stockpile to wipe out the whole of civilization. And they gave Schweitzer prizes because he had a little hospital in Africa, not because he coined the expression, and believed in, reverence for life. Reverence for life is honored only in the negative.

Ben-Gurion is a fascinating man, and I could talk for hours about him. I recently spent a month with him in the Negev Desert at Sde Bokar, a kibbutz where he lives. He's eighty years old and still stands on his head for fifteen minutes every day — part of his yoga exercises. He's a man who seems to grow younger each year. He has, in some respects, feet of clay, and some blind spots. As his biographer I think that his recent political activity discloses a blind spot. But his place in history is made, and he is the most fortunate man on my list because he lived to see his life's dream come true. As a small boy, you know, he became a Zionist, meaning a Jew who was interested in working for the repopulation of the ancient Jewish homeland. He not only lived to see this realized, but he played a vital part in the most important episode in the two thousand years of Jewish history since the birth of Christ.

Although my biography of Ben-Gurion has not sold more copies

than any book I've written, it has been my most successful because it's
been translated into ten languages. Doubleday still keeps it in print,
years after it was written, and has agreed to keep it in print almost
indefinitely.

After the favorable treatment *Ben-Gurion* received at the hands of
the critics, I had offers from two or three other publishers to do what
actors and actresses in Hollywood often do, leave home base for one
book. This is legitimate in the publishing business, just as it is in
Hollywood, and Doubleday was very kind. They told me I could leave
them for one book. Macmillan wanted me to do a definitive biography
of de Gaulle. It had not been done. There have been a number of
biographies since then, but at the time there was a void. I answered this
invitation by telling the Macmillan editor I didn't quite know how I felt
about de Gaulle, and I think a biographer has to have definite feelings,
preferably positive, so I turned that one down.

Another publisher wanted me to do a biography of the head of the
American Tobacco Company. They offered me a fantastic amount
because the subject of the book was going to buy ten thousand copies. It
would be profitable for everybody. *That* was an easy one to turn down.

Finally McGraw-Hill approached me to do a biography of Nasser.
The idea of doing a book on Nasser immediately after I'd written about
Ben-Gurion intrigued me because I was curious about Nasser's motivations. (I think the biographer *must* find his subject's motivation.) There
were two rather tricky clauses in the contract McGraw-Hill offered, but
I was intrigued enough to go into the project. The first clause read that I
would return the advance if I failed to get into Egypt; the second that
I would return the advance if I failed to obtain a series of personal
interviews with Nasser. This made it tough, but I countered with a
clause stating that they had to get me an interview with the Egyptian
ambassador in Washington without telling him my name, because I felt
sure he wouldn't see me if he knew who I was. So they made the
arrangement.

I arrived one morning in Washington and went to the U.A.R.
embassy as a McGraw-Hill author with an appointment to see the
ambassador. I walked in trembling, much more than I'd trembled under
gunfire. I was very nervous because a lot depended on this. I really
wanted to do this, but I was sure the ambassador would regard me as an
enemy. When I was presented to him I said, "Mr. Ambassador, you
probably have never heard of me, but my name is Robert St. John and
I'm the author of *Shalom Means Peace, Tongue of the Prophets*, and *Ben-
Gurion*. Worse than that, I've done a great deal of lecturing and fund-
raising for organizations such as Hadassah and Histadruth, Bonds for
Israel, the United Jewish Appeal, and..."

The ambassador held up his hand and said, "Just a moment." He pressed a buzzer, his secretary came in, and he said, "Would you see if any of St. John's copies of *Ben-Gurion* are in the embassy? I would like him to autograph one for me." Then he turned to me and said, "What do you want from me?" I said, "I have in my pocket a contract to do a biography of your man Nasser, and I would like your help." He said, "Why should I help you after what you have just told me?" I didn't tell him about the two clauses in the contract. I said, "Mr. Ambassador, I'm going to do this book in any event. There are three places I can do my research. The easiest place would be in the New York Public Library, where, by spending fifteen cents in subway fare, I can go day after day to read everything that has ever been written about Nasser. Then I would write a book. I've never written a book this way; I'm a reporter, essentially, and I think that is the worst way to write a book. The best way to write it would be to have you give me a visa and a letter to Nasser, with the assurance that I will see him many times, that I will see his wife, his uncle, his brothers, and go to his birthplace. There is still a third way I could write it. There is a city in the Middle East where they have a great deal of information about Mr. Nasser. I have a lot of friends in that city, and I'm sure they'd be glad to cooperate with me and tell me everything they know of him. In which of the three places do you think I ought to do my research?"

He smiled and said, "You're going to get a visa, and you're going to see Nasser, not once, but many times. First I want to give you a little talking-to, a little orientation."

So I went to Egypt. I had many, many interviews with Nasser. Most of these interviews took place after midnight because Nasser believes that he thinks better, clearer, more sharply after midnight than he does during the day. He knows that nobody else does, and he wants to practice this bit of one-upmanship.

I found him to be one of the most charming and personable men I have met in my life. He never fails to inquire about your wife, or about how you feel. He has the charm of a matinee idol, in contrast to Ben-Gurion, who is diametrically the opposite. You hold out your hand to shake hands with Ben-Gurion and he just looks at your hand and says, "What's that for?" You say, "I'm trying to shake hands with you." He says, "What for? Don't you know where that custom originated? It started when one man wanted to show another that he didn't have a dagger in his hand. I don't think you've got a dagger."

I had a terrible time trying to find out when Ben-Gurion was born. I said, "When is your birthday?" I knew the year, but I didn't know the month or the day. He said, "I don't know. I never celebrate my birthday." I said, "Why don't you?" and he said, "Why do you celebrate yours? Celebrate on a day when you did something. Let your mother celebrate your birthday. *You* didn't do anything on that day."

He seriously does not celebrate his birthday, and he never asks you how your wife is, or about your health. He hates small talk. Small talk is the oil which lubricates the machine of social intercourse, and Ben-Gurion isn't interested.

While Ben-Gurion was prime minister his aides had a terrible time getting him to attend a limited number of receptions and cocktail parties each year, and even when he did attend he would frustrate them by standing in the doorway, looking around the room with his bright little eyes. He would pick out one man he thought would be interesting to talk to, then take that man off into a corner and spend the entire two hours with him. Why should he waste his time making small talk with some American clubwoman?

Nasser will talk about the weather; he will talk about your children. When I was there the correspondents used to say that it took a half-hour after you left Nasser before you would come to your senses. I would say, "Mr. President, what is your fight with Israel really about? Why are you so antagonistic? Why do you constantly threaten Israel with extermination?" In a very pal-like, confidential, warm voice he would say, "Look, St. John, you're a very intelligent man and you've been around and you can put yourself in other people's places. Just imagine my situation. Imagine if you were in my position . . ." and he takes you right down the garden path and gives you one of two choices, and before you know it, you're trapped. But on the plus side he has managed to maintain a very stable regime, quite a feat in view of the fact that he has two or three million members of the Moslem Brotherhood, an organization of fanatics that believe in holy war, that you go immediately to heaven if you die in a holy war, plus a large Communist party. He has managed to keep both of these groups under control; in fact, if he were only to stick to internals, I would have no quarrel with him.

After the Nasser book I did one I wish I had drawn royalties on, because it has sold about half a million copies. I did a book on Israel for the Life World Library. It was done for a flat fee, and I enjoyed doing it. It was an interesting book to write because it had to follow the format of the series, one chapter on history, another on the arts, and so on — quite rigid. But I wish I'd been able to draw royalties. *They Came From Everywhere* followed, containing twelve short biographies of the most important people in the making of modern Israel, followed by *The Man Who Played God*, a long novel set in Hungary and Israel which followed fairly closely an actual case that came up during the Eichmann trial, the Kastner case, about the man who bought 1,681 Jewish lives from

Eichmann, put them on a train and sent them to Switzerland. Like Eichmann, who said he wasn't interested in little deals, he'd make a big deal; he'd give them a million Jews for ten thousand military trucks. This was actually the start of the Cold War, you know, because Washington sent a man to Istanbul to talk about the deal. Eichmann wanted to make sure that these trucks came from America. Kastner, the man who played God, said that the only place he could get those trucks *would* be America, and he said, "Why would the Americans give us ten thousand military trucks to give to you, their mortal enemy?" Eichmann said, "I am instructed to tell you that they will be used only on the Eastern front against the Russians." Well, we didn't go through with the deal, but the Russians found out that we considered it, and it was the wedge that started the Cold War.

Most recently — *Roll, Jordan, Roll*, a very large book that presents the history of the Jordan River from four and one-half million B.C., when the star hit, to the present.

Next, I'm doing a book on Judaism. It's for Doubleday's Main-stream of America series. Cannon, the editor of the *Christian Science Monitor*, will do one on Christian Science, a very prominent Catholic will write on Catholicism in America, and I'm covering Judaism. I'll be the only one in the series doing a book on a religion that isn't his own. It will be a challenge. (I hate that word; like all clichés it became a cliché because it is a good word, and now it's almost meaningless.) At any rate the book on Judaism is the first I've done that will attempt to be somewhat profound. It requires deep research and a great deal of thought.

N: *How would you define your objectives as a writer, either in terms of goals or principles?*

ST. JOHN: Well, I have lived in sixty-five countries and traveled three million miles or more since the end of World War II. I know bits and pieces of a great many languages. During the London blitz I tried to report on what was happening over there in terms of people. I am not much interested in events; I'm interested in the similarities and the dissimilarities of people. I'm interested in the victims of such things as fascism and apartheid, not in fascism and apartheid in themselves.

At any rate, I have tried books on various parts of the world and on various colors and nationalities and creeds of people, and I've constantly tried to pour them into one mold — not to make them look and smell and sound alike, but to make it clear that we are all victims of the same uglinesses, of the same horrors in life, whether it's that little Greek girl with her arm blown off, or the black African living in those horrible slums on the edge of Johannesburg, or the people who now live in a block on the near West Side of Chicago where I was born.

I hate to use the word "humanitarian" (we've run so many good words into the ground; some ugly forces have even run words like "peace" into disrepute), but I think my principles are those of a humanitarian.

Now, I've been called quite a few things during my life. I've written fifteen books and done thousands of broadcasts and a considerable number of magazine articles, and I've paid rather heavily, along the way, for some of my principles. Yet I have one prevailing satisfaction, even though some of the books have been so badly written I wish I could go back to rewrite them. I think I've matured as a writer; I seriously believe that my last book is the best I've done as far as the style is concerned. But that isn't important.

What *is* important to me is the fact that I don't know of one sentence I've written that I want to retract. I might wish to rewrite some stylistically, but I don't know of a sentence I'm ashamed of having written. I wrote about Yugoslavia at a time when, if you said one decent thing about that country, you were called a dirty name. Yet six or eight months after my book came out, the State Department was trying to sell my point of view to the American public. Things changed. I wrote what I saw, felt, heard, and smelled about Yugoslavia. It wasn't a book of opinion; I don't pretend to be a Walter Lippmann. But this doesn't mean for a minute that I pretend to be objective.

I'm not objective. I have absolutely no use for objectivity. I loathe objectivity. My definition of an objective reporter is a man who goes into a room and interviews two men; one man says, "It's raining outside," and the other says, "He's a liar. The sun is shining." So the objective reporter tells his readers what the two men said, but he doesn't tell whether it was raining or the sun was shining.

I can't be objective, perhaps because I'm an American. I've lived a great many other places, but I'm essentially a Middle-West American, and just as I can't ever lose my Middle-Western accent, neither can I lose my American principles. One of the distinctive things about Americans is that we are instinctively against bullies and for the underdog. Look at this New York Mets business. No baseball team in the world has had such enthusiastic supporters while losing all the time. I don't have any objective feelings about South Africa, or Hitler, or Castro.

I think there is a place in literature and in life for people with strong feelings. I miss Heywood Broun terribly, and Mencken, and even Will Rogers, who had bits of vitriol. We are all trying too hard to be intellectually objective. You can't be intellectually objective about

Adolf Hitler, or about an extermination camp. *I can't be.* I told you that my first book was picked by several pacifist societies for one set of reasons, and cited by Goebbels for quite another. My biography of Nasser is the only book I know of that was on sale simultaneously in Tel Aviv and Cairo. (I think Nasser read only the first half of the book, which was sympathetic toward him when he was fighting Farouk and the corruption in Egyptian government.)

But beliefs and points of view have been taken in my books; they have not been objective, and I've been roundly condemned. But I wouldn't change a thing.

N: *In this incendiary world, where do you think we should stand, as a people, and what should our government do toward building a secure peace?*

ST. JOHN: I think the Peace Corps and the Friends Service Committee are two organizations that exemplify the best of intentions, of altruism combined with good works. This is internationalism, one worldism, international humanitarianism, of the kind so desperately needed.

The tragedy one constantly sees abroad is the way we export the worst of our civilization. We have so many things to be proud of, but we don't export those—no Ralph Waldo Emerson, but plenty of sexy, violent movies.

The French rather scathingly denounce our "colonization" of Europe. We *are* colonizing, culturally (or anti-culturally most of the time) and economically. We'll send Franklin Roosevelt to speak before the International Labor Organization to denounce South Africa in the most scathing terms, yet American investments have doubled in South Africa, and our State Department policy is based entirely on the fact that we have ever-growing investments in South Africa. We're talking out of both sides of our mouth, and we're not fooling people. The day World War II ended the United States had the greatest goodwill any nation in the world had known. Year by year we've lost that goodwill. We've lost the goodwill of Africa, of a great deal of Europe, of much of the Far East and Middle East—not through individual action, but through the policies of our State Department.

The State Department is one branch of our government that simply does not represent the thinking of the Americans I know—the Americans I come in contact with on my annual three-month lecture tour. It's the State Department that gives us our bad reputation abroad. We have consistently been on the wrong side, backing little villains the world over ever since the end of World War II. The people we play footsy with, to whom we give aid, are the Francos and Nassers, Chiang Kai-shek and Syngman Rhee, Salazar and the Diem family—all bad people.

But these are our friends, the State Department favorites. I am constantly trying to explain to foreigners, particularly to sophisticated Europeans, how such things happen. They say, "You do have a democracy, don't you?" and I say, "Yes." "Then, if you have a democracy, the State Department must represent the people." Then I have to shy away. Because we only have a democracy at those periods when we care enough to really get on our hind legs and tell them off in Washington. Most of the time we have only a representative form of government, which is something quite different; we allow the rascals to do what they will while we're busy raising children and buying a new automobile and going to P.T.A. meetings. We're too busy to be concerned, so we hire experts who go to Washington to run things for us. I think we are the victim of experts, and it's hell to try to explain to Europeans or Africans or Asians how Washington does and does not represent us.

I do not think that we are as bad as the image we create. I believe in America. I believe in the tradition of Thoreau and Emerson and Jefferson, and I believe that fundamentally our civilization is good. I simply do not believe in the image we are creating around the world.

Pierre Salinger

Since its release, Pierre Salinger's *With Kennedy* has won a favorable verdict from the majority of press outlets and a strong acceptance by the public.

It has seldom been criticized as "yet another" book dealing with the late John F. Kennedy, despite the flood of volumes that has followed the tragedy at Dallas. Those who have taken Salinger to task have focused upon his firm stand on the press vs. President battles. Salinger has spoken in behalf of the President, basing his views quite solidly upon experiences incurred during office.

Salinger is quick of wit, intelligent, and charming. The meeting was also something of a shock; I saw him on television in California in 1964 when he ran for Congress against song-and-dance-man George Murphy, and my impression was anything but favorable. He seemed like a very plump, sardonic member of the Mafia, while Murphy projected a boy-next-door wholesomeness.

Perhaps a considerable loss of weight, a chance to relax with a cheeseburger and beer, and a whole new set of circumstances added to the contrast.

I asked him what motivated his writing of the book.

"I waited for a whole year after Dallas to make up my mind about doing it. There were so many other important Kennedy books in the works. Finally, I decided that I had something to say regarding the working relationship between the President and the press—something no one else could say because they hadn't been so involved.

"There were other areas in which my experiences were totally different from others close to JFK. My dealings with the Russians, for example, and incidents during the campaign, and some of the inside on the handling of the Cuba missile crisis. I simply felt that I could offer some fresh disclosures, and hoped they would be important."

How does he feel about the many other Kennedy books?

"In the long run, all are helpful, even though they've been written by people who are admittedly prejudiced. It may take twenty years for a writer or historian to produce an unbiased look at the Kennedy Administration, but all of the books written until now contain something of value. Different men close to Kennedy saw different things, were impressed by different things. There's bound to be a varying emphasis in their views, perhaps in their interpretations.

"From the historical standpoint I think that Sorensen's book is the best. It's closer to the heart of the matter, the real truth, because of his inner knowledge and interest."

How does he compare the late President with brother Bobby?

"They are two different personalities, two different men. JFK possessed a pleasant exterior and a public personality; he was totally charming, but he was a tough man. A very tough man.

"Bobby, on the other hand, gives an impression of toughness, but he has great spirit—a truly sensitive concern and regard for people. He's thoughtful and understanding.

"Unfortunately for Bobby, his jobs have required toughness, particularly when he was Attorney General. They were unpopular jobs, you might say, and gave the impression of a ruthless man, yet he is the opposite.

"Frankly, I don't know another man who has grown so much in ten years. A decade ago Bobby saw the world in black and white; now he sees it as it is, in all its shades of gray."

How does he feel toward the popularity of "glamour" candidates for office like George Murphy and Ronald Reagan?

"You've got to remember that they called me a glamour candidate when I ran against Murphy in California." He grinned. "I think the glamour thing will run its course, probably in 1966. They can only succeed as long as they are demonstrably successful. As far as the public is concerned, I think they should heed this warning: If you want to elect a governor or senator who has not had five minutes of administrative experience, you'll bear the consequences."

"...we must realistically and frankly accept the book as a commodity, a product, an article of commerce... and not confuse that fact with the... ephemeral business of words, reviews, communication, education. All those things are fine and true and beautiful and correct, but books are products, like a piece of soap or a loaf of bread."

Leon Shimkin

Leon Shimkin

SHIMKIN: I was born in Brooklyn, the youngest of a family of six—three boys, three girls. Early in life I developed an interest in becoming a professional businessman, a student of the science of commerce, to develop a knowledge of the principles upon which our business life develops. Having an older brother a lawyer and another a physician, I planned to become a professional man, to have a license to practice business. In that spirit I planned a course in the School of Commerce at New York University, which at that time combined academic and vocational undergraduate training. We had philosophy and history as well as accounting and finance and the principles of sales and marketing, plus, of course, those important psychological aspects of human relationships—why people react one way or another, and how to project oneself to get results.

During the first summer vacation I decided to seek temporary employment to get business experience to complement what I had been studying in college. I asked myself, "Why should anyone hire me for the summer in the first place? How can I design a job to suit my specifications—to get around the entire organization in one summer?" I decided that the way to approach the problem was to establish the basis for value, to make the prospect of employing me worthwhile for the firm I approached. I was referred to Arthur Pell, then the business manager of a book-publishing company, Boni and Liveright, located in a very pleasant brownstone house on West Forty-eighth Street. At the time it was a thriving publishing firm, responsible for some of the best-selling authors of the time—Hendrik Willem Van Loon and Eugene O'Neill, among others.

I decided to frame my approach by using, as my opening, the fact that I offered my services as a summertime pinch hitter (emphasis on the last two words). Mr. Pell reacted according to the laws of human behavior; he asked the logical question, "What do you mean by pinch hitter?" I had rehearsed this the previous night in front of the mirror, so I knew what he was going to ask and what I was going to say. "By summertime pinch hitter I mean that when your bookkeeper is on vacation I can do bookkeeping, when your credit-collection man is on vacation I can take over because I'm trained in credit and collections, when your secretary is on vacation I can type and take shorthand," then I paused for appropriate emphasis, "and when your switchboard operator is on vacation I can handle the board."

As I think back I think it was "handle the board" that put the idea across and nailed the job down. He came back with the answer I couldn't have rehearsed: "That sounds like a good idea. Would $25.00 a week be all right?" I said, "Yes, thank you," and he asked me to start work as soon as possible.

I got the satisfaction of being able to put into practice the principles I had been studying. What is the value involved? Why should the other person do something I want them to do? The obvious answer: To make it worth their while to do it.

This brought me into the book-publishing field, the magic world that has enthralled me for the last forty-two years. That summer I did go through three of the steps, including bookkeeping and the handling of credit and collections.

I recall one day, while I was handling the credit collections, one of our sales representatives came in with a batch of orders. I took his orders and went through the ledgers to find out if the accounts were up-to-date and discovered that most of them hadn't paid their bills for many, many months. I told the salesman that these accounts were overdue, and he said, "What can I do about that?" I said, "The customary practice is to write a letter asking them to pay before a new order is shipped. You write the letter; I'll be glad to take it down." So he paced back and forth and dictated to me. I got to the typewriter and discovered that this man did not know the proper form of business correspondence for pressing past-due payments, so I rephrased it as I though it should be and handed the letter to him. He signed it, "Bennett Cerf."

They were the first orders Bennett Cerf took in his life, the first orders I checked for credit, and neither of us knew the other was a neophyte. Every time we see each other now, we laugh at the way he put on airs as an experienced sales representative and the way I was so official about credit collecting, neither of us knowing a thing. But we found our way.

In the early part of August during that summer of 1924, Mr. Pell called me into his office and told me that a publishing company, Simon and Schuster, had just been founded, and that they were looking for someone to handle their business affairs. He had the feeling that I would be just the man for them, and wondered if I would like to go see them. I was a boy who couldn't say no, so it was a "Yes, thank you."

I then called upon Mr. Simon and Mr. Schuster. Dick Simon seemed to be about ten feet tall, and Max Schuster was an extremely philosophical-looking gentleman with dark-rimmed glasses. I seemed very small. They told me that I had been highly recommended to them, and they were seeking someone to handle their business affairs since neither of them had been trained in business. Dick Simon had come up from Columbia with a great personal interest in music; he'd tried to make a vocation of it by selling pianos. He couldn't quite make the grade, but he did meet a prospective customer one day, Max Schuster, who could not afford to buy a piano but who could afford to have several wonderful conversations with him about the various authors they loved and the ideas they shared. Schuster, at the time just out of the Columbia University School of Journalism, was involved in public relations and doing some writing; he also did a column for the *Boston Evening Transcript*. He had been a copyboy for the *New York Evening World* during Joseph Pulitzer's days. His interest in journalism led him to the world of books, as did Dick Simon's interests in music and literature. Dick had spent some time at Boni and Liveright in the sales department; in fact, he had taken Bennett Cerf on his first selling trip. At any rate, the men had established this company, and they were seeking someone to help on the business end. They asked me if I could come to work Monday morning, and I, as always, said, "Yes, thank you."

On the way home to Brooklyn I realized that I was scheduled to go back to college in September, the very next month. I obviously couldn't go to college during the daytime, and also work through the day, so it was solved as a business problem: by doing both. I decided to finish my college education at night.

Fortunately, they had the complete business course at night. Most of the students in the School of Commerce couldn't afford to go to day school. The day school did offer more opportunities for combining liberal arts with business subjects, but by that time I was ready to concentrate on just the business courses. I valued that night school very much because there was a definite correlation between the practices of the day and the discussions of the evening. It was doubly valuable because the professors at night were practitioners; accountants who came fresh from their accounting offices, bankers who came from their banks, advertising men and sales managers and marketing experts, all practicing their professions during the day. They taught from a fund of real knowledge, not by staying a chapter ahead of the student textbook. For me it was ideal — I practiced as I learned.

I also learned why Mr. Pell felt that Simon and Schuster needed someone with my experience and background. One day Mr. Schuster opened an envelope with a check in it, and said, "What do you do with a check?" I said, "Let me have it, please," and he never saw another check for the forty-two years following. And Dick Simon came back from a visit to a bookseller with some orders, and I said, "Let me take care of them," and he never saw another order processed for the next forty-two years. He saw plenty of orders, naturally, but what happened after they came into the shop was something that went on behind the business curtain.

It was an exciting experience, being in the world of business. There were just five of us at Simon and Schuster to begin with. One girl acted as secretary and assistant to Max Schuster, another as secretary and assistant to Dick Simon, and there was me. It was so casual that one night the head of Leggitt's Grand Central Bookshop called me at quarter to five. He had an urgent need for twenty-five copies of a crossword puzzle book, the number-one seller at the moment. He had evening trade he'd miss if he couldn't get the books right away. So I sat at the typewriter, made out a bill, went to the stockroom, took down the books, and delivered them by five-thirty. I think back to those days rather wistfully when I hear that our IBM machines at the Buffalo warehouse, and all the other data-processing systems and procedures, take from today until doomsday to get a single order filled. It might be nice to go back to the time when you could go to the stockroom, get the books, and deliver them.

In any event, I obtained a license to practice business in the form of a Bachelor of Science degree in Commerce — appropriately named, since I've always approached business as a science.

The principles of business I learned as a student have stayed with me in this exciting world of book publishing. I believe they have been responsible for some rather interesting developments in the book-publishing field.

In the early days the ideas of Max Schuster, who had a passion for the humanization of knowledge, led to such books as *The Story of Philosophy* by Will Durant, a book that made the ideas and achievements of the philosophers live and breathe for the average reader. That, in turn, led to the monumental Durant series, *The Story of Civilization*. Schuster had a sort of encyclopedic mind, a built-in Dewey-decimal system that touched all types of learning, all fields of knowledge. By using, for the most part, the biographical approach, he brought to people an understanding of the achievements of great men. He launched a series of *Treasuries — Treasury of Science, Treasury of Grand*

Opera, even a *Treasury of Art Masterpieces*, which brought color reproductions of the world's finest paintings into the home. *Treasury of the World's Great Prints*, *Treasury of the Theatre*, *Treasury of the World's Great Speeches* — all emanated from his approach to publishing.

Dick Simon hunted for and published the kind of books he would like to buy and read. His special interests included golf, bridge, music, and photography, and the firm of Simon and Schuster became specialists in those fields. In addition, of course, we published fiction, but it was a rather erratic type of publishing. It brought about success, but the problems built into the success made it questionable. By good fortune we had quite a number of best sellers in both the fiction and nonfiction fields, like *Cradle of the Deep*, *Trader Horn*, and later *The Man in the Gray Flannel Suit* and the works of Hendrik Willem Van Loon; books on music by the best in the field — Deems Taylor, in the early days, did *Of Men and Music*, and currently Leonard Bernstein is doing books on music for us.

Rather early I began to feel that best sellers, from the point of view of the business organization, posed serious problems. Many of them represented what I called fads, and when you think back to the way the word "fad" was formed out of three words, "for a day," the problems seem obvious. While the fad lasted we expanded our staff and our facilities; at the end of the fad we had to reorganize our business. We couldn't afford to keep the organization we had built. We didn't know when the next best seller was coming or if it was coming. These peaks and valleys represented, to me, an unsound way of building a business. I approached Mr. Simon and Mr. Schuster with the idea that we endeavor to find some way to build a basic library of books which would give us a steady supply of bread. Then, when a best seller came along, we would have butter, perhaps jam, and maybe, with a really big best seller, a cherry on top. We could live without the cherry, we could live without the jam and, if necessary, without the butter, but at least we would always have bread. Everyone agreed that this was a good idea, but what to do? I narrowed it down to the possibility of acquiring Modern Library, which at the time represented the soundest approach to the publishing of low-priced books with perennial sales activity. I made a proposal to Bennett Cerf and his partner, Don Klopfer. They were tremendously impressed with my appraisal of the value of their property; it gave them quite a thrill to realize it was worth as much as I thought, but the answer was, "No, we're too young to sell. We wouldn't know what to do with ourselves if we sold the Modern Library." So that idea didn't work.

Some years later, while we were still trying to create a solid foundation for the business and were anxious to avoid the volatility of peaks and valleys, another idea came into the air. Alan Lane had started a paperback library in England called Penguin Books. Dick Simon, returning from London one time, described this new development in book publishing. Max Schuster, independently, had dreamed of an idea he was to call the Twentieth Century Library — low-priced books to be sold at twenty cents each to match "twentieth century." But these were amorphous ideas; we didn't know how to go about following through.

One day Dick Simon had lunch with Robert De Graff, who had been developing the field of the reprint book. He started the Star Library for Doubleday, which distributed reprints of books that had originally been published at $3.00 to $5.00 for $1.00 in hard-cover form. They were quite successful. Later, with a group of publishers, he formed Blue Ribbon Books — again full-size, hard-cover reprints at lower prices. He decided, at the age of forty, to go off and start a company of his own. Dick Simon suggested that he might be interested in joining forces with us in bringing down to earth the idea of the low-priced paperback; to do in the United States what Alan Lane had done in England. Since Robert De Graff was not associated with Simon and Schuster, and wanted to have a separate unit of his own, we formed another corporation to share ownership and development work. De Graff came up with the name "Pocket Books" and the twenty-five cent price. This appealed to us, because the concept of "Pocket Books" suggested portability — a book that would fit into the pocket and be kind to the pocketbook by virtue of the low price. My role at that time involved the economics of that operation. I did this as Bob De Graff gathered the titles and made arrangements for rights from various publishers, Dick Simon dealt with the selling function, and Max Schuster organized the publicity and promotion.

I recall a rainy Sunday afternoon in my home at Larchmont, when I decided to tackle the problem of establishing a profitable business basis for publishing paperback books at twenty-five cents retail. I took out a ream of yellow second sheets and began figuring. My first question was: How many copies of how many titles at what cost would provide a profit? It turned out to be millions of copies of thousands of books at a cost so high we couldn't afford to invest in it.

So I started the second half of the ream, but with the opposite approach. How few copies could we print at what cost to find out whether the American public would accept the paperback? You've got to remember that the concept of the paperback was really new. I recall in June, 1939, when a lawyer friend who frequently came to my home to say, "Any new books?" (I usually said, "Go to the shelves and find them.") I replied that evening, with great pride, "Take a look at these," and displayed our new brainchild, the very first advance Pocket Books. He said, "I'm looking for a book, not a pamphlet." This is how Pocket Books were first regarded. Interestingly enough, if I may digress, twenty-five years have changed the status of the paperback from the dirty book found in drugstores to highly respected books found throughout the school systems. Today a student who carries a full-size hard-cover book under his arm is regarded as a square. Only those who wear jeans and carry paperbacks are "in."

I guess that's the story of the paperback cycle. Most of the teachers of the country grew up with paperback books, just as children today grow up with radio and television. Paperbacks have caused a revolution, not only in book publishing, but in the reading habits of everyone.

At any rate, in 1939, we decided we would have to find out whether our Pocket Books would be accepted before we plunged into full production. So on June 19, 1939, we came out with ten thousand copies of ten books and distributed them in New York City. On the second half of that ream of yellow paper I'd found that if we could produce ten thousand each of ten titles it would cost us twenty-five cents each for paper, printing, and binding. If we sold them at twenty-five cents retail we would get fifteen cents from the bookseller; therefore, we would incur a loss of ten cents per copy. But that loss, in total dollars, was within our means if we were to answer the big question: Would the American public accept Pocket Books?

That business principle (we now call it "research and development" — the concept of finding out how little you must invest, rather than how much, to make a profit) was a basic of business thinking.

Just prior to the advent of Pocket Books a very wealthy man spent a million dollars transferring the Alan Lane concept over to the United States. He printed a million copies of books that would help people become better citizens, understand the society in which they lived, comprehend the political system, etc. He soon discovered that he had a million books but no place to distribute them, nor was everybody interested in buying books on better citizenship. So he lost his million dollars. This same idea, with research and development, might have succeeded.

I referred to the Pocket Book, originally, as a bookazine. (Incidentally, in a recent article in *Time*, I was called a "glottologist." I went to the dictionary to find out what that was, and learned that it is a philologist, one who invents terms.) Pocket Books as a bookazine was a hybrid of a book with every word as the author wrote it, sold at a price generally associated with a magazine.

The display of the first Pocket Books in New York showed an avid interest on the part of the American public in our concept. People took to them immediately, and it was obvious that we could sell millions of copies if we could find places to display them. We found that they sold best in areas where magazines were displayed. So we took that basic idea, the bookazine concept, and piggybacked on the magazine distribution system throughout the country. There were then some 750 points of distribution through independent distributors of magazines, many of whom also handled the local newspapers. This was a built-in, ready-made mass distribution device which we latched onto. Today we manufacture well over seventy million Pocket Books or pocket-sized books each year, and they are distributed with the dispatch of magazines. They're issued, reissued, and hold a consistent, firm place in the market.

We use the word "book" so frequently I am intrigued by the way Pocket Books work both with and against the concept of the word. After Gutenberg developed the movable type, we shifted from the scroll to the printed page. The ingenious Germans found it necessary to encase the separate pages to keep them intact. So they took a slab of wood and put it on top, and another on the bottom, and bound the pages between these slabs with leather thongs. The wood they found most effective for the job was from the beech tree. The word "beech" in German is "buche." So a "buche" became a package of pages enclosed with beechwood slabs. The cover gave the name to the whole thing.

With Pocket Books we took the "buche" away: we took off the wood. We also took off a very large margin of waste paper by narrowing the margins, saving considerable amounts on paper cost, which comprises the largest share of book production expenses. By reducing costs of paper and binding we were obviously able to bring the book down in unit costs; we were again able to bring costs down through the design of special presses. Thus quantity enabled us to make a business in millions and a profit in pennies.

Incidentally, the first ten Pocket Books we brought out were titles that enabled us to find out what kind of book the American public preferred. (Again, research and development.) We had the basic novel, like Pearl Buck's *The Good Earth*, and adventure like the classic *Lost Horizon*. We had the tragedies of Shakespeare, a book of humorous verse by Dorothy Parker, *The Bridge of San Luis Rey* by Thornton Wilder, *Bambi* by Felix Salten, the romantic *Wuthering Heights* and *The Chinese Orange Mystery*. Later we found that the mystery would develop all by itself; we've sold over 120 million copies of the Erle Stanley Gardner mysteries, for example, making the genre a virtual property in itself.

Shortly after Pocket Books had been established and I was still immersed in its business aspects while Bob De Graff busily collected more titles, and Max and Dick worked in their areas, we realized that Pocket Books had grown so fast it had to be separated from Simon and Schuster. We had our foundation, the core of business that would offset the fluctuation of the hard-cover best seller. In fact, what has happened to our first Pocket Book title, *Lost Horizon*, illustrates the way a new form of best seller came to be. We have reprinted *Lost Horizon* thirty-nine times in twenty-seven years. It has not been a book for a day; it has been a perennial best seller. Many titles in the Pocket Book library may have been only for a day had they not become paperbacks to become books for the years. Thus we have extended the life of many, many books, and the influence of the author, for generations.

After Pocket Books was firmly established, another idea came to me, again more or less by accident and coincidence. I had two small children by this time, a daughter Emily and a son Michael. I used to come home and tell them bedtime stories after work (this was before they could read). One evening I took that last telephone call from some irate bookseller or author and missed my train at Grand Central Station. I decided to browse at the Doubleday Bookshop; I didn't want to miss the next train because I wouldn't have time to tell the children their stories. As sort of an apology for keeping them waiting, I browsed about in the children's book section, picking up a book here and a book there. Rather hastily I turned them over to the clerk who wrapped them and said, "Twelve dollars and fifty cents, thank you." I did a double take. Twelve-fifty! I loved my children, but at that time twelve dollars and fifty cents was a lot of money. I sheepishly paid it and got out to the train and opened the package to find out why these few books cost all that money. There was a book for $1.75, another for $2.50, and so on. I looked to see how many pages were in the books, but the pages weren't numbered. I found out later that they didn't number them because there were so few. So I counted through to the middle, found thirty-two pages in one-half the book. Sixty-four pages and some pretty pictures for $2.50! I said to myself, "Why? We're publishing three- and four- and five-hundred-page books in paperback for twenty-five cents."

I felt that we could put together sixty-four pages for a fraction of our Pocket Book costs, a bit more, perhaps, because of the color and art, though even those costs would be offset by the fact that there were so few pages. I thought of how wonderful it would be to play the proud papa, to come home at night with four books for one dollar.

My first idea was to have a Pocket Book Junior series. As so often happens in life, if an idea is generated, and you don't quite know where to go with it, and it stays in the mind, something comes along to connect and act as a catalyst. A few days later, Albert Leventhal, then Simon and Schuster's Sales Manager, said, "Leon, a man came to call on me and asked whether we'd be interested in doing a series of children's books." I asked if he'd found out the price level the man had in mind. Albert said, "They could be a $1.00 or $1.50 series. He represents the Western Printing Company." I said, "We've never done any children's books, but I dreamt the other night that we should be doing low-priced children's books. Would you ask him whether he could produce a line to retail at twenty-five cents?" (At the time the concept of a quarter was so low in relation to average retail price it was like bringing a dollar down to a dime.)

Soon after Georges Duplaix came to call on me. He explained that he was the director of a unit of Western Printing Company called Artists and Writers. The unit created ideas for books and endeavored to find publishers for them. I told him I had an idea for a series of low-priced children's books to sell for a quarter, but realized that we would have to develop a plan to produce millions of them in contrast to the thousands that were now printed of the average children's book. He told me that they had developed a plan for a certain kind of binding, developed by a Swede, therefore known as Swedish binding. He felt that if we were prepared to plan on very large quantities, we would enable them to use this new binding method to produce books at low prices. Western had a great deal of experience in low-priced children's books of the varieties sold at Woolworth's etc., published by the Whitman Publishing Company. These ranged from coloring books to what might be called pamphlets. I told Mr. Duplaix that if he could produce books at twenty-five cents we would be prepared to test them. He said, "We've had this plan for years, and we've been hoping that someday a publisher would ask us to do this." I said, "I'm a publisher and I'm asking the question. Let's go."

This started the development of what later became known as the Little Golden Books. I took the first titles home and tried them out on my children; in fact, I remember sitting next to Emily's bed to read *The Pokey Little Puppy*. Twenty years later I walked into her apartment on Central Park West and found Emily sitting next to her daughter's bed reading *The Pokey Little Puppy*. But by that time we had sold some 250 million Little Golden Books; there would hardly be a child in the United States who hadn't been exposed to one or more titles.

But the really exciting aspect of the Golden Books is how books came into the lives of millions of children before they could read. The book became something between parent and child that brought them together. The child got undivided attention from the parent, with the warmth and comfort of the parent's voice and presence, all attending the most important person in the world, the child. A book brought this about. This is why I believe that the most important contribution to book publishing with which I have been indirectly associated has been to change the connotation of the word "book." In the earliest ages the word had always come with association to duty, with the schoolbook, homework, responsibility. With all the pressures books applied it is no wonder that so many of the early students read their last book in their last class at school.

Today a child, by the time he gets into school, has the world of books well known to him. He learns to read faster as the result of the availability of books. A book becomes a known and loved object; try to make a mistake reading a familiar book to a child, and he will immediately tell you what word you forgot. Golden Books have helped develop an interest in books in general, and have opened worlds about the child — worlds of nature, literature, music, and art. This is why I believe that the more of us who are interested in the business of publishing and of publishing as a business, think in terms of business principles — of mass marketing and mass distribution and low prices — the greater our contribution to the entire field of communication.

At any rate, the distribution system built for Pocket Books proved to be perfect for the distribution of the low-priced twenty-five-cent children's books. So Golden Books grew rapidly on the basis of our prior experience. Where do we go from there?

About fifteen years ago it seemed desirable to take another road off the main highway of book publishing, this time trying to find a way to get the pocket-sized book established in the schools. After thorough research we decided to enter the junior and senior high-school field, where there was a great need for collateral reading, particularly in English classes for book reviews and reports. We sent letters to the members of the National Council of Teachers of English, and with their help developed a list of titles most highly recommended for reading at the junior and senior high-school levels. But when we first went to the schools to offer the books, the reaction was, "Do you mean that those dirty books should go into the hands of schoolchildren?" It took quite a few years to get around the concept of paperbacks as something more than "dirty books sold in drugstores." We redesigned the covers. (In fact, paperback covers now compete for art awards.) Then, happily, I acquired the New York University Press, Inc., a private corporation the university couldn't afford to keep because of tax complications. I changed the name to Washington Square Press, and made that our school imprint to get away from the connotation of Pocket Books as "dirty books." And we brought the Pocket Book to school, a vast market.

Because of the low price, children began to buy the books to build their own home libraries as distinguished from the occasional, temporary relationship with the borrowed hard-cover. We believe that by virtue of the modern business approach to book publishing in the paperback field, we've inculcated the habit of building home libraries. This should spread to succeeding generations, make important contributions to the solid place of the book in the home, and distinguish the book publisher as a member of the family of communication. But not all of my activity was with Pocket Books and Little Golden Books.

What happened in the course of my career was that I became more and more involved with publishing per se in addition to the facts of life of book publishing. The sort of creativity employed in solving business problems (a study of cause and effect) and my increasing interest in the marketing of books led to a recognition of certain needs for certain kinds of books. My personal interest in human relationships, starting with my early interest in how to project oneself and how to get the proper response from the other person by using logic and mental discipline, also extended to other areas where I had some degree of personal interest and knowledge.

One evening I was asked by a friend to come to his home to meet a man coming out to Larchmont. I came and was surprised to find quite a number of people there. The evening turned out to be not a small party, but a presentation by a man who was trying to start a course in public speaking in our town at the local country club.

I was impressed with the effectiveness of his technique. I recall him saying, "I've been talking to the public for over twenty-five years, and can speak with the eloquence of William Jennings Bryan. Because of my experience, this should not impress you one bit. So instead of me talking, let me present a few of your neighbors who have taken my course in New York." My friend got up and stuttered and stammered a bit, then explained that when he first tried to speak he got so nervous he couldn't even say his own name. He found that he could now talk before the board of directors and the local Boy Scout organization, and he felt that he'd gotten a great deal out of the course. Another fellow got up and spoke with similar imperfections, but did get words out before a group. I thought it was particularly clever of the man running the thing, psychologically, because you said to yourself, "If that's what they can do I could certainly do a lot better." It built up sort of a challenge.

I became very interested in this man, and attended his lectures and meetings. He was a local man, certainly not at all well-known, but in the techniques of human relationships he seemed extraordinarily capable. His name was Dale Carnegie, and it occurred to me that he should write a book, a book that would certainly help the vast public that couldn't hear him speak or take his courses.

I had hurdles to overcome, selling what I called a biblio-therapeutic book within my own organization, and selling Mr. Carnegie on the idea of writing one. I approached Carnegie after a lecture and asked him if he would consider writing a book dealing with the subject of getting along with people. He asked me what firm I represented, and I said, "Simon and Schuster." He said, "I would never dream of writing a book for Simon and Schuster; I wrote two books, one on Lincoln, one a collection of short radio talks, and they rejected both of them."

I explained how important I felt such a book would be to the millions of people who could not be exposed to his lectures. He said, "I know all that, but I just don't want to take all the time and trouble." I said, "I don't want to impose on your time at all, Mr. Carnegie, but if I could have a stenotypist come to your next lecture, we could see what we come up with," and he said, "If you want to waste your time and money, it's all right with me." So I sent a stenotypist out to Long Island City, had a transcript made, and sent a copy to Mr. Carnegie. He called me the next day and said, "I read that stuff you sent me. You know, I found it very fascinating. Don't you think it's well-done?" and I said, "Not only is it well-done; it's magnificent. It needs other material before it can be put into book form, but the ideas are there. That's why I think it's so exciting to contemplate. The man in Oshkosh or Peoria will get the benefit of your lecture." He said, "Gee, you're right, but I can't get to it. I have too many things to do. But if you want to work on it, I'll put my notes and papers at your disposal, plus a secretary who has written some radio talks for me." So I found the answer of how to win friends and influence Dale Carnegie, and Dale Carnegie's *How to Win Friends and Influence People* has won and influenced millions of persons in the years that followed.

There was another innovation involved in this book. It was the first "How To," and became a mother lode concept for titles thereafter. The "How To" titles became involved in specifics, as well as therapeutics, and they've made a mark. But the second innovation was in the length of the title. I recall getting a phone call from the jacket designer saying, "Look, do you want me to put a picture of the author with the title? It's hard to get anything else on, with a title that long." We finally succeeded in getting both on the jacket, and we've been getting long "How To" titles on jackets ever since, including *How to Succeed in Business Without Really Trying*.

Another interest that stemmed from my business education was in the field of taxes. I took courses in taxes and was familiar with them, in general and specific terms, through my business experience. One evening, again at my home in Larchmont, we had some young couples in for drinks and conversation, and one man said, "You know, I just learned I could deduct the real estate taxes on the home I just bought on my income tax." The fellow next to him said, "Wait a minute. I pay rent on a house; why can't I deduct the portion of my rent which the owner uses to pay taxes?" So I, the tax expert, spent the next hour futilely trying to explain that the law does permit the deduction if you directly pay the taxes, but not if you pay them indirectly.

After everyone left I told my wife that it seemed to me there must be a lot of people who quite naturally don't know the rules and regulations, particularly the exemptions, regarding income tax. I said, "Someday I'm going to find a man who can work with me in developing a translation of the tax law into simple English to tell people what they can and can't deduct and how they should prepare their tax return."

Shortly thereafter I received a bulletin from the American Book Publishers Council, a memorandum on taxes for book publishers by J. K. Lasser. I asked my secretary to call Mr. Lasser, and I introduced myself to him over the telephone and outlined my idea. He thought it was a good idea and said he'd like to work on it. We got together, became fast friends — in fact, we bought our lake property together, and he lived at the lake until he died. We used to spend our summers going over the new edition of the annual *Your Income Tax*, which has sold over fifteen million copies. It was an intimate collaboration in that he was the specialist, I the reader, and if he made things clear to me, I could feel certain that millions of readers would also understand it.

Even my country place became part of a publishing world. This sort of experience has been expanded into other fields. For example, I'm working currently on a book that will help people plan their estates, to get a more efficient job done and save money in taxes and avoid unnecessary complications. Again I'm working with an expert, and I'm the reader's representative.

One of the interesting things that has happened consistently throughout my publishing career is that authors have so often honored me with requests to handle their financial affairs. They have left their money to their widows, their widows to me, and I have had a good list of widows as clients over the years. Hendrik Willem Van Loon, who did *The Story of the Bible*, *The Story of Mankind*, and many other major best sellers, was a genius at writing, but almost childish in caring for financial affairs. He'd make a large sum of money one year and be a pauper the next, until another book came out to make him rich again.

He'd give his money away; he just couldn't hang onto it. So one day I suggested that I put him on a budget and actually parcel out $200 a week to his wife so that she could take care of the household. If he made $50,000 one year, he would only get about $10,000 for household expenses. I would save the rest of it to fill in the valleys between the peaks. He liked that idea very much; he appreciated being taken care of. But once in a while he'd come into my office looking very unhappy, very angry, and I'd say, "What is it, Hendrik?" He'd say, "Well, a former neighbor of mine in Holland has come over here with his six children and he's very poor and I think a few thousand dollars would help the poor man out, but I don't have it to give to him, the way you keep me." Then he'd take his shoe off and carefully show me the big hole in his sock. "After all, with the little money you give me, how can I take care of my friends?" I'd say, "Tell me, Hendrik, where can I reach him? Why not send him in to see me?" I'd settle with the Dutch neighbor for $500. The man was very grateful, and was told that he could get more later if he needed it. More often than not that amount would get a man started on a job and he was able to take care of himself. Hendrik always wanted to give all his money away.

Another adventure that led me from the concept of business to ideas involving book publishing started on the day a mutual friend introduced me to Rabbi Joshua Liebman of Boston. We were to meet at the Plaza Hotel for lunch at the Oak Room, and as I approached the rabbi to be introduced something happened. A chemical reaction took place, and we both instinctively put out both hands to each other in a brotherly embrace. We sat down at the table and tried to find out what had caused this. No family association, no geographical proximity, no school ties, no mutual relatives of any sort. But we discovered that we were born on the same day of the same month of the same year, April 7, 1907. We realized that something had intuitively made us feel we were brothers. Thereafter we celebrated our birthdays together every year. I would go to Boston and be assistant rabbi for the day, going with him on pastoral calls; on the alternate year he would come to New York (Look, Ma, I'm a publisher!) and stay at my office all morning and go with me on whatever business I had to conduct in the afternoon.

I am simply grateful for the happiness I've found in working with authors who become lifelong friends after meeting, originally, as part of the author-publisher relationship. Contrary to popular fallacy — the belief that the usual publisher-author relationship is a knife at the throat — some of my best friends are authors.

One birthday Joshua told me that although many members of his congregation played golf, he had never been free enough to play; he didn't know anything about the game. It was a sunny, spring day, and he was with me in New York and had the right to do anything he wanted for the day. So I took him up to the country club in Westchester and out onto the green. I took out the driver, identified it, and the ball and the tee, and showed him how to swing a golf club. I was very careful, slow and deliberate in my backswing, equally slow coming down, just to demonstrate the technique. To my surprise, the ball went to the middle of the fairway. We walked toward it, talking about a mutual friend suffering a depression. I found myself saying, "Tell me, Josh, how would you define a happy man?" and he said, "Your golf swing." I said, "Now you're talking like a rabbi. How does my golf swing define happiness or a happy man?" He said, "You remember when I asked you how it was that your ball went to the middle of the fairway, and you modestly explained that you must have made two or three mistakes in the backswing, and offset them with two or three mistakes when you hit the ball?" I said, "That's very interesting, but how does that define happiness or a happy man?" He said, "A happy man is one who has adjusted to his maladjustments, accepting, realistically, the fact that there are imperfections but also compensations. A happy medium as distinguished from the extreme of agony on one end, ecstasy on the other." I tell you this anecdote because it led to a very interesting episode in my publishing life. Rabbi Liebman died after the success of *Peace of Mind*, which followed this early association. I don't want to indicate that I was primarily responsible for *Peace of Mind*. Actually, it came through a mutual friend as a suggestion. Dick Simon played a very important role in developing what was originally a book of sermons, and with the help of Henry Morton Robinson, the author of *The Cardinal*, blended the material into a reconciliation of religion and psychiatry. The rabbi died very early in life, at the age of forty-two.

I had several talks with Joshua Liebman before he passed away regarding a sequel to *Peace of Mind*, which would be called *Hope for Man*. It would work from the psychological point of view rather than the philosophical, tied in with the art of living. We didn't reach the point of rough manuscript, but after he died, as part of my effort to continue financing his widow, I inquired as to what had happened to the material he had prepared for *Hope for Man*. I found that it was part of a great number of cases of personal belongings stored in a warehouse outside of Boston. I then engaged Mrs. Selma Stone, his former secretary and assistant while he was at the temple, to arrange for an office in Boston, gather together all the files, and locate the sermons and addresses and notes dealing with this particular area—the area that had been at least roughly defined by Joshua through our informal talks. I found a great deal more material than I had anticipated—enough, in fact, to weed out the weakest stuff and still have a fairly good-sized book.

For two or three years, as a labor of love, I personally undertook to prepare this book. My objectives were to carry out the objectives of the book as the author had intended it, and to have every word in the book written by him, then to organize it in a manner that would be cohesive and lead, logically, from his basic philosophy of life to the art of living and the various areas of life where people so often need help. The author, in this case, was a friend, guide, and philosopher—the man who takes the individual reader by the hand and leads him along a path to inner serenity and emotional maturity.

I found that the logical thing to do was to start with his brilliant essays that analyzed, interpreted, and explained the nihilists, the existentialists, the Sartre-Kierkegaard group. He had superbly explained the philosophy of these negativistic philosophers, clarified them, and made them interesting to read about in terms of how they arrived at their points of view through analysis of their personal lives. I thought these would be wonderful for the many people who have a vague idea of this hard-to-pronounce existentialism, the whole negativistic approach.

Then I found an equally eloquent series of papers rebutting the negativistic philosophies, setting forth his own positive philosophy, his yea-say—his urge to reach out aggressively to make life a good one, to live with affirmation. I couldn't help but think of myself as a coach for a high-school debating team, setting up a two-part program where the presentation of the negativists was put forth clearly, then smashed to pieces. This led, logically, to various sections on the art of living. As the reader's representative, I had not only to present the material clearly, but to give the reader handles to hold on to, to lead from general to specific to application. I recalled the one word that explains the success of *The Reader's Digest*. When DeWitt Wallace was asked for his secret in developing the most successful magazine in the world he said, "Applicability." I endeavored to apply that word to the so-called biblio-therapeutic books I became involved in.

In the area of books where I've worked as a combination of publisher and editor and merchant, I've worked primarily with books to help people. People apparently have needed the help I believed these books would provide. Dale Carnegie's *How to Win Friends and Influence People* has sold over fifteen million copies, and is extremely popular in countries as diverse as the United States, India, and Australia. To a great extent it is a pertinent reinterpretation of certain biblical precepts. Instead of saying, for example, "Do unto others as you would have others do unto you," as in the Golden Rule, it says, "Look at it from the other fellow's point of view." It doesn't deal with tricks to seduce or influence people; Carnegie's principles won't work, in fact, if not applied with sincerity. Paying respect to a fellowman is not a matter of affectation; it won't work if it is.

Basic truths underlie all of Dale Carnegie, no matter how unsophisticated they often sound. For example, he says that the way to approach a problem in which there is a broad difference of opinion is to find some area of agreement. If you start with an attitude of, "What can I agree to?" rather than, "You're all wrong about the subject," you find that the other person is inclined to want to agree on another aspect, and it's possible to build a bridge between two diverse viewpoints and arrive at an understanding. This is an important approach to life, as well as business — it applies to husband and wife, parent and child. And when I work on a book, either as editor or collaborator, I effectively try to use the medium of the book to lay a pipeline between the mind of one man and the minds of many. This, to me, is the role of the publisher — to multiply the effectiveness of the communication device known as the book.

Years ago I started a course at New York University called "The Practice of Book Publishing." It was the first university course in book publishing given in this country. It has since become the core of the Graphic Arts center at New York University, which I helped found. At the time I recall saying to classes:

"The objective of a book is to communicate. The size of the sheet of paper or the texture of the cloth binding have no logical connection with a book. Its total value lies in how well it communicates.

"If you could find a way to inject an idea with a needle in the arm, I would tell you to consider yourself a publisher because you see it as a way to get across to the minds of others. Strip your mind of all the form and format and get to the heart of the nature of your function as a publisher. The extension from mind to mind calls for manufacturing equipment, machinery, promotion, and so forth. You are publisher, editor, and merchant. You are, above all, a communicator.

"When you work on a book designed to deal with a specific problem that people face, presenting the best of one mind to their minds, ask yourself, 'Why should I read this book? What will it do for me as an individual?' Look at the other person's point of view to create a product to be sold to a mass market."

In the case of *Hope for Man*, after setting up a debate over the negativistic philosophies with Joshua Liebman's presentation and rebuttal, I had to ask myself how I brought it down to earth to relate to others. On a television program where I appeared recently, "The Mike

Douglas Show," I was on with Arthur Godfrey and Eartha Kitt as sort of a panel, discussing *Hope for Man*. I was trying to get down from the lofty level of Kierkegaard, Kafka, and Sartre, lest I lose my audience, and I suddenly turned to panelist, Miss Kitt, and said, "I believe you'll agree, when you read this book, that Dr. Liebman has brought the subject down to *Eartha*." The public got it. The public will get the book, because Joshua communicates with the individual reader.

For example, he talks about the parent and the child. He addresses the adult reader in the terms of his own childhood to better understand his children. He discusses the turbulence of the adolescent years, and the early years of maturity, in terms of the parent—making it easy to understand what is going on with the generation coming up. He involves the reader in the psychology of living with himself, accepting his limitations, and understanding the limitations of others to the point where he will like other people more. The more he likes other people, the more people will like him, and this is where he reaches the virtuous cycle that leads to greater self-fulfillment, to an adjustment with living values as distinguished with negative ones such as depression, unhappiness, anger, a feeling of failure, and frustration.

This is a selling technique, in one sense, but the objective is a worthy one. Particularly worthy from the point of view of the editor, publisher, and merchant, who anticipates that readers will say, "I learned something from this book. It has helped me."—worthy if that magic formula of success in book publishing, word of mouth, leads one satisfied customer to others. The higher the degree of articulation the higher the sales, but this must be done with a book eligible to qualify for that high level of reader satisfaction.

None of the biblio-therapeutic books I've already published have sold less than a million copies. Dale Carnegie's tops fifteen million, and J. K. Lasser's is near thirteen million. Those very large sales compete with the distribution of the Bible and far exceed *Gone with the Wind*. These are the dimensions I'm referring to when I talk in terms of the mass publisher who fits the needs of a mass audience.

I'm impressed with the fact that most people think of publishing as some combination of editing, writing, printing, and distributing. Actually, the dictionary defines publishing as "to make public and to disseminate, to spread, to circulate." Frequently people say, "Oh, but that's a mass-distributed book," inferring that "mass" can't have class. In terms of publishing, the fact that a book has been accepted by millions gives it a higher quality if only because publishing, in essence, is dissemination. The greater the dissemination, the greater the quality of publishing. I like to think of this not just because I prefer to be a higher-quality publisher, and use this phrase as a device, but it has been my good fortune to be involved, for the past forty-two years, in a wide variety of publishing activities: trade publishing of original hard-cover books; reprint publishing of the paperback; original publishing in various formats; materials developed for the schools; low-priced books for children.

I consider the role of the publisher important to the community, the family. A publisher has the duty to help people buy, select, furnish, and decorate their homes. In the homes there are people — father, mother, children. There are books to help them with knowledge, relationships, career development, entertainment, child rearing. A family unit is a unit within society. There are books to help them in their relationships with others. There are books for the schools and books for the teachers in that school. There is an auditorium; there are books on music, current events, art, philosophy. There is also a motion picture theater, and books for entertainment — westerns, mysteries, novels, adventure stories.

There are also books for training, not only of the academic variety, but for supplemental or home-study training in science, engineering, technology, electronics, business management. And there are religious books, and books that deal with archaeology and the future.

A publisher thus has a multifaceted approach. I point this out because as a result of my involvements in various types of publishing, tied in with the business developments thereof, I find myself having an interest in a series of enterprises. And after forty-two years I have been able to put my interests together into one cohesive form under the title "Simon and Schuster."

One of my pleasures in life is expressing myself through business design. My background in business has enabled me to develop ideas for mergers, acquisitions, consolidations, and the design of business organizations. I thought I would get a personal thrill, a great deal of satisfaction, a "charge," so to speak, by putting under one roof my various interests in hard-cover adult publishing, low-priced paperbacks, children's books, and so on, to be, frankly, a sort of General Motors of book publishing in which each unit would be a division of one company, serving an individual product for an individual market need. It would furnish books of the highest degree of excellence, like GM's Cadillac Division, produce serviceable books with the emphasis on utility and economy, like GM's Chevrolet Division, and hit all of the varying markets in between. Thus I have books that range from twenty-five dollars to twenty-five cents, designed for the oldest to the youngest — books to help people in daily life, books to entertain and educate people, all in one happy complex.

The art of designing a complex of this nature starts with a philosophical approach. We must bear in mind that the objective of the
design is to form a combination of units which will not only be effective
as a business enterprise, but will effectively meet the needs of the kind
of enterprise it is. The book-publishing firm has a unique relationship
between author and editor. Often it is a highly personal one, frequently
very intimate, and always one that must be separated from the mass
concept of standardization and routinization considered essential to run
a modern business.

How to blend these two came to me in the form of a visual image. In
May, 1924, I went to visit a brownstone house at 61 West Forty-eighth
Street. The people in that building, editors and designers and production people, all worked very happily at their pleasant pastime of book
publishing. This vision came back to me, and I thought that instead of
erecting a skyscraper, with its monolithic, vertical concept and its built-
in dangers, I would avoid the tower. The man at the top with a view
from the fortieth floor could be dangerous; if something happened to his
brain or his bowel it would affect the whole structure more seriously
than if something went wrong with the elevators at the thirty-second
floor. Even an elevator breakdown would seriously affect all that went
on in the skyscraper.

So I took this concept and transposed it into a horizontal layout, a
series of brownstone houses broken up into compartments, watertight
compartments, at that, such as a steamship has for protection. Each
compartment contains a group of people dedicated to a particular kind
of publishing, supplying a particular series of services. There is the
trade division, Simon and Schuster hard-cover. There's the Messner
division, with inspirational biographies for junior and senior high-
school students, and a series of intermediate books called Essandess
special editions. There's the paperback library, the Washington Square
Press with books for schools, and Trident Press promotional books on
their way to paperback. Another unit, Associated Educational Services,
supplies learning materials for schools. There's a Special Products
Division for distributing what I call the "nonbought book," which is
distributed in millions of copies as premiums. Each of these units has
specialists who devote themselves wholly to their particular area.

The business part of the publishing combination — the furnishing of
supplies, removal of garbage, window washing, sweeping, advertising,
promotion, order filling, credit and collections, comptrolling, payroll, all
records and reports — is removed from this series of brownstone houses.
All this is in a high-rise with machinery and mechanics and method-
ology, everything you need these days to run an efficient enterprise.

We also have a law factory to deal with the government bureaus, the FTC, FCA, SEC, XYZ. Fantastic, the machinery that's needed. But all this is removed from the brownstones, permitting those minds to be devoted to dreaming, sleeping, and living with the essence of publishing.

What I've done, in effect, is to take the vertical concept of the giant corporation and straighten the complexes out into a series of simplexes. Together they represent (again remembering the quantity of dissemination being the quality of publishing) the world's largest book-publishing company. Imagine this in terms of units of reading matter.

The fact that we publish Shakespeare's *Hamlet* for fifty cents doesn't change the play. That it's on a small piece of paper rather than a large one, has a paper cover instead of beechwood, has nothing to do with it. Every word Shakespeare wrote is the same as in any other edition, with only minor changes incurred from one annotator to the next. In our Folger Shakespeare Library, words are explained to the reader beside the text, in the most convenient place, another functional quality at low cost.

Another reason for founding this series of simplexes is to assure the writer the personal attention he deserves. When the publisher takes a book, he assumes responsibility for the brainchild of the writer. He has an unwritten contract that calls for him to give that child tender, loving care. Unless he does that he is not discharging his proper role as a publisher, and he is not going to be a very effective and successful publisher.

I turn down books which I can truthfully say are publishable, and the reason is this: If I send a manuscript down the line to a series of editors, and find no editor sufficiently interested in spending a part of his life working on that book, I believe it would be unwise to impose that book upon them; it would become an orphan, and I would be doing harm to the author and performing an unsound business practice. Therefore I suggest that the author find another publisher for the book.

You can never give a book enough time to satisfy an author in any case. But to neglect a book, to have nobody interested in it, is like taking in a foster child and not caring for the child.

The other reason for establishing all this is the fact that I am by no means finished with my career. This company is a public company, with stock listed on the over-the-counter market. I have just acquired another company on the basis of exchanging of stock. It's the Regents Publishing Company. A group of young men have built a moderate-size business with a variety of educational approaches. *English as a Second Language* is their principal series, highly accepted and accredited in school systems. I'm backing these young men with the additional capital they need, giving them the benefit of our larger organization. They have a small one now, and I'm hoping to give the sapling enough air and sunshine to enable it to grow into a giant oak in the area of educational publishing, which I'm emphasizing, to establish a balance between the stability of educational publishing and the volatility and excitement of general publishing.

Recently I was asked how long I've been in book publishing, and I said, "I have just passed my ninety-second year." The person looked startled and said, "How do you figure that out? You don't look that old." I said, "The figures you read in a paper about a criminal being convicted of a crime and sentenced on a series of counts—ten on this one, fifteen on that, twenty-five on another, and so on, totaling 150 years—apply to me. My concurrent sentence in publishing adds up to ninety-two years. Forty-two at Simon and Schuster, twenty-seven with Pocket Books, twenty-four or five with Golden Books." I'm leaving out the shorter stretches to keep the figure from getting too high. During these ninety-two years in the book-publishing business I have developed a versatility of approach to the various types of publishing, and the business organization around me is doing the same. I have a son Michael, approaching thirty, who has been with me for five years and is being groomed to carry on, and I hope his son, Tommy, will come on after him. Looks like a dynasty is in the making, but that's fine with me. Somebody has to start one.

Most importantly, the real joy and satisfaction of all this is the fact that it came out of my mind. I sensed the need, I found that I could make a contribution to this field by virtue of experience and knowledge, and I have been able to lay a pipeline to others which, in turn, effectively carried to millions and millions of *others:* To take a conceptual idea and develop a business organization around it that affects tens of thousands of lives. We have now, in our connected businesses, about a thousand employees. I think of the breakfast tables in a thousand homes, the number of glasses of milk, the number of eggs and bowls of Wheaties and pots of coffee that are supplied every morning. This is part of the responsibility of a publisher running a business enterprise. The publisher is providing a means of living to families, and there's satisfaction in doing this.

The satisfaction that comes to an artist who finishes a painting, or a writer who finishes a novel, comes to a publisher in terms of the method by which he creates his design. There's a narrow difference between the architect of a building and the architect of a business design. They're both based on structural elements. In the first case they're physical elements, but in the second the more difficult element: human beings as structural units. If you have the right skills and, more importantly, the right personalities to blend together, building a business enterprise is an art in itself. You can't have a house stand no matter how beautiful the individual units are if they aren't in the right place and supported with the proper strengths.

Now, to refer to the criticism of my building a "corporate giant" in the book-publishing field. I view myself as a businessman in publishing, and a publisher in business. I think that is a realistic viewpoint of the two needs. The popular fallacy, the nostalgic recollections, regarding the good old days in publishing, aren't too valid: they weren't so good. You find that most publishers — the Harpers, the Appletons, the Scribners, the Boston group that founded Little, Brown, and Houghton, Mifflin, the Philadelphians, like the Lippincotts — were originally booksellers; they were merchants. Or they were printers who became publishers. It was the business mind that started the book-publishing industry in America, and the business mind at that time, living within the mores of the business community at that time, was a far cry from the business mind adhering to today's standards of ethics. I'm not being derogatory to the people of that period, those intrepid pioneers; I'm explaining that the mores of the time were quite different. It was the author who paid the publisher to have a book printed, not the other way around. The author frequently got a raw deal from the publisher. If the publisher could pirate a book instead of paying royalty to a publisher in England or elsewhere, he would cheerfully pirate it because the laws were not strict, and his sense of morality did not restrict him from taking advantage of other people's properties. If he could find a way to pay the author a stipend rather than a royalty on a successful book, he'd do it.

This was right at the time — right in the sense meaning "customary" or "normal." Out of that little bookshop and that little printshop came the magnificent houses that are now publishing books to help children in school and entertain them at home, books to instruct and entertain adults. I'm not saying there is anything wrong with the founding methods. My point is that we did not get very many successful publishing companies from editors or from book designers or from book salesmen. Though I must say that book salesmen are second in the order of sources of background that led to successful publishing.

I believe that we must realistically and frankly accept the book as a commodity, a product, an article of commerce. The publisher must act as a purveyor of commerce and not confuse that fact with the particular property, with the ephemeral business of words, reviews, communication, education. All those things are fine and true and beautiful and correct, but his books are products, like a piece of soap or a loaf of bread. As a matter of fact we happen to offer food for the mind just as the grocer offers food for the body.

I see no difficulty in reconciling a book as a product, even though it contains that magic blend of ideas and mind-conditioning that makes the pen mightier than the sword. The reason I don't find the reconciliation difficult is because I think that if you do accept it as a fact of life, you can more effectively extend the limits of literature to the minds of people; you can more effectively get their minds conditioned to the extent where they properly interact with other sound minds. You can more effectively help teach children in school and train people in their vocational careers.

Thus the effectiveness of the publishing process as a business, as an act of commerce, as a form of the extension of one mind to many, as an interplay of marketing and distribution and profit, is all one entity. The more effectively we distribute our books, the higher the quality of publishing. Most people think of the publisher as a pipe-smoking gentleman sitting in a plush chair, wearing a Chesterfield vest, poring over great works of literature. Let's face it: the modern publisher is a man who has a job and is working with people who have ideas and talents to contribute. The publisher's role is similar to that of the leader of an orchestra. He has instrumentalists—they're called editors and artists and designers, production and sales and marketing personnel, promotion and public relations and publicity people, office workers—all sorts of instrumentalists. His function is to select the best possible instrumentalist to fill each chair. He must also pay close attention to the interpersonal relationships between the instrumentalists; after all, they are highly imaginative, talented people with unique personalities and egos. There are adjustments to be made. Just as you have prima donnas in musical organizations, you have them in publishing staffs.

The obligation of the publisher as the orchestra leader is to blend the positive talents of all these people to create harmony; then you have a successful business organization. What comes out of a successful orchestra? Good music. What comes from a successful publishing organization? Good books.

Edith Sitwell

Taken Care Of is an autobiography few readers can forget. It is remarkable for its candor, its literary excellence, and for the fact that Dame Edith was so highly selective in recall that she never quite got around to telling us more than a fraction of the richly-embroidered lives she and her brothers led.

I saw her in London a few months before her death. Though wasted by illness, the imperious, invincible Dame Edith was still a force to reckon with.

"I know you'll misquote me," she said upon introduction. "People always do because I shock them by saying precisely what I think. Nowadays nobody has courage to say what he thinks; he only says what someone else wants to hear. That's why civilization is going down the drain.

"I've done my autobiography, you know, and it's causing quite a fuss because I'm not putting tea cozies over the negatives. I've known many loathsome people during my life, some who have actually gone out of their way to wound me, and I see no reason to remember them fondly. But I'm not judging them — only God can do that. I'm simply recalling them as they were in my eyes.

"On the other hand, the people who have been dear to me are treated as gloriously as they deserve to be. But that isn't noticed; it's only the negative bits that stand out."

How did Dame Edith and her brothers achieve such eminence?

"To begin with, we're extraordinary people. I don't mean that we're lovely in a physical sense — I've always looked a fright — but we're extremely intelligent, we have breeding and taste and manners and a great flair for appreciating beauty and truth.

"In addition, our childhoods were wretched, and this rather threw us in on ourselves, and we grew up longing to travel and meet interesting people and find challenge and stimulation. We cannot stand boors, and because the larger share of mankind is boorish we have purposely surrounded ourselves with persons we could admire for accomplishment and love for the quality of 'presence.'

" 'Presence' means so much, doesn't it? A person does have an aura. I honestly believe you can tell, almost at a first meeting, the extent of honor and talent and intelligence a person has. I learned long ago that if a person's presence disturbs me, it is wise to dispense with that presence. Life is too sweet to spend on unnecessary irritation.

"For example, if I'd found you disturbing I'd have sent you packing before I said twenty words."

We talked about her travels in America. She said:

"I love your country—two cities in particular. Los Angeles because so many parts of it are beautiful, the film people are fascinating, and it is becoming so civilized. The last time I was there I got to know that young actress, Marilyn Monroe. She was the sweetest thing, a truly glorious person, and it's a tragedy that she was driven to that awful end.

"Chicago is another city I adore. I have many good friends there, and it's such a sincere city, and so beautiful along the waterfront. And such splendid shops—better than any in New York or London.

"But about my autobiography—a mere memoir, really. I hope you don't find it offensive because I don't mean to be unkind. I've merely chosen, in this life, to surround myself with the things that are right and interesting and beautiful.

"God gives us that right, and I've taken advantage of it."

"One of the things that makes all the work we do, all of the frustrations we encounter, all of the distress we endure, all of our shortcomings, worthwhile, is the feeling that not only can one do something worth doing with a magazine but that magazines are peculiarly suited for keeping people human in a society where it is more and more difficult to stay human."

Robert Stein

Robert Stein

STEIN: Birth, rearing, education—all can be answered in one phrase: New York City—except for a brief period during the war when I was in the Army.

There's a story I'd like to tell about how people become magazine editors. It's really a takeoff on Walter Slezak's story about how people become prompters in the theater. He said, "Isn't it strange that no one sets out to be a prompter? Nobody looks at a child in the cradle and says, 'That boy is going to be a great prompter someday.'" Well, nobody looks at a child in the cradle and says, "That boy is going to grow up to be a magazine editor someday." It always happens accidentally. You more or less drift into it, or find your way into it through accident or circumstance. At least this is true of everyone I know who is a magazine editor. Even graduates of journalism schools think in terms of newspapers rather than magazines, then find their way into magazines.

I started on this road when I was in second grade. When I first learned to write I began writing essays after school, all about imaginary cats and imaginary dogs and things of that nature. Then, a few years later, some neighborhood friends and I put out little periodicals, duplicated by hectograph, typed and transferred to a bed of gelatin. We distributed our faint purple reproductions of little stories, neighborhood news, cartoons, etc.

I was a sophomore at City College when the wartime draft age was lowered to eighteen. Realizing that the Army was imminent, I decided to get some working experience for a few months rather than being deferred to the end of the year. I went to work as a copyboy on the New York *Daily News,* and stuck it out there for the few months before the Army called me.

I was in the Army for three and one-half years, ending up in Europe with the 80th Division, Infantry. It turned out that my three months of experience as copyboy on the *Daily News* was the only experience anyone in the entire division had in publications work, so I was immediately qualified to be editor of the regimental newspaper once the war was over. I spent my last six months in the Army after VE-Day, putting out a newspaper and a history of the regiment. I worked with German printers who didn't know how to insert hyphens when they broke an English word. Needless to say, I had all sorts of fascinating experiences with them.

I discovered magazines when I was a senior in college. A friend who had graduated a bit ahead of me was working in the college public relations department. He had apparently taken a course in the English department I had somehow missed. He had discovered or been told — neither of us really believed it — that you could write articles for magazines without being on the staff; that a magazine would accept articles from anyone. He investigated this and sold an article or two, so we started collaborating. After a few joint efforts we started writing individually and actually sold our articles to magazines. I sold *Coronet* first, then *This Week* and *Popular Science*. By this time I was prepared to graduate; they offered me a job at the college doing publicity work and eventually editing the alumni magazine, so I combined this free-lance work with the employment at college. I did this for three or four years, then decided that perhaps I could get a job with a magazine. I had written about fifty articles by then for *Reader's Digest, Collier's,* and virtually all other "mass" magazines. When I went out to look for a job my working experience didn't count for anything, but the free-lance articles I'd sold were impressive enough to get me job interviews. I took a job as *Argosy's* feature editor. The gist of the job interview was this: I was asked a succession of questions about whether I was interested in hunting, fishing, outdoor cookery, photography, and several other esoteric male subjects, and in each case my answer was, "No, I'm not. I don't know anything about it." Finally I was asked, "Well, you know your job would involve editing in all these fields. What makes you think you could handle it?" And I said, "Well, if I can get the material so that I can understand it, anybody will be able to." That turned out to be persuasive enough, and they hired me, and I remained *Argosy's* feature editor for over a year. I don't remember a word about what I wrote or printed on hunting and fishing, but apparently I was able to get it into shape for people who were interested.

After *Argosy* I took a job with a small magazine that went out of existence after four or five months, and I was then offered a job at *Redbook* in the middle of 1953 as associate editor in the articles department. I started there and went through three or four promotions, through articles and managing editor, and when Wade Nichols left to become editor of *Good Housekeeping* in 1958, I became editor of *Redbook*. I remained that until January of 1965, when I became editor of *McCall's*.

N: *How would you define your objectives as editor of* McCall's?

STEIN: When you answer questions regarding your objectives, you really have to answer on several different levels at once, at least on two crucially important levels.

You have to start with recognition of the fact that a commercial magazine is a business enterprise. You have to look at it on that level. The job of the editor of the mass-circulation magazine is to attract and hold an audience of millions—in our case, millions of women. So this sets the framework for what the job is.

Now, I happen to believe that women's interests, particularly during the last ten years, have been expanding at a tremendous rate, that the cycles of discussion about "a woman's role" are rather wearisome. The feeling of the early 1950's, based on the book *Modern Woman, the Lost Sex,* was that women should do nothing but bake bread and have babies. This was typified by the plot of *Lady in the Dark,* which found the woman executive unhappy because she wasn't really a "woman." She found happiness by giving up her job and becoming a conventional housewife. Then the discussion turned full cycle, as best exemplified by Betty Friedan's *The Feminine Mystique,* which took an opposite view— that women can be fulfilled only if they become men in disguise and hold full-time jobs. This view regarded all the talk about femininity as a device to keep them trapped, to prevent them from finding total fulfillment.

It seems to me that both of these arguments are rather extreme and foolish, yet both are useful in crystallizing the issues. The reason why everyone debated—and debates—about woman's role is because women, in a large sense, have come into their freedom as people in this last generation. They're now debating how to use this freedom. The debate involves the confusion about what the individual woman should do with opportunities and advantages unprecedented in history.

In past generations women were literally kept within the home, confined within a narrow range of possible activities. The women of this past generation have been suddenly liberated to find their own way in life through any combination of career, home life, marriage, and motherhood—whatever elements or activities they find congenial.

It seems to me that a magazine addressed to all women is an exhilarating prospect, particularly when you remember that women's magazines used to be rather narrowly-defined publications that printed a few recipes, showed a few of the latest fashions, possibly added a chitchat article, and stopped there. Now we can take the conventional areas of interest which are unchanging—interest in food, fashions, their appearances and the appearances of the home, child-rearing, and harmony with husbands—and go on from there in a remarkable fashion. We can be a lot more sophisticated in the basic areas, for that matter, because we're talking to better-educated, more sophisticated women. But we can discuss serious subjects that have to do with our society and culture and the world in general—how things run, what the problems are, how we're going to survive. The possibilities are much broader and deeper than they ever have been. What is exciting about the mass magazine for women—and this has become apparent only in the past few years—is how far we can go, how wide we can range, how seriously we can approach our subject matter. It's an extremely liberating feeling for an editor. But it must be done within the commercial framework with the need to attract and to hold a mass audience of women rather than a "special" audience.

There have always been magazines on different levels. The smaller the circulation, the more precisely we can define the interests of readers, the more can be taken for granted by the editor. But as the editor of a mass magazine, I must constantly try to find out what the limits of our readers are. Hopefully, I try to please these readers. I also try to please minorities of readers with a particular article or story and hope to please them in a way that will make an impression on them, at the risk of displeasing or boring the majority of readers. But each month if we put together enough things that have value for different minorities within our circulation, we begin to make an impression on these people. They don't suffer from the confusion of wondering whether they read a particular piece in our magazine or in our competitor's. They begin to understand our point of view and what we're trying to do in general; they identify with that, and if they find it congenial or attractive or exciting they will come back. Those who don't, won't; this is one of the facts of life. We can't try to reach every single person—in my case, every single woman—with a magazine. We're trying to reach a co-herent, large body of readers and, if we do our job with some con-sistency of point of view, we will eventually find those readers who want the magazine we produce and eventually lose those readers who find our product unattractive or disturbing or unsatisfying in one or more respects.

We must identify the strengths of our medium. I think that maga-zine people have gotten over their initial fear that television was a monster that was going to destroy them—just as newspaper people got over this fear of radio and, earlier, magazines got over their dread of radio and the movies. Each medium that comes along doesn't destroy all other media; it simply changes the range of possibilities.

One of the things television has done for us is to relieve us of being the mass-entertainment medium. Television supplies that need superbly. This has made the "possibilities" I mentioned "necessities."

To gauge the difference in the mediums: If you're producing something on television you're faced with the necessity of attracting an audience on a given hour of a given night, which means that your solution must be conditioned by what your competition is doing. If the other two networks are doing something particularly attractive at the time, it doesn't matter how valuable what you have in mind may be — you're faced with the job of attracting people in the face of that. In a way it's a sort of hopeless problem in terms of the quality of what you do, since you constantly have to respond to what the other fellow is doing.

In magazines you're relatively free of this because you can find your readers where they make the choice of time and place. It's perfectly possible that they may value your magazine, and value equally a magazine that's in direct competition with you. There's no need to address yourself directly to what competing magazines are doing; this means you are much freer to define your own way and decide what you're doing, than you would be under the pressures exerted by the kind of mass-medium television is. Think of what it must be like to have a marvelous idea, a thing worth saying — but if you have to go against "Bonanza" and Ed Sullivan it's going to be difficult, if not impossible, to find enough of an audience to make it worthwhile for a network to have you say it at that time.

On the other hand, if you have something to say in a magazine addressed to women, it doesn't matter that there are now more than a dozen large magazines of different kinds for women. You can still find the audience for whom your magazine can be valuable. In a way, you invent your readership by having an idea and a conviction, then having the skill and imagination — or having a group of editors with the skill and imagination — to make it materialize. Then you can find the people for whom your magazine will be valuable, interesting, exciting. You do this without regard for what anyone else is doing. In a way, you're in competition with everything — paperback books, newspapers, everything that takes up people's time and attention — but in another sense you're in competition with nothing except your own ability to do something that will warrant the time and money people are going to give you.

N: *But isn't the competition among women's magazines intense?*

STEIN: In one sense the competition is not as intense as it used to be — the competition for readers, that is. Most magazines have had the good sense and good fortune to develop their own directions and their own personalities. What is significant is the fact that the three largest women's magazines have, over the last five years—and as a group—added several million readers. We don't seem to be taking readers away from each other, and I don't think this will be our main problem as time goes on.

The competition is much more direct in terms of advertisers; advertising does, to a large extent, subsidize a mass magazine. Here I think we are very directly competitive, and in a way that I hope will be remedied by time. It's a misguided competition in a way. An analogy would be this: if we were airlines we would be saying to potential customers that you're going to go down in flames unless you fly with us. I think this is very destructive. If airlines did this it would be destructive to flying, in general.

The kind of competition we conduct for advertisers is destructive to all magazines, but there are some signs that we're outgrowing it. But I don't think we're outgrowing it fast enough. To attempt to convince advertisers that magazine "X" is not only better than magazine "Y," but that magazine "Y" is worthless, becomes stupid and insidious and venal —a very destructive form of competition. It isn't true to begin with, because magazines have grown and survived during a period of intense pressures to attract people's attention. Each magazine has to have its own virtues, and it's unfortunate that there is a hangover from an earlier day in that we compete with each other for advertisers in a destructive manner. We don't, by and large, compete so fiercely for readers. For readers we proclaim our own virtues, produce the best magazine we can each month. All of us seem to be finding readers without doing so at the direct expense of each other.

Hopefully, the time will come when we will do the same thing in competing for advertisers.

N: *To turn to you in a more personal sense, many of the more publicized activities seem to be beyond your immediate role as an editor. I'm referring to areas where national welfare is involved.*

STEIN: There's no way to draw a line between the two areas; they fuse into each other.

All good editors I know start with their own convictions and their own interests. They use these convictions and interests with as much imagination as they can within the framework of what their magazine is trying to accomplish. Now, they sometimes don't do things they feel are worthwhile because their judgment tells them they can't find a way of reaching enough of their readers with a particular idea. But they're constantly trying to find ways to translate things that are important to them, as citizens, as human beings, into terms that are effective and meaningful to their readers.

You cannot make a distinction between what is important to a man as a person and what is important to him as an editor. The only distinction you can make is in how he translates the first into the proper form for the second. And it takes a great deal of imagination to leap from the things he feels, to a point of view from which readers can be interested. No good editor does the obverse of this—takes things he disbelieves or things which go against his own basic convictions, and tries to exploit them because they might be commercially viable. Eventually those editors who try, lose the confidence of their readers. Readers can sense whether an editor is doing things because he believes they're worth doing or because he believes he can exploit them. I'm not saying that no editor ever does anything he doesn't believe to be true and useful. But I don't think any *good* editor exploits things which run contrary to his beliefs, because he's aware of how badly he would do it in the first place, and because there's so much else to do that he *does* find useful and true.

I mentioned that women's magazines have grown up to the extent that they don't indulge in juvenile competition for the attention of readers. I guess this is best typified by what we, as editors of women's magazines, did with President Kennedy in 1963. At the time I was editor of *Redbook*. I had been doing articles in the magazine over a two or three year period about the dangers of nuclear war and some of the very practical problems of nuclear testing—because I was editing a magazine addressed to young women, most of whom had young children. I felt certain that they were concerned with the dangers, and I published a number of different articles from different points of view which helped to clarify the problem and also, I hoped, give them some indication of what they might do about it all as individuals.

Then we went through the Cuban missile crisis, which I think was a major turning point in modern history, and I was involved, as an individual, in President Kennedy's effort to secure a nuclear test ban, which went on over the following six months. It occurred to me that perhaps I should be doing something about my concern that went beyond my own magazine. I knew most of the editors of the other women's magazines, though I'd never had the occasion to meet several of them. I simply sent a letter (in a few cases, I called) asking if they would come and join me at the end of a day, that I had invited Dr. Spock who was just then beginning to write for *Redbook*, and that we had something to propose to them. They all agreed. We seven editors met and asked Dr. Spock to explain his concern about the dangers of nuclear testing and the possibilities of nuclear war, and then we discussed the subjects among ourselves. I suggested that perhaps one way to dramatize this concern on the part of all women was to ask President Kennedy if we as editors could come to see him, representing most of the women in this country who are our readers. We asked if we could ask him some very detailed questions that were troubling them and get answers directly from him. After an hour or so of discussion all of these intensely creative people, who superficially seem to be in such life-and-death competition, had agreed to this. What was more significant, we agreed that we would publish the results jointly, that no one magazine would get any individual benefit or advantage from it, that we were doing it to dramatize our own concern and answer questions for women who were concerned with this all-important problem.

We suggested it to the President, he immediately agreed, and we went through a series of complicated arrangements that resulted in our going to Washington to spend a few hours with President Kennedy, questioning him from every point of view. It was put on the record. A few weeks later the test ban was actually signed. We went back and interviewed him again, and we published the results in November of 1963, just a few days before the assassination. The last I heard was that President Kennedy had read all the reports and was very pleased at the way it worked out, that he felt it was a useful thing to have done.

This gives me hope that there are overriding concerns which editors of magazines, even mass magazines, have that go beyond selfish interests. I know this is true of them as individuals. You have only to look at their magazines to see that they do things which couldn't be calculated simply to be "popular." Magazines have to reflect the editor's feeling of what is valuable and important, and here was a case where seven editors jointly did something they felt immensely worthwhile.

Interestingly enough, we attempted to do something similar with President Johnson some months after he became President, on the civil rights issue. It would have worked out, but we ran into some complications making arrangements, so the project never materialized. What was interesting was that the same group of editors, plus a few more, were ready to make another joint effort.

N: *How do you feel about the general level of material that comes your way for consideration by* McCall's?

STEIN: I suppose that editors are habitually dissatisfied by what they get. Perhaps this is the necessary mark of a good editor, but in many cases they have good reason to be dissatisfied because the requirements are much higher than they used to be. As I said earlier, people in general — women in particular — are better-educated, more sophisticated and aware, and they aren't satisfied with the superficial job that was once considered satisfactory in magazines. The reporting must go deeper, the writer's perception has to be more acute, he must write with more grace and style. He simply has to be better at every level.

In many cases the best writers for magazines have been very properly attracted to other fields. There is something very seductive about writing books, especially when the possibility of a very large success with a single book promises wealth and fame, all at one crack. A certain amount of the best writing is attracted to the theater and various other entertainment media. And there is simply more demand for good writing and good reporting than there used to be; thus it is harder to find the quality of work we want.

In the last year or more we have found ourselves often turning to novelists, playwrights, and critics for articles, rather than to the professional magazine writer. In many cases this involves a great risk, especially where good reporting is involved, because novelists, playwrights, and critics are not usually trained as reporters. But we're willing to take that risk because many subjects require the qualities the creative writer has that the conventional magazine writer lacks.

On the other hand, many of the best magazine writers are meeting the challenge, are working harder.

Part of the challenge, of course, must be resolved by editors. Good reporting and good editing simply take more time than mediocre reporting and mediocre editing. We have to invest more time to get better results. But we've got to make writers aware that we are serious in asking them to do better work. It's traditional, you know, for editors to talk out of both sides of their mouth, to say their standards are this high, then reveal they are lower when involved in a specific article or story. We may still deceive ourselves when we speak in generalities about what our level of aspiration is, but I think we mean what we say more than we ever have because our readers demand more. This makes the need for higher quality a necessity rather than choice.

From the editor's standpoint, it involves being inventive and imaginative about what we set out to do in a given article, whom we ask to do it, what point of view is taken, and how we go about helping the writer do his job. It isn't enough to have a subject of interest, of obvious appeal, then simply throw it into the lap of a writer and ask him to come back with three to five thousand words. Now we have to know why the subject is of interest to our readers; we have to explore every possible approach; we have to, sometimes, try unconventional or even new techniques for getting at it. And, as I indicated, we have to be very selective about whom we ask to do it. Otherwise the results will be predictable, and it's predictability that kills magazines.

It used to be that we could cover almost any subject in a popular magazine by assigning a very good writer to go to a number of obvious sources, get the necessary facts and figures and dramatize them with a few anecdotes or individual experiences, then put it all together in a neat, well-rounded way. The result would be that the reader would be superficially informed, would quite possibly be entertained by reading the article, but would be left with very little of real value to him.

Now, on some of the most serious subjects, we find that we are investing as much as two years of time; that we're using not only writers, but (often) teams of researchers to help them. In some cases we're working with research organizations and foundations to do basic research which goes far beyond reporting, simply to find out what the reality of the situation is before we can begin to figure out what we're going to say about it, how we're going to treat it in a magazine. This is a growing trend, because readers can discern the difference between an exploitation of their interest on the part of the magazine and the magazine's desire to serve their interests by clarifying confusion about issues that are important to them. We have to get beneath clichés, myths, and easy answers.

When I first started writing magazine articles on almost any subject of direct concern to the reader, I finished with ten rules on how to handle the subject. Well, the ten-easy-rules days are over, because any issue that can be treated with ten easy rules isn't worth considering in the first place. The best you can hope to do now is to find those subjects and issues that really concern readers, really confuse them, then clarify the subject, pinpoint the problem, and give them some sense of what the range of possible solutions might be. It can never be so simple that a set of easy rules will work for all individuals. We must give them something they can interpret in light of their own interests, attitudes, and needs. Then we've done our job well.

No more ten easy rules.

The same thing is true, on a different level, when we deal with people, personalities. We used to be able to take some popular movie star, politician, or public figure, and string together a few colorful anecdotes that would pass as a profile of the person involved. Nowadays, if we're going to interview someone, we're going to interview him in depth, go through hours and hours of preparation before the actual interviewing is begun, then more hours and hours of editing to make the interview effective and coherent and to get across what the person being interviewed really has to say. There may still be some magazines that still get by with the superficial interview, and we may fall into that error occasionally, but it is to be desperately avoided.

Similarly, if we're doing an article about the person, it's going to be done by someone who has spent a great deal of time on the subject and brings to bear a great deal of talent in his observation. It's a different kind of reporting and writing, and another reason why so many of the best things that appear in magazines these days are either ultimately published as books, or are advance excerpts from books, simply because books in general, though there are notable exceptions, attract the best writers, and the terms under which they're allowed to write enables them to do their job well.

In many cases magazine editors now find that they are working in collaboration with book publishers in subsidizing writers over a period of two or three years; in this manner they can do their work well enough to develop a series of two or three articles for a magazine and a book for the book publisher. This is very healthy. And again, it's in the direction of doing things better and in greater depth.

I haven't said anything about fiction. It used to be that magazine fiction was light, easy, conventional — especially in a woman's magazine. It used to be a joke around the offices of some women's magazines that the illustrations were done first, the stories written afterward. This was not simply a joke, either. It was true, in some cases, because you could get the illustrator to do an infinite number of variations of men and women embracing each other and be sure that sooner or later a story you ran would fit the particular illustration. They were all the same.

Now television has come along. Considered on the level of light entertainment, television is magnificent; thus the opportunities for magazines do not lie in that direction. As the articles have become more serious, the fiction has had to go in the same direction. Now it's not surprising to find that stories from mass magazines are beginning to appear in the anthologies of the best short stories of the year. Once they came from the literary quarterlies, or from commercial magazines of small circulation — *The New Yorker, Esquire*, etc. But this is no longer true. They come from *The Saturday Evening Post, McCall's, Redbook*, etc. This again is because the level of interest and comprehension of the reader has changed; consequently the functions of the mass magazine have changed. The fiction we publish again underscores the fact that we simply cannot settle for a superficial, easy sort of entertainment.

To make a reader come back to your particular magazine, something has to stay with that reader. Something that goes deeper than light entertainment, though this is not to say that one of the great responsibilities of the magazine isn't to entertain. It is, but to define entertainment as we must provide it, we have to work in a manner similar to the range of theater — from the lightest musical to *Oklahoma!* to the starkest drama. We cannot compete as magazine editors by presenting the equivalent of a TV variety program.

We do have, as a medium of information, one advantage over television. No matter how well television treats serious subjects, no matter how well the medium attempts to inform, it is under a handicap because it comes across in a very impressionistic way. It provides images which are then associated with ideas, but the audience doesn't have to digest these images at individual rates of speed, nor to go back to think about what was said ten minutes ago. How did the argument proceed? There's no page to turn back to. Thus television can only work in an impressionistic way, cannot compete with magazines because magazines can treat subjects at greater depth, with more organization, and with more lasting effect because people can absorb at their own rate of speed and interest. They can refer back; they can reread. Thus television's strength is in the light and superficial aspects of entertainment, whereas entertainment in the sense of presenting that which is more substantial, of lasting value, belongs to the printed word.

I think we are growing intelligent enough to know what our strengths are and to use them and to avoid competing with the strengths of other media. This is why I think that our competition with television to gain people's attention never was too direct and has become less so.

The competition is direct, of course, in competing for advertisers. But I don't know of any magazine editor who thinks of himself as a serious competitor of a television producer. We're simply doing different things.

N: *If you were to advise the young writer coming up who wishes to do work for a magazine, what would that advice be? What would you hope for him?*

STEIN: To begin with, I wouldn't put much emphasis on preparation in terms of specific skills. I think these skills are sharpened with experience, though I do think it is valuable to learn the techniques of writing, research, and interviewing. What I think is more important for the young writer—and it sounds banal to say it—is that he should develop himself as a person, and his range of interests, because it's an awareness of himself and his possibilities that will lead him in the direction of what he can do best. It's trite to say, as we once said to the aspiring novelist, "Write about that which you know best," but this should be said to aspiring reporters and magazine journalists. Write not only about what you know best, but what interests you most.

I've watched some very good writers develop in magazines, and the best were always those who followed their own instincts and their own interests, who did not try to tailor-make their work for what they thought were the requirements of magazine editors. They sometimes suffered a material loss—they certainly did at the beginning, before they were recognized—but they always turned out to be not only more effective, but more successful in a commercial sense.

I'm not saying that it is always possible to take what you're most interested in and most excited about — especially the beginning writer — and use it directly to publish in the largest and best-paying magazines. But if you take what you care about most, what you know best, and try to find those publications whose needs most closely coincide with your own interests and your own talents — even though they be small magazines that do not pay so well — they will give you the opportunity to develop in the best possible direction for you. Sooner or later you can move on to larger magazines and better-paying work.

I think a fatal mistake is to try to prefabricate for a given market. By the time you learn to prefabricate for it, the market may have changed; it very seldom appears to be what you think it is. If you look at an issue of a magazine and decide that you're going to produce such-and-such a piece for an editor because it will be close to what he's already published, you have no way of knowing whether he considers it one of his successes or one of his failures or one of his compromises. Every issue of a magazine is made up of all three, and you have no way of knowing which is which. Even if he considers it one of his successes and his readers will want more of same six months or a year from now, the piece you're planning for him may already be written. So it's fatal for a young writer to take literally what he sees and try to imitate it. If you read with a knowing eye and try to understand some of the underlying points of view — what the piece reflects about the magazine's interests — and try to extract from it more than what it literally is, then that sort of reading can be useful.

But to read with an eye toward imitation is disastrous; you're failing to use most effectively whatever talent you have, attempting a self-exploitation that doesn't really work out well.

This leads to something I didn't say before, about what magazines really are. This is true of mass magazines and specialized magazines, true on different levels in different ways, but nonetheless true.

One of the things that makes all the work we do, all of the frustrations we encounter, all of the distress we endure, all of our shortcomings, worthwhile, is the feeling that not only can one do something worth doing with a magazine, but that magazines are peculiarly suited for keeping people human in a society where it is more and more difficult to stay human, where everything has a tendency to become more mechanical, where everything has a tendency to get larger, where everything has a tendency to negate individual choice and individual action. I think this is one of the underlying strengths of magazines, one of the truly fine opportunities a magazine editor has.

When I go off to our printing plant and see eight or nine million magazines stacked in one place, I must admit it's an awesome sight. But I cannot work from that concept. What I work from day to day — what other editors work from day to day — is a sense of talking to one individual at a time, trying to say something we think is of some use, some value, whether it's a piece on religion or a recipe. We try to transmit this to another individual in such a way that it will be effective and useful. I think the result of this — if we do it well, with conscience and responsibility — is that we do one of the most valuable things needed in a society getting so large and complicated and noisy and mechanized. I think this is a constant challenge to bear in mind, and one of the burdens as well as the joys.

Each month we have to produce a completely new magazine. We have behind us our own experiences, our own general approach. But each article has to be different, and each picture. Not only must we avoid repeating, mechanically or by rote, what we did before, or restricting ourselves to what has been done before, but we must, in a sense, be dissatisfied with ourselves deeply enough to try to do better than repeat past successes and avoid past failures. We have to learn what our past successes rest upon, then go beyond them; we also must learn the real sources of our failures and try to do better the next time.

But even failures are debatable. A resounding one — in the sense that a particular issue of a magazine may not have sold enough copies or that too many complaints came from irritated readers — may not be a failure per se. The issue or the article may not have meant much to a majority of readers, yet it may have touched a few lives with great effectiveness. This may be much more important.

Jacqueline Susann

The "dolls" of the best-selling novel *Valley of the Dolls* are the pills that flood the entertainment world. Some of them offer sleep, others dewy-eyed wakefulness, still others a hypo'd stimulation. And in recent months they've made news, as one celebrity after another has succumbed to a combination of a supposedly innocent handful of "dolls" combined with a moderate amount of alcohol.

But there are other dolls, live ones, in Jacqueline Susann's highly-sexed novel of life at and near the top of the theatrical world and, to Miss Susann's credit, they are quite unforgettable, particularly since we play guessing-games with possible real-life doubles.

How did she come to write the novel?

"I started out to be an actress," she explained. "My childhood in Philadelphia was divided between a desire to star on Broadway and a desire to write. I was doing fairly well as an actress when my poodle, the love, turned out to be the star of the family in *Every Night, Josephine!* —a book which was a surprising best seller.

"For the second book, instead of writing a Josephine sequel and becoming typed as a writer of dog books, I turned to the world I knew best: show business. A rather glorious, fearful world my husband knows even better than I do. A world that had come to rely more and more on pills.

"Perhaps people in business gulp pills the way they do in Hollywood and on Broadway; I don't know. But I do know the pressures of show business. People watch an Academy Award telecast and say, 'It must be marvelous to be an actress.' I say, 'If you only knew what it takes, and what it takes out of them, you wouldn't be so envious.'

"Show business is tough. Cruel, unkind, competitive. For example, one writer will be genuinely pleased when another writer has a success. But Broadway openings are crowded with actors who are hoping that the play is a flop and that the star, their dear friend Henry or George, will fall flat on his ass.

"This constant jockeying for position, knifing, struggling, fearing, brings on the pills.

"You see, the pills aren't taken to escape reality, they're taken so a person can cope with reality. Alcohol ruins careers, but the pills can help for a long while. They induce sleep, so the actor, after he's shrugged off the aftereffects, can look refreshed. Add Dexedrine, and he can actually sparkle.

"But this does nothing to help the actor's private life—to replace the wife or husband who's been divorced through lack of time or place for personal love, the children who've been custodied away. The loneliness at the top brings on more pills and, perhaps, more of the drink that speeds the pills' effects. One drink becomes three, two pills become six or twelve, and then there's the night when the performer didn't know how many pills she took, how many drinks she had, and she dies.

"I'm convinced that Marilyn Monroe died that way."

Some readers have criticized *Valley of the Dolls* for its strong emphasis on sex, the extremes to which pill-taking was carried.

"I did not set out to write a book that shocks. The characters are composites, of course, of people I've known and watched in show business, but nothing that happens to them, sexually, is distorted or exaggerated.

"The same with pills. If anything, the book underplays the quantity of pills taken by many performers. I've seen an actress take sixteen at a time, and I've also seen some of the tragic effects."

Should barbiturates and amphetamines be banned?

"I don't think they should be taken off the market, but I think they must be controlled more carefully, and that people must be educated regarding their effects.

"Some drugstores find ways to sell them without prescription. Some doctors prescribe too many. Some people find ways to forge prescriptions, or find pills on the black market. It's all insidious, but if the purveyors of pills were always honest and people knew the real dangers, this much horrible damage wouldn't be done."

Some months later, when *Valley of the Dolls* was still riding high as our number one best seller, I saw Miss Susann again. Still expertly guided by her husband, television producer Irving Mansfield, her promotion efforts continued—with obvious results.

Again I questioned her about motivation, and her reaction to the "dirty book" criticisms coming her way.

"I didn't set out to write a so-called dirty book. I don't think it is a dirty book. I do believe, however, that you cannot define characters without identifying them with the sexual acts they would commit and the language they would use.

"For example, it is one sort of person who would say, 'Oh, for goodness' sake!' when a rehearsal went wrong. You would know that woman has restraint, a basic dignity, and is likely to be in command of a given situation. But when a performer blows sky-high, loses control of herself and her tongue, and lashes out at everyone in sight, then you are aware of the deficiencies in personality and character that will play themselves out in later events in the novel.

"It's hard to explain, but I do think that words and acts, sometimes shocking words and acts, are essential to a novel that treats life as realistically as my book does. And my book does deal honestly with show business and some of the truly vicious things that happen in a world where you have to wade through horseshit to get to the foot-lights."

Is it necessary to portray such a world?

"I spent many years as an actress. My husband has been a success-ful radio and television producer for even more years. We know show business—the good sides, the rewards, the bad sides with all the attendant tragedies and disappointments.

"*Valley of the Dolls* is an honest picture, a composite of the things I've seen happen, the people these things have happened to. Actors and singers do terrible things, often to achieve success. They can turn into monsters, quite capable of destroying themselves as well as each other.

"If I didn't sometimes show these characters at their more bestial, weaker moments, I'd have written a dishonest book. Frankly, I'd rather risk being called the author of a dirty book than the author of a weak or inaccurate one.

"As a matter of fact, all this talk about *Valley of the Dolls* being a shocking, dirty book hasn't hurt the sales one goddam bit."

I saw Jacqueline Susann once more, this time in London, the day before *Valley of the Dolls* catapulted onto British best-seller lists.

This is the speech that won the British press, and helped launch her book on a transatlantic basis.

"I want to thank you all for coming here to this party for *Valley of the Dolls* in London. It's very thrilling, the success that *Valley of the Dolls* has had in America. I hope it has the same success here. You know my first book, *Every Night, Josephine!* was about my poodle, and what we call a "mild success." It made number eight on the best-seller list in *Time* magazine. My mother was very thrilled. She used to sit around in Philadelphia in the park with her friends. (My mother is a retired school-teacher.) And she'd take bows and her friends would say, 'Isn't it marvelous, Mrs. Susann, that in a time and age like this your daughter writes such a pure and sweet, clean book.' So then she began getting very interested in *Valley of the Dolls*, and she'd say, 'What is it about? Is it a whole bunch of little dolls like poodles?' And I said, 'Mother, I'll show it to you later.' So when I finished it, I sat her down and gave her the galleys. Her eyebrows shot up to her hairline and she turned to me and said, 'Well, what am I going to do? How can I face anyone in Philadelphia after this?'

"My husband said, 'Rose, you might as well face it, you've gained a writer, but lost a city. Move.' Well, Mother did go out-of-town for a few weeks and when she came back, *Valley of the Dolls* was on all the best-seller lists. Before this she had prepared her friends. She started going around before she went out of town, saying, 'Now look, things are different in writing today.' She started carrying copies of Norman Mailer under her arm when she'd go to her bridge games, and she'd say, 'You know, writers are realistic, and whatever words you read in Jackie's book, it doesn't mean Jackie says them, it means her characters say them.'

"Well, when she came back, people greeted her at the concerts and said, 'Oh, Mrs. Susann, your daughter has written such an earthy book, it's marvelous.' And, of course, that's the great thing about success and Mother now says to me, 'What's your new one about? Is *The Love Machine* going to be juicy?' And she's really carried away with all this although she's still a little shocked. Because my mother thinks that none of these people exist in Philadelphia. All these things that happen, happen in cities other than Philadelphia.

"And you know when I wrote *Every Night, Josephine!* I used to get wonderful letters from people with poodles. They'd write from different cities and say, 'My little Bobo wants to know about Josephine,' and I got birthday cards from poodles and everything. And my husband never really paid much attention to my mail, because how many times can you open a letter and stare at a cocker spaniel's picture falling out, or a French poodle's? It wasn't very exciting. I used to envy him because he's a different kind of person and I longed to get exciting mail, like he did. But at that time when I got my mail about Josephine from all the poodle lovers, I used to go to his office. One day there was a large envelope, and I started reading his mail as wives often do, and out of this envelope, a picture of a girl, an eight by ten glossy, fell out. She was in a bikini, and she was really built. And she said, 'Mr. Mansfield, I would do anything to get on one of your shows, and when I say "anything," I mean anything. P.S.: I also sing.' So I got a picture of myself and enclosed it to this young lady, and I said, 'I am Mrs. Mansfield. I do everything for Mr. Mansfield, and when I say "every-thing," I mean everything.'

"Well, now since *Valley of the Dolls*, I get also equally interesting mail, and I want to thank you all for being here."

How did she feel about the reception of the book in England?

"There aren't any reviews yet, but the press reception has been fantastic, and it's amazing. Have you seen the press? And the word of mouth is so tremendous. It's the same thing I said about in my book, our jet age has made communication instant and people in England have been buying the American edition at airports. People in London were asking for this book long before it came out. They had heard about it. Just like when some big hit plays here in London, we kind of know about it in America, and wait for it. I went to several bookstores yesterday and they said, 'It's unusual about this book. Usually people wait until the reviews come out before buying, but they aren't this time.' They stick to the 'pub' date rather strictly in England. I was at Harrods on Wednesday and the publishing date was Thursday, and the woman who runs the book department said, 'Oh, it's crated downstairs. We can't open it until tomorrow, but the phone's been ringing all day, people asking "Is it there yet?" and they'll be coming in tomorrow. We've taken orders.'

"So I'm really terribly thrilled about it."

"It is very important in all countries ... that the individual citizen should feel that he does count, that he has responsibility, that he does make a difference by exerting his pressure on the government. This is his duty."

Arnold Toynbee

Arnold Toynbee

TOYNBEE: I was born into a family who hadn't much money. My father was a social worker; my grandfather, a doctor; my great-grand-father, a farmer. I had an old-fashioned education, extremely thorough in Greek and Latin, but rather sketchy in other things, and this led me, as soon as I finished at the university, to travel in Greece. I traveled in Greece in 1911-1912. I went in order to study ancient history, with the objective of coming back and teaching Greek and Roman history at Oxford.

I discovered present-day international affairs because every Greek person was talking about whether the war would come next autumn or next spring. They knew the war was coming and they debated whether Greece would get Macedonia or Crete. I used to sit in the village store in the evening listening to the men talk about these things. This was the beginning of my education in international affairs. I contracted dysentery and this is why I wasn't killed in the war, I suppose—why I am speaking to you now when half of my friends were killed.

By the end of the war, I was deeply interested in international affairs, and because I knew about the present-day Near East, I got into the Foreign Office temporarily, and then into the Turkish section and went to the Peace Conference.

Since then I have kept a foot in the present and a foot in the past. I have never lost my interest in ancient history. I spent most of my life in this Institute with my wife, writing a current survey of international affairs.

N: *Very few husbands and wives have worked together, professionally, for the length of time you and Mrs. Toynbee did. How did this collaboration work?*

TOYNBEE: We were colleagues before we were married—for a long time, as a matter of fact. I suppose this is a fairly new thing in the life of most countries, the enormous part women are taking in the professional life of the world. In the early stages women and children took too great a part in the industrial life of this country; women were actually down in the mines in the early 1800's, and they worked under pitiful conditions in the mills long after that. The two world wars promoted women, in effect. Even in Muslim countries like Turkey, the lack of manpower during the first war helped toward emancipation of women. It is a big change, an important step forward, and a good one. I notice this in America especially—the number of married women with children who hold down jobs. I don't know how they do it. The exertion must be tremendous. As to my wife—we are retired, so she is not now actively working beside me; but all the while we were working, we were actually partners—equal partners.

N: *Does the historian have an obligation to the public?*

TOYNBEE: I think he has a great obligation. I think historians have had quite an influence on affairs in the past, sometimes for good and sometimes for evil.

An obvious case is the breakup of the Austrian empire. This was largely the work of the historians who rediscovered the past histories of the different nations in the Austrian empire and made these nations conscious of their identity.

I am afraid that, on the whole, historians in recent times have thought in national terms and led the world to think in national terms instead of universal terms. There have been times in the past where the traditional Christian view of history was the universal view. It didn't break up the human race into nations. It thought of mankind as a whole, and Christ came to save the whole of mankind, not just the Czechoslovak nation or the Yugoslav nation. Now this traditional view has been succeeded recently by the national view, and just at the time when technology has been really linking up the nations into a single human race rather effectively, for the first time in history. This nationalism which historians have encouraged has gone against the natural tendencies. This is one of the dangerous things in the present-day world. I think we are de facto linked up together and thinking more and more in terms of separate national units. But nations don't make sense in the space age. Cutting up the surface of one tiny planet into 125 sovereign national states, when we're reaching out to outer space, is really senseless—it doesn't fit.

N: *I remember from reading your twelve-volume study of history, that you have thought of the West as declining since—roughly—the time of the Reformation. Have your views changed to a measurable extent?*

TOYNBEE: When one is in the middle of the story, it's very hard to see where one is, isn't it? The story of the West isn't finished, so we can't tell whether or not we are in decline. I try to keep an open mind, and I can see parallels to things in the past—particularly where we know the whole story, as with Greek and Roman and Chinese history—but though they ended in decline and fall, I still think we may recover.

Of course, all this is particularly serious because the West has now engulfed the whole world, and if the West were to decline, the effects would be disastrous for the human race. All the eggs, as it were, are in the Western basket.

N: *How do you feel about America's ability to keep, or help keep, those eggs from being scrambled?*

TOYNBEE: It's almost obligatory for the United States to revolutionize its relations with the rest of the world, isn't it? You see, through most of your short history—up until the Second World War, in fact—people emigrated to the United States to cut clear from the Old World and to start a kind of earthly paradise in the New World. This has now been reversed. America is not only implicated in the rest of the world, but is positively reaching out into it.

For example, there couldn't be a country more remote from the United States than Vietnam. Not only is it physically remote, but from the traditional American point of view, it has no bearing on American security in the traditional sense. It must be astonishing to congressmen, who in 1939 passed the neutrality legislation, to realize that in 1965 America would regard winning a war in South Vietnam as being a vital interest to the United States. Neither America nor Vietnam would have thought this credible if prophesied. But it's part of the great revolution in the American attitude toward the world.

N: *How do you regard our action in South Vietnam?*

TOYNBEE: If I may speak frankly, I think American pride—not a good kind of pride, at that—plays a great part. America isn't accustomed to accepting reverses. Most of the nations in the world have had big reverses—France in 1815, 1870, 1940; Britain with the Revolutionary War and the loss of the thirteen colonies—but we've digested the inescapable fact that, in public life and private life, mistakes are occasionally made and disasters occasionally incurred.

America finds it hard to accept this. What happens is that a very minor motive, prestige—prestige in one's own eyes—takes precedence over reason. America might run into big disasters that would involve the rest of the human race.

But America has always been a warlike nation, hasn't she? It is significant that every American citizen has the right to bear arms, whereas in Britain the very last thing that could happen would be to grant such permission. After you conquered your country from the Indians—by force—you founded your independence via war, and you maintained your unity through another war, the Civil War.

Now, you haven't suffered from a war in your own country since that time, and then only the defeated party, the South, suffered at all, if we except a ravaged corner of Pennsylvania. Thus the effect of war in one's own country hasn't really got into your bones yet. The rest of the world feels that America does not understand what war really means, or what it may mean to a country that is fought over and is bombed. Certainly, Hiroshima thinks that the rest of the world doesn't understand what even a primitive nuclear war means.

Did you observe that Mr. McNamara stated, just when you were starting to bomb North Vietnam, that in case of a nuclear war between Russia and America, the deaths in the United States would—I think— be 149 million and the deaths in the Soviet Union 80 million? This was published in the press, but very few of you paid much attention to it— yet Mr. McNamara must have said it for a purpose.

This is the sort of thing that causes concern in the rest of the world. The American government is acting as if it could still have its limited type of war that it had in the past, in the preatomic age. You apparently assume that you can have war without nuclear war. The rest of the world doesn't believe this, and the rest of the world is frightened by American policies and actions.

N: *What is your hope for our policies and actions?*

TOYNBEE: I think you must endeavor to put first things first. In any human action, there is always a choice of priorities, a consideration of what is important and what isn't important. It seems to me that America is sacrificing a big opportunity for the sake of a smaller thing. The smaller thing is what I call "American pride" or "prestige" or "face," as it is called in China. The big thing you seem to be missing is the possibility of a détente with Russia, a chance to prevent the proliferation of nuclear weapons, a point that is of vital interest to both countries. The fact that China is spitting in the face of Russia as well as of the United States has put Russia into a difficult position, and this should provide an excellent opportunity for America and Russia to get together to keep China down; they should cooperate to put the world in order and to put an end to international anarchy.

America is not pursuing this opportunity at the present. Russia seems to be open to the idea of improving her relations with America. After all, China, in the long view, is a more serious threat to Russia than to America.

N: *In view of these American actions, what do you think of the prospects for world peace?*

TOYNBEE: I'm much less optimistic than I was about a year ago. At the time of the last American Presidential election, I thought that we would now have a moderate administration in power, an opportunity, created by China, for America and Russia to get together. It hasn't turned out this way. One thing I'm very apprehensive about is the fact that the American people don't seem to be concerned about the escalation of the war very much at all. A small minority is rightly alarmed, but the great mass of people doesn't seem to notice what is happening. This is alarming. In fact, for the first time since the Second World War, I have become pessimistic. You *can* and you *must* change.

N: *In the area of foreign relations—and since principles of government as well as actions seem to be involved—how do you feel about the true ideological differences between the United States and Russia?*

TOYNBEE: The differences are much slighter than meet the eye. I believe that every people in the world are nationalists first and ideologists second. America and Russia are very much alike in being nationalists. Also, the economic and social systems on which the ideologies are supposedly founded are becoming less and less at variance. For a worldwide force is playing upon us, and this is modern technology, which has no concern for ideologies and is compelling every nation to organize its social and economic structure on the same pattern. I think we are converging, but I think that people will go on, for a long time, proclaiming their ideological differences, even though those differences become smaller and less important, just as Catholics and Protestants stopped fighting each other a long time *before* they began to make friends with each other.

N: *Do any actual parallels in history exist with relationship to the situation the U.S. and the U.S.S.R. now face?*

TOYNBEE: Oh, I think so. I think those religious wars between Protestants and Catholics and between Christians and Muslims are direct parallels. Each side said that the world would be an impossible place for them and for everybody if the other side continued to exist; yet they found, in each case, that they had to and could coexist. When they accepted that fact, and they did so very unwillingly, they shook down together and simply *did* coexist. I think that this state of coexistence is going to come about between communism and capitalism.

N: *But doesn't China add a rather fierce and indefinable element?*

TOYNBEE: China's fierceness is really nationalistic rather than ideological. I think that, for China, communism is a sort of weapon for getting back her normal important place in the world. The cause of China's present state of mind isn't that she went Communist, but that she was trampled on and deposed from her normal great position in the world back in the nineteenth century. The essence of China's state of mind, and my hope, is that when China is again given her proper place in the world, which she is bound to achieve, she will calm down a bit.

N: *All of America's allies are engaged in trade with mainland China. Do you think that some kind of trade in nonstrategic materials would help ease the tensions between the two nations?*

TOYNBEE: Definitely. After all, America is trying to do as much harm to continental China as she can, isn't she? To persuade other nations, as far as she is able, not to trade with her? To keep her out of the United Nations?

Now, these are the acts of an enemy. To do these things to a country is to make that country regard you as an enemy and in return they will do you all the harm they can. Now, China is more than just a fact in the world; they say that by the year 2000 more than half the human race will be citizens of continental China. Looking ahead and even considering the unreasonableness of present Chinese attitudes, isn't it really a mistake on America's part to try to injure China?

Now, the Chinese are aggressive and unreasonable, but it's easy to see why. Ever since 1840, when my country attacked them and forced them to buy opium in that horrible war, they've been trampled on by England and France, and then by Japan, and their present state of mind is a comeback from that. One must take cognizance of China's history, and of the awful shock it was for China (who had been, for about two thousand years, the important civilized nation in her half of the world) to be treated as natives. What would the effect be on ourselves if this happened to us?

Our object should be to try to bring China back into the family of nations, to try to make her again behave like a good citizen of the world. The Chinese in the past have been rather moderate and unmilitaristic. It's the West that has made them militaristic. We hit them and hit them again, until the only thing they could do was fight us with our own weapons. The tragedy is that nineteenth-century America was the only nation in the world that didn't bully China; Russia, Britain, France, Japan — all bullied her. But now America has made herself China's Enemy Number One, and it's a tragic story. I don't know what the end will be, but there is still time to change the drift of events.

N: *You are known as a strong advocate of world government. Could you explain how world government would help minimize the chances of another world war?*

TOYNBEE: What I've been advocating — and I think this concerns America and Russia most directly — is that a world government has to be practical, and it must be based upon the realities of power.

The realities of power in the present world are that 90 percent of the world's power is held by America and Russia, though between them they have only 15 percent of the world's population. This means that

America and Russia could put the world in order if you could only agree together to run the world. It wouldn't be democracy, but it *would* be peace and order, and it *would* mean the survival of the human race. These things are even more important than democracy. We might, of course, get democracy in world government later on; but we'd get the survival of the human race immediately, and that is what we need most.

Now, I don't believe in these rather theoretical blueprints — constituent assemblies, etc., for forming a world constitution. I don't think world government will come in the way in which federal government came in the United States, through a constitutional convention, but I'd be glad to have world government on virtually *any* terms. Then we'd have *time* to see about the democractic aspects, which we would wish to do, of course.

N: *To bring the prospect of world government close to home, what elements of national sovereignty would the United States retain?*

TOYNBEE: I presume you would retain all that were not essential to the survival of the human race. Isn't the principle of the United States Constitution the fact that the states retain all sovereign powers except those that must be yielded to keep the union together? We know that when we get a federal government, power tends to increase at the center and diminish at the branches. This is one of those burning issues for American conservatives who are now up in arms against the growing power of the federal government and against the weakening of the state governments. But wasn't the federal government founded to cover the bare essentials, to set a united front to the rest of the world?

I would say that world government should be primarily constructed to deal with the three great problems of our time. First, it must present a united front to the great common enemy — nuclear weapons, those weapons that are poised to destroy our world. We must deal with the business of preventing war, and also deal with the population problem and the food problem. World government would be concerned with these pressing issues, and the national governments would assume roles comparable to that held by the sovereign states in the United States.

I would say that world government should be content with the immediate essentials to begin with. But I think, as technology increases, that the world will grow closer and closer together, and then we shall find it a matter of utility to give more administrative power to the central world government and less to the local governments, if only because being a member of the *human race* will count more than membership in the tribe, as time goes on. We shall feel more loyalty to *humanity*, less to our local state.

Didn't this happen in America? At one time, a Virginian was a

Virginian first and an American second; now he is an American first and a Virginian second. It was a gradual evolution. But, as I have said, I wouldn't try to found world government through the constitutional-convention method. I'd start with a Russian-American combine; that's where the power lies.

N: *An interesting aspect of one-world solidarity is the emphasis on unity and peace as advanced by the Roman Catholic Church. How do you view the actions and attitudes of the Church?*

TOYNBEE: I'm not a Catholic, but I think that Pope John — though he had such a short time as pope — made a permanent mark on history, not only in terms of the actions of the Catholic Church but in his effect on the attitudes of all religions toward each other. I presume the time was ripe for this sort of thing, but Pope John really started it off.

It's obvious, I think, that one of the reasons religion has lost popular interest and has been losing hold all over the world, and I mean *all* religions, is that they have seemed to be out of touch with the real problems and questions facing the contemporary world. The religions just haven't been biting into things that really matter to human beings — the propagation of peace and charity and goodwill toward each other, which are vital matters now that we have nuclear weapons in our hands.

If the churches take up these ideals and come to stand for the unity of the human race — not necessarily unity in the formal sense, but also not merely tolerating a negative coexistence — if the churches help us get on with each other as members of one family, feeling regard and affection for each other, this would have an enormous effect upon people's attitudes toward religion. The faiths would then stand for something that matters.

Thus I think that what is happening in all religions, this show of greater loving kindness toward each other, is one of the most hopeful, and also one of the most unexpected, trends that have followed the Second World War. Pope John was the catalyst. Not only Christianity has been affected. When I visited Burma recently, I found scores of Buddhist pilgrims from Ceylon, Japan, and Thailand, which is something unknown until recently, because even though Burma is the center of southern Buddhism, the southern and northern Buddhists had nothing to do with each other for centuries; they were split as far apart as Catholics and Protestants. But now they're coming together again and are making friends with each other. This is so new.

Take the reception that Pope Paul got from a Muslim crowd when he landed at Amman, the capital of Jordan, on his way to Jerusalem, or the reception he got in Bombay when he went to the Eucharistic Congress there. A few years ago, this would have been unthinkable — that a mass of people of other religions should shower the head of the Catholic Church with welcome and goodwill. It was spontaneous, unorganized, a mass movement, as though something rare and wonderful were running through the human race. I think they felt that the pope was concerned for the human race as a whole, not just for Catholics, so they were determined to show their gratitude.

N: *Can we turn for a moment to a number of Americans with whom you have had contact or of whom you have knowledge? How would you evaluate Presidents Wilson, Roosevelt, Truman, and Eisenhower?*

TOYNBEE: Wilson was a very great man, with very great ideals. But he was insensitive to the public, with fatal results—both for himself and the public, I fear. If he had yielded a little bit to Congress over the League of Nations, given in to them just the slightest, they wouldn't have chipped off much from the League. But he wouldn't yield an inch, so he got nothing. Then, not to have brought Republican representatives over to the Peace Conference was a terrible mistake.

My opposite number at the conference, Will Westermann, had come over on the S.S. *George Washington* with Wilson and expected that the members of the "inquiry," an organization that had been preparing for the Peace Conference during the previous twelve months, would have a chance of meeting the President on the ship. He expected the President to tell all the delegation what his policy would be, so that they would know his personal views and therefore know how to serve as his instruments. Wilson didn't see any of them. He shut himself up in his stateroom for a whole week. This was very obtuse, and it's strange that such a big man should have made such elementary mistakes in his relations with other people. I suppose these things have happened all through history, but because they have happened and do follow patterns, I think President Johnson should observe closely what happens to a leader who removes himself from counsel.

President Roosevelt was a hero to non-German Europeans. He was bound to be a hero because we felt that he understood what so many Americans didn't understand—the attempt of Germany to conquer the world. He educated the American people, if I may say so, into seeing that the war *was* their affair, and he did this with great political skill. In America, of course, he was, and is, a very controversial character; outside America, he was a hero, just as President Kennedy was the hero outside America, but a controversial personality—though less so than Roosevelt—at home.

Truman is rather a favorite of mine. I think he has an engaging character, with a compelling straightforwardness and simplicity. I think he is a very brave man. He did realize his duties and responsibilities and his obligation to make decisions. "The buck," he said, "ends here." The bomb situation, whether he did right or wrong, was a big decision. To fight the war in Korea—a big decision, and he made it. To dismiss MacArthur—another bold undertaking. These were hazardous decisions, but he made them, and these things lead me to admire him.

Eisenhower—I was astonished when I heard that he had agreed to run for President. He didn't run into as much trouble as Grant did, but after all, he will be remembered, like Grant, for being a general rather than for being a President. I think it is probably a mistake to run for the Presidency after being a top military commander. There's likely to be an anticlimax. Eisenhower did have an anticlimax, I suppose, and I don't think he's going to rank as one of the great Presidents.

N: *Do you find a great difference in our international policies between the Kennedy and Johnson Administrations?*

TOYNBEE: I do think that President Kennedy had a surer touch and also a greater sense of the importance of keeping of human relationship with the rest of the world as well as with the American people. What is upsetting to the rest of the world now is that we feel that President Johnson doesn't want to meet the heads of foreign governments or to take notice of foreign opinion. In fact, he gets rather annoyed when he's told that foreign opinion is critical of his policy. This seems to us unreasonable because our eggs are in America's basket. We might not lose, in a nuclear war, the number of lives that America would lose, but our world would be wrecked too.

You see, we did feel that President Kennedy stood for the human race as a whole. He was thinking of all of us, and not just of the American voters who elected him, and he won the hearts of people throughout the world as a consequence. Take the extraordinary outbreak of feeling in England when he was assassinated. And not only in this country. The Sunday following his death, my wife and I went to the American embassy to write our names in the book. There were queues and queues of people waiting to do the same, to express their feelings. A farmer's wife who lives next door to us in the country said, "I can't think of anything else."

I'm afraid that President Johnson hasn't this sensitivity to the rest of the world. In fact, he has aroused hostility, and this is very unfortunate for the United States and for the world. It could be put right, but he seems to resent criticism from within his own nation as well. This, as I see it, is different from the American tradition. In the past, everything in American political life has been done openly and publicly, and it has been assumed that the American people have a right to discuss and to criticize. This seems to have changed under the present administration, and I think this is unfortunate.

Nor do I think that this is a logical way to manage America, and

President Johnson is presumably an expert politician. We hope that sooner or later he will realize that his present line clashes with the politician's sense of his relationship to the American people. Right now, he seems to be moving toward something that the American people haven't intended and don't want.

N: *Do you think that the job of President of the United States may have become too big a job for one man, under the standing delegation of power?*

TOYNBEE: It almost seems so, doesn't it? He does have two functions. He is the representative head of state, the sort of position filled by a crowned head in Britain or Holland. Yet he is the executive head of a responsible government as well. Now, it does lighten the load to divide these two jobs, and they can be divided. As it is, it's almost superhuman to be both of these Presidents. In addition, on his executive side he is the leader of his party. He has much more power than, say, a prime minister in Great Britain. He's more like a four-year King George III than he is like a British prime minister. Ironically, the American Constitution gives the President the very powers that the colonists objected to in King George. The limitation is only in the sense of the four-year length of administration, but within those four years, the President is a king. Actually, by the time he became President, Washington had more power than George III, whose wings he helped clip.

In short, the Americans helped liberalize the British Constitution, yet gave themselves a sort of absolute ruler. Even the President's cabinet — his inner circle — is rather small and really quite private. The President has few advisers. I'm rather surprised that Congress has been so quiet; the Senate has always been jealous of Presidential power in the area of foreign relations. But now it's passive.

N: *I'd like to turn now to West Germany, today a strong economic force with, perhaps, some traces of German nationalism. Does England, on the whole, share Russia's apprehension about Germany as a resurgent power?*

TOYNBEE: Every European nation that has been invaded by Germany or, in Britain's case, fought by Germany, shares this apprehension. You've just seen in Holland what happened when a Dutch princess became engaged to a German. The Dutch — and the Norwegians, for what matter — were outraged by German aggression. They'd been neutral for so long, yet they were invaded and bombed in cold blood. You don't forget that sort of thing.

There's the same feeling in England. We hope that the Germans are going to stop being militaristic. People can learn from experience, after all. The French were militaristic for about two centuries, but 1815 and 1870 put a stop to that. But we don't know about the Germans. I think they will probably change. They seem to be devoting their energies to economic prosperity. Yet power has always gone to their heads, and they've repeatedly lost their sense of balance, so I think you'll find a general and continuing anxiety in Europe about the prospect of German nationalism.

This is something that people in America don't seem to understand. They've never had this feeling about Germany. I don't know why; Germany was quite a threat to the United States if the Americans had realized it.

I think that all Europeans are thankful for the existence of Russia, if only because of our apprehension over Germany. This is equally difficult for Americans to understand—the fact that we wouldn't like to see Russia abolished, not at all.

N: *I'd like to discuss a totally different area—education. You are well acquainted with American colleges and universities through your frequent lectures. How would you appraise our standards of higher education?*

TOYNBEE: I would say that the American student is more spoon-fed to begin with, than the British or continental European student is. The British student is made to feel that he's got to put himself to work by the time he's reached the university stage. The professor is a consultant, not a schoolmaster. There is a sharp distinction between the schoolmaster who dictates, so to speak, and the university professor who advises. You're expected to come of age at a British university, and it's your own responsibility to educate yourself with advice from the professors, but without spoon-feeding.

In America, it seems to me, the teacher-pupil relationship has been extended into the university much farther. But I think there are serious efforts being made to change this. During the last few months of my last visit, I was at a very new college at Sarasota, Florida—only a hundred or so students in its first year. The intent of this new college is to adopt the European system of making the students stand on their own feet more, making them do their own work and be responsible for it. No credit system. The students are examined after a year or three years, and the results will be on their heads. If they haven't worked, that will be too bad. They will have to take the consequences. I think this is rather good. One ought to learn at the university stage to be intellectually independent.

But there is such a wide variety of American colleges that one oversimplifies by generalizing. This is a strength of American education.

N: *How do you find the curriculum balance—or imbalance—between the technical side and the humanities?*

TOYNBEE: Well, the emphasis on technology is another defect, to my way of thinking, in American education, but this is going on all over the world. I'm prejudiced on the side of the humanities, yet the emphasis on the technical side was bound to increase. A century ago, technology and science had no position in the university, and it's only right that they should gain a position.

But they shouldn't push the humanities so far to the wall. Unfortunately, science and technology stand for power, especially military power, so it's rather simpleminded to think that they can be denied dominance in the curriculum. Yet, because as far as technology and science are concerned, the human race is gifted and successful, whereas in our human relations we are extremely unsuccessful, I think we should equalize things a bit. We have a natural genius for technology. We have to be *taught* humanity.

But this isn't especially American; it's worldwide. In Egypt a few years ago, I visited a new university in upper Egypt where they were concentrating almost exclusively on their scientific and technological faculties and were letting the humanities take care of themselves. I'd have done it the other way around.

N: *Do you think students today can find educational opportunities comparable to those made available to the young Englishman of your generation?*

TOYNBEE: The more widely education is spread, the more difficult it is to keep the personal relationship between faculty and students. In my generation, those relationships were very close at Oxford, but the number of students was very small. Enrollment was limited to a privileged small class, people who could either pay the fees or win scholarships—as I did—against very fierce competition. I think this was wrong.

On the other hand, when you get universities the size of the University of London or some of the colleges in New York or California, or the American Midwest, it's very hard to maintain personal relations. The administrative machine seems to take hold and get between the students and the professor. This does take away part of the value of an education.

But I don't know what the cure is either. I suppose you should try to break up the huge universities into human-size units, perhaps smaller colleges, to restore the personal relationships. But this would require the recruitment of enormous faculties, and the trouble is, we can't raise a new crop of professors as quickly as we can raise a new crop of students. In this generation, everyone wants to be a student, but it takes a whole generation to educate professors.

Yet we mustn't yield to the temptation of mechanizing education by

laying on lectures with public-address systems. This is really destroying the purpose of education.

N: *Did you pay attention to the Berkeley affair at the University of
California? What were your impressions?*

TOYNBEE: It looked to me as if the administration was rather out of
touch with the faculty as well as with the students, which can happen at
very large universities. The thing oughtn't to have arisen. It seemed that
they revived some old regulation and announced that it would be in
force again and perhaps hadn't considered the possible effects.

Now, there's a lot to be said for and against students' taking a part in
active politics, especially on the campus; in fact, it's a sign of bad times
when students do become restless and political. It's important that
people raise their voices to protest against inequity, but when other
people won't, and the students and professors are left to do it, this is
better than if no one did it. Of course, they should do it in as objective
and orderly a way as possible; but, being young, students tend to be a
bit boisterous.

N: *What books would you include on a list for high-school students to read?*

TOYNBEE: One very recent book I would include is *The Rise of the
West* by William MacNeill, professor at the University of Chicago. *The
Rise of the West* is too narrow a title; it is really the history of the world,
taking in all different civilizations, all the way through from the
beginning. It is a college-level book, but I think the better students of
high-school age can take it all right.

Also, a very, very good history by Samuel Eliot Morison of Harvard
[*Oxford History of the American People*] has just come out. This is really a
first-rate book, amusing and interesting, as well as full of information.
Again it is rather big and solid, but I think a good high-school student
could tackle and get a lot out of it.

What I am getting at, of course, is the comprehensive book, not the
specialized book. Probably there are shorter and smaller books that are
good that I don't know much about.

N: *You have visited America a number of times and resided in several parts
of the country for rather extended periods. Could you give us your impressions of
American women?*

TOYNBEE: I think that most women of most countries would regard
the American woman with envy as a privileged person. She has more of
the national income in her pocketbook to spend than the woman of any
other country. Some years ago, I was at Houston, Texas, staying at a
residential hotel. There were seventeen widows of oil kings living in that
hotel. A short time before that I had been in Australia, and I thought
how an Australian oil king would laugh at the idea of seventeen rich

widows. He'd say, "I'm not going to work myself to death in order to leave a fortune for her to spend."

In a sense, women are the dominant sex in America. They have money to spend; their clubs are strong and are centers of eager activity. At the same time, I think American women are very brave; they manage to bring up their children, run their house and, at the same time, partake in all sorts of outside activities. They are more ambitious about these outside activities than women in other countries, and a large number of married women are in some kind of profession, as well as taking part in these outside activities and minding their homes. And when one is entertained in their homes and sees the elaborate dinners they serve — which no European woman would think of doing without help — one is *amazed*. American women have tremendous energy and spirit. They do more than a European woman would think possible for a wife and mother to tackle.

Do they do too much? I don't know how it is with their children. Children may suffer from mothers who carry on too many activities outside the home. It isn't that the mothers don't do what is necessary for the child, but I suppose there are children who need special attention that they don't get.

But we need women who go into public life.

N: *As far as women in American history are concerned, which do you find most influential?*

TOYNBEE: The first name that comes to mind is Eleanor Roosevelt, of course; she was truly outstanding. But there are many, many others; in fact, it's striking, the part women have played in America. I don't know when their strong role began — when they got their independence, so to speak. They didn't get the vote particulary early; but then, a woman doesn't need the vote in order to be a force in life and destiny.

Women's movements of various kinds have been important in all stages of your history, haven't they? Some unwise movements, included. I suppose the prohibition movement was largely a woman's effort. They tried to force something on men that men weren't ready to accept. But Harriet Beecher Stowe, the little woman who made the big war, did have a great influence upon American history. Of all women, I suppose she is the Churchill of American history. And in education and social welfare, one is struck by one great woman after another, like Jane Addams.

N: *If you were to live in America, what area or city would you prefer to make your residence?*

TOYNBEE: I couldn't live in New York. I would die of exhaustion in the first few days. People say that if you live there, it's not so exhausting, that it's bad when you come in for a few days of business — so maybe I've caught the pace at its worst.

Washington is a beautiful city, but I wouldn't like to have to work there every summer.

I have lived for several months at a time at Princeton, New Jersey, which has great advantages. It is easily accessible to New York, Philadelphia, and Washington; it's a beautiful city, and the people who live there are friendly and nice.

I fell in love with Denver, Colorado, last fall. The climate is beautiful, and the people are kind and sunny, as warmhearted as the sunshine they get in the fall. I think I could live there quite happily.

I shouldn't want to live in the Old South. It's so backward-looking and can't even forget the War Between the States. Seriously — some place like Princeton, New Jersey, is where I'd be inclined to live.

N: *If you had your life to live over again, are there any dramatic changes you'd make?*

TOYNBEE: No, I'd live it the same way. I'm devoted to history, and I'd be an historian again. But with the knowledge from my present life in my mind, I think I would have broadened the base of my education. I wouldn't have given up mathematics so early. Of course, I wouldn't have wished to be brought into practical life by two world wars, though I am grateful for having been forced by these wars to do some administration, to have taken time for temporary government service. This was valuable; the historian saw history being made in action, instead of looking at it from the outside. But I wouldn't wish to have gained that experience at the price of wars.

But — I'm an historian, and I'd be it again.

N: *Now here's a big question: If you were to give a lecture to a large American audience, what is the most important message you would like to put across?*

TOYNBEE: That the American people, together with the Russian people, constitute only 15 percent of the world's population, but since things are not equal, you have 90 percent of the power in your hands. This places a great responsibility on your shoulders. It's rather an unwelcome and even annoying responsibility to know that you are accountable not just to yourselves but to the rest of the world — but there it is.

The Presidential election in America is a *world* event. You talk about a World Series in baseball, but the Presidential election really *is* a World Series. The whole world realizes now that its fate hangs on the election, and it takes the same degree of interest as the American electorate takes.

In a way, this is annoying for the American people, but just to be annoyed at it is, I think, the wrong reaction. I think the right reaction would be to realize that although this wasn't what Americans thought was going to come to them, this is the situation they're in, and they have this responsibility toward the world. America possesses enormous power, and power brings responsibility with it.

I'd say these same things to the Russians, and I'd say to the older generation in both nations: Be sorry and concerned for the younger generation, because it's the young people, now in or just out of the universities, who are going to have to take on, as electors, the big life-and-death decisions for the world.

I would also say this: Don't think that because the scale of life is now so large, and everything is so highly mechanized, and it's so difficult to know the facts, because the facts are so complicated and often secret — don't think that it is no good being a citizen, that you might as well not vote, that you might as well take no part in political affairs.

It is very important in all countries, especially in those countries that have a democratic tradition, that the individual citizen should feel that he does count, that he has responsibility, that he does make a difference by exerting his pressure on the government. This is his duty.

These are some of the things that I'd say to the American people, whom I love.

"I would like [my books] to be associated, in however humble a way, with all the traditional fairy tales. I couldn't ask for more."

P. L. Travers

P. L. Travers

TRAVERS: I can quote Blake: "My mother bore in the southern wild"—in the north of Australia. It happened that my father was Irish, my mother of Scottish and Irish descent, though Australian born. They went to live in the north of Australia, but they brought their own Celtic "aura," so to speak, with them.

N: *But you went to England at a rather young age?*

TRAVERS: I was eighteen when I came to England, a rather grown-up woman. All my life, because I had been brought up by a father who was a very poetic Irishman, it seemed nothing but Ireland would do. Everything around us was Irish. If we had a servant, it was an Irish one; if we had a horse, it had an Irish name and an Irish pedigree. The lace for our clothes was bought from Ireland, and I grew up and was nurtured on "the Celtic twilight," Yeats and all. Therefore, Australia never seemed to be the place where I wanted to be.

But back in Australia I was educated, for a time, by governesses, then attended private school.

N: *Did you begin writing when you were a child?*

TRAVERS: I can't remember a time when I didn't write, but then, I never called it "writing." It never seemed important in that sense. I thought of it more as listening, then putting down what I heard. Nobody in my family called it writing; in fact, nobody was very pleased or proud. I feel that was rather a good thing for me because I was never made to feel that I was anything special.

Actually, I had two loves when I was a child. Writing seemed to me a part of daily life, but my real love was the stage. I began writing poems when I was very young and told stories to the rest of the children in my family, but that was just like breathing. The things I really wanted to do were all connected with the theater, and in my boarding school I used to write the school plays and act in them and produce them.

Then one day a real director happened to attend my school, and he said, "I want a child who will play in my production of *A Midsummer Night's Dream* and she must be small and round and have a good voice."

The headmistress showed him around and said, "We have lots of children here and one who is rather good at acting; let's have a look at her." So he watched me running across the playground and said, "That one will do." So that was my first real part, that of Bottom, when I was about ten.

This director offered to take me and train me for the stage, but this was quite impossible in my kind of family at that time—shocking, in fact—so I had to wait until I grew up before I returned to the stage. I began in Shakespearean companies, playing all sorts of parts and gaining all sorts of experience, much against my family's wishes. All this time I was writing. Then, while I was still touring, I happened to meet a young man who was a journalist on a newspaper and I showed him an article. (Very shyly; I didn't think much of it.) He brought this to his editor who sent for me and said, "Have you any more pieces like this?" and I said, "No, I haven't, but I could do some more." He said, "All you can do I will buy and I will give you five pounds for each of them."

Then it occurred to me to try to do something with my poems, so I showed these to a rather good literary paper and they were taken, too. I never set out to be a writer, but after these blushes of success there was nothing else I could do. Oddly, back in Australia, I always felt reluctant to judge my bits of success. *They* praised my poems and *they* liked my writing, but how can *they* judge? I'm afraid I felt that way about Australia, that there was nobody who could be quite sure, and consequently I couldn't be quite sure.

So I saved money, deciding quite secretly that I would save enough money by my writing and by the acting I was doing at the same time, to go to England. And I did. I came to England with ten pounds in my pocket—two five pound notes, one of which was immediately stolen by someone. So there I was, fresh in England with five pounds to my name. I had to get a job immediately, and luck was with me, for I picked up a journalistic job. It paid enough to keep me going, and I went on with my own writing, tackling comparatively challenging articles and poems which were soon being published in the English papers.

I then decided that I would like to go to see my father's people in Ireland. I don't know whether you've heard of him, but a great contemporary of W. B. Yeats was the poet Æ, [George William Russell], a poet and editor, actually. I wrote to Æ, having been brought up on him and Yeats by my father, and sent him a poem, but without a covering letter. I was rather proud in those days; I wanted the poem to stand on its own feet. I sent a stamped envelope for its return, but shortly I got back a check for two guineas. Two guineas was quite a lot then, but I was more thrilled by the letter that came from Æ saying, "I accept your poem. If you have any more, I'm pretty sure I will accept those. I have a strong suspicion that you are Irish; if you are, and if you are ever coming to Ireland, will you come to see me?" He was wonderful to young people.

So I went to Ireland and saw Æ in his wonderful great room in Marion Square, the room he had painted with all sorts of mythological figures. He talked to me about literature and made all sorts of suggestions regarding my work and said, "I know you're going on now, to stay with your uncle in the south of Ireland. On your way back to London come and see me again." Well, I stayed with my family and met all my Irish people and on the way back I thought, "Oh, so great a man, I can't disturb him; I'm sure he was only being polite." I was too shy to knock at his door again, so I went on back to London without seeing him.

A few days later I got a letter from him and he said, "By this time you should be back in London, and I believe you just bypassed me. I'm coming to London and I will come to see you." In a few days he stood at my door with all his books under his arm, signed and dedicated, and a friendship began which became a very great thing in my life.

N: *How did Mary Poppins enter the picture?*

TRAVERS: That is a long story. And I'm asked the question so often. Especially here in the United States.

N: *We're nosy.*

TRAVERS: No, you're not nosy, but you ask questions that take me back to a period when I was too young and too inexperienced to answer. I used to put people off by saying, "I'm not sure how I came to think of Mary Poppins."

I think the only possible answer, even now, must be put this way: Hendrik Willem Van Loon became a friend; I can't remember how I met him, but I remember once when he invited me to luncheon, and during luncheon he was busy drawing some elephants for me on the back of a menu. He always drew things on the backs of menus. Anyway, he was drawing elephants and I said, "You know, people are always asking me how I came to think of Mary Poppins and I just don't know. I don't know how to answer them." And he went on drawing with his head down. He was silent for a moment and then he shrugged his shoulders and said, "Doesn't interest me; doesn't interest me at all."

After having been asked about Mary Poppins by so many people, I was a bit peeved and said, "Not at all?" Van Loon said, "No, not at all. What interests me is how Mary Poppins came to think of you," and he handed me a little drawing of dancing elephants. Suddenly something came clear to me, and this belief has stayed with me ever since. Perhaps ideas go hunting for people, for writers. You see, I never felt that Mary Poppins had very much to do with me. I've never been able to puff out my chest and swagger and say, "I did this." I've never felt any pride of possession.

While we're on this subject, when children ask me, "Where did you get that idea?" I throw the question back to them by saying, "Where does anybody get an idea? Where do you get an idea that you want candy, a new penknife, that you'd like to go for a walk or see a particular friend?" And they always say that they don't know where those ideas come from.

Well, I don't know where ideas come from either; I never know where I get an idea for a poem or a story. I have the attitude, the feeling, I had as a child: It is not so much inventing as listening. I think that Mary Poppins just fell into me at a time when I was particularly open, and I'm grateful that she did.

N: Mary Poppins, *for which you are so extremely well-known, has become a classic for children. What distinction do you draw between children's literature and literature for adults?*

TRAVERS: I don't think there's any such thing as a children's book. I think all books are children's books or, to put it the other way, all books are grown-up's books. I dislike the distinction very much. People come to me and say, "Tell us the secret; how do you write for children?" I have to say that I don't know because I don't write for children.

You may remember Beatrix Potter saying, "I write to please myself." This is exactly the way I write. I never have children in mind. I never have grown-ups in mind.

But I do have a listener present — inside me, I think — and if that person is pleased or moved or amused then I assume someone else will be. Often, when I'm at the typewriter putting things down, I laugh at something I see on the paper. The thought strikes me, "Now, how did she think of that?" Then I realize that the "she" is myself.

N: *Then you resent the distinction?*

TRAVERS: I don't exactly resent it; that isn't a word I would normally use. But I really think that books usually classified as children's books, those that have lasted, have always been books that grown-ups liked, too. Even nursery rhymes, you know, are very grown-up.

Now, *Mary Poppins* has been in the world a comparatively long time. Therefore, people who read it as children, and are now quite grown-up, will write to me at both levels. For example, "You won't remember that I wrote you a fan letter when I was a child and told you how much the books amused me and how I wanted to reread and reread," or, "Ah, now

I see what you really meant." It isn't that *Mary Poppins* is written on several levels. I didn't hide anything in it. There has been no deliberation, no inventiveness, in that sense. It's the recording technique again, though I do see that it is a book on various levels. You can take it absolutely on the surface or you can take it with some underneath meaning.

N: *You mention letters—*

TRAVERS: They're so important. To begin with, one is pleased to get them, pleased to hear that someone has enjoyed. Yet the letters I like best are those that have some criticism in them. The most critical ones are nearly always from boys. Sometimes people are surprised to learn that boys read *Mary Poppins*, but remember, boys take as large a part in fairy tales as girls. Boys are apt to give me a new slant on the books themselves.

For instance, after the third *Mary Poppins* you will remember that she goes away for good. There are five *Mary Poppins* books, but the last two are supposed to have taken place while she was down there visiting the Banks family. Well, after the third one a little boy wrote me a very touching letter. It began: "Madum: I have just finished reading *Mary Poppins Opens the Door*. She has gone away. Did you know? You are awful. You shouldn't have done that. You have made the children cry." A marvelous letter, really, because there was such praise in that reproach. So I wrote back, "I'm not surprised that you cried. I cried bitterly. My typewriter was rained with tears when I was writing it."

I wonder if writers would go on writing if they didn't hear from people. It's the only tangible proof you have that they're reading and enjoying your work.

N: *Do you feel an obligation to the audience you presume you're reaching?*

TRAVERS: Absolutely not. I would be immobile if I thought I had an audience waiting. I would be terrified at the thought of people waiting; I don't think it's a suitable obligation for a writer to have.

The writer's only obligation is to the idea he has. He must be as truthful as possible, as faithful to the idea, but it would be inhibiting to think of any real or imaginary reader. I can't imagine working this way.

N: *This is an offbeat question, but I wonder if you could define the very special lyric gift so many Irish writers seem to have.*

TRAVERS: I think "lyric" is absolutely the right word; it's a word I use very often. The Irish are lyricists; contrary to this is their lack of success as epic writers. It's the caught, quick moment, the flash of a wind going past, kissing the joy as it flies. I can't tell you why, but it seems essentially part of the Irish temperament. People have asked me why I don't write one long story or one long poem, and I know it simply isn't in me. The emotion comes quickly, like a rush of water or the bubbling of a spring, and then it's finished. There's never a broad, rolling river.

I have to have the end come fairly close to the beginning. That may be Irish, but don't forget that there is a great deal of lyricism in lyric poetry in English literature, and that they are capable of the epic, in addition, which we are not.

N: *I'd like to turn to* Mary Poppins *as a movie now, the most highly regarded motion picture Walt Disney has turned out in many years. How do you react to seeing your own product on the screen?*

TRAVERS: When I first saw the film I had an emotional shock. I don't quite know where it sprang from. I was deeply disturbed and had to ask myself, "Am I so identified with Mary Poppins?" Well, I know myself *not* to be identified with her; I don't feel that she is me or part of me. I don't feel that I invented her. She's one of those joys that do fly and brush you as they pass. So I don't feel that was what disturbed me. I think I was disturbed at seeing it so externalized, so oversimplified, so generalized. Not vulgarized, really; it isn't exactly that. The movie hasn't simplicity; it has simplification. I think that *Mary Poppins* needs a subtle reader, in many respects, to grasp all its implications, and I understand that these cannot be translated in terms of the film.

I went out to Hollywood probably, oh, bound to a promise made to myself, if you like, that I would feel that the book hadn't got onto the screen. I was intellectually prepared for a jar, but even so it was a shock —and I don't mean a shock of disappointment. Parts of the film, those that refer to the human family, are not exactly like my story, but it seems to me that the dramatic shape that the Disney writers have made is viable. Yet I can't understand why—with five books of imaginative ideas to choose from—the writers or the director should have had to introduce a quite different sort of fantasy, a fantasy on a totally new level.

The film, to me, falls into two halves, and the halves don't entirely blend. I'm not saying that I'm against the film; it's charmingly acted. Julie Andrews gives a beautifully understated performance; she's very great indeed. And there is a lovely performance by an English actor, David Tomlinson, in the part of the papa, that pleased me. The little children are very good, too.

I'm bound to say that Mr. Disney has been faithful in all of his promises to me. He agreed to my suggestion that it should be put into the Edwardian period. I wanted that because I thought that if it were to be a timeless tale, it could not have a contemporary look. It would soon seem old-fashioned, but a period would be recognized as a period a hundred years from now. It would still be Edwardian and retain its freshness. Anyway, Mr. Disney agreed to this and faithfully carried out his promise. He also agreed that there should be no love affair for Mary Poppins. I knew this would be difficult for him because most musical comedies thrive on love affairs, but he was faithful in this matter, too.

However, I don't think it was at all necessary to increase the fantasy. The whole point of *Mary Poppins* is the fact that she's a down-to-earth and very solid person, serious and even commonplace, and it's from this character that the fantastic things spring. To my point of view the fantastic things must be rooted in something that's of an everyday nature. But in the film there are long sequences of pop tunes in which the human figures mix with the cartoon characters. I know that Mr. Disney is essentially a cartoonist and that one of his cherished dreams is to mix human and cartoon characters to create a new art form. I think many people like this, but I feel that it rather breaks the film in two, that it would be even funnier and more like *Mary Poppins* if the cartooned figures, such as the dancing penguins and the racehorses, had been real. There's a scene where Mary Poppins rides a race with cartooned racehorses and says to one of the riders, "Will you let me by, please?" and of course they let her by because she is Mary Poppins. Imagine if they had used real horses and real riders, how much funnier it would have been. The incongruity would have been immense.

At the same time, in spite of the introduction of what, to me, are extraneous measures, I think there is enough of the spirit of Mary Poppins in the film to persuade people to want to know more about her by reading the books. The film is splendid in its own right and deserves the success it is having, yet I hope, in the end, that its effect will be to bring more people to the books.

N: *In looking at the creative world today what do you most admire? Conversely, what do you most deplore?*

TRAVERS: Heavens, what a question. If you don't mind I'd rather look at the world in general, and not creative activity specifically; they do rather come together in the end, don't they? I think I most admire today's young people; mind you, this is what most people deplore. I think the young, if they would only realize it, have been born into a wonderful world in which they are made very important. Too important, really. But I wish I could be young in this period. The generation that is growing up, children and adolescents, seem just wonderful. So full of life and so unafraid. I'm always hearing bad things about them and reading startling things in newspapers, but when I meet them I always find that they are a new and beautiful race. Perhaps it's because I'm getting older that they seem so beautiful, but I don't think that's quite the case.

Children today are so much freer than I ever was. They're not so downtrodden by grown-ups. It was a grown-up world I was born into, and now children get born into a world of their own. I think that what I most deplore is the fact that grown-ups seem to have rather less place in it. Perhaps that isn't altogether true; perhaps I should state it differently. I do deplore the declining grandmothers. It's a small subject, at first glance, but actually it's quite a large one. For instance, I was told today that certain American parents are so anxious to keep children away from the notion of old age and sickness and sadness that they keep them away from their grandparents.

Remember, when the Buddha was a young man his father kept him away from everything that was not sublimely beautiful; he was hemmed in, in the walls of the palace with nothing but beautiful wives and dancing girls. All life was to be lovely, and the king, his father, would let him see nothing else. One night the young Buddha said to his servant, "Disguise me. I'm going out beyond these walls." And he went out and met with old age, with sickness, and with death, three of the most real things there are. And from then on the Buddha cast aside the other things.

We do such harm to children if we don't let them know the realities of life. It's my idea that it should be every woman's aim to be a grandmother; I don't mean necessarily a physical grandmother, but an ancient, a crone, who's gathered up all her experiences, the stories and tales and traditions, and is there at hand, like a full cup, when the children want her. It's the grandmothers who tell the stories, you know.

The great sorrow in my childhood is the fact that my grandmothers had passed on before I was born. And don't forget, childhood is a sorrowful time; people think it's so wonderful, the best years of life, but they're wrong. Childhood is sorrowful or at least it was sorrowful before it became so cushioned. Even now, children don't have money; everybody who is adult is right and they are wrong; they don't know that the minor disasters in their lives will have an ending in fact and in memory. They are like an occupied country with the adults being the occupiers. But to get back to grandmothers: I was always wanting somebody who could tell me the answers — who I was, why was I born, how did I get born? Ordinary childhood questions, but important ones. I wanted the important answers, but the grown-ups around me were disappointing in their answers and I came to the conclusion that they didn't know, either. I used to feel, "Oh, if I only had a grandmother, she would know all these things." This is why I think grandmothers are so very useful. They ought to be able to be there in the background, waiting for children's questions such as I asked. They are the carriers of tradition, and we lose them at our peril. They are carrying the thread. A child sees where he comes from and gathers, to some extent, an idea of where he is going.

In somewhat the same context I'm sorry that the fairy tale is so very much out of fashion. Not long ago I went to a very famous library, and in the children's section I noticed that there were no fairy tales. I asked the librarian if she had any Grimms' and she said, "Yes, we do, but they're in a separate room." And there was a little room filled with fairy tales. I said, "Why are they separate?" and she said, "Parents really don't like to have their children read fairy tales and we only give them to children when they're specifically requested. Parents feel that fairy tales encourage wishful thinking."

I thought about this for a while. I don't like the phrase "wishful thinking." It's a phony phrase. And I wondered if those parents had ever thought of what trials and tribulations and tasks and labors the fairy-tale heroes go through before they get to the "happily ever after." If children could go through such trials they'd be entitled to get what they wished for. Fairy tales do not give something for nothing. They require the most tremendous labors before the reward is granted.

N: *This is a personal question, but why do you use the initials P. L. instead of your full name?*

TRAVERS: From a desire for anonymity—and this isn't humility. Perhaps it's backhanded pride.

The poems I've liked best are those signed "Anonymous." In a sense, these poems have something very special about them, as though they're written by the same person. Frankly, I think of my work as the work of an anonym.

I have always wanted to be as anonymous as possible. I'm rather shy of publicity; it pulls me out of my socket. It makes me feel disjointed, so I've felt that if I just used initials nobody would know whether I was a man or a woman, a dog or a tiger. I could hide from view, like a bat on the underside of a branch. I thought too, that if I signed myself as a woman, people would feel that the *Mary Poppins* books were sentimental books, and this was the last thing I wanted. Few people wondered what Milne's A. A. stood for, or Yeats' W. B. Yet everybody wants to plunge into my secret world and find out what those two initials mean. They mean simply, "Don't come in. Stay out!"

N: *If you were to project a century ahead, how would you like to have the works of P. L. Travers regarded?*

TRAVERS: I would like them to be associated, in however humble a way, with all of the traditional fairy tales. I couldn't ask for more. I've never felt that an author matters. I've never felt that the person behind the book is the thing to search for. Of course it's true that sometimes, after reading a book, I've fallen so in love with the person behind it that I thought I'd like to meet him.

I don't think that children, if left to themselves, feel that there is an author behind a book, a somebody who wrote it. Grown-ups have fostered this quotient of identity, particularly teachers. Write a letter to your favorite author and so forth. When I was a child I never realized that there were authors behind books. Books were there as living things, with identities of their own.

Not very long ago a young man came to interview me who had said rather breathlessly on the phone, "I read your books when I was a child," and I said, "Well, good; now you know what to ask me and what we can talk about." He came into the room and took both my hands in his and said, "I'm so glad you're alive; all these years I've been thinking you were dead." And you know, I could have embraced him because I was so delighted he had thought I was dead. I had gone into the world of timelessness. All authors are dead. Blake said, "The authors are in eternity," and that's where I'd like to go.

"Every creative person who attained fame and freedom did so in the historic literary way — by sitting in a lonely room for ceaseless lonely hours, and sweating and cursing and writing word after word, sentence after sentence, alone.... The most glamorous, brilliant, prestigious authors still sit by themselves with their tortured psyches and numbed fingers and write and labor under conditions resembling solitary confinement."

Irving Wallace

Irving Wallace

WALLACE: I was born in Chicago, but when I was a year and a half old my father moved us to Kenosha, Wisconsin, about fifty miles north of Chicago. Kenosha is a lovely place to have been from, and I say that in the nicest way. It's great until you're seventeen or eighteen, and then, if you have any creative bent at all, you have to get away. Kenosha didn't even have a bookstore in those days, though it did have stationery shops that sold a few books. My father ran a clothing store—they called it a general store then.

Ben Hecht, you know, was reared in Racine, right above Kenosha. An odd thing—and a bit of a digression. My wife comes from New York City; she was a magazine editor and she ran into a good deal of anti-Semitism as a rising young career girl in New York, and when she met me, she simply couldn't understand that I hadn't ever encountered any anti-Semitism during my Midwestern upbringing. I told her it had not existed in Kenosha, at least among people I knew. My closest friends had been Italian, Polish, Lithuanian, German, Swedish, and anti-Semitism did not exist. My wife always believed that my memory of those days was faulty. But years later, I read Ben Hecht's memoirs— he'd been raised ten miles from where I had been raised—and he made the statement that not until he had left Racine and gone on to Chicago had he encountered anti-Semitism for the first time. This confirmed my remembrance of times past.

Perhaps this condition existed because a great segment of my hometown population was composed of immigrants who had come over in the same period and were, so to speak, in the same boat. They were segregated from the old settler native population to some extent, but because they were a minority with common problems, they didn't segregate within their group. (I haven't thought about this before; it would make an interesting sociological study.) I attended high school in Kenosha. I was a debater—the negative side, naturally—at Kenosha Central High. I was ranked by the National Forensic League as one of the top ten debaters in the country, and I won a fantastic number of writing contests on the prep-school level. As a result of the debating and journalism contests, I was offered six or seven different college scholar-ships—Wisconsin, Northwestern, Ripon, Drake, I recall—but I didn't take any of them because I wanted to get away from the Midwest. So after I took my first big trip away from home at the age of eighteen—it was an expedition down through Mexico, Central America, part of South America—I accepted a scholarship from a little college in Berkeley, California, called the Williams Institute.

Williams was an attractive school, a sort of avante garde writing college with a psychiatric-oriented approach to creativity. I mean, you started in the morning sitting at a desk and doing stream-of-conscious-ness writing. But the accent was on control and marketing stories. This was in the mid-thirties, and the guest lecturers were well-known and stimulating personalities such as Alfred Korzybski, the father of seman-tics, and even young William Saroyan lectured there just after he'd done *The Daring Young Man on the Flying Trapeze.*

Why Williams Institute? It was a geographic change, far from home. It was an odd school, unorthodox. Above all, it had strong courses for writers. You see, my parents were not literary people at all. They read in a limited way only, but they had respect for literature. Unlike the parents of many of my friends, they were the only ones who encouraged their son to become a writer. In other words, most of my friends who wanted to write met nothing but parental resistance. "Make a living from telling stories? Ridiculous!" Writing as a vocation was a foolish, impractical indulgence that you either got over with early or that you did on the side after you had become a lawyer or a dentist. But my parents—especially my mother, who had been raised on Tolstoy's *Anna Karenina* and similar novels—was very romantic about writing and encouraged me. So I was permitted, when I was dead broke and my parents had to support me, to keep on making up stories. This went on because even when I went to college I didn't have money. And even when my future was bleakest (I had an aunt who kept saying, "Writing, sure, but what do you do for a living?"), my parents continued to believe that writing was a wonderful, honorable, even sensible profession; and their attitude was a great thing for me.

While I attended college, I wrote free-lance fiction and nonfiction for magazines, worked late into every night, but I simply couldn't make enough eating money, and my parents kept sending small amounts because they were as determined as I was that I should be an author. (I repeat, this is not the story I usually hear from others. I have friends who are in analysis today—men who started out to be writers, but could not overcome family resistance, and who were thereafter forced into becoming businessmen or some other damn thing, which may be fine, but it wasn't what they wanted; and in the end, their inner conflicts landed them on the couch.) But as I said, my parents gave me an extremely lucky break. They were an up-and-down family. My father would make a lot of money (I don't mean in the really big sense) and then he'd become very careless with it and be flat broke a few years later. But up or down, they always were for me. Today, they're pleased at what has happened to me (they keep my books on display in their dining room), and they read the reviews, though not *all* the reviews. (I see to that.)

After comparing early youths with friends I've decided that I would not trade my Kenosha boyhood for any other anywhere else on earth. Kenosha was a wonderful, easy, rural place. And for a while it was intellectually stimulating — we had a good group of young men interested in the same things: books, ideas, sports, girls. I've only been back to where I came from once, and that was on my honeymoon in 1941. I took my wife there for two hours. She was dismayed, New Yorker that she was. I'm not sure she'd ever seen a farmer or cow or one-hotel town before. She simply couldn't understand this sort of small-town Main Street community, this end of the world. But to me it was beautiful. Yet, I haven't been back since — though I want to return, because somehow I'm always writing about it, in little ways, and I'd like to go back and recapture more of the past, and (hopefully) find Thomas Wolfe wrong. I still correspond erratically with several of my high-school teachers, and I feel close to my Midwestern roots in many respects, so I suppose I'll chance it and go back one day.

But let's return to Berkeley. I got restless in school. You couldn't smoke in class; you had to listen to too many dreary lectures on the theory of writing when you were already being published and dying to get off on your own and have whole gobs of days not to listen but to tell, to storytell. I was actually selling then to magazines, earning from $5.00 to $25.00 occasionally, from lesser periodicals like *All-American Sports, Thrilling Detective, Modern Mechanics, American Farm Youth, Current Psychology*. Also, I was doing the obligatory adolescent-author thing, writing cynical imitative Hemingway or impressionistic short fiction about encounters with prostitutes, with Life, for the little magazines and having them deservedly rejected. Anyway, I became restless, revolted against student discipline, and decided I could learn and progress on my own much faster and better, so I quit college when I received an offer to do a series of magazine interviews with movie personalities.

The idea of going down to Los Angeles sounded very glamorous to me, and I had a large number of relatives on my mother's side living there (so I knew I would not starve), and at last I went down to Southern California and resumed going to school another year (at Los Angeles City College) while I did the interviews and wrote plays for little theaters on the side and had several love affairs, all the while feeling very adult, at last.

Anyway, I've devoted all of my work time to writing ever since, never ever having any other vocation. I think I began serious writing when I was eight or nine (I've noticed, in your interviews, how many others started with words and drawings at those ages. My daughter was doing this even earlier; now she's nine and writes wonderfully imaginative yet controlled stories) and at thirteen I began submitting to magazines and at fifteen I sold my first article to a turf periodical for $5.00. In Los Angeles, I continued to free-lance (I'd never met an agent, editor, or been to New York; it was all through the mail) and I tried, also, to sell to the movies—novelettes, you know, that are called "film originals" or "treatments." Failing all the time, in all areas of writing, until I was twenty-two.

My wife recently went through the things we save—and we seem to save everything—and she found three cartons of rejection slips—*cartons*, mind you. She said, "If people who say you made it overnight or that you were simply lucky could see this, they'd be stunned." I can remember one summer day in Kenosha when I received fifteen rejection slips in a single mail.

In any event, I finally achieved publication in the better magazines in 1938. I sold political articles to *Ken*—one on the Vatican's fight against the Nazis, another on Hitler's takeover of Memel, that little slice of land near Estonia. But it was not until 1940, after I had gone on my own to Japan and China, that I really began to be accepted regularly by national magazines. I did numerous stories for *Liberty* magazine, which was one of the "big three" weekly periodicals and widely read in those days. I ghostwrote articles for a variety of entertainment, sporting world, and political figures—W. C. Fields, Jim Thorpe, Kid McCoy, President Camacho of Mexico, many more. Above all, I wrote articles on offbeat personalities and places under my own by-line. Many of these were published in *Esquire, Coronet, Pageant, American Legion*, and similar periodicals. Then, in 1945, and the years immediately following, I began to appear in the biggest popular magazines—*Saturday Evening Post, Cosmopolitan, Collier's, Reader's Digest*.

Now, almost all of this was nonfiction. I did write short stories and some were published, but I was never successful with them; I felt terribly hampered by the length and the necessity to adhere to formula, and I had a tendency to get gimmicky or tricky. But I became quite good at doing the articles, particularly the profiles of people I'd met—because I am persistently curious about and fascinated by human beings.

In 1941 I was married in Santa Barbara, California. After the war, and after three and a half years in the service as an enlisted man, I was honorably discharged. My wife, Sylvia, quit her editorial job and we went to Europe for a year. I had a number of assignments that led to some of the best stories I've done. A number of these are included now in *The Sunday Gentleman*, which is about to be published.

N: *I wanted to ask you about the content of that book, and the rather enigmatic title.*

WALLACE: Well, I must have had over five hundred articles published during those years and it has bothered me that a number of those pieces have been lost. I mean, I felt some of the best of them deserved to appear in book form, be brought to life again. For example, an article I once wrote for *Saturday Evening Post*. I think it was one of the last articles I did before I turned to motion pictures and resumed writing books. I called it, "They Cut Away His Conscience," and the magazine called it "Operation of the Last Resort." It was the case history of a prefrontal lobotomy patient whom I knew, what happened to this Princeton genius who became a serious depressive, then suicidal, and to save himself tried everything from faith healing and psychiatry to shock treatments. The young man's story was a wild and touching adventure. His life was really the Odyssey as if it had been written by Kafka. The case history was complex and fascinating. I had to learn all about the subject before and after his lobotomy, and I had to learn all about this brain surgery that alters a human being's personality so drastically. It ran as a double-length feature in the *Post*, in 1951, and its appearance provoked one of the greatest reader responses in the magazine's history. The letters were unbelievable, really. Strangers would write and ask, "Should we give our daughter a lobotomy?" or castigate me and say, "No scalpel should be allowed to tamper with God's handiwork." The letters were a cross-section of the intelligence and sensitivity, the blindness and utter stupidity, of Man.

Well, I always felt that this piece, along with others, should be in book form; so I took about nine published stories that I felt stood up over the years, and added eleven more that had never been published for reasons of censorship, editorial prejudice, or because they were too unusual to fit into commercial magazine formula, and I gathered these together as a book. But the idea of a paste-up collection did not appeal to me. So I began to write in 1963. I partially or fully rewrote every piece —but then, as I worked, I began to wonder what had happened to the

subject of every article since I had first done it. What had happened to
the prefrontal lobotomy patient since 1951? What had happened to the
two most fabulous and notorious bordello madams in American history,
the Everleigh sisters, since the time I knew them, when they were
posing as New York socialites? What had happened to the Nobel Prize
judge in literature who had told me he loved Hitler and who had never
heard of James Joyce? I suddenly determined to find out. So during
1964, I did a sort of detective job, located each subject, traced the person
up to the present, and then wrote a series of detailed, highly personal
postscripts to each chapter—sometimes the postscripts are longer than
the original articles—bringing each story up to date.

I did many other things, too. I told how exciting the life of a magazine writer can be. I also told how shabby and mean and dishonest an
existence it can be. And I also told how many of my magazine
adventures planted the seeds for some of my future novels.

The title, *The Sunday Gentleman*, goes back to the seventeenth
century, the day of Daniel Defoe. At that time, if you were in financial
trouble and threatened with debtor's prison, you could be arrested any
day of the week but one—the only day you were exempt from arrest
was Sunday—so on Sunday you could emerge from hiding, immune
from arrest, and safely go out and appear as a gentleman. Defoe,
bankrupt, was such a Sunday gentleman in Bristol for a period. Well, I
related that to my magazine years. Six days a week I used to write what
I had to write to support my family and keep myself from our modern
version of debtor's prison. But on Sundays I took off, I wrote as I
pleased entirely, and could appear in my own eyes as a literary
gentleman. And many of these stories are in *The Sunday Gentleman*.

Now, as I have said, my novels have grown, or parts of them have
grown, out of the trips I took and the people and places I encountered in
the course of magazine assignments. *The Prize* grew out of that first trip
to Scandinavia and Europe in 1946 and 1947—I spent almost two
months in Stockholm, got the idea for the novel, although it was fifteen
years before I actually found the approach, the freedom, to undertake
writing it.

Oddly enough, I finally became involved with motion pictures
because they didn't know what to do with me in the Army. I had been
living in or near the Hollywood section of Los Angeles all those years,
and I had never gone near a studio after that first little monkey business
with original treatments, so after I enlisted in the Army they asked my
profession and I said, "Writer," and instead of making me a cook, as
might have been expected, they placed me in a documentary film unit
called The First Motion Picture Unit of the Army Air Force.

The conditions were schizophrenic because all of us had to live and behave as soldiers, yet we were stationed in the old Hal Roach Studio in Culver City and were ordered to perform as disciplined writers. Some very successful writers were in our group—Norman Krasna, Robert Carson, Jerome Chodorov come to mind. Our job was to write training movies about flying—I would be given an assignment like, "How To Fly Lazy Eights." Well, for me it was madness, because I don't fly (I have a phobia about airplanes; I've only flown three times in my life), so I wasn't of much use to the Air Force. But then the Army learned that I had been one of the last correspondents out of Japan before Pearl Harbor, and I was transferred to the Signal Corps Photographic Center where they were having trouble with an orientation film called, "Know Your Enemy Japan." Colonel Frank Capra was heading this unit elsewhere in Los Angeles, and I went with that outfit two and one-half years more (as a corporal) working with remarkable talents such as John Huston, Ted Geisel who is Dr. Seuss, and others.

Eventually, I wound up on Long Island with another Signal Corps photographic unit just before the group dissolved—William Saroyan, Irwin Shaw, John Cheever, a great many fine writers were there when I was there. Anyway, I learned about scenario-writing in the Army, because they taught a prose writer how to create movie scripts, how to be visual, write for the camera eye, dramatize.

After my discharge from the service, I was offered screenwriting jobs, but I turned them down to take my magazine trips to Europe. But magazine writing was always a financial struggle, and when Warner Brothers offered me an assignment at $750 a week—this was in 1948—I was glad to accept it. That was and is an awful lot of money. At that time, you worked seemingly forever on a magazine piece to make that much, and at the studio you'd get it every Friday. No one was ever happier to be seduced. Besides, being creative visually seemed a challenge.

N: *What movies did you work on?*

WALLACE: I've drawn a veil over that. Although, I did write a few very good movies. But from 1948 until 1957, off and on, I worked on salary in every major studio at least once. I'd never had a Social Security number until I was at Warner Brothers, where I worked many times. The first picture I was assigned to was a big one starring James Cagney and Doris Day—*The West Point Story*. I was sent to West Point twice to obtain factual background; that was interesting because I was doing what was familiar. At the start, I guess I was really excited about the movie medium—not just the money, but the creative form fascinated me. I studied the form. I wanted to become a great movie writer, but it fast became apparent, after two scripts, that this could never be. I'm a loner. One of my highest values is independence, freedom to do as I please. In the studios, writing by committee appalled me. I just can't work with other people, so then my work in Hollywood became a long battle to get out of what I'd got into. I had given up magazines. I had a family now, son and daughter. I had to start somewhere else or go insane, and so I began writing books at night, after eight hours at the studio, and I tried to write books between jobs and on weekends. It was rough.

Actually, I had always written books. I had a passion about books, reading them, touching them, collecting them, the freedom to write as one pleased which they promised. I wrote them in my adolescence, in my twenties, in my thirties, in dozens of strange places and lonely rooms, in my spare hours. I wrote five full books, perhaps twice as many half-finished ones, before I was thirty, and while I sometimes received encouragement, all my efforts were rejected. Temporarily, I gave up. But when I was thirty-seven, and determined to counteract my unhappiness in the movie studios and determined to escape and be on my own, I went back to books.

I started with nonfiction, my love at the time, and it's hard, as you know, to make a living in nonfiction books. You have to teach and write them on the side, or have a wealthy wife and write them on the side. Otherwise you will starve. Alfred A. Knopf was my publisher, and he brought out my first three biographies. We did fairly well, actually — two of the hard-covers sold ten to twelve thousand copies, and the third was a Literary Guild choice of which Knopf kept half the money. The second of these, *The Square Pegs*, briefly made the best-seller lists, and the third, *The Fabulous Showman*, sold three hundred thousand in the book club, or some damn figure like that.

But this wasn't a living in the way I had been living when I wrote for films, or even magazines. In fact, one might do better as a grocery store manager or executive secretary. I had spent more on researching and writing time on those three books than I had made from them.

I'll go back a bit. In 1953 I determined to write books, and eventually nothing else — I remember the time well because one of my best friends died then, and it grieved me that this young man, who was a wonderful magazine short-story writer and always meant to write novels, had died at thirty-two and had not written those books, and didn't have a book he could leave behind. I think this tragic event was one of several that helped push me over the literary edge; otherwise, I might never have been able to summon up the courage to leave the relative safety of a salaried studio life.

My first book advance was $1,000 from Knopf for *The Fabulous Originals*, a collective biography of real people who inspired enduring characters of classical fiction (as the real Delphine Delamare inspired Flaubert to create Emma Bovary). I can't tell you how many years went into that $1,000 advance. Eventually, I earned a little more in royalties from that first book, but not much more. (I had to keep on in movies. It's hard to turn your back on steady income when suddenly there's a son and a daughter as well as a wife. There is responsibility and maturity. You have to live with your family, and your family has to live with you — and depend on you.)

Then, *The Square Pegs*. I turned down some film assignments to do this second one, which was not easy, but I burned to write a book about nonconformity and eccentricity in America. Then I wrote a novel. I did ten television shows first to support myself while I wrote that novel, *The Sins of Philip Fleming*, about a hero who suffers temporary impotency while having an affair. I didn't pull it off, but I think I could today. I was too fearful of the novel form. Perhaps I'd been scared by Tolstoy, Flaubert, Balzac at an early age. My standards, demands on self, were so high, it inhibited me when I wrote. The novel was published, after a half dozen rejections, but sank without a trace, until recently, when it has been rather popular in American paperback, and in English and Italian editions. Anyway, I went back to nonfiction to do *The Fabulous Showman* on Phineas T. Barnum, the book club selection; and then, feeling I'd had my first dip in the novel and feeling more confident and brimming with characters and an idea that obsessed me, I wrote *The Chapman Report*.

To my surprise, that one was an overnight success, as you know, an international best seller; but instead of capitalizing on it by writing another novel, I went back for another turn at nonfiction, *The Twenty-Seventh Wife*. Everyone around me was appalled. There I was, plunging into Mormonism, attempting to recreate American polygamy in a scholarly way, and publishing people saying to me, "Can't you make it fiction instead? As a historical novel it could be another best seller and you could sell it to movies." But it was too delicious a thing, having all the fascinating true material that would have been diluted in fiction. As my literary agent, Paul R. Reynolds, always said, "If you have fact that reads like fiction, stick to fact, for as fiction it would be unbelievable." That long-lost material about Brigham Young's multiple wives was so rich that it had to be done my way — even if the commercial prospects were poorer, which they were.

N: *Before we leave your nonfiction, I'd like to ask you if you've been conscious of specific obligations or objectives in your work in that area.*

WALLACE: I don't really know if I can answer your question, but I'll try. The only strain of similarity in my first three books is that they all involved unusual or offbeat persons. *The Fabulous Originals* presented real people who inspired great characters of fiction. Who was the real Sherlock Holmes? Who was the real Robinson Crusoe? Camille? Marie Roget? I tried to search behind the classical characters of fiction and locate the once-living prototypes. It was quite a sleuthing job, but it was intriguing to discover these little-known people and try to bring them back to life and show how authors had drawn upon the living to develop fictional heroes and heroines.

The Square Pegs dealt with eccentric Americans who had been forgotten by our history books. You know, against-the-grain people like Victoria Woodhull, who managed a Wall Street stock brokerage and ran for President in the late nineteenth century. To me, these were important people whose nonconformity had given American culture irritants it sorely needed, people time has erased, for the most part unfairly. Phineas T. Barnum was quite another matter. There had been some fine books published on Barnum, including an excellent one by Werner. But these dealt largely with his public career, and only hinted that he had a private life. So I went after his private life like a hungry tiger. I wanted to find out what Barnum was like as a human being—not just the superficial aspects, his public life, but the *whole* man. I had a hell of a time finding what was missing, but almost at the last moment, when I was ready to give up, I came upon the key portions of his very private life. I found out that he'd had two wives—this had never been published in any biography. I learned that one of his daughters was cut out of his will for having love affairs, and that he himself had been an alcoholic who'd gone through all sorts of secret horrors. Plus a lot of other facts I found new and meaningful. These things interested me and motivated *The Fabulous Showman*.

Does any of this answer your question?

N: *No. Once you have this material, do you feel any obligation to it in creating the book?*

WALLACE: Your basic obligation is to be true to your material, honest, stick to fact, and not romanticize. Unless, of course, you are writing a fictionalized biography or historical novel, where known facts are rounded out with thoughts and scenes you feel are logically in character and might have occurred. But here you are usually working in an area where only the skeleton of a life is known, but where all else that gives the skeleton flesh must be a matter of surmise.

When you are writing really factual books, as I was, the point is to dig up important information that has not been used before, to supplement what is known. But the validity of facts is questionable after a long period of time has passed. Here is a new and illuminating anecdote about Lincoln or Napoleon or Brigham Young. What is the source? Should you accept a sensational disclosure at face value and use it to enhance the readability of your biography, when three other sources which seem closer to the subject, and more reliable, don't mention it? Or did the three suppress it because they were *too* close to the subject? You have to evaluate these factors very carefully, apply all the intelligence, perception, and knowledge you can, and fight down the desire to accept the most exciting fact rather than the one that might be more accurate.

I was truly interested in trying to resurrect people who were dead and neglected, reviving long-buried facets of personality so that the subject could be seen more completely. I'm extremely proud of *The Twenty-Seventh Wife* because Ann Eliza Young, Brigham's last polygamous wife (who revolted against the harem and helped end multiple marriage in America) was absolutely dead in history. I had to dig and dig and dig to resurrect her. There were none of the primary sources normally available to the writer-historian. I researched thoroughly and soundly, and I believe I came up with a valid and balanced biography. The reviews were highly favorable everywhere. The only really bad review I got was from the big Mormon newspaper in Salt Lake City; the Mormon authorities, touchy about the old polygamy, were upset by the book. Rather, some of them were. I received many interesting letters from hard-core Mormons who enjoyed it. Yet, apparently the officials of the Mormon Church condoned publication of a silly, angry book called *Sounding Brass* (a selection of a Mormon book club) by a Brigham Young University professor last year — a work devoted largely to dissecting *The Twenty-Seventh Wife* from the point of view of the orthodox Mormon line and its dogma, possibly to straighten out readers who may have been led astray by This Monster.

The other obligation of the nonfiction writer is to write interestingly, to try to be a storyteller within the boundaries of his fact-finding. You know, W. Somerset Maugham once said that a book is incomplete until it has a reader. I agree. A book that is unreadable, does not hold the reader, should not have been written or published. A book, fact or fiction, must be honest above all, and after that it must communicate, grip, entrance someone else. Otherwise it has no reason to exist, beyond the author's self-indulgence and vanity. It takes not one but two to make a book: the writer *and* the reader.

N: *I'd like to turn to your novels, now. Did* The Chapman Report *follow directly in the wake of the Kinsey report in the sense of capitalizing on it? I read somewhere that you wondered what would happen to the community after a team of Kinsey researchers came through.*

WALLACE: That absolutely isn't true at all. When the novel's publication and its film sale were announced in advance, we were actually threatened with an injunction and possible lawsuit by the late Dr. Kinsey's Institute in Indiana. The law offices of Morris Ernst were retained by the Kinsey team to learn if the novel was libelous. Before the novel was available, the Kinsey team, agitated by publicity about it, wanted to read it, and they threatened Simon and Schuster and the Darryl F. Zanuck Company with an injunction. It was all very serious; there were some bad weeks, but I was able to prove that the novel was based on neither Dr. Kinsey nor his investigators.

In any case, that is *not* how I got the idea. For a number of years, I'd had the notion of writing a novel about the married or once-married young women who live in my community, Brentwood, the West Los Angeles area.

It is an upper-middle class residential area. The women's husbands have money, and the women have too much leisure and too few hopeful dreams. I used to meet them at parties. Some were acquaintances, some were friends, and a lot of these young ladies told me about themselves and their husbands and lovers. These were women who had thought that marital and financial security would make life perfect, and when they had both, they were surprised at their restlessness and unhappiness. Well, I always have been fascinated by what goes on behind closed doors — the doors of houses, rooms, minds — what goes on behind the facade and the obvious, and here, first-hand, was marvelous, dramatic material. For ten years before that, you know, we'd had a flood of novels about suburbia (although mostly about the Eastern suburbs) and even though I wanted to write this particular book, I didn't want to create just another one to follow the worn pattern. Anybody can follow footsteps. But even if you impose your own unique point of view, the story itself won't be compelling because the approach you are using, the backdrop and platform for your characters, won't be that different.

So there I was, with this rich material and no way to use it, no unique storyteller's framework to make it exciting for me. Well, one afternoon I was reading galley proofs on the Barnum biography in the study outside my house. I had recently read several articles in newspaper supplements based on sociological surveys of women's sex lives, and I guess something had lodged inside my head. For, as I started pacing back and forth, thinking of my women again, I suddenly stopped and said to myself, "My God, what if a couple of sociologists came into Los Angeles and interviewed the young women I've been talking to for an official sex survey?" I had the texts and reports Dickinson, Kinsey, several others had published, but I'd never read them or paid any attention to them, so I went to the books to see how they conducted their surveys—not to get their statistics, but to see how they went at it, their procedures. Then I wrote down a list of the names of the women I knew who had talked to me over the years, and alongside their names described them and their problems in detail. After that I cut off the real names and threw them away. I then combined the various true case histories and superimposed imagination and invention, and then began to create a fictional frame for my women. I did this to make the novel more plausible, because some of the actual material I had was unbelievable. Parallel to my creation of characters and plot I began to learn how the sex survey operation worked under university and government grants. I studied over thirty of them, found their methods, studied the statistics they contained so that any statistics I might make up would not be widely at variance with reality. From then on, I just wrote the book.

In memory, the writing of *The Chapman Report* does not seem to have been as difficult as novels I've worked on since. But the passage of time often blots out pain. I suppose it was difficult when I was writing it. This was only my second novel, remember, and my first had been a failure; but fortunately I was really fired up and I wrote it in a great sustained burst. Then I was overwhelmed by what happened afterward, because until then my books had not been successful, least of all my first novel which had been considerably more candid about sexual matters, and I thought those things, all the facets of success, would never happen to me. Or, at least, not with this book. The only straw in the wind was the size of the advance against royalties from Simon and Schuster. I didn't know that an advance on a novel could be over $4,000. It could and was. Then my motion picture agent made advance copies of the manuscript and submitted them to various studios and independent producers and overnight there were nine bidders. I had never been through an experience like this. It was heady. Everybody, it seemed, wanted *The Chapman Report*, and the book wasn't even out yet. The money from my publisher had partially liberated me. The money from the studio and foreign publishers liberated me entirely. I could now afford to do anything I wanted to do as a ﹍ author—and all I wanted to do was to write books, nothing but books, write books full-time. Then the novel came out and my first experience of success was intensified, because *The Chapman Report* seemed to be everywhere, written about, talked about, and it became such a worldwide best seller that I was literally dizzied by the excitement.

N: *What were your reactions to the fuss stirred up by* The Chapman Report?

WALLACE: When it first began, I was quite pleased that anyone paid any attention to the book. Don't let pretentious literary talk fool you into believing that writers just write for themselves. Writing for yourself alone is creative masturbation. We do write to please ourselves, but basically we write to be read. Writing is not only a means of self-expression and catharsis, it is also a compulsive form of egotistical and infantile exhibitionism. So being singled out as one of the few authors among the twenty to thirty thousand to be published that year meant a book of mine might have readers in great numbers for the first time, and I was thrilled. I would have an audience. They might want to read more of my stories. *The Chapman Report* appeared and, as I have said, was doing wonderfully well. Reviews were good, reviews were bad. Margaret Meade defended the novel in a public quote, which was thrilling; Elizabeth Taylor and Jacqueline Kennedy read it, which was gratifying; and the Kinsey lawsuit had been withdrawn. Then, for an author enjoying his first success, a terrible thing happened.

My wife and I had celebrated by going to Europe, taking the children. I was in Rome, walking with the family on the Via Veneto, when a new issue of *Time* magazine came out. I picked up the thing, turned to the book section, and came upon this clever but cheap gimmick about the non-book, a book supposedly invented by the publisher and assigned to a writer to develop on order, a prefabricated commercial product. There were a number of examples given, and my book was one of them. I repeat, it was clever, no matter how dishonest, of *Time* to have dreamt it up, for the label caught on and has never ceased being bandied about.

The Big Lie trailed me around for some years, and was elaborated upon: that publishers or film producers gave me ideas for novels, that I manufactured my books on order, that I had a formula for unliterary best sellers. When Malcolm Cowley and Colin Wilson perpetuated the myth, I wrote them the facts and received their private apologies. But it is difficult to stop a lie entirely. A reader will write me, distressed, that a Brooklyn library will not stock my novels because they are prefabricated. An English teacher in my son's high school will tell her class, and my son, that my novels are not creative and should not be read.

Even more recently, I read a piece in *The Saturday Review*, a piece by Kubly, a recognized nonfiction writer but an unsuccessful fiction writer, in which he mentioned me, along with several other authors, and claimed that we sat with film producers over Bloody Marys and concocted books for the movie factories. He was a too-willing victim of the Big Lie, perhaps because of his own frustrations, and he never bothered to find out the truth. Nor did *The Saturday Review*, and thousands of more readers, librarians, professors were deceived. I wrote Kubly a letter that I never mailed and probably won't, though I may publish it one day in a book collection of unmailed letters. In any event, it was all utterly stupid or dishonest. Those people who write about books and authors don't know anything about what really goes on. And *Time* knew the least. If my publisher had enough creative talent to conceive and develop *The Chapman Report*, I suspect he'd cease publishing and start writing. If a formula existed by which a successful novel could be manufactured, authors who possessed it would not have so many failures following their successes, and they would not have suffered so many years to achieve independence. I cabled a correction to *Time* from Rome; they ran half of my cable, and said underneath it, in one line, something to this effect: "We stand by our sources." Whatever their so-called sources, the story was a complete falsehood, and since I anticipated that a sensational story like that would be picked up all over the country, I was deeply disturbed. It was by far the worst single incident that happened regarding this novel.

Now, I was not very concerned about the mixed reviews, because there were so many good and interesting ones — even if they, too, picked on the fact that the novel leaned too heavily on overt sex. That didn't upset me. I objected to the misrepresentations contained in other items that were written. But there is no way to answer back — all you can do is try to forget it, and write another book — yet the past follows you into the present, and old lies often drown out the sounds of your new words in your new book. Even with *The Man* I've had my personal motivations questioned rather than the book itself judged as a creative effort. It is unreasonable and unfortunate, but I understand it now. A collage of old clippings present a certain image of the author, and although distorted and misshapen, the old image cannot easily be removed. Sometimes, I suppose, there is even a certain justification for this image because of the way a novelist handles himself, or the way his book promotion is handled, but mostly the image is accepted because of the natural resentment generated by anyone who is successful and whose integrity is suspect. Although any image at all may be better than being faceless — having your books ignored — still, you are human, you suffer small agonies, especially if you're sensitive about attacks on your personal motives, which I am.

However, I'm not sensitive about honest reviews. If an unbiased reviewer really reads a book he's assigned to read, and doesn't like it, well and good. You've offered your creative work for judgment. It is judged. The verdict must be accepted without complaint. The only thing I do object to, and strongly, is when they start reviewing me, the author as a person. The private life of an author should not be related to the book he writes, nor should his motivations, drives, the mystic feelings that made him undertake the book. How can the reviewer know about these? Usually the author, himself, doesn't. Reviewers don't know me, and even if they did, what does their specific knowledge of me have to do with the book I have completed? The book should stand alone, with a life of its own without me. After I'm dead nobody will remember me, but here and there one of my books will be around — and somewhere, someday, some interested reader may read one of the news pieces that inaccurately reviewed me instead of the book, and make unwarranted prejudgment, and ignore the book. That's the ultimate unfairness of it.

N: *Then came* The Prize —

WALLACE: Actually, *The Three Sirens* was supposed to come next, but I was scared off writing it by all this controversy. I'm ashamed to admit it now, but it's true. I really was upset. After I paid my income tax and my publishers took half my subsidiary income and my agents had their percentages, I had little money in the bank, and I had behind me a successful book I was suppose not to have created, a book I was supposed to have filled with sex for commercial reasons — and the ill effects of a frightful emotional reaction. So, though I had *The Three Sirens* outlined, I turned away from it. I knew the major characters very well, I knew the story, I knew what I wanted to say about our society, I was eager to go ahead, yet I was afraid to write another novel right then that dealt primarily and forthrightly with love and sex.

At the same time, I had always wanted to write *The Prize* but I had never known how to do it. Over the years, I'd had many approaches. Contrived ones. Like taking a group of Nobel prizewinners to Stockholm on one plane, and the plane crashes in East Germany where the refugee physicist laureate is wanted, and how, through their ingenuity, the winners save him and reach Stockholm safely. All wrong. I approached the subject this way and other ways, but all the while I was avoiding the real story. Then suddenly I told myself, "The only way to write this novel is to write about what really happens to those who give the award and those who receive it," but I was scared of tackling it head-on. It was too complex and challenging, and the canvas was awesome.

The Chapman Report didn't compare to it in scope, of what you have to know or imagine. But I had been living with the hero of *The Prize* for years, and several other characters, and two Nobel judges in Stockholm somewhat based on fact, and I finally got up the guts to undertake the book. Once into it, I was so committed that it became the only reality in my life.

You see, I originally had the idea for *The Prize* in Stockholm, fifteen years before, when I was interviewing a Swede who was trying to impress me with his importance. He was not very interesting, and I wasn't impressed at all until he told me that he was an official Nobel judge who voted annually on the literary and physics prizes. I became excited, and forgot about the interview I was after (we were discussing Swedish science) and I said, "What happens when you vote for a Nobel winner? How do you do it? What do you mean, you're a judge? How did you become one?" He began to talk, candidly, and then I hurried back to the Grand Hotel and made loads of notes. I asked to see him again about the Nobel awards, and I boned up on the Nobel Prize background, and then went back to him and acquired some marvelous material. He, in turn, sent me to other Nobel judges, so by the time I was through, I had an incredible amount of inside background, but I didn't know how to handle it for a novel.

When I put aside *Sirens* and decided I was going to try *The Prize*, I went back to Stockholm in 1960; this is what I did with my hero in the novel, having him see Stockholm in two different periods. I could be quite accurate about that. This is how *The Prize* came to be. When I finished that book, while I could never make it all I hoped it would be, I was proud of it. Then the news magazines appeared with the first reviews. Again, I was stunned. They had been so antagonized by *The Chapman Report*, that they treated *The Prize* as no more than an extension of the other novel. But highly favorable reviews on *The Prize* began coming in from all over the country. The book sold extremely well in hardback, and the paperback reprint keeps going on and on, and I continue to receive wonderful letters from students, housewives, professional people. By my own standards, I felt that it was the best writing I had done to that date.

N: *Then*, The Three Sirens. *Did you do it next?*

WALLACE: Yes. Now there was a new me, so to speak. I felt secure because of the way *The Prize* had been accepted in every nation. No fuss about Kinsey, non-books, or anything else, and though the book had sex in it, the story was about something else, and sex was never an issue. *The Prize* was a far greater success than *Chapman*. I had the confidence, finally, to say to myself, "To hell with those few critics and the news magazines. I'm going to continue writing exactly what I want to write, and I'm not going to rest until I finish *The Three Sirens*." In a sense, that may have been a mistake. I don't think so, but some people feel it is the long-range literary image a novelist builds that matters. And many friends felt that by going back to a sex-oriented subject, I was retarding my building of a new image. What happened was this. A lot of reviewers who did not like *Chapman* had forgiven me for it after *The Prize*, because they enjoyed the latter book so much. But when I undertook *The Three Sirens*, they felt I had let them down, reverted to writing about sex for commercial reasons (which was anything but true), and many reviewers were disappointed in me and some were angry.

Still, I'm glad that I wrote *The Three Sirens* because I wanted to say those things and develop those characters, bring them to life, and get it all out of my system. But in terms of my career, the timing was off. Ideally, that book should have followed *Chapman*.

N: *Now for* The Man. *And if you don't mind, I'd like to go into both the genesis of the novel, and also into some of the financial aspects that caused such a confused hue and cry.*

WALLACE: Let me just ramble on about *The Man* and perhaps both of your questions will be answered. Genesis: I've always been an active liberal, with a fierce belief in equality under the law and civil rights. I don't mean that I join anything, but I constantly feel that I want to write about a national or international human issue about which I feel deeply. I'm sure most of us have felt pain, alarm, even horror, about this whole Negro situation in America, the scandalous plight of the "second-class citizen," and at least twice I wanted to write novels about it. But you just don't write novels about a subject, you write them about people. Twice, in the last seven or eight years, I've had ideas for novels that dealt with American Negroes, with Negroes and whites in social and political contact, but each time I realized that though the ideas could convey my feelings, the ideas really weren't good novels. They were ordinary. Other writers, especially Negro ones, had said the same things before, and better than I could. And I didn't want to write a mammoth tract or pamphlet. (I'm ruthless with myself before I undertake a novel, commit myself to one. I know that once I become involved in writing a novel, I have to live with it for a long, long time, it has to become my entire life, it has to draw upon my feelings and imaginings and intellect, and it would be hell to be tied to a novel that you discovered, after a year, you didn't want to do, after all.)

Normally, a book gestates inside me for some time—the way *The Prize* did. (I have a dozen ideas for novels I've been thinking about, making notes on, for at least as many years.) But *The Man* just came to me, and when it came I knew it was right. The characters were there. A fresh approach to the whole subject was there. Every major ingredient of the book came early. This was important, for when you have a strikingly unusual idea to superimpose upon your characters, there's always a danger that you'll get into trouble in the last part of the book, because the idea begins to dominate the characters, suffocate them, so that the characters can't evolve through the novel naturally, and you are left with an overwhelming idea that can't be resolved in the end.

I knew from the first day I began working on *The Man*, that I wanted it to end with an impeachment trial. The characters were heading that way. The trial seemed as vital as my opening idea. And also, an impeachment trial appealed to my sense of theatrics. And I had my Negro President, Douglass Dilman, whole, right away. I got him while I was sitting in the dining room one Saturday night, reading, and I can't explain how he got there. But suddenly there he was, a Negro President, and I jumped up and went into the kitchen to tell my wife and son about him. They were equally enthusiastic. Then my wife said, "It's a great idea; it should be done, if you can make it plausible. But how can you do it right now? You're planning to do the other novel." She was referring to an international novel I'd been preparing for over a year. But I was so highly charged by *The Man* in its initial concept that I began making voluminous notes that night, and went right on making notes for days—loads of them. There were countless stumbling blocks. The numerous characters who surrounded Dilman must not be completely overshadowed by him. The necessity to root the story in reality, make the reader suspend disbelief. Unless it could be made believable, it would be pointless. But I do think I eventually succeeded in that, because I believed it all from the start, and still do. The modern impeachment trial before the Senate was another problem. Was it too big and improbable? Would it throw the novel out of balance? Would it impede the whole movement of the characters? But I thought: No, the characters are logically moving into that climax and it is a dramatic means of bringing the story to a head. So I searched and I obtained transcripts of actual impeachments in our history—there have been many, you know, since President Andrew Johnson was acquitted by one vote. I had a librarian duplicating the trial records and sending them to me to study. I examined the Johnson impeachment minutes against the modern ones. I found the procedures similar, and once these were set in my mind, I knew what I could do, could not do, and I had to discard some fictional ideas I had planned to use. So here I was with notes, outlines, some of the research completed. What happened then?

I went to Europe. I had to go to conclude research on the previous international novel I'd been working on. But insistently *The Man* took

over. At last I put the other novel aside and gave over all my energies to
The Man. I buried myself in research books, deluged government
officials and Negro leaders with inquiries by mail, interviewed well-
known people and little-known people, experts and bystanders. And the
minute I reached Europe, I began to write biographies of my characters,
and bits and pieces of scenes that came to mind. A large amount of the
novel, in separate parts, was done that summer. While I was in Europe,
I told my literary agent to advise my publisher what I was up to. And
Peter Schwed, Vice-President of Simon and Schuster, even though
probably uncertain about the commercial potential of such a novel, said
he loved it, thought it was a wonderful idea, and that if I felt I could
manage it that was enough for him. He wanted a contract for it right
away, and I signed one. I told him how much I had written, but I added,
"I prefer not to reveal or show a word of it until it is completed." I told
him I would have to go to Washington, D.C., to see activity in the
White House firsthand before I started writing chronologically.

You mentioned the financial aspects of *The Man* which you say
caused such "a hue and cry." That came next. When I returned to New
York from France in 1963, I had a meeting with the heads of Simon and
Schuster, and Schwed said, "As you know, we announced in *Publishers'
Weekly* that we are going to publish your new book, and we released the
title and a paragraph about the idea. There was a great response to the
announcement. Five or six major paperback companies want to buy the
reprint rights this minute, sight unseen." I was surprised, because I
didn't know anyone could make a blind offer on what I hoped would be
a major novel. I said, "I'm not sure I want a reprint commitment yet.
You know, I'm not going to show them anything I've written or
planned. I haven't shown you, and I'm not about to show them.
Frankly, I think it would be wiser for me to finish the novel first."
Someone from Simon and Schuster said, "We don't feel that is necessary, Irving. You have no idea how determined those reprinters are to
have the book. They're willing to gamble. They are betting on you, on
your writing record, on the unique idea behind *The Man*. Look, we have
nothing to lose. Let us go out and ask a certain advance, and if we can
get that advance we'll all be happy, so what's the difference?" So I said,
"Fine, do it your way, go ahead." Then I remember someone saying,
"Now all we know about the novel is this short publicity release, and
that is all the paperback companies have seen to date. Is there anything
more you'd want them to see?" I glanced at the release and said, "This is
fine." It was next to nothing. It said I was preparing a dramatic novel
about a Negro senator who, by accident, becomes President of the
United States to fill an unexpired term. That, and no more. Suddenly,

because the cryptic announcement offended my sense of thoroughness (and fairness), I said, "Wait. Give me an hour to write another page, expanding what you have. I still won't give away a great deal, but it'll let the paperback people know it is a whole book I'm working on."

I'm relating what actually happened. But this is the way, to the best of my memory, it was told in *Life* magazine: "Wallace went up to his hotel room and knocked out a few pages and made a deal for the biggest reprint advance in history." Well, I did go up to my hotel room in the Plaza, and I did take the publisher's release and expand it to not quite two pages (not even mentioning the impeachment trial as the climax of my novel). The implication in *Life*, however, was that I merely put down an idea that had come to my head in a few minutes on a few pages and made a mint. It was made to sound almost mad and frivolous, on my part, on the part of the publishers. But as you know, when I did those two pages, somewhat reluctantly, I had already been on *The Man* for months and had written much of it and had it all outlined. I simply have a phobia about anyone seeing any of my writing before a novel is done. I have never in my life shown any part of any novel I've been working on until the manuscript was completed, and then rewritten to my satisfaction. That's why, when anyone has been eager to contract for one of my novels in advance, I've always said they'd have to do so with knowledge of no more than the title and basic idea.

Anyway, I sent this two page memorandum back to Simon and Schuster; they made five or six copies and delivered them to the foremost reprinters who'd been after us like Dell, New American Library, Pocket Books, Fawcett, saying, "Here is a memorandum on Wallace's new book. Here is the minimum advance and royalty agreement we want. Give us a reply in seventy-two hours."

Then, without awaiting the outcome of the negotiations, I took the train to Washington, D.C., which represented the last link in my researches. The missing link had been my lack of insight into the Presidency. I had no firsthand experience of it, only a backlog of reading. I'd written Pierre Salinger from Rome of my need, and he invited me to the White House. Apparently not only Salinger, but some of the Kennedys knew my novels. When I met Salinger I told him I did not want to see the White House as a tourist or even newspaperman. I'd done that before. I was writing about a Negro President, inside him, and I had to know how it *felt* to be President. Salinger spoke to President Kennedy, and Kennedy, somewhat apprehensively (knowing of the controversy surrounding my earlier books, uncertain what I would do with this one) gave his generous approval. So for ten days I was in and out of the Oval Office, the private apartments where the

First Family lived, sitting where the President sat, observing and listening to what he saw and heard, watching him in action three times, interviewing his secretary, his Secret Service guards, soaking it all in. As I was leaving, Salinger wanted to know if I'd like to observe a Presidential junket firsthand. He said President Kennedy was going to Dallas in nine weeks, and I could meet up with the party there. I was tempted, but I didn't think I had need for such an experience in my book, and I was bursting to resume on the book as soon as possible, so I did not go to Dallas to see President Kennedy.

I returned to my home in Los Angeles. An hour after my return, I learned that the paperback reprint houses in New York had bid far more for *The Man* than Simon and Schuster had asked, and that Fawcett Crest Books had been the highest bidder. I remember Simon and Schuster's message to me: "The reprint terms for *The Man* have set a record and this is a tribute to everyone's faith in you. Nobody wants to see anymore about the book than you've already presented. Repeat, Fawcett took it on faith, as we did, and we all know it will be as good a novel as your others. It is a brilliant idea, the characters sound great, and we all are happy. Now finish it." I was delighted. But so was Simon and Schuster, and no wonder. Under their contract with me, they kept 50 percent of these reprint earnings (and when the novel was done, and became a Book-of-the-Month Club selection and a Reader's Digest Book Club choice, my publisher kept half of that money, too—a practice the general public knows little about when they read news stories of rich authors).

Now I locked myself in my study and continued writing *The Man*. The word is "continued," not "started." I worked mornings, afternoons, nights—no luncheons, no cocktails, almost no social engagements, and very little family, except on Sundays. For me, the clock had no hands. I had to do this novel. I was obsessed by it. As I once told someone, I was afraid I might die before it was finished. I felt that the body of work I left behind to represent my passage on earth, should include *The Man*.

Looking back, I can sort out two factors that apparently drove and inspired me. One was the Negro revolution, in full force by then. Wright, Baldwin, Ellison had been among the voices that impressed the revolution on whites. I felt I might supplement what they had done, as a white writer with a wide audience, as an author accepted as a storyteller, and that I might reach a whole segment of whites, readers of goodwill but with too much fear and not yet enough understanding, as yet unmoved by Negro writers, but who might be moved in a different way by *The Man*. And indeed, since, I have had so many whites come up to me, or send me letters saying, "I loved Dilman. I had so much sympathy for him, I forgot he was a Negro." All meant well, no matter how it sounds. But important because it also meant, perhaps for the first time in their lives, those readers, who had unconsciously considered black men inferiors, could now see that a Negro was like one of them, no different, a human being with similar fears, aspirations, problems, reactions, a Man like all men.

The second factor that spurred me on was my brief contact with President Kennedy and his Administration. I came away enormously stimulated by Kennedy and his team. (I've written about this experience in the last chapter of *The Sunday Gentleman*.) My God, I told myself, here was a President who read books, who was smart, steady, vibrant, and tempered gravity with natural humor. I'm not speaking this way because he's dead now. I'm a romanticist, but hell, I'm no sentimentalist. I can see through sham and hypocrisy and pretense as well as the next man. I was simply excited by Kennedy. He restored my belief in the Presidency and democratic government. While I had always been a Kennedy enthusiast, I had faltered once. Early in his Administration I'd had a moment of uncertainty, a slight impatience with what I thought were Kennedy defects: too little decisiveness, too much caution and compromise and committee, too much effort to please everyone. When I spoke of this one evening over drinks with Dr. Allan Nevins, a friend, a wise, objective human being and a great historian, he told me to wait. He told me this was the preliminary period, and this was JFK's tempo and style, and that he was sure Kennedy's second term would be memorable and touch upon greatness. I'm sure Nevins would have been proved correct. On the eve of his death, when I saw him in action, Kennedy was becoming his own man, and that was a lot of man. Anyway, my experience in the White House was something I could give to Dilman, my hero in *The Man*, and I tried.

There were starts and stops, all kinds of agonizing, but for the most, the novel poured out of me. The book was written, then rewritten, and rewritten again in first galleys and again in final page proofs. I'd never done that much revising; I kept changing and changing. My publisher was kind enough to let me do this, because it can be very expensive to reset final page proofs. But I wanted it right, and so did they. So there it is, how I wrote *The Man*, how publishers contracted for it; those are the facts, certain newspaper and news magazine accounts notwithstanding.

N: *Then there wasn't a movie deal tied in at the very beginning?*

WALLACE: God, no. On *The Man*? With all its commercial movie taboos? Anyone who says that knows nothing about the mentality of the bankers who finance movies. Like you, I read that nonsense about a pre-film deal somewhere, and I was quite fascinated because I hope there is a movie made of the book one day. It should be done by daring and creative persons. It could be unforgettable. About film rights—the moviemakers like to see possible properties early, in advance; they hate to wait for galleys or publication of a novel, which they feel is too easily available to all their competitors—or so my movie agent informs me. My Hollywood agent believes that once a novel is complete, and being readied for print by the publisher, copies of the manuscript should be shown in advance to a limited number of film studios and producers. I presume it is a sales technique, and not too unusual a one. He sent manuscript copies of *The Chapman Report* and *The Prize* to studios in advance of publication, and sold the movie rights. He tried the same with *The Man*. He ran into a wall, because here was a controversial subject, and from the point of view of commercial filmmakers, *really* controversial and dynamite. For book publishers—no problem. Authors write, and if it is good, they publish. But a motion picture costs a fortune to make and the risk is tremendous; and *The Man*—the mixture of Negroes and politics, both box office blights, some thought—seemed too dangerous. The major studios, conservative, were fearful of undertaking it themselves. Most of them were enthusiastic about *The Man*, but they wanted creative talent to underwrite their enthusiasm. If a successful star, director, independent producer said, "Let's do it, we must do it," the major studios would take the risk.

Right now, with the novel out and heading the best-seller lists, we have many talented movie people coming to us to discuss putting it on the screen. Sidney Poitier for one. He read it and contacted my agent. I don't know him but I admire him, and I was nervous because I wondered, "How will a sensitive Negro react to the book?" Fortunately, he loved it. He thought Dilman was a role he wanted to play. I don't know what will happen. I have confidence a movie of *The Man* will be made. I'd sell it for Confederate money, if the right people would transfer it to the screen honestly. I want it to be made so the story reaches vast audiences. We'll have to wait and see.

Note: At the time of this interview, movie rights had not yet been sold. Six months later, the movie rights to The Man *were acquired by an independent company, Joint Venture Productions of New York, the major stockholders being Sammy Davis, Jr., and Milton Greene. And they announced that Sidney Poitier would star in it.*

N: *How do you feel about the critical reaction to* The Man?

WALLACE: Sixty percent of the reviews were very good, 40 percent were mixed good and bad, or bad. The "money thing" seems to prevail to some extent in the unfavorable reviews, doesn't it? Unfortunately, publication of *The Man* was preceded by a *Life* magazine article on America's big money writers, which was strongly (and ridiculously) angled to show that a small group of popular novelists in this country become best sellers and make considerable income because they have evolved a formula. I was used as the case history in the article. Actually, for the most, the writer was kind to me; but the overall tone was damaging, and it impugned the sincerity and honesty of *The Man* and affected many reviewers, who referred to the talk of commercialism in the *Life* piece.

That kind of story hurts a book, because the story makes you unliterary. Coupling an author with his income is unliterary and dangerous for the author. Any other type of creative artist, on any level, can make all the money on earth, you know, and have it publicized — even Picasso, Giacometti, Stravinsky, Nureyev, Bernstein — and somehow it is all right. It doesn't tarnish the creativity of the artist. Money only proves his acceptance and value. He remains pure. But somehow, among the literary opinion makers, there is a strong feeling that a writer shouldn't make too much money or, if he does, it should be kept a dark secret. A novelist may possess other things — homosexuality, addiction to drugs, alcoholism, a predilection toward beating women — and somehow this is laudable and literary, and gives him cachet. But not money, the root of evil reviews.

You know, there is an old saying in the world of sports, that a hungry fighter is the best fighter. Perhaps this is true in pugilism because fighting is a form of savagery, of contained survival of the fittest. But creative writing has little to do with bashing another fellow's head in. Yet, as in sports, there exists a stupid literary tradition fostered by publishers, understandably, and by English professors, naïvely, that a hungry writer is the best writer — an empty stomach and slum dwelling being considered most conducive to good books, honest books, uncorrupted books. Revolting nonsense, I say. Why can a better novel be produced in a grimy attic than in a Riviera villa? Tolstoy and Flaubert did very well without attics or hunger pangs. The really hungry writer, I truly believe, is the one most susceptible to corruption and dishonesty, for he has a problem that must intrude upon his creativity. The problem is: he must eat. And to eat, he must often put aside writing as he pleases, to write potboilers for the marketplace, to write what he is told to write.

The writer who has money, enough or a lot, has to compromise with no one, do nothing he does not want to do. He can afford to write as he pleases. There are exceptions, of course. Hungry writers can survive on bread and water, by begging and stealing, and never compromise, and produce fine works. And financially secure writers can lose touch with life or repeat themselves because of a neurotic need for more and more wealth. But generally, I suggest, better books are written by men who have survived starvation, have bank accounts, and are beholden to no one. And in the end, I suspect, rich or poor has nothing to do with it; for if hunger is the driving force behind literary honesty, then the real writer is always hungry, a hunger in the mind, the heart, the conscience.

Another factor, too, has perhaps influenced some reviews of *The Man*. When you bring out a new book, the reception you receive often depends on who you are and what you've written before. A case in point —Mary McCarthy can do *The Group*, a novel very explicit about the sex act, and her novel will not be castigated for its sexuality because she has such a solid, long-established literary background built on learned essays, *Catholic Girlhood*, *Stones of Florence*. When she turns from this to a book weighted with sex, her critics are more likely than not to feel her use of sex was not a commercial one, spelled out to sell books, but an honest one in an enlightened time.

But when you've written controversial books that have handled sex with candor such as *The Chapman Report* and *The Three Sirens* and even, to a far lesser extent, *The Prize*, and these books have been successful, the critics are suspicious of any new novel you publish, no matter what the theme and are ready to consider it an effort tailor-made for sales and nothing else. I am sure if I had not written the other novels, had stayed with nonfiction, with biography, and then suddenly written *The Man* as my first novel, my critical reception would have been different, far more favorable.

While good reviews of *The Man* have outweighed the bad ones, the bad ones have troubled me more than reviews usually do because many have appeared in national publications which have millions of readers. What has troubled me about these mass-read reviews is that they are apt to stand between my book and many potential readers—readers who might really enjoy the book, but will never get to it, because "somewhere" they read it is another "commercial book" turned out through a "best-seller formula." Still, this may be a needless concern of mine. *The Man* is getting through to great numbers of readers, and these people are telling their friends that they like the book, and so their friends are reading it, and in the end, perhaps, it is not the critics but the public and its "word of mouth" that determines the fate of a published work.

As to my feelings about specific critical reactions to *The Man*, I don't mind citing a few book-reviewing customs that my writing friends and myself find particularly unreasonable. One is the practice of book review editors giving a new biography or novel to a specialist in the field which is covered by the new biography or novel. Although the author may have spent a decade producing his biography or novel, the specialist, who has funnel vision, may devote his entire review to pointing out a minor inaccuracy in the book (the better to show his own erudition) and ignore the book as a whole. In a small way, this happened to *The Man*. Several book review editors gave my novel to their Washington political correspondents to review, and these correspondents, to display their veteran knowledge of the capital city, devoted a large amount of their space to proving that so-and-so would not have worn an overcoat in Washington at that time of the year, and more of that sort of nonsense. Here was the too-familiar problem of specialists being allowed to review a book, men who were not interested in any overall novel but only in their own specialties, and so one has to endure a column of nitpicking rather than balanced criticism.

But far worse is the prevailing practice of giving a working novelist another man's novel to review. Here we have madness. The novelist as reviewer, and more often than not he is an unsuccessful or embittered one, has to be a saint, yes, superhuman, a man without impurity—all objectivity—to pass clear, cool judgment on another novelist's new book, especially if the new book comes from a widely read author. Most human beings possess the frailties of prejudice, envy, malice, competitiveness, and in novelists all these weaknesses are accentuated. Often, the worst reviews of novels are written by fellow novelists. Of course, that is not always so. A novelist named James Kelly, whom I've never met, wrote a highly favorable if critical review of *The Prize* for the *New York Times Book Review*. But this is rare. Usually the novelist-turned-reviewer is Madame Defarge with a vengeful pen.

Those reviewers who were prejudiced against *The Man* because of the sums of money it earned in advance of publication know nothing about my deepest motives for writing. Naturally, writing is one means of making a living, surviving, on earth—writers since the days of Richardson and Defoe and Dickens wrote for their keep as well as their souls. But you have to want to write a book desperately to do it at all, because the effort is a torture you have to live with so long a time. A book must come out of your gut. You must write it because you can't help not writing it. That's the motivation for a novel, the only one I know. After that, you hope that your instinct and storytelling experience have produced a work of fiction that has some connection with a vast public out there, people who have interests and feelings similar to your own which they cannot articulate or define. The bridge from you to the reader is made up of a story, of ideas, of emotions, and if the reading public is interested in that bridge, the public will cross it in great numbers, and enjoy the crossing, and join you.

N: *You've discussed your reactions to some specific reviews and reviewers. Now, in a broader way, I'd like to know what you think of the prevailing standards of book reviewing?*

WALLACE: I think it's no secret that they're very low. But I don't think the problem is a lack of talented reviewers, but rather the lack of a measuring stick that the book review audience can go by. It's confusing to read a book review page or section in any American city (and there aren't too many cities with book review pages) and observe the indiscriminate way new books are passed out for review. Frequently, the reviewer is a close friend of the author who wrote the book he is reviewing. Sometimes, he is an enemy. There is a good deal of back-patting—"You love me and I'll love you"—a kind of understanding among an inner clique, a mutual admiration society—"You give me a good review on this book and I'll repay you by reviewing your next book the same way." These cliques, cults, circles, whose members promote one another and hold grudges against outsiders or defectors, are widespread. All this is unknown to the trusting reader who can't know if a review that has sent him out to pay hard cash for a new book is a prejudiced or unprejudiced review.

I feel there should be some kind of standards and uniformity in literary criticism and reviewing. The innocent public deserves to know the reviewer's credentials. As I have already said, a novelist competing for public favor should not be permitted to review another novelist's work, nor should a specialist in a particular field outside literature be permitted to review a book even remotely in the same field. And if this is permitted, the backgrounds of the reviewers should be made very, very clear to the reading public.

Then, too, the public should know a reviewer's personal standards. When a reviewer discusses a new book, is he judging it against established modern classics or against contemporary popular books? In other words, if the reviewer is discussing a new novel about a modern woman's psyche, is he pitting the new novel's characterization, style, readability against *Anna Karenina* or against *Fanny Hill* or against *Marjorie Morningstar*? Furthermore, is the reviewer measuring the modern novelist under discussion against his admiration or distaste for Henry James or Saul Bellow or James Michener or, indeed, Himself, Author-of-an-Unfinished-Epic-in-the-Trunk? Once these factors are known, the reading public can better understand and find meaningful the critic's praise or damning of any given novel or novelist. Without that, a great amount of criticism and reviewing of books in the United

States is valueless and, worse, a cheat — especially in those book sections of newspapers and magazines where so many reviewers are allowed to use columns not for objective studies of new novels but as personal showcases for their own sophomoric word acrobatics and otherwise repressed erudition. The only book reviewing I find honest and acceptable in the United States or Great Britain is that done by a personality, whose primary vocation is book reviewing, and who reviews regularly under his own by-line. In such cases, the public has the opportunity to know the personality of the reviewer, his standards, his prejudices, his fancies; and while I may not always agree with them, I will read and respect and be guided by such regulars in England as Prichitt and Connolly, or Edmund Wilson, Orville Prescott, John Barkham in the United States.

I've tried to be as impersonal as possible in what I've just said. For my own part, I have antagonism only for book reviewers who are hypocrites, self-serving, unqualified, or who misrepresent the author and his work or who discuss the author and not his book. The real reviewers, the honest and objective and qualified ones, I feel serve a good purpose and I respect them. Sometimes they like my work, sometimes they dislike it, and sometimes they ignore it completely. I would love to have them all praise my writing, all give me attention, but they have the right not to, and that is fair enough.

Essentially, I am getting what I want: a large number of people reading my books and telling me directly how they feel about them. Not to be writing in a void, but to be reaching and touching people, this is the greatest encouragement of all.

N: *Can you state your objectives as a writer in terms of what you want to accomplish and how you would like your work regarded long after you, yourself, are gone?*

WALLACE: I want to tell stories, my stories. I want to organize in some form all of my highly personal observations, thoughts, imaginings, perceptions, learning during my time on earth, and recount them artfully to my fellows. Above all, I want to write books as I wish to write them, freely and independently — and always I want to write better and better books. It maddens me, sometimes, how brilliant are the fancies in my mind, yet how clumsily they translate to the limitations of words on sheets of paper. For me, the greatest distance on earth is from my brain to a piece of paper, a voyage so long and perilous that creative thoughts are shrunken and altered in transit.

My fundamental objective is to try to please myself. I can't start out by writing for anyone else, for whatever reasons — I can't divert from my goal to please or impress any segment of audience. I write to be read, but I won't make concessions to be read. Last week, a close friend of mine said to me, "Why in the devil don't you write a sensitive slender little novel about a boy growing up in Wisconsin, about the boy and his parents and all the difficulties and problems he has maturing? It would be gentle, tender, nostalgic, it wouldn't be too long, it would be about one character not twenty, it wouldn't be controversial, or widely read, or sell to movies. Then you might have a chance of pleasing all of the suspicious literary people at least once in your lifetime, although I think it's too late."

My God.

I told him that doing such a book would be my first dishonesty, for I don't want to write such a book right now; I'm not interested in it, and if I did write it for the reasons given it would be a disownment of the sincerity and honesty of all the books I'd written to date.

As to how I would like my work regarded long after I'm gone? Perhaps that's the primary question of being alive as a writer. What do I want?

I would love to know that in a future time, another generation of readers might be curious to pick up the written products of my erratic career and find that there was in them, in some way or another, parts of a picture (shown nowhere else, by no one else) of the way we truly lived and felt in our time. But on the other hand, just the mere thought of anything of myself surviving is heady enough. You know, Arthur Koestler wrote of this very well in one of his autobiographical series of books. He considered what he really wanted for himself as an author. And then he said — well, the essence of it was — he'd trade one hundred readers one year from now for one reader one hundred years from now. Maybe that's what most of us honestly want. That one reader.

As to the future, you are probably aware that most contemporary writers are requested by major universities to donate their manuscripts, notes, letters, personal papers. I've had numerous universities request mine, and beginning some years ago, I gave a considerable collection of raw material to the Humanities Center in the University of Texas at Austin. Recently, I've agreed to give more of my papers and future materials to Brandeis University in Waltham, Massachusetts, where there will be a special room devoted to these papers as well as other materials relating to the popular American novel in the twentieth century. There is always a sense of secret embarrassment in making such gifts, for I ask myself a question: not whether my work will last, but does it have meaning, is it worth preserving? Though, of course, it is pleasing to know that all these papers, a crazy autobiography of a writer's career on earth, will be safely stored somewhere, and that in some distant day, someone, rummaging around, might quite by accident come across these cryptic notes, tortured outlines, revised manuscripts, research papers and books, and read them—and for fleeting moments give their creator a return to life. But when I wonder if all this is worth preserving, I remind myself that it won't ever be a question of someone, some scholar, attending the collected papers of Irving Wallace, to study him. Not a bit. The value of all this may be that students, graduate students, scholars, even popular writers in the future, may want to write about our time, about the authors who were read in our time, and by chance I'll be there with all the others who are banked in other universities, and my papers will make some minor contribution to the whole, and the idea of this pleases me as much as Koestler's dream of one reader one hundred years from now.

N: *If you were to give advice to the aspiring writer, the one with a future yet to come, what would that advice be?*

WALLACE: That's a difficult question. Because for one thing, I would hope for the aspiring writer's sake, that he would have sufficient desire to write, as well as drive, confidence, ambition not to have to ask for any advice. I mean, if a young man is determined to become a writer, he is going to go ahead along that terrible road and make his own way, and no advice will set him on the right turning. He'll *know*. He'll have the ego and the passion.

But if advice is wanted, it can only be offered in the broadest way. The one thing I believe in for the aspiring writer—and the thing most of my published author friends believe in—is the absolute necessity to write, I mean to write every day and not merely when the Muse moves you. And you have to read tremendously, all your life, to know what has come before you, what is going on around you, and to learn how other writers achieve what they do in their works. Reading can often be as important as personal experiences. Then you have to learn to understand yourself, and those around you, and to interpret what you see and perceive what you cannot see. You have to learn to give absolute freedom to your imagination, your daydreams, and then learn to catch and tame these dreams so they can be transmitted to paper. Perception and imagination, too, may be more important than the experience of an event one wishes to write about. Da Vinci did not have to attend "The Last Supper" to paint it. Intellect is a lesser asset. Most great writers were not great intellects; they were, instead, great feelers, they were instinct-people.

But the main necessity for the beginner is to write regularly, steadily, and not to be put off. Many young aspiring writers I've talked to never get to write or complete their first book or their second because they are frightened—frightened by a literature instructor, or by the classics. These beginners often read only the very best novels that have survived several centuries; they read these and little else and they are mesmerized by genius or near genius and become word paralyzed because they don't feel they can match the masters. They must be made to realize they don't have to. There was only one Balzac, one Melville, one Hemingway. And the new writer is unique—there is only one of himself in the world, only one with his original vision of what goes on inside him and outside.

I think one thing that kept me from writing a novel for many years was the fact that I was so occupied reading nonfiction, I rarely had time for fiction; and when I did read fiction, I rarely read popular contemporary novels. I was always trying to catch up on the so-called classics, and some of them were so great, such masterpieces, that I was humbled by them and thought, "This is the novel, and this is something I can't do."

Of course, the novel is more than that. The novel is also every contemporary work of fiction, no matter how skillfully or crudely done and no matter how brief its stay. The novel is the modern book that reflects our time and our lives, or from the point of view of our time probes our past and our tomorrows. One-third of all new books published every year in America—perhaps ten thousand annually—are novels, and whatever their ultimate worth, each is part of a mosaic of our era.

There came a period when I began reading these novels as well as the classics, reading the books that were coming out, the best sellers and the also-rans, and what I found was a revelation to me. There were so few novels of any merit. There was such general mediocrity. There was so much about so very little. And there were very few who could tell me a story, force me to say, "Yes—yes—but what happens next?" I saw at once that the new novelist should not be frightened into paralysis. His contemporaries are not geniuses. Their words are not magical. And almost none of them possesses the gifts of sensitivity and perception that make one's own seem shallow and dull. This revelation overcame my fear of trying to write a novel. I plunged. And if the aspiring writer will now read my novels, as well as Stendhal's or Faulkner's, he'll have the courage to take the plunge, too.

I often suspect, however, that not too many aspiring writers really want to write—they just want to be authors, Instant Authors. I can remember, when I was very young, I used to read Ray Long's *Cosmopolitan* or the old *College Humor*. You turned the pages, and there was always a picture of Louis Bromfield wearing a beret against some

Riviera setting, or the then much younger W. Somerset Maugham sitting in some exotic locale dressed in an exotic robe, or F. Scott Fitzgerald and a bottle of champagne in Paris, and I would sigh and think, "This is being an author."

Fortunately, I didn't wish only to be an author; I wished also to write, to record my feelings and observations, to put black on white, as de Maupassant used to say. But I think there have always been too many young people who look at the Bromfields, Maughams, Fitzgeralds of their time and say, "That's what I want," forgetting what comes before. Today, many aspirants want to travel on a yacht like Irwin Shaw, live on an island like Herman Wouk, have a Paris apartment like James Jones, enjoy the money so-and-so has, the glamorous reputation so-and-so has, wallow in the excitement of cocktail parties, beautiful women, reporters. What these aspirants forget is that every creative person who attained such fame and freedom did so in the historic literary way—by applying the seat of the pants to the chair—by sitting in a little lonely room or a big lonely room for ceaseless lonely hours, and sweating and cursing and writing word after word, sentence after sentence, alone. Nor is there ever an end to it. The most successful authors will advise newcomers that the money in the bank draws interest—but it does not write books for them. If there is to be a next book, it has to be written—alone. The most glamorous, brilliant, prestigious authors still sit by themselves with their tortured psyches and numbed fingers and write and labor under conditions resembling solitary confinement. Tell the boys who want to be authors that that's the name of the game—work.

There is one last thing an aspiring young American writer should be told before he chooses to give over his life to writing, and that is this: he is volunteering to enter into a strange kind of exile. I am constantly fascinated by the relationship of the writer in America to his fellows, his society, his culture. One final story, which should make my point.

Several years ago, a prominent French psychoanalyst, from Paris, was a guest at our home in Los Angeles. There was stimulating conversation, and finally we came to discuss creative people, their problems and conflicts, and I told him that as many as three-fourths of my writer-acquaintances were or had been in analysis. I asked the French psychoanalyst what I presumed was a rhetorical question: "I suppose most of your patients are writers?" He replied, "No, I have no writers. Most of my patients are businessmen." I found it hard to believe. Then the French psychoanalyst explained it. "In France, the writer is accepted by society, so he has no conflict with society and he does not need help. But in France the businessman is not accepted by society; he is the one in conflict with his culture, and he ends up on the couch. On the other hand, in America you have a money-oriented culture. The businessman is the symbol of success and it is he who is accepted by society—whereas the American writer is a stranger to conformity, rather an odd one who is held suspect and who is not accepted by his society, and so he suffers conflicts; in America it is he, the writer, who needs analytical help."

I've thought about that many times since. Eventually, I came to think that the French psychoanalyst was wrong, until lately when I came to see that he was probably right. At first I thought the French analyst was wrong, because there are so many creative people, writers among them, who are accepted by American society, who are admired and emulated. But lately I've come to understand that the French analyst was probably right, after all—for writers are accepted by American society *only* if they are very successful, if they are important, famous, wealthy, powerful—in short, if they are as solid as American business-men. If the American writer is as successful as the American business-man, our society understands and appreciates him, for he has achieved Everyman's aspirations, and so he is safe and a worthy. But to be an unsuccessful author in America—well, anywhere, but in America especially—that's really hell. Still, being a successful writer in America is a sort of hell, too, because of guilts about being accepted by society for the wrong reasons.

That was a clever psychoanalyst, that French one.

"I assume that the busy man or woman sitting down to read my book must be hit over the head with some sentence or other to make them stop worrying about their family, their housekeeping, their business, their finances, to listen to my story."

Alec Waugh

Alec Waugh

N: Island in the Sun, My Place in the Bazaar, *and* Fuel for the Flame *are some of the recent books by Alec Waugh which afford pleasure as well as candid insight into life. But the most of Mr. Waugh is seen in an autobiography of his early years, called, appropriately enough,* The Early Years of Alec Waugh. *This is a remarkable book, not only well written, but totally realistic — first in view of the precocity of Mr. Waugh's very early years, and second, with regard to the impulses and ambitions which make it so pleasant to be young. In starting to talk to Mr. Waugh, I'll pass up reference to a brother who also wrote — named Evelyn — to ask him about his father's publishing house with which he more or less came of age.*

WAUGH: Publishing was very different from what it is today. It was even a different kind of life, perhaps more like the sort of thing that would go on in an accounting firm. There was no publicity of any sort. Authors didn't have interviews. My father didn't even have an expense account. If he was going to see Arnold Bennett or H. G. Wells, both of whom were on his list, he'd make an appointment with them as though he was a solicitor. They would call at 11:15 and be out of the office by 11:30, having completed whatever business was at hand. Nevertheless, relations were very cordial. A great many of his authors dedicated books to him.

There was little telephoning in those days. I'm talking now about the way Chapman and Hall's office operated when I went to work there in 1919. The only telephone in the office was in a ground floor passage; my father had an extension in his study. A call could be put through to him, but he could not initiate a call himself. He would blow down on a whistle and say, "Please get me Tinker," or Watt or whoever the agent was. He was more concerned with correspondence, and frankly loathed the telephone.

Books came out more quickly then. Manuscripts arrived and seven or eight weeks later were on the market. There was no special advertising; the list was inserted in the newspapers. Now it takes a year to publish a book, and a great deal of high-pressure salesmanship goes on during and after the publication.

In those early British days, authors didn't even have editors. They delivered the manuscript and that was that. The publisher sent it off to be printed, though he might read it first if he thought something indecent or scandalous might be contained.

But it's much more fun now. It's very nice being taken around by an attractive young woman from Farrar, Straus, and hauled off to cocktail parties and TV interviews. It makes the author feel important.

N: *Though you worked for your father, you left the firm after* The Loom of Youth *was published, didn't you?*

WAUGH: No, I wrote *The Loom of Youth* when I was in the army during the First World War. It was published in 1917. I was twenty when the war ended and I transferred to the reserve army. I was not earning enough to support myself, so I went into publishing and spent six or seven years in my father's firm. It was a half-time job. I would go there on Mondays and Fridays, and in the middle of the week I went into the country to write my own stories and novels.

The Loom of Youth was a best seller by the standards of 1917, though it didn't sell more than 15,000 copies in a hardback edition. It wasn't a book that appealed to women, but it was a center of controversy because it criticized the public-school system. In those days the public-school system was considered sacrosanct. It was one of the two main pillars vaulted high on which the British Empire rested. If anyone criticized his public school, it was somewhat like casting aspersions on the virtue of his mother. He was considered a cad, a bounder. I was taken off the roll of my own school — so was my father, as the begetter of the beast. My brother couldn't go to that school. But we've made friends since, and both my sons went there.

N: *Was the criticism of* The Loom of Youth *very harsh?*

WAUGH: The criticism was very fierce from the schoolmasters. The parents wrote and asked if the things I'd described could really happen in public schools. The schoolmasters replied, "Only in a very bad house, in a very bad school, at a very bad time." I was a shocking fellow to have written about my public school with anything less than devoted admiration.

N: *After you resigned from your father's firm — I'm considering now the backgrounds of many of your books — have you spent the majority of your time in the West Indies?*

WAUGH: Oh no, not by any means. I've been in the West Indies quite a lot. I can say, "I've been going down to the West Indies for thirty years" and perhaps I give the impression that I'm there all the time. Actually, I go for five weeks one year, then for two months three years later, but I keep in touch with the West Indies all the time and I read a great deal about these islands when I'm not there.

N: *Could you review your career as a writer, not chronologically, but in terms of things you consider as highlights?*

WAUGH: *The Loom of Youth* came out in 1917, and that was the start of everything. A novel called *Kept*, which was published in 1925, did rather nicely, and was my first book to sell well in the United States. It was laid in postwar London, and a kept woman was the central character, but it showed various characters kept in different ways— living on the past, living on a title, living on gallantry in the war. The general idea was that the British Empire itself was being kept on what it had done in the past. It was a lively book, it told a story, and I'm fond of it.

During the thirties I did family-saga novels. *The Balliols* and *Jill Somerset* were in the Galsworthy tradition. They didn't do badly. They are dated now, but they were solid sociological jobs of work. During the Second World War, when I was again in the army, I thought I should get some of my old books and read them to see what they were like, what sort of writer I was, what standards I had set for myself. Actually, I was rather shocked. I thought I had written a great deal better than I actually had, and I vowed that in the future I would not only publish a good deal less but take more trouble with what I was doing. I have taken more trouble, and I hope the books are better.

N: *What about* Island in the Sun *and* My Place in the Bazaar?

WAUGH: *Island in the Sun* was a very lucky book for me. It was a novel about the West Indies, and the timing was right. It was published when colonialism was being discussed and criticized, and when racial problems were beginning to come into the open. Perhaps the thing that helped it most in the United States was the fact that the story was set in an English colony. It wasn't personal to the American audience; they could be impartial about it. I had a very lucky break with *Island in the Sun* as far as serialization and book clubs and motion pictures were concerned. It's the best book I've ever done, and by a long way.

N: *How did you react to the motion-picture version?*

WAUGH: I thought it kept to the theme of the book very well. It didn't say something I hadn't said. It may have been a little long— maybe they tried to put too much into it—but I've seen it seven times and I've thoroughly enjoyed it. Dorothy Dandridge and Joan Collins and Joan Fontaine were all delightful to look at, and the scenery was superb.

As a matter of fact, I've just been down to Granada, where the film was made, and many people came up to me and said that they had acted as fishermen or had been in a crowd scene. Normally you go to a place after you've written about it and people have angry faces and say, "You libeled me," but in Granada they were very happy because they had had money put in their pockets. They were only getting two or three dollars a day for acting in crowd scenes, but they had never been so rich in their lives.

After I'd written the book my agent, Carl Brandt, didn't think we had much chance of serializing it because of the racial problem, but *Ladies' Home Journal* took it. We were all surprised and delighted; it just happened to be on the stack at precisely the right time, when it had become possible to discuss racial things.

N: *Could you discuss* My Place in the Bazaar?

WAUGH: Well, that's a favorite book of mine because it's a collection of short stories written over the years, arranged with autobiographical notes saying where I was and what I was doing at the time each was written. Some of the things in it are definite favorites, for one reason or another. But you can't pass a writer's sentiment on to the reader; he's approaching the book without benefit of these sentiments after all, so I shouldn't really go on about it.

N: *Could you discuss* Fuel for the Flame?

WAUGH: That is a story about an oil camp, and it's set in the Far East, and I think it's fairly exciting. The trouble is, I didn't put it in one particular place — I invented an island and I've often wondered, despite the book's success, if it really rang quite true. One is never sure about such inventions.

N: *You did a book on wines, didn't you?*

WAUGH: That is one of my favorite books. I've always been a wine drinker. I drink much more wine than spirits. Two cocktails are enough for me, but I always take wine with meals. The book deals with the eight or nine special wines that you can get only in one place, like the table wines of Burgundy, the Medoc and the Rhine and dessert wines like port, sherry and Madeira, with Cognac to close the meal. I need hardly say the research on that book was very pleasant. I went around to all those places to gather material. But it's a special kind of book; it's not for everyone, but the people who like it like it very much, and they write to compare notes. It's opened up some very gay avenues of correspondence.

N: *I gathered, from your autobiography, that you were the first publisher of your brother Evelyn's works.*

WAUGH: Yes. In the early 1920's I was editing an anthology called *Georgian Stories*. It ran for five or six numbers and I only did one of them and included one of Evelyn's stories. He has never put that story into a collection of his own, so he can't think it was a very good one. Yet it was the most exciting story in that volume. It seemed very good, I think it was very good, and it introduced a new, fresh voice. So I could say that I discovered my brother, although Evelyn, with his talent, would have been discovered well enough without me.

N: *While you've traveled a great deal, has Evelyn always stayed in England?*

WAUGH: Evelyn traveled a lot during one period. He went to Africa a great deal. He did two novels about Abyssinia and one about South America. For seven years he traveled continuously, then in 1937 he married. He has six children and a lovely house in the country and a splendid library; he loves his home. But he makes one big trip a year.

We've often told this story, Evelyn and myself. We arranged, at one time, to go to different countries — not that we didn't want to meet each other, but because we didn't want to use the same material. So we divided the world in two, the same way the pope once divided the New World between Spain and Portugal. I as the elder got the better part of the deal. He got South America, Central America, and Africa, and I got the West Indies, the Far East, and the South Seas. We left the Middle East to be discussed later; oddly enough, we were both sent there during the war, so it is common ground and, of course, the United States was common ground.

N: *In your writing, do you feel an obligation to the materials you use and to the public for which you're writing?*

WAUGH: I don't know what public I'm addressing, so I can't say that I write for a public. I suppose I think of my reader as someone like myself, and write the kind of story I myself would like to read. I don't either write up to an imaginary intellectual nor down to someone uneducated. I take my story along the general road of my own tastes.

I try to make things easier for the reader; for instance, I'll introduce my leading characters as quickly as possible. I assume that the busy man or woman sitting down to read my book must be hit over the head with some sentence or other to make them stop worrying about their family, their housekeeping, their business, their finances, to listen to my story. I want to lead them into my story as quickly as possible and I want to keep them so interested in it that they won't stop reading.

N: *In looking at today's culture — our literature and theater — what do you find most admirable and most regrettable?*

WAUGH: As far as literature is concerned, I think we're in a rather good state. This psychological thing — well, I think it's fine for writers who feel this way, who are interested in describing minute differences. If one is a psychological writer and wants to show various nerve states, it must be all right because a great many readers are interested in these nerve states.

As far as theater is concerned, I'm afraid I don't see as many plays as I'd like to. I really prefer films. They come on at a more convenient hour. If I go to the theater after dinner I will most likely fall asleep, and if I go before dinner I'll get hungry. I like to go to the cinema about six— then I know I shall be awake. This sounds as though I'm dozing all the time, but really, theater hours are a problem. Perhaps they should serve popcorn.

N: *Will there be a sequel to your autobiography?*

WAUGH: I very much doubt it. You can tell the truth only up to a certain point in your life. As I say in my book, I don't see how a man with children can tell the truth about the marriage that has produced them. I don't say anything about my children or my marriage in *Early Years*, and I don't think I shall ever want to.

Toward the end of *Early Years* I write about a love affair with an American woman; I think it was movingly told, but I couldn't tell it until both she and her husband were dead. If I were to write a sequel I should have to live to be 150 or so, to make sure that the recital of other love affairs did not embarrass anyone. I don't think I want to live that long.

Morris L. West

The Ambassador is a thoughtful, powerful, and often alarming novel, dealing with American action and intervention in South Vietnam and focusing upon the immediate and long-range problems of East-West relationship. I believe it is Morris L. West's best novel, but for the moment I would like to discuss content. Consequently, my first question to him is: How much time did you spend in South Vietnam, and how thoroughly would you say you researched the background for *The Ambassador*?

"First I must admit that my visit to South Vietnam was largely an accident. I had spent twelve months on some studies of Buddhism, Hinduism, other Eastern religions, politics, and Southeast Asian history. This was in preparation for a new approach to the novel based upon the point of view of Eastern belief.

"I had made several trips around the Far East beginning in Thailand and working through Laos, Cambodia, Vietnam to Hong Kong and Japan. Then the Buddhist burnings began to occur, and the Catholic press in Australia, where I was then living, took a very reactionary attitude toward Ngo Dinh Diem and his repression of the Buddhists. This shocked me very much, and I decided to go to South Vietnam myself to have a look. It so happened that I arrived in Vietnam during the last weeks of the Diem regime. I asked to see Diem and Nhu and members of the cabinet. I did see them, and I found a curious circumstance: they were very glad to see me. You see, my works are very well-known in France, and these men had read them in French.

"They thought they might be able to use me as they had used neutral correspondents from Sweden, Italy, and other nations — to push their own point of view.

"I resented this and I think it was largely because of this resentment that I agreed to report the substance of my discussions to my own embassy and to a member of the United States embassy (who, I gather, was a member of the CIA). I reported and I came out of the country with the opinion that Diem and his regime must go, more or less assenting to the rider that hung on the proposition, namely, that if they went they'd be knocked off one way or another.

"When I got back to Australia a letter was waiting for me, informing me that certain things I had said had been picked up and that I was no longer welcome in the country. When I got that letter Diem and Nhu were dead.

"The strange thing about it was the way I felt deeply involved in these deaths, not that what I had said or reported was of any great significance in the course of events, but because I had made a moral assent to a situation and to an act.

"Out of this measure of guilt, of participation and nonparticipation, grew the novel *The Ambassador*, an attempt to display the dilemma of a man who is charged with a public duty to make the best deal he can with a regime, and who at the same time is faced with a moral choice when the consequence of his dealings may be an assassination. I hope, of course, that this theme is amplified and explored and clarified in the novel."

In *The Ambassador* you seem to use much more fact than fiction especially in the burning of the Buddhist monks that led directly and indirectly to the ousting and assassination of Diem. Could you explain the novel's relationship to actual events?

"There's not only fact—far more fact than fiction—in the burning of the Buddhist, but there is also a great deal of fact in the background of the book, in the background events I use.

"I was faced with a curious choice. In constructing this novel I could not use real personages—such would involve laws of libel, defamation, and things worse. On the other hand I could not depart from the historic structure of events, so I empted for a very clear demarcation: I would use the total background of history that was available to me, and people it with new characters. For example, let me say very clearly that the ambassador in the book is not Henry Cabot Lodge. My ambassador has a completely different background, approach, mental attitude, and set of personal characteristics than Lodge, although he is faced with the same circumstances. Cung, in the book, is close to a portrait of Diem, but even this is not the whole portrait."

Your last statement in your *Counterpoint* interview (April, 1964) was this: "Now I want to enter into the great dialogue between East and West, to try first to understand it, then to dramatize it, if possible, in a novel. But this is so important that one cannot approach it lightly, as a writer of thrillers might. I think one must prepare himself thoroughly, with study and education and this is what I am trying to do." Is *The Ambassador* a product of this preparation?

"It is the first step in this dramatic dialogue, if that's what we wish to call it. The problem is the fact that one's entry into this dialogue has to be progressive. One has to realize that his equipment is vastly inadequate because of the fact that our thinking is oriented Westward, our emotional attitudes are oriented Westward, and that it is a difficult job to pick up the threads of history, philosophy, logic, emotional attitudes conditioned by Hinduism, Buddhism, Animism, by the crosscurrents of history in a continent where there is no finality if only because the contour and ethnography of the land forbids it.

"Oddly enough I think it is a job for the novelist and the artist more than for the historian, economist, or philosopher, because it is a great part of the artist's job to feel and work intuitively at a human level. I suppose that, in this regard, I was not wholly unprepared for the dialogue, though the more I entered into it the less I was prepared to count myself ready for it."

Could you define the contrary viewpoints of East and West that contribute to our problems in South Vietnam?

"First, we have the fact that we are an evolved people. We are an evolved product of the industrial revolution, and the industrial revolution has not yet had much impact in Southeast Asia.

"Picture an enormous flat delta rising slowly to the mountains in the north. Look closely at the delta and see how it is cut up by waterways. Small villages are dotted amongst vivid green paddy fields, hidden in clumps of bamboo, in mango and banana plantations. The only way you can get to these plantations is by water.

"The village headman is the chief who keeps tribal records and dispenses tribal justice. These people are everything from Buddhist or Taoist to any of a number of synthetic sects, but underneath all is the ancient Animism of Asia. Four generations of people live in one house.

"Now, you come in and say, 'This is democracy, this is government of the people, by the people, for the people.' They look at you and say, 'That's wonderful, but don't forget that there's a spirit in the lily pond.'

"You tell them to fight for freedom and liberty, to kill their cousin or brother, the man who comes over the wall of the fortified village at night, and they look at the lily pond which has been there for one thousand years, and the paddy, and they realize that whether they kill their brother or cousin or not they still have to eat by getting up to their hocks in heavy mud to plant and cultivate rice. So why kill anybody?

"Why commit themselves to an ideological struggle which in either

Buddhist or Animist terms — is simply like the ripple on the surface of the water, a ripple that does not touch the depths beneath?"

Do you have any specific recommendations for American conduct in South Vietnam?

"Yes. The first is that within the limits of American commitment in South Vietnam they must be strong in action. If they're hit they must hit back. What Asia does understand is '. . . a strong man armed who keepeth his court.'

"However, America cannot be committed to that dreadful albatross of a thing called a 'policy.' Once you have a policy you have a set of dogmas that become almost as irremediable as the laws of the Medes or Persians. Like the doctrine of the Two Chinas — suddenly you've got the dogma of the Two Chinas and you cannot talk to 800 million people because you've got an island with a few million people which is the second China.

"Therefore, when the American people demand, either through the press or through Congress, to be given a policy, they are asking for a dangerous thing. Suddenly you have a hard and fast formula by which a fluid situation must be measured, and I think this is dangerous and wrong.

"The proper attitude is the existentialist view — that this is the situation in which we live. A situation fraught with risk and danger, a situation of shifts and changes that must be dealt with as events occur. The Americans cannot be committed to a verbal definition which could ultimately strangle them. Don't demand the albatross.

How much of the present situation in South Vietnam is unique to that nation? Or can the pattern of action in South Vietnam be repeated elsewhere in Southeast Asia?

"The South Vietnam situation is at once typical and specialized. It is typical in that I believe that none of the problems of Southeast Asia will be solved by the intrusion of the West. You see, Southeast Asia is the rice bowl of Asia. This is where the great rivers run, where watersheds sustain the ricelands. This, traditionally, has been the trading ground of China; a mutual traffic has gone on for centuries.

"Now, we're not going to change all that or modify it. If we come in as political architects we are going to fail. Ultimately the nations of Southeast Asia will determine themselves, and the way in which they do it will not be the way we like or even approve of.

"But we'll have to live with it. Our learning should be dedicated to living with them, not to a role of playing architect with their futures."

Also, in direct reference to material in your book: Do you think Buddhism is truly capable of coming to living terms with communism?

"Buddhism thinks it can. This is a necessary consequence of the belief that ultimate perfection resides in a common nothingness, the nothingness of Nirvana. Thus obviously one can't come to terms on that ultimate term.

"I think that the Buddhists are nourishing an illusion if they think they can survive as an active religion under communism. They do survive in China, but they survive as a state-dominated religion, as an instrument of the state."

Do you think we can establish an enduring peace in Asia?

" 'Enduring' is the operative word. Remembering that there is no finality in the world, particularly in Asia, we must seek to establish a working arrangement as can be established in a marriage of individuals. It's going to be rough, abrasive, risky; sometimes peaceful, sometimes quarrelsome, but we must always regard the needs and attitudes of the people.

"Now, the one disposition in Asia which—by an extraordinary piece of blindness—we are attempting to ignore is the existence of 800 million Chinese who, like them or not, are all God's chillun.

"They're increasing at the rate of the population of France a year—47 million. That increase is going to go on. Now, China has a marginal economy that depends on 'night soil' to fertilize the crops that will feed these people. There will be no enduring peace in Asia if the Chinese don't eat, and the only way they can eat is by being brought into the commerce of nations.

"It's the height of sheer nonsense that an American tourist goes to Hong Kong to buy goods from China—goods like jade or ivory—and must come back with a comprehensive certificate of origin that says he hasn't bought a stick or stone from Communist China because we are blockading her.

"Can anybody blockade 800 million people indefinitely and refuse to admit them, however quarrelsome, intransigent, troublesome, tyrannical they may be, into the community of nations, into the commerce by which people eat and breathe?"

"I don't look on myself as a satirist at all. . . . Occasionally somebody says I'm satirizing the British aristocracy. That's rot! I just try to tell a good story, and if it comes out funny, fine."

P. G. Wodehouse

P. G. Wodehouse

N: *It is almost impossible to believe that P. G. Wodehouse is now eighty-five years old. Those of us who were literally weaned on the "Jeeves" books do not like to think it happened so long ago. We find no diminishing of freshness, no slowing of pace in rollicking humor — either in short story or novel form — in the current Wodehouse output.*

Anyone fortunate enough to visit him at his home in Remsenberg, Long Island will find a courtly, energetic, witty gentleman. The word "charm," so grossly overused and misused, comes to mind in the presence of Wodehouse. Where did it all begin?

WODEHOUSE: My people were in Hong Kong most of the time, so I was more or less farmed out along with my brothers. We lived with some people named Prince in South Croyden, just outside London, and I was there from the time I was five until I was eight. Then my oldest brother was supposed to have a weak chest and they thought he ought to go to a warmer climate, so he went off to school in Guernsey in the Channel Islands, and I followed him for two or three years.

After that I went to a small private school near Dover and finally to Dulwich College (I call it "Valley Fields" in some of my books). It's a curiously rural place, only about five miles out of London, but you really think you're in the country — beautiful grounds and everything. I loved the place.

I wrote for the school magazine. I used to report football games, that sort of thing, nothing serious in the way of writing. I was supposed to be going up for a scholarship at Oxford, but the family finances couldn't stretch far enough to send me there. My brother went.

I went into a bank, a Hong Kong-Shanghai bank, for two years. Then one of the masters at Dulwich, who had left the school and gone to work for an evening paper called *The Globe*, came across me, and I asked him if he could get me any work in the writing field. Every now and then he'd take a day or two off and I'd substitute for him. They ran a comic column, rather like F.P.A.'s [Franklin P. Adams] column used to be. Finally he wanted to take three or four weeks off, and I had to choose between staying at the bank and giving up this opportunity.

Naturally, I took a chance and did his work on *The Globe* for three weeks.

He came back, but after about six months he resigned and I got his job, with the result that I was on *The Globe* for about seven years. It involved writing a column of supposedly humorous paragraphs and a set of verses. I've always thought of it as excellent training. If you can write a set of verses every day between half past ten in the morning and twelve noon you can do anything.

In 1904 I took my holiday — we used to get five weeks — in America. I had always been very keen on coming here. I wanted to see the fair in St. Louis, so I came. I never got any farther than New York; I stayed there for three weeks, then had to go back to work on *The Globe*. The odd thing is, I saw much more of New York in those three weeks than I've seen since. I think you have to be a tourist to see New York properly.

I worked on at *The Globe* until 1909. Then I came to New York again, thinking I was going to spend another three-week holiday, but I brought two short stories with me. I sold one to *Collier's* and the other to *Cosmopolitan*, both on the same day and at rather good prices. I was getting about £10 for a short story in England, and *Collier's* paid me $300.

I thought this was very much worth looking into, so I resigned from *The Globe* and stayed on.

The years that followed were sometimes rather glorious, sometimes not so good, as far as income was concerned. I wrote a lot for the pulps, *Munsey's Magazine* and *Argosy*. They were a great source of revenue in those days.

Then I ran into an old friend I'd worked with in England on a little show in 1906 — Jerome Kern. I had done lyrics for some of his music, and I met him again on the first night of a very good show titled *Very Good, Eddie* that he had written with Guy Bolton.

We decided to team up. I'd do lyrics, Guy would do the vocal arrangements and Jerry would do the music. So we started what became known as the Princess Shows, very popular in their day — *Oh, Boy! Oh, Lady!* and one or two others. Then I did various other shows with Guy, some with Jerry, some with other composers.

Writing musical comedy was a much simpler thing in those days. One didn't have to wait for years for a production, getting together a million dollars or whatever. Costs were quite low. Guy and I actually had five shows running on Broadway at one time, simultaneously. A manager would say, "Do a show for me," and we'd do the show and the thing would be produced a month after that.

Those five shows: *Oh, Boy! Oh, Lady!*, *Miss 1917*, *The Riviera Girl*, and *Leave It to Jane. Miss 1917* was a terrible flop despite the fact that it was produced by Ziegfeld, but *Leave It to Jane* has just been revived and ran three years off-Broadway. It's a musicalization of George Ade's *College Widow*, actually. I'm crazy about Ade's stuff — remarkably fresh and penetrating. *In Babel* was so awfully good; one or two of the best short stories I've ever read were in that.

I suppose the turning point in my career was when I sold a serial to *The Saturday Evening Post*. That was in 1914, a thing titled *Something New*. I've never dreamed of getting into *The Post;* it just seemed impossible. But they took the story, and I wrote for them for the next twenty-five years.

In my day, remember, the American magazines were all publishing serials, so they got pretty good stuff. Nowadays you don't see more than two short stories and no serials at all, unless it's one of those awful long shockers or a seventy-thousand-word novel condensed into thirty thousand words and absolutely killed.

But I've been writing for *Playboy* for about four years, now. That magazine seems to have taken the place of the old *Saturday Evening Post*. It's open to all sorts of stuff, you know, as long as the material is original and interesting. It isn't like the other magazines.

N: *How did you create the immortal Jeeves?*

WODEHOUSE: Jeeves had a rather interesting birth. I was writing short stories in those early days about a sort of Bertie Wooster whom I called Reggie Pepper. He was always getting into difficulties, and he and a friend got into a scrape so serious that I felt it was impossible for either of these two birdbrains to think of a solution. I didn't know how to get them out of their mess. Somebody else would have to solve their difficulties. Then I thought, "Why not let one of them have a valet who is sort of omniscient, equal to anything?" And that's how Jeeves came into being. He had appeared in one story before, but he'd only had one line. Now he made a full-dress appearance, so to speak, and he rather stayed around. That first story was "The Artistic Career of Young Corky," if I remember correctly; remember, that was over fifty years ago.

N: *How many "Jeeves" books have there been, altogether?*

WODEHOUSE: There've been nine, and I'm now working on a long "Jeeves" story, a novelette. I'm afraid I can't get enough together to make a whole book; I suppose it will run twenty to thirty thousand words, but it will be the basis of a book of short stories I'm getting ready.

People ask me if I've been bothered by being identified too closely with Jeeves, but I haven't. Jeeves started off in that story I mentioned, and I don't think I wrote another "Jeeves" story for about a year. Then I wrote some at intervals of a month or so, but it wasn't until I wrote a full length novel that I really felt I had got hold of Jeeves. That was *Thank You, Jeeves* and it came out in *Cosmopolitan*. I think there have been nine "Blandings" books altogether.

N: *Are Jeeves or Bertie or any of the characters in the "Blandings Castle" books taken from persons known or incidents recorded?*

WODEHOUSE: I don't think so. I never consciously draw a character from real life. I suppose there are echoes of characters I've met. Certainly one character, Ukridge, I've used in two or three books. Oddly enough, he is drawn from two people. He's drawn first from a man I never met, but who was very elaborately described to me by a friend, and I drew the original character on that. Shortly afterward I met a man who became a great friend who was exactly like Ukridge. A fellow who was always hard up, putting the touch to everybody for a half crown, that sort of thing. Certainly Lord Emsworth isn't drawn from anybody.

Jeeves, of course, is rather like all the stage butlers and valets. He's like Lane, in Oscar Wilde's *The Importance of Being Earnest*. But I think the thing that differentiates him is the fact that he really does something. Stage butlers seldom do anything. They come in and say, "The carriage waits," or that sort of thing, but Jeeves goes out and solves problems.

N: *Do you feel that the humorist has an obligation?*

WODEHOUSE: Not consciously. You mean, do you feel that you ought not to write that sort of dirty humor? Or bitter stuff? Well, I do personally feel that I shouldn't. But that's only the way I look at it. I don't know whether you could say that a humorist is under any obligation to write any particular type of humor, but the kind I do is the only kind that appeals to me.

I dislike this Lenny Bruce type of humor very much. It tries to hurt somebody, and I don't see why a humorist has to do that. I don't look on myself as a satirist at all, so you might say I'm not trying anything at all significant. Occasionally somebody says I'm satirizing the British aristocracy. That's rot! I just try to tell a good story, and if it comes out funny, fine.

I think my books are more or less like historical novels now. I've never attempted to treat them as up-to-date, but I don't think that matters very much. For instance, this book that's just been published about Blandings Castle. I don't suppose there are any Blandings Castles left in England now, or any Bertie Woosters with valets, but that doesn't matter, really. I don't think I'm under an obligation to write about modern life. I always picture my stories taking place, oh, say, in the 1920's, between the wars.

Life was much freer then. After the First World War, country-house life flourished in England. It was only after the second war that it was all wiped out. There are still enormous houses, like the Duke of Bedford's, but they're kept going by charging entrance fees and jazzing up the place. Jeeves couldn't live there.

But I suppose the real old country-house life has absolutely disappeared.

N: *How did you happen to choose the United States as home?*

WODEHOUSE: I've practically always been an American. I've lived here virtually all the time since 1909. After visiting New York once, I wanted to come over to stay, to resume my writing life here, and I found that I quickly ended up with many more good friends over here than I had in England. I've been mixing in theatrical circles, writing circles, all satisfying. I don't think I've been in England since about 1934. During the war, of course, we had this house in France and it never occurred to us to leave, and the Germans overran us and we were interned. But our lives have rather largely been here.

N: *And there was a separate career as a motion picture script writer?*

WODEHOUSE: I went out to Hollywood under contract to Metro-Goldwyn-Mayer for six months, with an option for another six. Those were the boom days in Hollywood when they did that sort of thing. Now I imagine you are engaged for one picture, and when you're done with that, you're through.

When I got there they put me on a dreadful picture titled *Three French Girls*, which was nearly all written. That was the trouble with Hollywood. They never gave you a job you could start from scratch. Generally three or four other people had already worked on it.

They took up my option at the end of six months, but I hadn't really done any work. Then, there had been a Ziegfeld musical titled *Rosalie*, on which I'd done half the lyrics with Ira Gershwin. Metro had bought it for pictures, and the first thing they wanted to do, naturally, was to alter the entire story. It hung fire and various people worked on it and I was supposed to make a version of it, but nothing ever really came to a head.

Then I left Hollywood—that was in 1931—and I didn't go back again until 1936. The first thing they gave me to work on—*Rosalie*, all over again. Nothing much came of it again, even after six years of moldering in a drawer or somewhere.

However, I did work on a book of my own, a thing titled *A Damsel in Distress* which had appeared serially in *The Saturday Evening Post*. They wanted to make a musical out of it with music by George Gershwin. I think it came out rather well; it was quite a success. Fred Astaire starred in it, Joan Fontaine played the heroine, Burns and Allen were in it. I don't think they make musicals like that anymore—fresh and high-spirited. They try, but they spoil them with stories.

N: *What are your thoughts on the present state of humor?*

WODEHOUSE: Terrible, isn't it? But there aren't any markets for humor. I suppose *The New Yorker* is open for humorous contributions, but as far as newspapers are concerned everything seems to be written by staff people. Some of them are very good, but new humorous writers just don't seem to appear. When I first started out over here, so much very fine humor was being written—George Ade, Ring Lardner, Sullivan—all of them were going strong.

Now everything is so dreadfully serious.

N: *Finally, which are your own favorite Wodehouse works?*

WODEHOUSE: I'm very fond of *Leave It to Jane* and the Princess Shows. I like the "Jeeves" series and the "Blandings Castle" books. I'd say that *Quick Service* is the favorite of all the books I've written, though I'm not so sure but what my last book won't replace it. I read it again last night and I think it came out exactly as I wanted it to.

That is so satisfying, you know. Even if one lives forever—which I'm threatening to do, it seems—there aren't too many things in life that come out exactly as one wants.

Doctor X

In less than a month *Intern*—based upon a day-by-day diary kept by an intern during a truly rough year—was a nonfiction best seller. The layman may be jarred by the doctor's frank, inside view of hospital procedure, but *Intern* is far from a deliberate shocker or exposé. The doctor writes well, and his biggest ax is reserved for the almost inhuman way internships are managed rather than for professional practices and ethics.

How did he keep these close records?

"I just decided, before I started my year of internship, to put down my experiences and observations on tape. Often I was too tired to put down all I wanted to—sometimes too tired to put down anything at all—and the whole thing was a terrible chore for my wife, because we could only afford the two or three tapes I started with. This meant that she had to transcribe them right away so I could use the tape again. The whole thing was much harder on her than it was on me."

How did *Intern* actually become a book?

"Several years went by, with all these hundreds of pages stored away in a closet. I was practicing before I hauled them out one weekend and decided that if I was going to do anything with them that was the time. So I bundled them off to an agent, who got quite excited and told me to turn the first portion into manuscript.

"I did, he sent it all to Harper and Row. They took it. Here it is."

Why did he want to publish it?

"There are two reasons, actually. First, I believe that the intern's lot should be improved—the very low pay, the very long hours. I don't think he gets as much out of it as he should, and I don't think the patients get the best out of him.

"I don't know what the solution is. We aren't turning out medical-school graduates in numbers proportionate to the increase in population.

"The second thing is this: I don't think the mantle of silence surrounding the medical profession is advisable or useful. I think the public should know more about medicine and more about their doctors, especially in the human aspects. A great deal of ignorance, suspicion, and fear would be removed. And the public would get more from their doctors through his closer relationship.

"But it's a two-way street, and the doctor has to do his part, too. As busy as the average physician is, this is going to require some skill."

How has the medical profession reacted to the book?

"I haven't heard too many reactions yet, and I can't search for them while I'm staying incognito. But the book seems to be either liked tremendously or absolutely condemned; there's no in-between.

"Those who hate it think I've broken with every stated or implied medical rule and ethic. Which I haven't. I've broken with custom and I think this is all to the good."

I commented on the literary quality of *Intern* and asked if he had written it by himself.

"All by myself—every word of it.

"This shouldn't be too surprising. Chekhov, Cronin, and a great many other writers were or are physicians. Remember, we have to write detailed case reports, and we have to be very clear in these, both on medical and human levels. This is great training."

Why the anonymity?

"To avoid harassment and comment from fellow doctors; also the discomfort of former patients identifying themselves, or thinking they do. As anonymous as they're kept, and as careful as I've been to cloak their identities, things could get pretty sticky.

"I just don't want trouble, I guess. Not for myself, and not for anyone else."

"I do hope young writers coming up will write with beautiful prose at the same time they keep touch with reality. I would love to see the restoration of style because it is the most subjective, personal thing . . . and it gives a dimension to culture."

Marguerite Young

Marguerite Young

YOUNG: I was born in Indianapolis and received my education at Indiana University and Butler, my master's degree at the University of Chicago in the days when Thornton Wilder was on the campus. At that time I was a poet, a dedicated poet, and I had published in *Poetry, A Magazine of Verse* edited by Harriet Monroe of Chicago. One of my great joys was that I was there in time to know her and visit her in her beautiful apartment overlooking Lake Michigan. I remember the beautiful set of Chinese dolls upon the windowsill she had brought back after living in China when her sister was married to (I believe) the American ambassador to China. I didn't think of writing fiction then, but I used to visit Thornton Wilder's class in creative writing. The day I began writing my novel, many years later, I remembered one statement he frequently made to the class. He would say, speaking of obsession in fiction, "Remember — the patient loves his malady." So years later when I began to write about the Opium Lady and her dreams, that was one of the clues with which I worked — the patient loving the malady. Naturally, she does not wish to be cured. The malady itself is part of the creative life in many cases.

At that time, too, I was fortunate enough to be in Chicago when Gertrude Stein visited, and I spent twelve days in her small seminars where Thornton Wilder was the host and Paul Goodman one of the challengers, perhaps the only person who challenged Gertrude Stein. She used to pluck her earlobe and pretend to be deaf for a moment while waiting to make some witty reply to his challenges.

I also studied for a while with Robert Morrs Lovett, the very great professor. I was a Milton major and wrote my thesis on Elizabethan and Jacobean prose. I also studied with Ronald S. Crane, and this is one of the great, prophetic facts of my life. Crane was a man who believed in the novel as a poet, and we read *Tom Jones* thirteen times for its poetic structure. I have been grateful all my life for this beautiful discipline, for the adventure of spirit in regarding the novel as a poem and not merely a realistic or naturalistic document of some kind. The first great novels in the English language were poetic novels like *Tristram*

Shandy. (It happened that Crane was a *Tom Jones* man, so we emphasized *Tom Jones* at this point.) The idea that prose should be a very plain method of communication did not arrive until after the Industrial Revolution, when they were attempting to reach a different sort of reading public. But the great tradition in the English language and in all other languages is the poetic novel, because the novel grew out of the poem. Categories, after all, do not describe creative processes, but are rather quick little ways by which critics or commentators can divide them.

Actually, as the novel is a poem, so we know that the drama can be a poem. The novel is the equivalent of the epic poem, although it could also be the lyric.

I'm very happy that I had that fabulous training at the University of Chicago, especially because I did not know then that I was going to write a novel, but, you see, we live our fate before we realize exactly what it is. When I started to write my novel in New York years later, I had in mind the person who gave me the greatest insight into life, a very beautiful lady in Chicago, a famous character, an opium dreamer who stayed in bed for years. This was a medical fate, not psychological; it was before they knew as much about modern medicine as they do now, and she became, of course, addicted. But she was a beautiful lady of great brilliance in the neighborhood of the University of Chicago. She entertained in her bedroom the great people of her day. I was there often as a young girl, and so while the book is not about her, it was from her that I understand the psychology of opium and the dream. As a way that opium will keep time from passing, and if it is properly taken under medical supervision, it will keep the patient from aging for a long time, then suddenly you crumble into age or death, age and death.

It's like *The Picture of Dorian Gray*, and it's very Coleridgian; it's like a Coleridge nightmare, the whole affair. Through this woman, of course, I became very interested in Coleridge, and I began to see him in a different light. So when I started to write the novel I thought back to this lady in Chicago as being the most interesting and fascinating person I had known, and I decided I would write about reality. This is one of the most amusing things; people think I invent characters who are so out of this world, but I knew them all. I don't write about them exactly as they were. You never do if you're really a writer. You start with reality, then enter reality thematically into the whole work. I thought of laying my novel in the city of Chicago, which I knew intimately, but the reason I chose the East is that I felt it must be near an ocean instead of a lake. The ocean is symbolic, too, an "out there," the unconscious and the dream, the inner sea.

Also, another close connection I have with Chicago is that I feel myself a member of a family that has shown me such great love, the Charles Walgreen family. Mrs. Charles Walgreen is like a mother to me, and she always claims me as her other daughter. Her real daughter, Ruth is a Chicagoan, of course, now living in the East; poet, novelist, and historian, a woman who has done a great deal to establish poetry libraries throughout the United States, and has done so many beautiful things for the dissemination of poetry, bringing poetry to people who might otherwise never see a poetry book. In the South she has established libraries for CORE. For a time I was fiction editor of *Tiger's Eye*, which was her really famous magazine. Everyone is so glad that she gave it up because she has an executive ability like her father's, and it would have consumed too much of the time she spends so wonderfully in many places.

But after the University of Chicago—actually, I was "discovered" in a snowstorm in Iowa City. A talent scout came to the University of Iowa to call on Professor Austin Warren. He said, "Are there any poets in this neighborhood?" and Professor Warren said, "Oh, yes, we have a poet with manuscripts." I was studying philosophy in the advanced graduate school at the University of Iowa, and Austin said I was a poet with two books. I hadn't even thought of publishing, but the talent scout went out into the snowstorm and saw me standing there and said, "Are you the poet?" I don't know how he could pick me out, but I said, "Yes, I am," and that's how my first books were accepted, and how I came to New York shortly after that with a fellowship from the American Association of University Women. I had no idea of going to New York, but when I received the fellowship I decided suddenly I had to come East, the thing every writer dreams about.

I left Iowa, never finishing my Ph.D. I've gone back there to teach at the University of Iowa Arts and Letters, but I've forgotten about that degree.

But to come up to *Miss MacIntosh, My Darling*. I had thought of writing another nonfiction book, and I always had in the back of my mind the idea that I might want to write a novel some day. When I was a child I wanted to be a novelist and wrote short stories. Then, when I was seventeen, I woke up one morning and said, "I will be a poet." So for nine years I dedicated myself solely to poetry. And I became involved in writing a long poem about New Harmony, Indiana, which became *Angel in the Forest*. First I wrote sixty lyrics about the people of New Harmony today, and what they say about utopia. That did not work because the history, the facts, had to be told. So I thought I'd try a sort of epic poem in blank verse, and I wrote a two hundred-page epic which is lost. I don't know where these poems are—probably in some-body's basement in Indianapolis. The facts were still missing, so I thought I would have to write prose. It was like the tolling of bells. If I had known how many years all this would involve me it would never have occurred to me to throw away those sixty poems and those two hundred pages of blank verse. Yet they are all utilized, in some measure, in *Angel in the Forest*, so you can see that it is a very poetic epic, with all the images and content of the poem and the poetic style sustained throughout. At the time it was published, Mark Van Doren greeted it in his review as the most European book ever written by an American on a regional subject, the most intellectual and the most learned. It received a fabulous press.

By that time I was very much involved with prose, but I was still thinking in terms of nonfiction. I went out with a young agent who was actually an editor. I never drink, and we were going to spend the weekend at his house in Westport. We missed the train at eleven o'clock in the morning, and he said, "Let's have a glass of champagne while we're waiting for the next train. It leaves on the hour." So we did. And every hour we looked up at three minutes after the hour, until seven o'clock that evening. It was no plot or plan; it was just that we were exuberant and having a wonderful time. If we got to Westport I don't remember a thing about it. I'm told I had a wonderful evening, dinner and everything, but I don't know a thing. The next morning when I came down to breakfast, my hostess said, "Isn't it marvelous, Mar-guerite, that you're going to write a novel for us?" and I said, "What?" She said, "Yes, darling, they're all dancing around," and I said, "No novels for me." I was deferring the novel until I thought I was ready.

Then my host (who must remain anonymous) said, "Look in your purse," and I looked, and there was a contract I had signed and a fabulous check. I said, "Oh, my goodness," and he said, "When will you start it?" and I said, "Well, this is Sunday, and tomorrow I have to go to the bank, and shop, and—I'll start it Tuesday morning." And I did. I sat down Tuesday and stared at my desk and thought, "How do you write a novel? First I'll make a list of the most magnetic personalities I've ever known," and I did. The most central figure was the Opium Lady. All the other characters I had known somehow fell into place; they were all to be eccentric characters because I thought, "I will put myself under the influence of Charles Dickens. I will externalize all the inner life of the characers." I don't like these analytical novels where you don't know how people look, what they wear, what they say or think. Sometimes you can't tell the difference between a man and a saltshaker, especially in these modern French novels.

I had the choice of the setting. It was to be the whole idea of the dream carried over from my utopian book, only with concern for the individuals. Illusion and reality—how much is illusion, how much is reality, and do we ever confuse the two. This is the theme of *Don Quixote*. When he has encountered these people on the road he thinks they are going to be as they were the last time, as illusions, so he says, "This time I'm not afraid of these people; they're illusions, they're hallucinations." But they turn out to be real. There is this continual interplay, and throughout *Miss MacIntosh* I think you'll find this theme rather consistently. This gave me a rather broad horizon to work with, and then I thought, "I must have one character who seems normal in contrast to all those other people," but then I thought, "What kind of argument is that? I'd be defeating my own purpose, which is to prove that so much of life is a dream." So I decided to have her just *seem* to be normal. This was Miss MacIntosh, the old nursemaid, a character composed of four or five wonderful old maids in Indianapolis. I made her Scotch Presbyterian, a Calvinist occupying the Opium Lady's pagan, St. Augustinian dreamworld. She's in contrast, but she commits suicide on page six, and the whole book is the inquest: Why did this seemingly normal woman commit suicide? It's no secret, but it turns upon the fact that when she lost her wig and was the naked animal, like King Lear in the storm, she had lost illusion and could not live and had to go back to the sea for renewal of the unconscious and the dream; also, she was acquainted with immortality although the sea is a mortal image. Poe did this, too. He believed that the sea was a coexistence thing, that you don't go to some far-distant heaven, but the sea itself is immortal, part of man.

So the book is about the girl's quest. Having been conditioned to expect reality by Miss MacIntosh, then having been failed by Miss MacIntosh who had found reality failing for her, she finally comes to liberation and returns to her mother. When she recognizes that we must live with these problems of ambivalence all our lives, and cannot expect absolute certainty, I feel she is a mature human being. She meets the stone-deaf man, who is partially living in the world of the dream, because she would substitute for the dead ear other senses, which are heightened by the loss of the ear, and marry him. This is as near as she can come to reality, to marry a normal man who is almost supernormal because he has lost his hearing.

I knew such a character as this, this deaf painter, and I became deeply fascinated by the psychology of the deaf. I have written a long article on this for *Flair* magazine, and had done research by interviewing all the deaf people in New York. I probably met the only stone-deaf dentist in New York, and I have the makings of a book about ears, so I brought to her my feeling that I already have about these deaf people that I love. I don't know why, but I have a deep, deep feeling for deaf people. It's a fabulous world. If you've ever done research in their world it becomes marvelous and beautiful.

So Miss MacIntosh enters the dream and becomes a part of it. No longer is there that rigid search for absolute certainty which many neurotic people have. And you do notice that many of my people, even though obsessed, live and have a joyous time, and if they commit suicide it's almost a joke, because they don't really believe in death. Suicides don't believe in death; they are, as Dr. Menninger said, "the great optimists." He says that really neurotic people live in order to enjoy the feeling of how sad life really is.

You see his brother, who is actually a part of himself, is the quick suicide. The melancholic brother doesn't die; the gay brother goes. I notice that Henry James has a beautiful character; in *The American*, the playboy dies in a duel over a foolish woman, and he really looks on the whole thing as a wonderful joke, because a joke or comedy can be a mask for the greatest of all melancholies, as dear Henry James pointed out. (I love William and Henry.)

In the years of writing this book I have had dreams, and I am not a person to dream at night. When I do have them they are terribly normal and dull. I visit someone, have tea with a beloved friend, and everything is exactly as it is in one's life. Perhaps a picture frame will be changed in a dream. But while writing *Miss MacIntosh* I had dreams of being visited by Henry James, and he sometimes came and we talked about fiction, and he read a page or two of my novel and told me I was doing all right. In one dream I went to a party and Henry James was there, and he sat in a corner and poured whiskey into his high silk hat. A few months later I was passing along Fourth Street, the secondhand bookstall region, and found, for fifteen cents, an obscure book of memoirs by a very obscure person (I'm always buying these books). In it is a description of Henry James at a party pouring his drink into his high silk hat. I don't know what it all means; I don't suppose it means anything. My friends say, "Are you sure you didn't read it first?" but I know I absolutely did not, and there were months between.

And I never really have fantastic dreams; they all go into my novel. I have never taken a drug because if I did I'm sure I would become absolutely sensible, go in absolutely the wrong direction. I'm full of images and dreams while walking around in the daylight, and one aspirin leaves me unconscious for days. But isn't that lovely, the Henry James dream? When I was at the University of Iowa I studied with a

very great philosopher, Gustav Bergman, who introduced me to
William James, and I've been extremely grateful for this all my life,
because it seemed to radiate throughout my entire life, and it heightened
all consciousness for me. The gift of William James has been a light-
house, has illuminated all of America for me. He was so American
with his ideas of the pluralistic, the many consciousnesses, the many
worlds, the many ways of looking at life. He has beautiful analyses of
illusion and reality throughout all his work. I remember, from the
time when I was at the University of Chicago, T. V. Smith, with whom
I also studied, said that it would be a wonderful thing if poets would
open their minds to the vast realms of sources for art which are not art
— you know, history or philosophy or science. I think these things
happened to me through association with great professors.

  I know it was at the University of Chicago that I started reading
outside the field of literature. Writers have to know literature and to
become obsessed with it, but it's so wonderful if they can begin to
realize the beauties of other fields. For example, I'm a great fan of
Cleveland Amory, and books like *The Last Resorts* enthrall me. Henry
Ward Beecher fascinates me. I don't see how I can ever run out of
material because I keep seeing such a variety of things to write about.

  If you live in New York and watch the newspapers as I do, you
wonder how you can compete as a novelist with what happens. The
things that happen every day are so fabulous that if you could get little
gleams of them into fiction, you'd be doing a great deal. Life is always
greater than art.

  Friends were shocked because every night, before retiring, I read
all the news in the *Daily Mirror*. I couldn't live without the *Mirror* and
the other newspapers; they absolutely keep me going, and I get hundreds of ideas for characters, in some cases actual case histories. When
the *Mirror* folded they said, "Marguerite, what is this going to do to
your fiction?" and I said, "Never mind, they'll have a dream issue for
me every night, my own little issue." Actually, a great many of the
Mirror columnists and headline writers went over to the *News*, but they
don't seem quite the same. I do miss the *Mirror* and stories like the one
about a man who was suing a woman to produce, in court, his three
illegitimate children by her, because his wife said that he was in-
capable of fatherhood and he wished to prove it was her fault that they
had no children. The woman couldn't produce them because they were
imaginary; she never had them. She just wrote to him about the
pregnancies he'd left her with, and accepted support money for the
three fictitious children. This ended up in *Miss MacIntosh*, not quite the
same as it happened in real life, but fairly close to it.

I also read *True Detective* like mad. I met one of the editors from a detective story magazine a few years ago, and she was absolutely appalled. She said, "You know more about murder than anyone I have met outside my office," but I follow murder cases. Think of the marvelous fiction, the incredible stories, that come out of them.

Truman Capote followed one through superbly. Truman is a very good friend of mine; I've known him since he was an elf with his first short story, "Miriam." We spent a long summer together with Carson McCullers. We used to call it "the long and the short of it," and we discovered during that summer that all three of us are descendants of John Knox.

Oh, dear, back to *Miss MacIntosh*. The young man I'd gotten so drunk with really didn't belong to the right firm for me, so I returned that lovely advance and took the first forty pages to Scribner's, to Maxwell Perkins, who accepted it. Mr. Perkins could foresee the whole novel. After a few marvelous interviews with him, he died, and I went on to my next editor, John Hall Wheelock, who was great and beautiful and wrote me marvelous letters. He, too, could see what I was doing, and had the greatest reverence for it. He's in Zurich now, but he's written several letters to people about *Miss MacIntosh*, and he says, "This book is going to be a treasure house for poets for the next thousand years."

During all those years the people at Scribner's never wrote me a single letter asking me about the book, reminding me of a delivery date, and heavens, almost twenty years went by. Scribner's has been terribly important to me. I went there first because I loved John Hall Wheelock. I knew him socially. He always said that he gained an author and lost a friend because I didn't see him much after that. The beautiful thing about Scribner's has been their respect for my privacy. I know that many publishers drive a writer almost crazy with continual inquiries; if they had me, there would have been breakdowns. Scribner's never pushed me for time, partly because, I think, they have such a tradition of great books behind them — Henry James, Thomas Wolfe, Hemingway — great names. Scribner's has really treated me and the book in that beautiful way and, now, when Burroughs committed himself to *Miss MacIntosh*, it was with total heart. Promotion and advertising are things money can buy, but the kind of devotion Scribner's has is a spiritual thing that simply isn't for sale.

I must say that I'm quite pleased about the critical reactions to *Miss MacIntosh*. There have been very few negatives, thus far only four, and I would say that two of those are really not negatives but rather old-fashioned notices by men who have never liked the poetic novel. I wish that the dyed-in-the-wool, hard-boiled realists would leave *Miss MacIntosh* alone, because there is an audience for my book, and a rather large one, that shouldn't be misled.

After I was committed to the book, and I was two years along, I realized that it would be a major novel, and I had to believe an important contribution to American culture in order to write it. People would say, "Oh, who cares about beautiful writing; with television there's no audience for beautiful writing." But I had to believe in *Miss MacIntosh*, and I did, because I know thousands of people who would appreciate it. I'm too practical to have written it if I thought no one would read it; I don't think any work of art is created in a vacuum. The reader begets the writer; the audience begets the art.

But I love the reviews. I don't think I have an ego-relationship to reviews one way or another, but I am pleased that the book does communicate, does reach its readers. I would be terribly upset if everything were negative, not only for my own sake, but for the sake of Scribner's, who took such great risks.

I do hope young writers coming up will write with beautiful prose at the same time they keep touch with reality. I would love to see the restoration of style because it is the most subjective, personal thing. It's personal, but it is also cultural, and it gives a dimension to culture, and I think we are famous for style throughout the world. The Puritans were great stylists, and it was Hawthorne and Poe who really taught realism to the French. I don't believe in the antiliterary writer. We have some of those, and some of them will accidentally be great. I think there are gifted writers of the antiliterary sort, but a stylist—a real stylist, I don't mean the ornamental—brings such satisfaction.

I try to teach my students style, but always as a part of life, not as ornament. Style has to come out of communicating coherent thought, not in sticking little flowers on speeches. Style and substance and a sense of life are the things literature is composed of. One must use one's own personality in relationship to life and language, of course, and everyone has such a relationship. Some people find it, some don't find it, but it's there. It may take two or three months for a young writer to find out what his particular mode of expression is, but once he finds it he never departs from it; it's like learning the Australian crawl—hard to learn, but once learned, never forgotten.

There were things I had to learn at the beginning of *Miss MacIntosh*. When I first started I went to visit Richard Wright one evening, who was a friend, and I told him I was starting the novel, and I said, "Dick, what is a novel? How do you write a novel?" He rose from his chair and he said, "I'll tell you what it is: 'Love, oh careless love ...'" and he put on a phonograph record and then he said, "It's love, give yourself with love." He turned the record over and said, "This is the rest of what a novel is: 'Go down, Moses, drown, forget yourself, dream....'"

A few days later I bumped into Allen Tate on the street, and I said, "Allen, what is the form of a novel?" (I wanted to know what other people thought). He said, "Well, Marguerite, form is that which keeps the reader reading." I thought that was a beautiful definition; he didn't say anything rigid or conventional. And I said, "What is the style of a novel?" and he said, "Style is thinking ... thinking on paper."

I've talked to so many young writers who say, "I threw my best papers away because they were only random thoughts," or "I thought of it but didn't write it down because people would think I was foolish."

I've allowed myself to be thought foolish, and I've written everything down on paper, just to have it there. I always tell young writers they should be like shorthand reporters, the hand taking dictation without too much intervention of judgment. People are very cruel to themselves and throw out their best ideas. If they would just let them flow, and afterward evaluate and organize and discard, fine. But when we're writing we're too critical. We must be kind to ourselves, to our thoughts, to our words.

I have a friend, a beloved friend, Mari Sandoz, who is a great historian. She always reads her galleys in a crowded restaurant because she says her judgment, if she were isolated, would force her to throw out the whole book. If she has enough distraction around her she can read in a more relaxed way, and not be overly critical.

Mari is dying, you know, a rather massive cancer, but to visit her now is one of the greatest privileges on earth. We will never adjust to the loss of Mari; she is worshipped by so many artists, painters, writers. She may not be aware of it, but she is a great figure in the lives of the artistic people of this city.

She has always predicted a great reception for *Miss MacIntosh*, and when I was frightened or skeptical, as one is, she has said, "Mark my word, Marguerite, people will love it and understand it." I'm happy she lived long enough to see the reviews.

Mari and I had a bet on the book—I would have to pay her a dollar per thousand copies for figures over a certain number, she would have to pay me a dollar for every thousand copies under that figure. When she was first ill, and she was supposed to be dying at that moment, I walked into her hospital room ready to collapse, and she looked up from her bed, more radiant than I've ever seen her, and said, "I'd rather die than pay you that bet!" and she laughed.

NOTE: A large portion of the Katherine Anne Porter interview appeared in *McCall's* magazine. The interview with Maurice Girodias originally appeared in *Cavalier*.

The eleven vignettes are adapted from their initial appearance in *Chicago's American*. Most of these shorter pieces are in vignette form because of the limited accessibility of the interviewee, not because I wished to give them less space, though a few can be regarded as special, in the sense that their experience as writers has been limited to a singular issue or subject.

ABOUT THE AUTHOR:

Roy Newquist is literary editor for *Chicago's American* and a nationally syndicated book-review columnist for more than one hundred newspapers.

Born and reared in Ashland, Wisconsin, Mr. Newquist was educated at Marquette University and the University of Wisconsin. Private study under Sinclair Lewis was followed by creative writing courses directed by Mari Sandoz. His voracious reading and curiosity concerning writers led him to write in the format he has used for this book and his two earlier ones, COUNTERPOINT and SHOWCASE. He also writes and interviews for *McCall's* magazine.

Mr. Newquist lives in Park Forest, Illinois, with his wife and three children.